TERROR IN THE BIBLE

INTERNATIONAL VOICES IN BIBLICAL STUDIES

Jione Havea, General Editor

Editorial Board
Jin Young Choi
Emily Colgan
Musa Dube
Julián Andrés González,
David Joy
Gerald O. West

Number 14

TERROR IN THE BIBLE

Rhetoric, Gender, and Violence

Edited by
Monica Jyotsna Melanchthon and Robyn J. Whitaker

Foreword by Phyllis Trible

Atlanta

Copyright © 2021 by SBL Press

All rights reserved. No part of this work may be reproduced or transmitted in any form or by any means, electronic or mechanical, including photocopying and recording, or by means of any information storage or retrieval system, except as may be expressly permitted by the 1976 Copyright Act or in writing from the publisher. Requests for permission should be addressed in writing to the Rights and Permissions Office, SBL Press, 825 Houston Mill Road, Atlanta, GA 30329 USA.

Library of Congress Control Number: 2021950648

This book project came to birth on the unceded lands of the Wurundjeri clan of the Kulin Nation, custodians since time immemorial. We recognize and acknowledge the human sufferings and injustices that Aboriginal people have experienced as a result of colonization, discrimination, and marginalization. We offer our respects to elders, past and present, for their continuing culture and extend that respect to all First Nations people everywhere. May we strive to uphold the gospel of reconciliation and justice and work for right relationship with one another and the land.

We are grateful for the encouragement, support and kind contributions of the Australian Collaborators in Feminist Theologies, Pilgrim Theological College, and the University of Divinity (Melbourne), that made this book possible.

Contents

Foreword: Biblical Terrors Then and Now ix
Phyllis Trible

List of Abbreviations xiii

1. Introduction: Terrorizing and Traumatizing Texts in Context 1
Monica Jyotsna Melanchthon and Robyn J. Whitaker

2. Terrorizing Indigenous Women in the Contact Zone:
Placing Cozbi and the Midianites in Colonial Australia 17
Laura Griffin

3. Numbers 25: A Reading by a Queer Australian 37
Karen Eller

4. But He Would Not Listen to Her: Revisiting
the Story of Tamar in 2 Samuel 13 55
Rachelle Gilmour

5. Clean and Unclean: Multiple Readings of Mark 7:24–30/31 67
Dorothy A. Lee

6. Desolate, Devastated, Redeemed, Restored:
Feminist Visions of Daughter Zion in the Australian Context 89
Angela Sawyer

7. Invoking Jezebel, Invoking Terror: The Threat
of Sexual Violence in the Apocalypse to John 107
Robyn J. Whitaker

8. The Leadership of Women in Early Christianity 121
Adela Yarbro Collins

9. Reading Crucifixion Narratives as Texts of Terror 139
David Tombs

10. The Fruit of Others' Labor: How Judges 19 Stands
with Dehumanized Migrant Workers 161
Brent Pelton

11. Interrogating Ahithophel: Intersecting Gender and Class
in Biblical Text and South African Context 177
Gerald O. West

12. Terror of Texts: Orality and the Reclaiming of
Daughters' Land Rights (Numbers 27:1–11 and 36:1–12) 201
Jione Havea

13. Gender, Violence, and the Dalit Psyche:
The Jephthah Story (Judges 11–12) Reconsidered 215
Monica Jyotsna Melanchthon

Afterword: Scriptures of Terror 235
Jione Havea

Contributors 237

Ancient Sources Index 239

Foreword
Biblical Terrors Then and Now

Phyllis Trible

AT THE BEGINNING

In retrospect, *Texts of Terror* began to form years before the book entered my consciousness. The occasion, in 1971, was meeting a prominent feminist theologian (to remain unnamed) on the American scene. She asked what discipline I taught. When I replied "biblical studies" (or did I say "Old Testament"?), she recoiled with disdain. In uncompromising language, she lectured me. As I remember, she said: "If you are a feminist, you cannot give allegiance to the Bible. You may teach it as an academic subject, but you cannot approve of it or identify with it. You must choose between feminism and that patriarchal book."

What a dilemma this woman set before me. Yet immediately I knew that I would not—indeed, could not—accept it. Deep within me lay two affirmations, neither of which would I disavow. First, I am a feminist. Second, I love the Bible. For sure, to "love" need not mean to approve, sanction, or embrace *in toto*. But it does mean that the Bible provides the foundational stories, for weal and woe, by which I interpret life. Somewhere within that meaning lay *Texts of Terror*, although at the time I knew it not.

We live by stories. Growing up in a church that required children to memorize weekly select verses in the Bible—all carefully chosen by the so-called powers that be—I grew into faith. Along the way to adulthood, probably through the influence of certain teachers (or by the grace of God), I grew also into what we call "feminism." Never was there a conversion experience, only an impeachable conviction. In time, this seeming dilemma of loving the Bible and being a feminist required exploration. After all, one might declare that, "if no man can serve two masters" (Matt 6:24), no woman can serve two authorities—namely, a master called the "Bible" and a mistress called "feminism." Gradually within my consciousness arose the challenge to wrestle with the Bible and, like Jacob, to not let go without a blessing (Gen 32:26). That ancient patriarch provided a story of entry into a journey of discovery.

My first response to the challenge focused on examining biblical texts that in varying ways differ from, undercut, counter, or resist patriarchy. My choices included female images for God (especially the womb), equality in the creation of Eve and Adam, gender mutuality in the Song of Songs, and female prominence in the book of Ruth. From these explorations came *God and the Rhetoric of Sexuality* (1978), some seven years (a perfect biblical number) after the definitive challenge by that unnamed feminist theologian.

Yet, the entire time I was exploring biblical texts that counter patriarchy in different ways, I was asking myself what to do with texts that are not only male-dominated but also openly violate women. If I love the Bible, I am compelled to struggle with these negatives. An invitation to deliver the Lyman Beecher Lectures at Yale Divinity School in 1982 focused the task. When I told my friend at Yale, Professor Letty Russell, that I intended to lecture on texts about women that offer no redemption for the victims, she suggested that to retell such stories on behalf of the victims could itself be redemptive. Grateful for that insight and armed with the literary discipline of rhetorical criticism, I examined four stories in which women are denigrated—used, abused, raped, and more. The four chosen derived from different segments of my scholarly pursuits across years. They embraced the desolation of Hagar (Gen 16 and 21); the rape of Princess Tamar (2 Sam 13); the rape, murder, and dismemberment of an unnamed concubine (Judg 19); and the sacrifice of Jephthah's daughter (Judg 11). As I brought these stories together (not in their biblical order but in the order of my hermeneutical journeys), the phrase "texts of terror" came to mind (from where? from whom? a gift from God?). To this day, the phrase resonates, as the essays in this present book confirm.

AT THE PRESENT

Since the publication of *Texts of Terror* in 1984 (some thirty-six years ago), attention to the subject has developed in breadth and depth. Although core commitments and affirmations endure, the worlds of faith and feminism have understandably changed. With gratitude, then, I salute the diverse and compelling essays that comprise this present volume. A brief overview of four contributions, in conversation with my book, highlights some changes alongside continuities.

First, the canon spreads. I chose texts from only three books—Genesis, Judges, and Samuel—but this collection extends within the First Testament to Numbers and Isaiah. Further, it moves into the Second Testament, into the gospels, the Pauline epistles, the pastoral epistles, and Revelation.

Second, authorship and locations expand. Both females and males, the contributors range in age and experience from newcomers to seasoned scholars. They come from various religious, social, and cultural backgrounds, and they work, teaching and preaching, in diverse settings. The thirteen represent five continents, beginning with Australia and including Africa, Asia, Europe, and North America, plus New Zealand and Tonga. Their various uses of traditional biblical disciplines such as source criticism, historical criticism, and literary criticism aid in developing theological and hermeneutical observations that engage the here and now.

Third, vocabulary, concepts, and points of view expand. With ease, the authors of this volume employ terminology and perspectives not present or readily available for earlier scholarly writings. A partial listing of these terms (chosen at random and presented alphabetically) include the following: agency, binary, bisexual, cisgender, deconstruction, ethnicity, gender fluidity, intersectionality, LGBTQI+, misogyny, postcolonial, queering, racism, sexism, trauma, and womanist. The listing might continue with vocabulary and concepts calling attention to new occasions and new duties. Throughout these expansions, the terror of texts and the texts of terror endure. Appropriations by readers remain open and flexible.

Fourth, texts of terror allow for glimpses outside and/or beyond themselves. Negatives not only point the way to continuing problems within faith but also provide potential shifts to more excellent ways. Several essays in this book suggest new directions with caution and care. Samples include the struggle for land rights in Num 27 and 36, the domestic violence and reframing of "the daughter of Zion" motif in Deutero-Isaiah, the irony of imagery in the Markan account of the Syro-Phoenician woman, and the ministry of women in the early church. Directions taken in these and other texts remind me of the comment Dr. Russell made: to tell texts of terror on behalf of the victims may itself become a redemptive act.

MORE TO COME

As I continue to reflect on the diversity and depth of the chapters in this book, I sense how far the discussion has moved from the dichotomy set up at the beginning of my remarks, between feminism and the patriarchal Bible. The authors of these chapters pursue more excellent ways. They wrestle with the Bible, faith, and feminism. They do not let go without challenge and blessing.

Such movements bring to mind an unexpected incident. Once, after I had lectured on the concubine story in Judg 19, an unnamed woman approached me with tears flowing. She said, "I did not know that the Bible had a story like that. I myself have been gang raped, psychologically murdered and dismembered. To hear now that the Bible tells my story begins my healing." I was stunned at the working of the Spirit in and through this woman as she listened to and appropriated the biblical story.

Continuing reflections on this surprising appropriation led me to a divine speech near the close of the book of Deuteronomy (29:1–30:20). In the context of covenant renewal, God commands Israel through Moses to obey the commandments. "Behold, I set before you life and death, blessings and curses. Choose life that you and your descendants may live" (30:19). This declaration places responsibility upon us, hearers and heirs of the covenant. We choose. Surely one way we can make choices is to identify and confront terror in biblical texts, with the intention of working our way to life. As contributors to this book pursue the task, may blessings come to them and to us the readers.

Abbreviations

AB	Anchor Bible
ABD	*Anchor Bible Dictionary*. Edited by David Noel Freedman. 6 vols. New York: Doubleday, 1992.
ABRL	Anchor Bible Reference Library
AcT	*Acta Theologica*
AIL	Ancient Israel and Its Literature
AThR	*Anglican Theological Review*
BETL	Bibliotheca Ephemeridum Theologicarum Lovaniensium
BibInt	*Biblical Interpretation*
BTB	Biblical Theology Bulletin
BZAW	Beihefte zur Zeitschrift für die alttestamentliche Wissenschaft
CBQ	*Catholic Biblical Quarterly*
Colloq	*Colloquium*
ExpT	*Expository Times*
HALOT	*The Hebrew and Aramiac Lexicon of the Old Testament*. Ludwig Koehler, Walter Baumgartner, and Johann J. Stamm. Translated and edited under the supervision of Mervyn E. J. Richardson. 4 vols. Leiden: Brill, 1994–1999.
IEJ	*Israel Exploration Journal*
Int	*Interpretation: A Journal of Bible and Theology*
JAAR	*Journal of the American Academy of Religion*
JAJ	*Journal of Ancient Judaism*
JANES	*Journal of Ancient Near Eastern Society*
JAS	*Journal of Anglican Studies*
JBL	*Journal of Biblical Literature*
JBRev	*Journal of the Bible and Its Reception*
JQR	*Jewish Quarterly Review*
JSNT	*Journal for the Study of the New Testament*
JSNTSup	Journal for the Study of the New Testament Supplement Series
JSOT	*Journal for the Study of the Old Testament*
JSOTSup	Journal for the Study of the Old Testament Supplement Series

JTSA	*Journal of Theology for Southern Africa*
LCL	Loeb Classical Library
LHBOTS	Library of Hebrew Bible/Old Testament Studies
LNTS	Library of New Testament Studies
NIB	Keck, Leander E., ed. *The New Interpreter's Bible.* 12 vols. Nashville: Abingdon, 1994–2004.
NIGTC	New International Greek Testament Commentary
NIV	New International Version
NovT	*Novum Testamentum*
NRSV	New Revised Standard Version
NTL	New Testament Library
NTOA/SUNT	Novum Testamentum et orbis antiquus/Studien zur Umwelt des Neuen Testaments
NTS	*New Testament Studies*
OBT	Overtures to Biblical Theology
OTE	*Old Testament Essays*
OTL	Old Testament Library
Proof	*Prooftexts: A Journal of Jewish Literary History*
PSB	*Princeton Seminary Bulletin*
QD	Quaestiones Disputatae
RSV	Revised Standard Version
SBLDS	Society of Biblical Literature Dissertation Series
SBS	Stuttgarter Bibelstudien
SemeiaSt	Semeia Studies
SJ	*Studia Judaica*
SJOT	*Scandinavian Journal of the Old Testament*
SNTSMS	Society for New Testament Studies Monograph Series
SSN	Studia Semitica Neerlandica
STRev	*Sewanee Theological Review*
TOTC	Tyndale Old Testament Commentaries
TS	*Theological Studies*
VT	*Vetus Testamentum*
VTSup	Supplements to Vetus Testamentum
WBC	Word Biblical Commentary
WUNT	Wissenschaftliche Untersuchungen zum Neuen Testament
WW	*Word and World*

1

Introduction: Terrorizing and Traumatizing Texts in Context

Monica Jyotsna Melanchthon and Robyn J. Whitaker

> The Bible is man (*sic*) in a nutshell. Good and evil live side by side in the same book. That's why it's cherished. The good find in it encouragement, the weak solace, the evil, justification.
> —Bangambiki Habyarimana

> In Western culture, the Bible has provided the single most important sustaining rationale for the oppression of women
> —Pamela J. Milne

We are conscious of the pain and oppression in the world we inhabit, even as we are mindful of the social and moral efforts underway to combat them.[1] We are aware that the undoing of injustice is never quite fully achieved. COVID-19 has been testing us in ways most of us have never previously experienced, providing emotional and economic shocks that we are struggling to rise above. The global pandemic of violence against women and children that has raged for centuries has combined with this more recent pandemic of COVID-19 to create devastating intersecting consequences for women and children. COVID-19 and its effects—be they isolation, stress and anxiety, unemployment, poverty, or ill-health—have amplified the context in which abuse can continue and increase. The coexistence of these two pandemics has exacerbated the disproportionate impact of structural inequalities on women, children, and people in minoritized and diverse communities. The head of UN Women, Phumzile Mlambo-Ngcuka, declared that

---

[1] Epigraphs from Bangambiki Habyarimana, *The Great Pearl of Wisdom* (Createspace, 2015); Pamela J. Milne, "No Promised Land: Rejecting the Authority of the Bible," in *Feminist Approaches to the Bible: Symposium at the Smithsonian Institution, September 24, 1994*, ed. Hershel Shanks (Washington, DC: Biblical Archaeology Society, 1995), 47.

violence against women and girls is a *shadow pandemic* during the wider coronavirus crisis: "The violence that is emerging now as a dark feature of this pandemic is a mirror and a challenge to our values, our resilience and shared humanity."[2]

The Bible, a book of faith for many, saturates the cultures of communities all over the world. It is mined for insight and instruction to address the many issues that confront the world today and sadly has been proscriptive of women and minorities. The stories within the Bible are compelling and vivid tools, assimilated into our bodies, as manuscript and collage, often in collusion with cultural dictums, expectations, and sanctions.[3] But some of these stories have proven to validate and sanctify violence, triggering trauma in women, men, and children; the culturally and ethnically minoritized; and those excluded from mainstream cultures due to gender, sexual orientation, disability, or disease, to name a few. The many broken and bruised bodies of victims in biblical narratives speak into the material contexts of varied tyrannies, validating and sanctifying racism, sexism, colorism, caste oppression, classism, colonialism, and heteronormativity. These violated, abused, forgotten, and rejected bodies in the biblical text function as metonymic signs that evoke the real. "It is important to bear in mind, however, that the line between actual killing and verbal, symbolic or imaginary violence is thin and permeable. The threat of violence is a method of forceful coercion, even if no blood is actually shed."[4]

Feminist theory helps us understand traumatic stress on individuals as microcosmic—namely, as manifestations of larger societal and cultural forms involving power, domination, and victimization. The feminist theory of trauma contends that what is traumatizing to a person is not simply the experience of violence or threat to life and security. Rather, it is also what is symbolically evoked by the experience, including the community's response to the person who has been traumatized. A contextual and sociological approach to trauma recognizes that the violence and resulting trauma is symptomatic of a social pathology and therefore moves "the locus of the problem of interpersonal violence from its historical location in a victim's personality to the misogyny of the culture expressed through the actions of perpetrators of violence."[5] This approach to trauma also highlights the fact that experiences of violence, subjugation, and pain result not from the inadequacies of an individual but from the ways in which the culture, through its various

---

[2] Phumzile Mlambo-Ngcuka, "Violence against Women and Girls: The Shadow Pandemic," UN Women, April 6, 2020, https://tinyurl.com/2vvda994.

[3] Lori Hope Lefkovitz, *In Scripture: The First Stories of Jewish Sexual Identities* (Plymouth: Rowman & Littlefield, 2010), 1.

[4] John J. Collins, "The Zeal of Phinehas: The Bible and the Legitimation of Violence," *JBL* 122 (2003): 4.

[5] Laura Brown, "Feminist Paradigms of Trauma Treatment," *Psychotherapy: Theory Research Practice Training* 41 (2004): 465.

hierarchies and textual traditions, defines identity, silences, dominates, invalidates, and rejects a member by virtue of his/her status within a minoritized group in that culture.[6] There is little chance for an individual to escape this imposed identity because it is not an identity of their choosing or developed agentially. The trauma of interpersonal violence is an individual representation of societal or institutional forms of discrimination, repression, and oppression such as racism, sexism, ableism, or heterosexism.[7]

The concept of "insidious traumatization," introduced by Maria Primitiva Paz Root, suggests that subjugated individuals and groups experience "sub threshold traumatic stresses" daily.[8] Such insidious trauma is triggered by incidents of violence against someone who belongs to the group, by forms of institutional violence and discrimination, and also by "negative and stigmatizing images of one's group in media, textbooks and discourse of peers and co-workers."[9] Such thresholds, Root maintains, are cumulative and serve as instant reminders of the precariousness of one's safety in contexts where one's group is the target of bias.[10] Do biblical texts influence these thresholds? We believe they do; hence we recognize that the violent rhetoric prevalent within biblical texts helps to create or adds to the insidious trauma of the victims of violence, be they women, children, or men. Biblical texts have the capacity and potential to create, maintain, and sustain a state of fear and distress in an individual and trigger trauma. We seek to bring attention to the fact that the Bible, by virtue of some of its contents and in complicity with culture, plays a significant role in prescribing, producing, enabling, and triggering collective alarm and insidious trauma.

This book began its life first as a day-long conference (but not all presentations at the conference are included in this publication) on feminist readings of biblical texts that critically interact with Phyllis Trible's classic *Texts of Terror*, either by engaging her method or by revisiting a text in that volume.[11] Trible's book, initially published in 1984, has influenced several generations of biblical and feminist scholars and continues to do so. She not only highlighted and popularized texts that were often ignored or sidelined but also drew attention to the terrorizing

---

[6] Maria Primitiva Paz Root, "Reconstructing the Impact of Trauma on Personality," in *Personality and Psychopathology: Feminist Reappraisals*, ed. Laura S. Brown and M. Ballou (New York: Guilford, 1992), 240.
[7] Brown, "Feminist Paradigms," 465.
[8] Root, "Reconstructing," 240.
[9] Root, as cited by Brown, "Feminist Paradigms," 466.
[10] Root, "Reconstructing," 230, 240. See also Brown, "Feminist Paradigms," 466; L. Juliana M. Claassens, *Writing and Reading to Survive: Biblical and Contemporary Trauma Narratives in Conversation* (Sheffield: Sheffield Phoenix, 2020), 14–15.
[11] Phyllis Trible, *Texts of Terror: Literary-Feminist Readings of Biblical Narratives* (Philadelphia: Fortress, 1984).

potential of texts that were considered to have no redemptive value, "sad stories" and "sympathetic readings of abused women" that make one weep and mourn, especially as they intersect with issues of gender within the Hebrew Bible.[12] These disturbing stories continue to be ignored or rejected in the teaching and reflection of the faith communities to which many of us belong. They do not appear in lectionaries and are rarely, if ever, preached on, characteristics of what has recently come to be called "cancel culture."[13] These texts have polarized readers and interpreters alike and continue to contribute to some bad press, especially for the Hebrew Bible. What is perhaps overlooked in such a response is Trible's helpful suggestion that we read these texts *in memoriam*—in memory of these abused, victimized, violated, dehumanized, nameless, and murdered characters, and in continuum with similar victims today.[14]

We took our cue for this book project from Trible because of how her book induced further study of these violent texts and brought attention to aggression against women in society as it intersects with issues such as caste, domestic abuse, colonization and imperialism, sexual orientation, and migration. Our hope was to discover the impact her work had on Australian feminist biblical scholarship and the status of those texts in specifically Australian readings and academic reflections. With the inclusion of contributors from outside of Australia, the project shifted and resulted in some surprising results; several of the papers engage Trible by paying attention to the terrorizing potential of some of the same biblical texts but also by extending the repertoire of Trible's terrorizing texts to include those not always seen as texts of terror, and to texts from the New Testament as well as the Hebrew Bible.

Our book is not about Trible, yet she shadows these essays—or perhaps the authors are shadowing her, sometimes countering her, using her thoughts as a springboard to ask new questions of the same texts, engaging new texts, asking similar questions, and stretching and extending her interpretations into new contexts. This book therefore stands alongside the many scholarly attempts to recognize suffering in its fullness, individuality, power, and vulnerability and to seek to address how violence or injustice against women and marginalized communities is depicted, shared, listened to, and responded to.[15]

---

[12] Trible, *Texts*, 1–2 and 3, respectively.

[13] Cancel culture is certainly not a new phenomenon; see Brooke Kato, "What Is Cancel Culture? Everything to Know about the Toxic Trend Online," *New York Post*, July 10, 2020, https://tinyurl.com/4wkh5cdh.

[14] Trible, *Texts*, 3.

[15] See Trible, *Texts*; Claassens, *Writing and Reading*; Caroline Blyth, Emily Colgan, and Katie B. Edwards, eds., *Rape Culture, Gender Violence, and Religion: Biblical Perspectives* (Cham, Switzerland: Palgrave Macmillan, 2018); Carolyn Blyth, *The Narrative of Rape in Genesis 34: Interpreting Dinah's Silence* (Oxford: Oxford University Press, 2010); Susanne Scholz, *Sacred*

THE AUSTRALIAN CONTEXT

The Australian context has been defined as being "antipodean"—namely, "situated as an outpost of European and North American theology, culture and politics, geographically removed from the main metropolitan centres of scholarship and debate."[16] Being antipodean "also involves interpreting European traditions, perspectives and institutions in vastly different geographical, climatic and cultural circumstances," because the Australian culture is primarily a European and white culture.[17] Its remoteness makes possible and even encourages a degree of independence and self-reliance. But, because a majority within the academy are trained in or hired from the West, this independence and self-reliance is not always apparent.[18] Australia's historical, political, and cultural circumstances therefore pose a specific set of challenges that arise out of its violent history of settler colonialism and its reluctance to fully engage with indigenous peoples and with Australian landscapes and ecologies even today. The *rawness* of European colonialism persists through varied expressions of racism, in the physical degradation of land, and in the cultural degradation of indigenous peoples.

Recent decades have seen the challenge of refugees and migrant peoples resulting in debates over who or what an Australian is. This is a significant issue that needs to be reflected against the White Australia policy, a racially restrictive government immigration policy aimed at keeping the nation white, which was lifted only in 1972. The impact of immigration on the ethnic composition of Australia's population since then has been striking. As of 2019, 29.7 percent of the population

---

Witness: Rape in the Hebrew Bible (Minneapolis: Fortress, 2010); Mary Anna Bader, *Sexual Violation in the Hebrew Bible: A Multi-Methodological Study of Genesis 34 and 2 Samuel 13* (New York: Lang, 2006); Cheryl A. Kirk-Duggan, *Pregnant Passion: Gender, Sex and Violence* (Atlanta: Society of Biblical Literature, 2003); Cheryl J. Exum, *Fragmented Women: Feminist (Sub)versions of Biblical Narratives*, 2nd ed., T&T Cornerstones (London: Bloomsbury T&T Clark, 2015); Frank M. Yamada, *Configurations of Rape in the Hebrew Bible* (New York: Lang, 2008); Hilary B. Lipka, *Sexual Transgression in the Hebrew Bible* (Sheffield: Sheffield Phoenix, 2006); Joy A. Schroeder, *Dinah's Lament: The Biblical Legacy of Sexual Violence in Christian Interpretation* (Minneapolis: Fortress, 2007); Renita Weems, *Battered Love: Marriage, Sex and Violence in the Hebrew Prophets* (Minneapolis: Fortress, 1995); Jerome F. D. Creach, *Violence in Scripture*, Interpretation (Louisville: Westminster John Knox, 2013); Eric A. Siebert, *The Violence of Scripture: Overcoming the Old Testament's Troubling Legacy* (Minneapolis: Fortress, 2012); and Philip Jenkins, *Laying Down the Sword: Why We Can't Ignore the Bible's Violent Verses* (New York: HarperOne, 2011).

[16] Winifred Wing Han Lamb and Ian Barns, eds., *God Down Under: Theologies in the Antipodes* (Adelaide: ATF Press, 2003), viii.
[17] Lamb and Barns, *God*, viii.
[18] Lamb and Barns, *God*, ix.

was born overseas.[19] Yet debates over immigration, especially from Asia and Africa, and multiculturalism reveal that many still see Australia as white and that race is still a part of the cultural politics of nationalism.[20]

The struggles, issues, and paths forged by the Australian women's movement through first, second, and even third wave feminists seem to be lost on the current generation of women, who believe that they live in a postfeminist world.[21] Monica Dux and Zora Simic report on the postfeminist sentiments that featured prominently in their study, voiced mostly by younger women.

- Feminism was understood as "the movement that fought for equal rights for women and allowed me and my generation to believe that we can do, be, think anything we want."
- Feminism is not a dirty word … a little obsolete now…
- it is irrelevant because women have come so far
- perhaps I am a bit post-feminist, or even post-post-feminist because it [feminism] is a term I identify with an earlier era.[22]

While these sentiments do not constitute the majority opinion, they are familiar to those of us who teach feminist biblical studies even today. But feminism and feminist activism persist outside and within the academy. It continues to be essential if we are to address the high incidence of violence against women. In Australia, one in every three women (30.5 percent) has experienced physical violence since the age of fifteen, and, on average, one woman a week is murdered by her current or former partner.[23]

> According to the most recent Australian Bureau of Statistics Personal Safety Survey (ABS, 2017), 11% of women and 5% of men in Australia report having been

---

[19] Australian Bureau of Statistics, "Migration, Australia: Statistics on Australia's International Migration (Interstate and Intrastate), and the Population by Country of Birth—Reference Period 2018–2019 Financial Year," April 28, 2020, https://tinyurl.com/k5f52hrv.

[20] The face of the migrant in the media is always yellow, brown, or black! On race and cultural politics, see Peter Mares, *Not Quite Australian: How Temporary Migration Is Changing the Nation* (Melbourne: Text Publishing Company, 2016), 1–11.

[21] Emily Maguire, *This Is What a Feminist Looks Like: The Rise and Rise of Australian Feminism* (Canberra: NLA, 2019) and Chilla Bulbeck, *Living Feminism: The Impact of the Women's Movement on Three Generations of Australian Women* (Cambridge: Cambridge University Press, 1997).

[22] Monica Dux and Zora Simic, *The Great Feminist Denial* (Melbourne: Melbourne University Press, 2008), 19.

[23] For the first statistic on violence, see Victoria Health, "Violence against Women in Australia: An Overview of Research and Approaches to Primary Prevention," January 2017, https://tinyurl.com/5x54tzyk. For the second, on murder, see Our Watch, "Quick Facts," accessed December 15, 2020, https://tinyurl.com/7bwjep46.

sexually abused before the age of 15 years. In total, the ABS estimates that approximately 1,410,100 people living in Australia experienced sexual abuse before the age of 15. Greater than half of these respondents (58%) report being sexually abused for the first time before the age of 10 years.[24]

Child sex abuse is therefore a matter of not only concern but priority, and the seriousness with which this issue is being handled is evident in the establishment of the Royal Commission into Institutional Response to Child Sex Abuse and the naming of Grace Tame, a sexual assault survivor, as the 2021 Australian of the Year.[25] Australia is presently haunted and consumed by allegations of sexual assault, rape, and other brazen acts within Parliament House, highlighting "the toxic culture" and a "sexism crisis," and calling for urgent reforms in work place culture.[26] According to a 2018 Australian Human Rights Commission (AHRC) survey, 33 percent of respondents have experienced sexual harassment in their workplaces.[27] Studies have shown that the rate of sexual harassment is much higher among vulnerable groups including young women, queer women, Indigenous women, migrant women and nonbinary people.

Violence and discrimination against LGBQTI+ communities are continuing issues despite the legalization of same-gender marriage in 2017. Conversion practices continue, aiming to change or supress sexuality or gender. At the heart of these practices is the deep discrimination and prejudice that persists within communities and in religious institutions: they are "hidden in evangelical churches and ministries, taking the form of exorcisms, prayer groups or counselling disguised as pastoral care. They're also present in some religious schools or practised in the

---

[24] Bravehearts, "Child Sexual Assault: Facts and Statistics," October 2019, https://tinyurl.com/ufx7nphx.

[25] Royal Commission into Institutional Responses to Child Sex Abuse, https://tinyurl.com/4zfcxhuv. Grace Tame, 26, was groomed and raped by her fifty-eight-year-old math teacher. She was fifteen at that time; see "Grace Tame, Who Took on the Law over Rape Silencing, Named Australian of the Year," Nine News, January 25, 2021, https://tinyurl.com/2f6z2ewk.

[26] On "the toxic culture," see Cathy Humphreys, "Allegations of Sexual Harassment and Abuse an Urgent Test for Government," *Pursuit*, March 5, 2021, https://tinyurl.com/h37f55nz. On the "sexism crisis," see Dan Jervis-Bardy, "Senator Lidia Thorpe Speaks Out about Sexual Harassment in Parliament House," *Canberra Times*, March 23, 2021, https://tinyurl.com/4cjexfd2.

[27] Bridget Judd, "Sexual Harassment Affects Workplaces across Australia: So What Can We Do Better?," *ABC News*, 1 March 1, 2021, https://tinyurl.com/y373t844. See also Australian Human Rights Commission, "Respect@Work: Sexual Harassment National Inquiry Report (2020)," https://tinyurl.com/h6bzaky8.

private offices of health professionals."[28] Recent times have seen some Australian states ban conversion practices and pass laws that define them as a criminal offense.

The secularist nature of Australian society is perhaps a little overstated because one cannot discount the "profound impact of Christian missionaries, churches and Christian laypeople in shaping Australian institutions and values."[29] We live in times of heightened awareness of postcoloniality and postmodern sensibilities, yet we are sceptical about progress based on Enlightenment values. Despite the marginalization of Christianity as a religion in current times, the Bible is cited and debated in conversations on the issues highlighted here.

The challenge before us is to find a framework for addressing these and many other issues, to move beyond an acknowledgment of "complicity in colonial exploitation and cultural appropriation, in patriarchal expressions of male domination" and "forms of church practice and church governance that embody the power relations and ideology of the dominant culture" to something radically different, liberational, and transformative that enables the flourishing of human life.[30] This volume is an attempt to address this context and the issues confronting it and beyond through our reading of the Hebrew Bible and the New Testament.

CHAPTERS

The issues raised above require thoughtful and informed debate, in conversation with narratives within the biblical text that might speak to these issues. Consideration must be given to both the existence of these stories within our tradition and the uses to which they have been put within the evolving tradition of Christianity—that is, we must recognize, question, and challenge the lasting and negative impact of these stories in current times and interpretations. Despite their horror, when we engage these texts, they evoke conversation and contribute to the development of a consciousness, both political and religious, that allows us to look at acts of violence in earlier times and texts and, we believe, to confront our moral dilemmas and sharpen our political and religious stances in addressing violence as we encounter it today.

These readings are done *in memoriam* and in recognition of the countless women, men, and children who continue to experience similar violence today, some who have survived and many others who have not. Our audience is both the academy and the church, as these essays address live issues that dominate the

---

[28] Farah Tomazin, "'I Am Profoundly Unsettled': Inside the Hidden World of Gay Conversion Therapy," *The Age*, March 9, 2018, https://tinyurl.com/e9s6b39x.
[29] Lamb and Barns, *God*, ix.
[30] Quotations from Lamb and Barns, *God*, xi.

church and society but do so from an academic and contextual perspective. The feminist and liberative stance adopted herein reinforce the notion that interpretation of the biblical text is not only an academic pursuit but also a political and a pastoral project.

The contributors to the volume represent populations that make up Australia today: from South Africa, Tonga, India, the United States of America, Aotearoa, and European Australia, although not all these authors live in Australia. Several of us are first-generation migrants to this country and have become increasingly conscious of the fact that we live on another's land and are in the process of learning and coming to terms with the checkered history of this nation. Some have chosen to reflect in conversation with a very explicit context or issue, while others have not. But no self is ever naked of culture; culture and context are therefore implicit in all these readings. All essays are critical, creative, interdisciplinary, and ideologically charged biblical interpretations that engage feminism but also culture, economics, psychology, sociology, politics, and violence using varied, creative, and innovative methodological approaches (literary criticism, reading in juxtaposition or the contrapuntal method, letter writing) and diverse hermeneutical lenses (feminist, queer, islander, caste, contextual). The flow of this volume will lead you first to reflections that engage the more pressing issues raised by these texts within the Australian context and then take you further out into readings from within cultures and contexts beyond Australia before bringing you back. At the end, this work takes off again toward two of the subjects that mainline feminist scholarship has not fully engaged—novels and Dalits.

We recognize the absence and sorely miss reflections by Aboriginal scholars in this volume. The creation of Australia required Aboriginal dispossession. In the process, Aboriginal people were subject to large-scale violence and displacement from their homes and lands, and they were systematically excluded from the emerging nation physically, through confinement in reserves and settlements; legally, through subjection to a separate and inferior legal status; and culturally and psychologically, through an extraordinary forgetfulness, a voluntary amnesia that rendered them invisible within the nation. "Colonization created Australians and it also created Aborigines."[31] Aboriginal communities have borne the brunt of conquest, and they experience continuing vulnerability to governmental policies, interventions, and surveillance. The experience of Aboriginal women is distinct from that of other women affected by colonial relations, and we acknowledge the absence of these distinct voices.

Laura Griffin begins these reflections in chapter 2 by drawing a parallel between the biblical depiction of Midianite women in Num 25 and colonial

---

[31] Jan Pettman, *Living in the Margins: Racism, Sexism and Feminism in Australia* (Sydney: Allen & Unwin, 1992), 7.

authorities' views of Indigenous women in Australia. Using Trible's literary analysis as a method, Griffin builds upon Musa Dube's valuable analysis of the "contact zone" as the site of interaction between colonizer and colonized. Colonial/Israelite views of the Indigenous/Midianite woman are shown to arise from the simultaneous threat and opportunity posed by her reproductive body. Like the land they seek to occupy, the colonized/Midianite woman's body must be subdued and rendered productive for the colonial/Israelite nation. In parallel to the murder and sparing of Midianites in Numbers, we thus see in colonial Australia early prohibition of miscegenation give way to a logic of assimilation through intermarriage. In both Numbers and the Australian historical reality, these anxieties manifest as laws and terrorizing violence that seek to regulate allowable and prohibited forms of intercourse and assimilation.

Karen Eller analyzes Num 25 from a queer perspective in chapter 3. Disturbed and challenged by the silence and complicity of queer white Australians over indigenous Australians, Eller unpacks the use of some language within the text and uses the ambiguity found within it to suggest alternate meanings of the language that would be affirming of LGBQTI+ people. Eller also suggests that Num 25 is a national narrative that was adulterated for the purposes and advantage of the powerful and at the expense of the vulnerable, which is similar to how the stories of indigenous Australians and LGBQTI+ have been treated. She takes courage from the fact that, despite these attempts by the powerful to erase them, Midianites continue to exist, as do queers and indigenous Australians.

Chapter 4 finds Rachelle Gilmour asking, "Is Absalom Tamar's compassionate avenger?" as she revisits 2 Sam 13. Having established the fact that rape within the world of ancient Israel was not solely the violation of a woman but also the theft of a man's sexual property, Gilmour proceeds to show that Absalom's actions toward Tamar are not words of comfort but a means to his own political end. The revenge on Amnon is for Absalom's own injured masculinity. Engaging "patriarchal investments" in the story, Gilmour concludes that Tamar is the construction of a male author. Her violations begin in the house of her father, who has the power to send or withhold her, and end in the house of her brother, who has the power to silence her. She proposes that there is no good brother in the story, that the patriarchal underpinnings of culture, custom, and family are not subverted or challenged, but they are also not endorsed. The text narrates abuse and its terrible consequences with realism, leaving it open for interpreters to critique.

The story of the woman identified as a "Canaanite" in Matt 15 and as a "Syro-Phoenician" in Mark's gospel is troubling for many readers. The difference in identification in the two gospels is odd and has been commented on by interpreters. A juxtaposed reading of these gospel narratives alongside passages that describe treatment of the Canaanites in the Hebrew Bible is essential if we are to get a fuller picture and the significance of Jesus's response. In chapter 5, Dorothy

Lee reflects on Mark's version of the Syro-Phoenician woman and examines missional, pedagogical, paradigmatic, and christological readings of the text, with their diversity of viewpoints and arguments. She shows that, while the text is sometimes interpreted as a "chauvinistic" account of Jesus's attitude to the woman and her daughter, a fuller account of Mark's theology reveals it to be an exemplary and liberating faith narrative, with irony at the heart of its challenging imagery. In this sense, she concludes, this is a text of hope and promise rather than terror.

In chapter 6, Angela Sawyer brings together discourse on the public and private realities of domestic violence in Australia today with the portrayal of Zion in Deutero-Isaiah. She posits that Zion songs are a form of trauma literature that include metaphorical depictions of violent relationships with potential to speak into the contemporary conversation around domestic violence. Calling attention to domestic violence in Australia, Sawyer reframes Daughter Zion's journey in Deutero-Isaiah from desolate woman to restored bride and suggests that inherent to this image is a rhetorical resistance to stereotyped categorizations of mother and child, husband and wife. She sees a literary and pastoral resource in Deutero-Isaiah's Zion passages that would help conversation about domestic violence issues.

In chapter 7, Robyn Whitaker offers a reading of the conflict between the author of Revelation, John, and the prophet called "Jezebel" in Rev 2:20–23. She calls attention to the Jezebel text and its legacy in the way women today are silenced, disempowered, and threatened with sexualized violence when they dare to challenge male power and authority. She argues that the force of John's use of the name "Jezebel" and the accompanying rhetoric threatens sexual and rhetorical violence. The Christian tradition's continued invocation of Jezebel stands as a sobering reminder of the dangers that women face when authority is challenged.

In chapter 8, Adela Yabro Collins argues that women functioned as leaders in the communities founded by Paul, their leadership exercised in the setting of households and where practices of patronage played a significant role. Women who were heads of households exercised a high degree of leadership, but the most important role in Paul's view was that of apostles, like Junia, commissioned by the risen Christ. Collins unpacks the terminology of leadership in Pauline texts and suggests that women may have served in that capacity. Inscriptional evidence adds support for the ministry of women in antiquity. Collins identifies 1 Tim 2:9–15 as a text of terror because of its blatant attempt to silence women and exclude them from positions of authority. She calls into question the authority and power of such texts by showing that they were not normative in the early church and did not have their desired effect.

Chapter 9 delves into the world of early Christian literature. David Tombs offers a gendered rereading of the crucifixion narratives as texts of terror involving sexual violence. Deriving inspiration from Trible's analysis of Judg 19, Tombs notes that textual analysis needs to focus on both the text and the gaps in the text—

both what is said and what is left unsaid—if the extravagant violence and its meaning is to be properly recognized and remembered. By paying special attention to the features of text and silence in Matt 27:27–31 and drawing insight from contemporary torture reports that narrate the presence of sexual violence in torture practices, Tombs concludes that the repeated stripping and exposure of Jesus in Matt 27:27–31 deserves to be named as sexual abuse.

Development, be it industrial or agricultural, is driven by economics and reliant on transient and migrant labor in many countries of the world. There is an increasing trend globally toward the employment of short-term low-wage temporary migrant workers who are given rather limited political and legal privileges and protection against exploitation.[32] In chapter 10, Brent Pelton brings Judg 19 into conversation with issues of migrant labor in Australia. Drawing on insights from the book of Proverbs and the description of Woman Wisdom and Dame Folly, Pelton unpacks the identity of the female protagonist in Judg 19 as both wife and concubine. By referring to the woman as "concubine," the author is stripping her of her agency, value, and human dignity. Pelton sees the experience of the concubine as akin to the experience of the migrant worker—exploited, dehumanized, and disempowered; while the Levite acts in ways similar to that of the contractor in an Australian farm.

Chapter 11, by Gerald West, studies David's most trusted counsellor, Ahithophel, who betrays David and joins Absalom's rebellion. West pens two imaginary letters, one by Bathsheba to her grandfather Ahithopel, written after she was raped by David, and a second letter to Ahithopel from Tamar, written while in her brother Absalom's house, after she was raped by Amnon. West wonders if these letters prompted Ahithophel to resist David. West asks: "If gender-justice did play a role in his decision to resist, then why does he counsel Absalom to publicly rape the *Pilagshim* of David?" This is the question posed to Ahithophel in a third letter, this one written by the *Pilagshim* after they were raped by Absalom. West prompts us to consider how the grandfather of the raped Bathsheba could advocate the rape of other women—namely, the *Pilagshim*. Is Ahithophel engaging in resistance theology by siding with Absalom? How is it that he cannot see a contradiction between the injustices he is resisting and those he is perpetrating? West addresses these questions in a deconstructive narrative reading of 1 and 2 Sam, with Ahithophel as the ambiguous protagonist.

---

[32] "Based on current trends, Australia's projected population will be thirty-eight million by 2050 and migration will be contributing $1.625 billion (1.6 trillion) to Australia's GDP. Moreover, migration will have added 15.7 percent to our workforce participation rate and 5.9 percent in GDP per capita growth. Without migration, the population would stagnate, and our economy would go backwards" Henry Sherrell, "Economic Impact of Migration," n.d., https://tinyurl.com/2mpa5szs. See also Migration Council of Australia, "Economic Impact of Migration," https://tinyurl.com/57wmjpd4.

In Chapter 12, Jione Havea returns us to Australia. Havea offers a reading of the story of five sisters: Mahlah, Noah, Hoglah, Milcah, and Tirzah. The reading highlights the courage of these women to keep their dead father's name (Zelophehad) and memory alive (Num 27:1–11) and the issues that arise due to legal revisions (Num 36:1–12). The reading is presented in four letters (following West's theoretical positioning) addressed to Havea's Tongan relatives: a dead niece, a dead sister-in-law, a living four-year-old daughter, and an elder from the Kulin nations. These letters take advantage of the workings of orality and, in the process, expose how the two-part story of the five sisters manifests the "terror of texts." For example, what the sisters accomplished in Num 27 is rewritten in Num 36 in the interests of the tribal leaders. Among the upshots of these letters combined with the workings of orality is the realization that what happened to the five sisters is similar to the dispossession of the five indigenous nations—the Wurundjeri, Boonwurrung, Taungurong, Dja Dja Wurrung, and Wathaurung—that make up the Kulin nations and the proposal that the unnamed mother of the five sisters be given the name "Kulin." Havea emphasizes that these two moves are necessary responses to the terror of texts.

We know from personal experience and from testimonies of the marginalized that victimization and oppression can be internalized. In chapter 13, Monica Jyotsna Melanchthon journeys to India. Drawing inspiration and insights from the emotional and violent autobiography, *Outcaste*, by Dalit author Sharankumar Limbale, she analyzes the Jephthah narrative in which she sees parallels between Limbale's experience and that of Jephthah and his psyche. She decodes Jephthah's identity as the son of a prostitute—shamed, rejected, marginalized, and she considers the impact of the same on his unnamed daughter, as well as how the tyranny and mechanisms of the dominant group tame, neutralize, deflect, and suppress dissidence for that group's own ends.

FINAL QUESTIONS

We close this introductory chapter with an issue that was voiced when putting this volume together: Is it appropriate to include male scholars in the task of feminist interpretation, particularly when speaking of sexualized violence? Some participants at the one-day conference were offended that men were putting themselves in the shoes of victimized women and wondered if this was a form of cooptation of women's experience. Do men have the capacity to understand the eruptions and cries of female pain, anger, and distress? Should men wade into this debate? Now that women are speaking, should men not just listen? In conversation with two of the four male authors in this volume, it became clear that they did not intend to speak for women or on behalf of women. Rather, through their reflections they wrestle with the manner in which male aggression belittles women both in the text under study and in the world today. They attempt to understand why men do what they do and, in doing so, invite or perhaps compel all men to want to look at the nature of men and become part of the movement and transformative change that is so urgently required.

Engaging issues of violence within the biblical text risks inciting criticism and opposition because the very nature of the Bible as Scripture has the potential to polarize its readers, exacerbated by differences in approach and the hermeneutical principles employed by the interpreter. The experience of violence likewise extracts a variety of responses from its victims—from acknowledging violence to redefining it, to varied forms of resistance ranging from vigilance, protest, activism (both social and textual), advocacy, to armed struggle. Resistance and protest are, we believe, intrinsic to the experience of violence, and this volume calls attention to the complexity of violence as portrayed within the biblical text, especially when seen and analyzed through concrete experiences and realities. This book challenges readers to recognize how the Bible and its interpretations can reinforce the structures that underlie and renew violent systems—systems that marginalize, dehumanize, and subjugate. While it seeks to raise awareness and engender resistance among those who are the victims of violence, it also, on normative grounds, questions those that perpetrate and perpetuate violence. In so doing, this book is a modest but critical endeavor that seeks to assign political participation and agency to biblical studies and interpretation, rarely recognized or allowed an interventionalist role in everyday life.

BIBLIOGRAPHY

Australian Bureau of Statistics. "Migration, Australia: Statistics on Australia's International Migration (Interstate and Intrastate), and the Population by Country of Birth—Reference Period 2018–2019 Financial Year." April 28, 2020. https://tinyurl.com/k5f52hrv.

Australian Human Rights Commission. "Respect@Work: Sexual Harassment National Inquiry Report (2020)." https://tinyurl.com/h6bzaky8.

Bader, Mary Anna. *Sexual Violation in the Hebrew Bible: A Multi-Methodological Study of Genesis 34 and 2 Samuel 13*. New York: Lang, 2006.

Blyth, Caroline, Emily Colgan, and Katie B. Edwards, eds. *Rape Culture, Gender Violence, and Religion: Biblical Perspectives*. Cham, Switzerland: Palgrave Macmillan, 2018.

Blyth, Carolyn. *The Narrative of Rape in Genesis 34: Interpreting Dinah's Silence*. Oxford: Oxford University Press, 2010.

Bravehearts. "Child Sexual Assault: Facts and Statistics." October 2019. https://tinyurl.com/ufx7nphx.

Brown, Laura. "Feminist Paradigms of Trauma Treatment." *Psychotherapy: Theory Research Practice Training* 41 (2004): 464–71.

Bulbeck, Chilla. *Living Feminism: The Impact of the Women's Movement on Three Generations of Australian Women*. Cambridge: Cambridge University Press, 1997.
Claassens, L. Juliana M. *Writing and Reading to Survive: Biblical and Contemporary Trauma Narratives in Conversation*. Sheffield: Sheffield Phoenix, 2020.
Collins, John J. "The Zeal of Phinehas: The Bible and the Legitimation of Violence." *JBL* 122 (2003): 3–21.
Creach, Jerome F. D. *Violence in Scripture*. Interpretation. Louisville: Westminster John Knox, 2013.
Dux, Monica, and Zora Simic. *The Great Feminist Denial*. Melbourne: Melbourne University Press, 2008.
Exum, J. Cheryl. *Fragmented Women: Feminist (Sub)versions of Biblical Narratives*. 2nd ed. T&T Cornerstones. London: Bloomsbury T&T Clark, 2015.
"Grace Tame, Who Took on the Law over Rape Silencing, Named Australian of the Year." Nine News. January 25, 2021. https://tinyurl.com/2f6z2ewk.
Habyarimana, Bangambiki. *The Great Pearl of Wisdom*. Createspace, 2015. Kindle.
Humphreys, Cathy. "Allegations of Sexual Harassment and Abuse an Urgent Test for Government." *Pursuit*. March 5, 2021. https://tinyurl.com/h37f55nz.
Jenkins, Philip. *Laying Down the Sword: Why We Can't Ignore the Bible's Violent Verses*. New York: HarperOne, 2011.
Jervis-Bardy, Dan. "Senator Lidia Thorpe Speaks Out about Sexual Harassment in Parliament House." *Canberra Times*. March 23, 2021. https://tinyurl.com/4cjexfd2.
Judd, Bridget. "Sexual Harassment Affects Workplaces across Australia: So What Can We Do Better?" *ABC News*. March 1, 2021. https://tinyurl.com/y373t844.
Kato, Brooke. "What Is Cancel Culture? Everything to Know about the Toxic Online Trend." *New York Post*. July 10, 2020. https://tinyurl.com/4wkh5cdh.
Kirk-Duggan, Cheryl A. *Pregnant Passion: Gender, Sex and Violence*. Atlanta: Society of Biblical Literature, 2003.
Lamb, Winifred Wing Han, and Ian Barns, eds. *God Down Under: Theologies in the Antipodes*. Adelaide: ATF Press, 2003.
Lefkovitz, Lori Hope. *In Scripture: The First Stories of Jewish Sexual Identities* (Plymouth: Rowman & Littlefield, 2010),
Lipka, Hilary B. *Sexual Transgression in the Hebrew Bible*. Sheffield: Sheffield Phoenix, 2006.
Maguire, Emily. *This Is What a Feminist Looks Like: The Rise and Rise of Australian Feminism*. Canberra: NLA, 2019.
Mares, Peter. *Not Quite Australian: How Temporary Migration Is Changing the Nation*. Melbourne: Text Publishing Company, 2016.
Sherrell, Henry. "Economic Impact of Migration." n.d. https://tinyurl.com/2mpa5szs.
Migration Council of Australia. "Economic Impact of Migration." https://tinyurl.com/57wmjpd4.
Milne, Pamela J. "No Promised Land: Rejecting the Authority of the Bible." Pages 47–73 in *Feminist Approaches to the Bible: Symposium at the Smithsonian Institution, September 24, 1994*. Edited by Herschel Shanks. Washington, DC: Biblical Archaeology Society, 1995.
Mlambo-Ngcuka, Phumzile. "Violence against Women and Girls: The Shadow Pandemic." UN Women. April 6, 2020. https://tinyurl.com/2vvda994.

Pettman, Jan. *Living in the Margins: Racism, Sexism and Feminism in Australia.* London: Allen & Unwin, 1992.
Our Watch. "Quick Facts." https://tinyurl.com/7bwjep46.
Royal Commission into Institutional Responses to Child Sex Abuse. https://tinyurl.com/4zfcxhuv.
Root, Maria Primitiva Paz. "Reconstructing the Impact of Trauma on Personality" Pages 220–65 in *Personality and Psychopathology: Feminist Reappraisals.* Edited by Laura S. Brown and M. Ballou. New York: Guilford, 1992.
Scholz, Susanne. *Sacred Witness: Rape in the Hebrew Bible.* Minneapolis: Fortress, 2010.
Schroeder, Joy A. *Dinah's Lament: The Biblical Legacy of Sexual Violence in Christian Interpretation.* Minneapolis: Fortress, 2007.
Siebert, Eric A. *The Violence of Scripture: Overcoming the Old Testament's Troubling Legacy.* Minneapolis: Fortress, 2012.
Tomazin, Farah. "'I Am Profoundly Unsettled': Inside the Hidden World of Gay Conversion Therapy." *The Age.* March 9, 2018. https://tinyurl.com/e9s6b39x.
Trible, Phyllis. *Texts of Terror: Literary-Feminist Readings of Biblical Narratives.* OBT. Philadelphia: Fortress, 1984.
Victoria Health. "Violence against Women in Australia: An Overview of Research and Approaches to Primary Prevention." January 2017. https://tinyurl.com/5x54tzyk.
Weems, Renita J. *Battered Love: Marriage, Sex, and Violence in the Hebrew Prophets.* OBT. Minneapolis: Fortress, 1995.
Yamada, Frank M. *Configurations of Rape in the Hebrew Bible: A Literary Analysis of Three Rape Narratives.* New York: Lang, 2008.

2

Terrorizing Indigenous Women in the Contact Zone: Placing Cozbi and the Midianites in Colonial Australia

Laura Griffin

Israel ... began to have sexual relations with the women of Moab.... Moses said to the judges ... "Each of you shall kill any of your people who have yoked themselves to the Baal of Peor."... Moses said to them, "Have you allowed all the women to live?... kill every male among the little ones, and kill every woman who has known a man by sleeping with him. But all the young girls who have not known a man by sleeping with him, keep alive for yourselves.

— Numbers 25 and 31

Interracial relationships were both a source of anxiety about racial purity and a means through which the demise of the Aboriginal population could be imagined.... Politicians tried to engineer the "disappearance" of their Indigenous populations by physically dividing Aboriginal people from one another, removing families and individuals from the reserves, and removing children from their families.

— Katherine Ellinghaus, "Absorbing the 'Aboriginal Problem'"

This chapter reads Num 25 and 31 as texts of terror, extending the method employed by Phyllis Trible in her classic book.[1] When we attend to the characters of Cozbi and the Midianite women/girls, we see a contradiction between Cozbi's violent murder in Num 25 and the subsequent sparing of Midianite girls from

---

[1] The first epigraph is from Num 25:1, 6 and 31:15, 17. All biblical quotations and references in this chapter are from NRSV unless otherwise indicated. The second is from Katherine Ellinghaus, "Absorbing the 'Aboriginal Problem': Controlling Interracial Marriage in Australia in the Late Nineteenth and Early Twentieth Centuries," *Aboriginal History* 27 (2003): 186, 193.

slaughter in Num 31. In these texts, the Israelites (and their deity, YHWH) seem to hold inconsistent views of Midianite women: they are cast as dangerous, idolatrous, and to be expelled, yet they are also depicted as desirable and to be accepted into the nation of Israel.

My goal here is to unpack this contradiction and draw a parallel between the biblical depiction of Midianite women and colonial authorities' views of Indigenous women in Australia. I extend Trible's method in order to relate a literary analysis of the text to the parallel terrorizing of women in a specific social and historical context. While Trible's *Texts of Terror* focused on the biblical text and gestured only briefly toward women who may relate to the biblical characters, she acknowledged that to hear these ancient stories is to confess their present (and past) reality.[2] Taking up this challenge, I consider the story of the Midianite women of Numbers from my own location, that of a white (settler) woman living on stolen, unceded land—the land of the Wurundjeri people of the Kulin alliance—who seeks to understand the violence by which this came to be my family's home.

I also build upon the valuable work of postcolonial feminist biblical scholars, making particular use of Musa Dube's analysis of the "contact zone" as the site of interaction between colonizer and colonized.[3] Colonial/Israelite views of the Indigenous/Midianite woman are shown to arise from the simultaneous threat and opportunity posed by her reproductive body. Like the land they seek to occupy, the colonized/Midianite woman's body must be subdued and rendered productive for the colonial/Israelite nation. Parallel to the murder and sparing of Midianites in Numbers, we see in colonial Australia early prohibition of miscegenation

---

[2] Phyllis Trible, *Texts of Terror: Literary-Feminist Readings of Biblical Narratives*. SCM Classics (London: SCM, 2003), 23, 106.

[3] Musa W. Dube, "Dinah (Genesis 34) at the Contact Zone: 'Shall our Sister Become a Whore?,'" in *Feminist Frameworks: Power, Ambiguity, and Intersectionality*, ed. L. Juliana M. Claassens and Carolyn Sharp (London: Bloomsbury T&T Clark, 2017), 39–58. More generally, this chapter is informed by such postcolonial feminist biblical scholarship as Sharon H. Ringe, "Places at the Table: Feminist and Postcolonial Biblical Interpretation," in *The Postcolonial Bible*, ed. R. S. Sugirtharajah (Sheffield: Sheffield Academic, 1998); Alice Ogden Bellis, *Helpmates, Harlots, and Heroes: Women's Stories in the Hebrew Bible* (Louisville: Westminster John Knox, 2007); Pui-Lan Kwok, "Making the Connections: Postcolonial Studies and Feminist Biblical Interpretation," in *The Postcolonial Biblical Reader*, ed. R. S. Sugirtharajah (Oxford: Blackwell, 2006); Dube, "Intercultural Biblical Interpretations," *Swedish Missiological Themes* 98 (2010): 361–88; Dube, "Boundaries and Bridges: Journeys of a Postcolonial Feminist in Biblical Studies," *Journal of the European Society of Women in Theological Research* 22 (2014): 139–56; Dube, "Toward a Post-Colonial Feminist Interpretation of the Bible," *Semeia* 78 (1997): 11–26; Susanne Scholz, *Introducing the Women's Hebrew Bible* (London: Bloomsbury, 2014).

give way to a logic of assimilation through intermarriage.[4] In both the book of Numbers and colonial Australia, these anxieties manifest as laws and terrorizing violence that seek to regulate forms of intercourse, determining what is allowable and what prohibited; in both cases the logic of this violence is fixated on marriage/sexual relations, and children—particularly girls.

The first section of this chapter examines the biblical character of Cozbi in the literary context of Num 25, which leads to a broader discussion of foreign women in the Hebrew Bible more generally. I then move on to address the contradiction in the biblical text between exhortations against intermarriage and the assimilation of Midianite girls in Num 31. This contradiction is then explained using the concept of the colonial "contact zone," which enables me to then consider the Indigenous woman's reproductive body and address how we might go about reading these biblical texts in the context of colonial Australia. This requires discussion of colonial policies on miscegenation and on assimilation based on sanctioned intermarriage and removal of children. The common imperial logic underlying both the systemic violence of colonial authorities and the biblical narratives of Midianite women and girls are then analyzed before a brief conclusion.

THE MURDER OF COZBI THE MIDIANITE: NUMBERS 25

The biblical figure of Cozbi is found in Num 25, which is a composite text comprised of two main narratives. The first scene (verses 1–5) tells of Israel yoking itself to the Baal of Peor by engaging sexually and ritualistically with Moabite women and their cult. This angers YHWH, who commands Moses to impale Israel's chiefs in an effort at appeasement; Moses passes on a command to the judges to kill any member of the community who is involved in the wrong conduct. The second scene (verses 6-13) involves an Israelite man bringing a Midianite woman into his family before a weeping congregation. This sight angers Phinehas, who follows the couple and slays them by spearing them through the abdomen. This bloodshed is said to have stopped a plague which had killed 24,000. YHWH, speaking to Moses, condones Phinehas's actions and rewards him with a covenant of perpetual priesthood.

The remainder of the chapter (Num 25:14–18) attempts to consolidate the two narratives and draws connections to the historical context. This explanatory passage names the killed Israelite man—Zimri son of Salu—and Midianite

---

[4] The parallels between Num 25 and colonial forms of violence against Indigenous women are discussed in Anthony Rees, *[Re]reading Again: A Mosaic Reading of Numbers 25*, LHBOTS 589, Playing the Texts 19 (New York: Bloomsbury T&T Clark, 2015), 158–63. This chapter pursues this parallel in greater depth and detail, and it employs new conceptual frames in doing so.

woman—Cozbi daughter of Zur, a Midianite chief. Speaking again to Moses, YHWH orders an attack on the Midianites for their deception in both the yoking of Israel to the Baal of Peor and for the incident involving Cozbi. As a somewhat awkward final clarification, the plague is said to have resulted from the Peor affair from the beginning of the chapter.

We never hear Cozbi (or any other woman) speak in this chapter. Grammatically, Cozbi is an object, brought into the family (25:6). She is not even named until the end of the narrative, unlike her murderer, Phinehas, who is named and whose lineage is spelled out as soon as he enters the narrative. Cozbi's identity is depicted only in terms of her ethnicity (Midianite) and her relations to men—namely, her father, Zur, who is a clan leader, and her companion (perhaps captor or husband?), Zimri. The violence of the second scene is focused on Cozbi's body, and her belly (קבתה, *qovatah*) in particular. There is some ambiguity, as *qovatah* could refer to stomach, womb, or possibly even genitals; note also the wordplay with the *qubbah* (הקבה), the sanctuary or tent that is said to be entered by the couple (Num 25:8).[5]

The only verb directly attributed to the Moabite/Midianite women collectively is to "invite" or "call" in Num 25:2 (ותקראן, *vatiqrena*). Their action is thus hospitality and engagement—inviting the Israelites (presumably Israelite men, primarily if not exclusively) to engage sexually and ritualistically, joining in sex, eating, and worshipping.[6] As non-Israelites, these women are not bound by YHWH's commandments: they have committed no crime. Instead, it is Israelite men who have angered YHWH by "yoking Israel to the Baal of Peor" (Num 25:3). Nonetheless, it is the actions of the Moabite/Midianite women that are depicted as harassment, trickery, and deception. The women are explicitly blamed for the sinful conduct of Israelite men, and it is Cozbi (together with Zimri) who pays for this with her life, in order for the divine punishment, in the form of a plague, to be lifted.

Cozbi, whose name means "one who deceives or disappoints," is clearly treated in the text as a symbol of Midianite women more generally, who are themselves fused or confused with Moabite women.[7] This slippage is illustrative; this group of women is itself, like Cozbi, symbolic of a broader category: the non-Israelite (foreign) woman. The chapter also occupies a key position in the book. Numbers opens with a census of the generation who left Egypt but who are condemned to die in the wilderness, and chapter 26 gives a census of the new generation who will eventually occupy the promised land of Canaan. Chapter 25 is positioned as

---

[5] S. C. Reif, "What Enraged Phinehas?: A Study of Numbers 25:8," *JBL* 90 (1971): 202 notes that "an early tradition relates that Phinehas' spear pieced the woman's genitals."
[6] The possible connections between acts of worship and sexual engagement are discussed below in further detail.
[7] See Rees, *[Re]reading*, 130–31 on the meaning of Cozbi's name.

a climax to the narrative of the old generation, whose faith is shown to be faltering, and as a fulcrum to the book as a whole. Comparing the two censuses highlights the importance of Num 25, as it suggests that only two men of the old generation survive its plague. The position of the text is significant: the narratives in chapter 25 tell of a communal and cultic crisis for Israel and its relationship with YHWH. Cozbi's tale "comes at a moment when the great promise to the patriarchs is at risk of unfulfillment."[8] How this crisis comes about and how it is resolved are thus imbued with great theological and political significance. And the foreign woman's body is placed at the center of it all.

THE FOREIGN WOMAN IN THE HEBREW BIBLE

The sexualized body of the non-Israelite woman depicted in Num 25 is both the site of Israel's misconduct and the object of violence through which Israel is saved. Of course, the connection between sexual misconduct and treachery against YHWH repeats the marriage metaphor, which features throughout the Hebrew Bible as a symbol of Israel's oscillating relationship with YHWH (see for instance Jer 2–3; Hos 1–2; Ezek 16, 23). It emerges in Num 25 in language such as "to fornicate" (verse 1). The root of this word zanah (זנ״ה), carries the meaning of "whoring" or "harlotry":

> This understanding of the word is often used in a metaphorical sense in relation to Israel's relationship to Yahweh, so that when Israel is allured by other deities, this is understood as an act of *zanah* ("to whore"). In addition, when the people of Israel engage sexually with people of other nations, this is regarded as *zanah*.[9]

The "yoking" (attaching) of Israel to the Baal of Peor also adds to this sexual imagery.[10]

Readings of Cozbi, in particular, and her actions with Zimri tend to confirm or even conflate such interpretations. We see this in exegeses of the word *qubbah* (הקבה) at Num 25:8. As a *hapax legomenon*, this term has broad interpretive potential, yet readings of the word as "tent"—interpreted as a private dwelling or bedroom—tend to emphasize the nature of their misconduct as sexual and/or as cultic: "This is not simply an episode of inter-marriage which is potentially destabilising; it is a cultic act which directly, and perhaps deliberately, threatens the cult

---

[8] Helena Zlotnick Sivan, "The Rape Of Cozbi (Numbers XXV)," *VT* 51 (2001): 79. On the cultic nature of the intercourse between Cozbi and Zimri, see also Reif, "What Enraged Phinehas?"
[9] Rees, *[Re]reading*, 75–76, 122–24. Hence, *liznot*, לזנות is translated as "have sexual relations" in the NRSV.
[10] Rees, *[Re]reading*, 76.

of YHWH."[11] On this reading, Phinehas's attack is legitimated as a fulfilment of "his responsibility to safeguard the cult of YHWH as the only legitimate cult for Israel."[12] Is Cozbi possibly a priestess, who has set up the *qubbah* in order to attempt to stop the plague that is oppressing Israel? Might she be engaging ritualistically (possibly including sexually) with Zimri in order to help the Israelites?[13]

It is important to note here that even the language of interpretations that focus on the purported foreignness of non-Israelite women in the Hebrew Bible is problematic and arguably inappropriate. The Israelites are journeying through others' lands on their way to conquer and inhabit the promised land of Canaan (itself also otherwise settled and occupied), so they are the ones who are more rightly labelled "foreigners" or even potentially "invaders," were it not for the Midianites' gestures of hospitality. In Num 25, Israel is camping on Moabite/Midianite land. Zimri is the foreigner, Cozbi the local inhabitant. It is thus more accurate to refer to the non-Israelite women in this chapter as local, even Indigenous, women who interact in various ways with foreign Israelite men.[14]

THE AMBIGUITY OF INTERMARRIAGE AND ASSIMILATION OF MIDIANITE GIRLS

Numbers 25—the demise of Cozbi and Zimri in particular—is widely interpreted, whether approvingly or more critically, as an exhortation to Israel against

---

[11] Barbara E. Organ, "Pursuing Phinehas: A Synchronic Reading (Highlighting the Interaction, Composition and Purpose of Biblical Narrative)," *CBQ* 63 (2001): 208. Organ even goes so far as to consider Cozbi "as the oracular medium parallel to Moses himself, operating in her alternative *qûbbâh*. Her position and activity hit right at the core of the worship of YHWH" (209). See also Reif, "What Enraged Phinehas?," who discusses historical evidence for reading *qubbah* (הקבה) as a tent-shrine attended by a female priest and occupied by elite women, providing divination in times of crisis.
[12] Organ, "Pursuing."
[13] Reif, "What Enraged Phinehas?"
[14] Further on the question of language, I note that Musa W. Dube, whose scholarship is engaged below, uses "native" woman. Because this is an offensive term to many Indigenous people, including in Australia, I avoid it and instead adopt the language of "local" and "Indigenous" interchangeably (but I have not changed the language in direct quotations of Dube's work). I also acknowledge that the language of "colonized" to refer to people and lands is problematic, as it can be read to imply the colonial process as a *fait accompli*—namely, that a person or place is an already completely "colonized" object. This may be seen as not only objectifying but also arguably inaccurate, given the contested and open-ended nature of colonial practices and subjugation.

intermarriage with Indigenous women.[15] But this reading ignores the ambiguity in this text, and elsewhere in the Hebrew Bible, toward intermarriage with non-Israelite women in general and Midianite women in particular. For instance, the Midianite women/brides Cozbi and Zipporah sit in direct contrast: it was acceptable for Moses to take a Midianite woman as his wife (Exod 2:21), but for Zimri it was punishable by death.

The Hebrew Bible as a whole can be seen as displaying a repeated ambiguity regarding non-Israelite wives.[16] Throughout the canon (for example, in Malachi and Ezra-Nehemiah) we can see a cycle of Israel intermarrying with local women and then condemning and rejecting them, as well as their children (see Ezra 2:59–62; Neh 7:61–65; 1 Chr 2:3–55; Ps 108:34–36; Mal 2:10–16). Of course, as a recurring theme, intermarriage is intimately tied up with the narrative of Israel's faithfulness to YHWH, as explained above. Numbers 25 thus demonstrates an intermarriage exhortation and contradiction in the broader Hebrew Bible. In particular, the brutal slaying of Cozbi as the symbolic Midianite bride in Num 25 sits in stark contrast with YHWH's attitude to Midianite virgins in the ensuing massacre of the Midianites in Num 31. In the war against Midian, which seems to result from the events of chapter 25, the Israelite invaders have killed the men and taken the women and their children captive (Num 31:9) alongside other booty. Upon their return, they are chastised by Moses, who says to them:

> Have you allowed all the women to live? These women here, on Balaam's advice, made the Israelites act treacherously against the LORD in the affair of Peor, so that the plague came among the congregation of the LORD. Now, therefore, kill every male among the little ones, and kill every woman who has known a man by sleeping with him. But all the young girls who have not known a man by sleeping with him, keep alive for yourselves. (Num 31:15–18)

Cozbi is thus a dangerous Indigenous woman who threatens Israel's boundaries and purity—its very survival, even—but the surviving Midianite virgins are explicitly ordered to be incorporated into the people of Israel. As Helena Zlotnick Sivan observes, this is a "spectacular contrast."[17]

---

[15] Rees, *[Re]reading*, 134–37; Yonina Dor, "From the Well in Midian to the Baal of Peor: Different Attitudes to Marriage of Israelites to Midianite Women," in *Mixed Marriages: Intermarriage and Group Identity in the Second Temple Period*, ed. Christian Frevel (New York: T&T Clark, 2011).

[16] Indeed, the forewarning by YHWH in Exod 34:15–16 can also be interpreted as a prediction of precisely the events of Num 25; see Rees, *[Re]reading*, 76.

[17] Sivan, "Rape," 70.

LOCAL WOMEN AND ISRAELITE MEN IN THE CONTACT ZONE

We can make sense of this contradiction—a woman who is viewed as a threat yet absorbed by the very people who view her as such—if we view Moab/Midian as what Mary Louise Pratt called a colonial "contact zone." The term refers to

> the space of colonial encounters, the space in which peoples geographically and historically separated come into contact with each other and establish ongoing relations, usually involving conditions of coercion, radical inequality, and intractable conflict.... A "contact" perspective emphasizes how subjects are constituted in and by their relations to each other.[18]

The concept of "contact zone" can be used not only to offer an alternative to the image and ideology of separateness in colonial worlds, but also to focus upon and question the very production of the ideology itself. This is demonstrated by Dube, who takes up the concept in her postcolonial feminist analyses of biblical texts. Dube observes the tension between separation and interaction thus:

> The social, sexual, economic and political intercourse in the colonial context is characterised by a dynamic tension. That is, while it is a contact zone, it is simultaneously dependent on the ideological claim of keeping races apart on the basis of racial, religious or cultural superiority of the colonizer.... For the purpose of oppressing, exploiting, and controlling the colonized, the colonizer always peddles an ideology of superiority, separation and purity, when facts on the grounds attest to something else.[19]

This conceptualization of the contact zone is helpful for our purposes as we unpack the Israelite contradiction regarding intermarriage with Indigenous women as articulated above.

Dube helpfully situates the colonized woman within the ideologies and practices of the contact zone. In particular, the Indigenous woman's body is the center of the contradiction being analyzed, because the Indigenous woman is symbolic as well as more literally productive of the conquered land and the future of the colonizing nation:

> Although native women may be depicted negatively and intermarriages between the sons of colonizing heroes are seemingly discouraged, the interaction is nevertheless permitted. The native woman can and should cross the boundaries

---

[18] Mary L. Pratt, *Imperial Eyes: Travel Writing and Transculturation* (New York: Routledge, 1992), 6–7.
[19] Dube, "Dinah," 41.

towards the colonizing heroes, for she represents the desires of the colonial dreams. She is the land that must exchange hands, from native to the colonizing heroes.[20]

This movement is one-way; despite any sexual or other intercourse, the foreign man does not become a subject of the local woman's family or community. It is the Indigenous woman who is objectified as an entity to be transferred.

However, as Cozbi's slaughter demonstrates, the Indigenous woman's coming to the colonizers cannot simply take any form. The modes of intercourse and the relations such women create in the contact zone are an important target of struggle and control. Cozbi approaches Israel as an elite, powerful at least politically if not also cultically; as such, she presents a threat, even even though she is "brought" by Zimri. Their union suggests relations of alliance and even equality between Israel and Midian.[21] In contrast, the Midianite virgins of Num 31 are captives, victims of dispossession and terrorizing violence by Israel. As young girls, they occupy perhaps the lowest social role within the community.

POWER TO PRODUCE THE NEW NATION

The contradictory and unstable place of local women in the contact zone reflects their reproductive power, as this makes them alternatively dangerous and/or valuable. Cozbi was speared through her belly—possibly her womb—in a symbolic rejection of her potential progeny with Zimri.[22] In contrast, the Midianite virgins represent not merely war plunder as chattel or labor but wombs for bearing the future Israel. Crucially, the Midianite virgins will not raise Midianite children. The desirability of their reproductive power depends upon the abandonment of their prior identity and kinship relations, as their own mothers, fathers, and male siblings have all been slaughtered.

This point is key to understanding the acceptance or disavowal of local women in the Hebrew Bible more broadly. Local women who wed Israelite men—who come to worship YHWH and thus accept and validate the Israelite power structure as well as Israel's occupation of the land—are cast as heroines and rewarded with powerful progeny.[23] But those who resist YHWH and Israelite

---

[20] Dube, "Dinah," 53–54.
[21] A number of parallels can be drawn between this and the Dinah narrative: relations of equality and alliance in the form of intermarriage by offering of elite daughters are rejected in favor of unilateral destruction and conquest; see Dube, "Dinah," 53–55.
[22] Rees, *[Re]reading*, 84–85.
[23] For instance, Ruth, a Moabite woman whose great grandchildren included King David; Zipporah, who bore Shebuel son of Gershom and Rehabiah son of Eliezer (1 Chr 23:16–

law/authority and instead seek to retain their native identity and cultic practices are denounced and even subjected to various forms of violence—the classic example being Jezebel.[24] This is because they present a threat to the legitimacy of the colonizers and the colonizing mission more generally. The Indigenous woman who is sexually welcoming to the colonizer in a passive, objectified sense is approved. The Indigenous woman whose sexuality poses (or is seen to be wielded as) a threat to Israel because it tempts them to worship foreign gods is reviled.

Under the logic of empire, the reproductive capacities of the Indigenous woman's body, as with the productive capacities of the land, must be contained, controlled, and put to use for the colonizing group. Maintaining this dynamic requires one to vacillate between notions and practices of purity and separation, on the one hand, and engagement and assimilation on the other. This explanation deciphers the colonizers' ideology of purity and separation. The local woman's threat to the group purity of the colonizers is not biological, racial, or genetic; it is political and cultural. As long as her sexuality and reproductive potential is controlled and possessed by the colonizers, she serves to legitimate their occupation of the land and perpetuate their group. Her children, as long as they are borne to a colonizing man, will be accepted as part of the new people—hence the emphasis on the Midianite girls' virginity in Num 31:18.

My analysis of local women in the contact zone has thus far focused upon the world within the text of Num 25 (and the Hebrew Bible more generally) and articulated the colonial ideologies contained therein. Of course, these ideologies are not merely contained in textual worlds. They have materialized, and continue to materialize, in the real-life colonial contact zones of various times and geographies. As Dube has shown in her work on the Dinah narrative in the biblical text, it involves striking parallels with the historical realities of the colonial contact zone of the Cape Colony of nineteenth-century southern Africa. Inspired by Dube's reading, I here extend Trible's methodology in order to argue that contradictory depictions of the Indigenous woman as analyzed in the texts of Num 25 and 31 can be observed in the colonizers' ideology, law, and practices in the contact zone of colonial Australia. The terrorizing violence exacted upon Cozbi and the other Midianite women and girls has played out in the genocidal practices of Australia's colonial authorities against Indigenous women and girls.

---

17); and Asenath, who became Joseph's wife (Gen 41:45) and mother to Manasseh and Ephraim (Gen 41:50; 46:20).

[24] 1 Kgs 17–19, 21; 2 Kgs 9:30–37.

READING COZBI AND THE MIDIANITE GIRLS IN COLONIAL AUSTRALIA

Before proceeding with the analysis, it is worth reflecting on the appropriateness of drawing comparisons between the contact zone of Moab/Midian in Num 25 and 31 and that of colonial Australia. While the two illustrate many parallels, as I will outline in detail, there are also important differences. For instance, the fate of the Midianites according to the biblical account is one of near complete decimation (and total assimilation of all young girls). There is no space in the Israelite narrative for (effective) resistance or any ongoing community with a Midianite identity. By comparison, the ongoing struggles of Aboriginal people and communities in Australia are undeniably more complex.

I cannot purport to speak on behalf of Indigenous people or communities of any place or time, to represent their perspectives, understandings, and lived experiences. A rich array of other sources, academic and otherwise, record and give voice to Aboriginal women's stories of survival, strategy, and resistance in the Australian contact zone.[25] Rather, I am concerned with the views of Indigenous women that were held and propagated by colonial authorities in Australia, and with how such views served to legitimate colonizing violence and terror of various kinds against these women and their families. My focus on the colonizers' ideology is not meant as an endorsement of it; on the contrary, my aim is to critique and deconstruct it. But there is nonetheless an inherent risk of reiterating or confirming the colonizers' objectifying views of Indigenous women unless a space is maintained for the possibility, always, of resistance in multiple forms.

PURITY AND SEPARATION: THE THREAT OF MISCEGENATION

The same central contradiction concerning Indigenous women that we saw play out in Num 25 and 31 can be clearly seen in ideological views about and treatment of Indigenous women in colonial Australia.[26] This is evident in the shifting colonial

---

[25] See, e.g., the important work of Palawa scholar Lee Miena Skye: Skye, "How Australian Aboriginal Christian Womanist *Tiddas* (Sisters) Theologians Celebrate the Eucharist," in *Reinterpreting the Eucharist: Explorations in Feminist Theology and Ethics*, ed. Anne Elvey et al. (London: Routledge, 2014), 283–307; Skye, "How Australian Aboriginal *Tiddas* (Sisters) Theologians Deal with the Threat of Genocide," *Feminist Theology* 23 (2015): 128–42; Skye, "Australian Aboriginal Catholic Women Seek Wholeness: Hearts Are Still Burning," *Pacifica* 19 (2006): 283–307; Skye, "Australian Aboriginal Women's Christologies," in *The Strength of Her Witness: Jesus Christ in the Global Voices of Women*, ed. Elisabeth A. Johnson (Maryknoll, NY: Orbis Books, 2016).

[26] It is difficult to define "colonial" Australia in both time and space, because structures and practices of colonization are ongoing. Notably, many of the policies and forms of violence

laws on miscegenation—that is, sexual intercourse or intermarriage between races. While such sexual unions were officially discouraged or prohibited, they were nonetheless unofficially accepted as inevitable, at least between Indigenous women and European men. A shift then occurred, at different times in the different states and territories, to official sanction for "constructive miscegenation" as a strategy for biological absorption and cultural assimilation.[27] This was accompanied by the targeting of so-called mixed-race children for removal from families.

Practically from the first colonial encounters and attacks by Europeans on Indigenous people on land that would become known as Australia in the late eighteenth century, colonizer men and local women engaged sexually—that is to say, the contact zone was always one of sexual encounter and intercourse, and this continued throughout the colonial period: "Many [Indigenous] women worked as prostitutes or were coerced into sex with white men. Sexual pleasures were in strong demand by the predominantly male population."[28] While not all sexual relations were forced, any question of consent or agency on the part of Indigenous women in this contact zone must be appreciated in the broader "political, economic and social context of their actions [which] makes the concept of choice problematical."[29] This broader context was one of extreme and ongoing frontier violence, deadly epidemics, and mass dispossession of land and resources. Colonizers' views of Indigenous women perpetuated and purportedly legitimated such sexual violence and terror; as these women were constructed by colonizing discourse as "universal whores" simply "there for the taking," rape of Indigenous women by colonizer men was regarded by colonial authorities as "inconsequential."[30]

Of course, such intercourse was not inconsequential. Beyond experiences of trauma and exploitation, intercourse between colonizer men and Indigenous women also threatened to produce legal, economic, and kinship relations and obligations, often in Indigenous laws if not also colonial ones.[31] Official colonial laws

---

referred to in this chapter have taken place not (only) in the nineteenth and early twentieth centuries but also in living memory, and they remain ongoing conditions for many Aboriginal women and their families.

[27] Ellinghaus, "Absorbing."

[28] Patricia Grimshaw et al., *Creating a Nation* (Perth: API Network, Curtin University of Technology, Australian Research Institute, 2006), 136–37.

[29] Mary A. Jebb and Ann Haebich, "Across the Great Divide: Gender Relations on Australian Frontiers," in *Gender Relations in Australia: Domination and Negotiation*, ed. Kay Saunders and Robert Evans (Sydney: Harcourt Brace Jovanovich, 1992), 36.

[30] Grimshaw et al., *Creating*, 145. On the sexualizing of Indigenous women and their bodies, see also Hannah Robert, "Disciplining the Female Aboriginal Body: Inter-racial Sex and the Pretence of Separation," *Australian Feminist Studies* 16 (2001): 69–81.

[31] Robert, "Disciplining."

and policies thus attempted to suppress and deny such consequences by ensuring the freedom of European men to use Aboriginal women and walk away with their social status intact. Intermarriages were made illegal, in part to protect white men from responsibility rather than to protect Aboriginal women from abuse.[32]

The pretense of separation maintained through the constructed illicit nature of miscegenation was a thin one, or at least contradictory.[33] Although liaisons between colonizing men and Indigenous women were seen as morally dangerous indulgences on the part of the men, they were largely dismissed as long as they were fleeting. This was partly because turning a blind eye allowed white men to continue to rape and exploit Aboriginal women without real fear of reproach. But it was also partly because the colonizers believed that the Aboriginal race was proceeding along an inevitable path to extinction. Thus, policies of segregation and so-called protection of Aboriginal communities on reserves were "based on the premise that Aborigines were a dying or doomed race."[34]

THE HALF-CASTE MENACE AND BREEDING OUT THE COLOR

The problem with this premise is rather predictable given that sexual unions were not without consequence, despite the best efforts of the colonial authorities. As Patrick Wolfe summarizes, "the single most important practical contradiction to have obstructed the logic of elimination was quintessentially gendered. This was the sexual abuse that male colonisers visited upon Aboriginal women everywhere."[35] The products of such unions were, of course, mixed-race children. And, given that white men were unwilling to take on responsibility for these children (or were even legally prohibited from doing so), the result was a growth rather than a dwindling away of Indigenous families and communities.

"The romance of the dying race steadily gave way to the spectre of the 'half-caste menace.'"[36] That so-called menace did not comprise any organized political or direct economic threat to the colonial presence or endeavor. Rather, the growth of Indigenous communities lay in direct contrast to the colonial vision of a "white Australia." Anxieties thus also arose at this time in relation to infant mortality and declining birth rates among white women in Australia. In a sense, then, the specter

---

[32] Aborigines Department, Battye Library: 827/1906, as quoted in Jebb and Haebich, "Across the Great Divide," 36.
[33] This pretence was also the basis for a continued "contrast between civilised selves and uncivilised Others" according to Robert, "Disciplining," 72.
[34] Grimshaw et al., *Creating*, 274; see also Ellinghaus, "Absorbing."
[35] Patrick Wolfe, "Nation and MiscegeNation: Discursive Continuity in the Post-Mabo Era," *Social Analysis: The International Journal of Social and Cultural Practice* 36 (1994): 93–152.
[36] Wolfe, "Nation and MiscegeNation," 101.

of mixed-race Aboriginal children was numerical, as "this section of the Aboriginal population threatened to expand exponentially."[37]

Containing this threat meant introducing the possibility that mixed-race progeny could be absorbed within the colonizer community. Laws on miscegenation shifted to reflect this new logic of assimilation. Rather than ceasing with this shift, controls over intermarriage played a crucial new role. Specifically, there was now one acceptable interracial pairing: that of a mixed-race Indigenous woman with a white man. As Indigenous people already required approval from colonial authorities to marry, this played out as recently as 1940, as colonial authorities denied permission for unions deemed undesirable and granted permission for desirable ones:

> In the Territory the mating of Aboriginals with any person other than an Aboriginal is prohibited. The mating of coloured aliens with any female of part Aboriginal blood is also prohibited. Every endeavour is being made to breed out the colour by elevating female half-castes to white standard with a view to their absorption by mating into the white population. The adoption of a similar policy throughout the Commonwealth is, in my opinion, a matter of vital importance.[38]

The act of "breeding out the colour" through constructive miscegenation centered on the capacity of mixed-race Aboriginal women to (eventually) bear white sons for the colonial nation. The dehumanization of Indigenous women as mere wombs for realizing this colonial vision is reflected in figure 1.

Putting this assimilation strategy into effect meant removing mixed-race children from their Aboriginal mothers, which gave rise to the "Stolen Generations" of Indigenous children. The means by which children were taken, justifications for doing so, and laws relating to removal have been well documented.[39] Most significant for my analysis, the strategy focused particularly on girls:

---

[37] Wolfe, "Nation and MiscegeNation," 100.

[38] C. E. Cook, Chief Protector of Aborigines, to Administrator of the Northern Territory, February 7, 1933, National Archives of Australia, Commonwealth Records Series, Department of the Interior file A659/1; 1940/1/408, as quoted in P. R. Bartrop, "The Holocaust, the Aborigines, and the Bureaucracy of Destruction: An Australian Dimension of Genocide," *Journal of Genocide Research* 3 (2001): 75–87; see also Grimshaw et al., *Creating*. As Ellinghaus, "Absorbing," 192 summarizes: "Legislators fought a losing battle to create a society which would eventually be 'bred' white."

[39] Ellinghaus, "Absorbing."

Figure 1. Three generations of "breeding out the colour." From A. O. Neville, *Australia's Coloured Minority, Its Place in the Community* (Sydney: Currawong, 1947), 72.

"It was a presumption for many years that we girls would grow up and marry nice white boys," says Aboriginal woman Barbara Cummings, a member of the Stolen Generations. "We would have nice fairer children who, if they were girls, would marry white boys again and eventually the colour would die out. That was the original plan—the whole removal policy was based on the women because the women could breed."[40]

One scholar has calculated "that 72 percent of all the children over 12 who were removed from 1912 to 1928 were girls" and described this as "an intervention to restrict and control young Aboriginal women's sexual activity."[41] The impacts of this genocidal policy are difficult to overstate: "It is probably fair to say that except for the remotest regions of the nation, there was not a single Aboriginal family which had not been touched by the policy of removal. Everybody had lost someone."[42]

CONTAMINATION, CONQUEST, AND CONVERSION

Having traced the complexities of intermarriage between colonizer men and Aboriginal women in the contact zone of colonial Australia, we can now see the

---

[40] Jens Korff, "A Guide to Australia's Stolen Generations," *Creative Spirits*, January 14, 2021, https://tinyurl.com/ezmztz8x.
[41] Peter Read, "The Myth of the Stolen Generations—A Rebuttal," *ABC Online*, October 4, 2010, https://tinyurl.com/3686wwcv. See also Heather Goodall, "'Saving the Children': Gender and the Colonization of Aboriginal Australian Children in NSW, 1788 to 1990," *Aboriginal Law Bulletin* 44 (1990): 6–9.
[42] Peter Read, *A Hundred Years War: The Wiradjuri People and the State* (Canberra: Australian National University Press, 1988). See also Korff, "Guide."

parallels with the analysis of the biblical texts as above. In both settings, local women—at least as seen by foreign authorities—are the focus of a tension or contradiction that arises from their reproductive power. On the one hand, such women are seen as dangerous and threatening to the legitimacy of the colonizer's presence, as well as the security and integrity of the colonizing nation. This is particularly so where they may seek to engage with colonizing men on terms of equality or mutual dependence, as perhaps Cozbi did. On the other hand, local women are constructed as potential vessels for the future of the colonizing nation, as in the case of the Midianite virgins and Indigenous girls stolen from their families by colonial authorities.

The key to an Indigenous woman's placement in either of these two roles is the nature of her relations both to the colonizing man and to her traditional community. The Indigenous woman who welcomes the colonizing man and desires his presence is obviously privileged in these narratives.[43] As argued above, the language of purity and separation is employed in colonial ideology not to preclude intercourse altogether, but to quash relations of equality or resistance. Australian colonial strategies of assimilation were not based on notions of genetic purity or immaculacy. If they were, no miscegenation would ever have a sanctioned place in the colonizing agenda. Just as the threat of the Moabite women was cultic rather than genetic, in Australia the threat of miscegenation was a political and cultural one—a threat to the colonizing endeavor rather than merely the genetic composition of the colonizing people.

In this imperial ideology, what is threatening is not the local woman herself. It is her connection to (and potential continuation of) her Indigenous or Midianite identity, and thus her tradition and culture. The Indigenous woman, like the colonized land she represents, is not simply to be avoided. She must be absorbed into the colonizer's identity and mission. Of course, in the Australian context, this fits with a broader program of conversion and civilization, which involved active destruction of Indigenous traditions and practices and instruction in Western ways of life and thinking.[44] For an individual Indigenous woman, then, her "right to be treated as an adult or 'exempted' from Aboriginal status was only granted if … [she] stopped associating with and living an Aboriginal lifestyle."[45] Only in such

---

[43] As Dube, "Dinah," 52 observes of the "contact zone" more generally, "indigenous populations/land are constructed as desiring if not adoring their colonising partner."

[44] This chapter has analyzed the world of the biblical text and the world of colonial Australia in parallel rather than making any explicit argument that the biblical text itself played any causative or facilitative role in the colonization of Australia. This is certainly a strong possibility but not a question that I have taken up here. For instance, see Jebb and Haebich, "Across the Great Divide," 30–31 on the influence of Christian values and the Christianizing/civilizing mission on the colonial Australian view of Aboriginal gender relations.

[45] Grimshaw et al., *Creating*, 275.

circumstances, and only if she partnered with a white man, would her progeny be secured as within the colonizing nation.

CONCLUSION

This chapter has analyzed the parallels between the tales of the Moabite/Midianite women in Num 25 and 31 and the ideologies and policies of colonial Australia. I have employed the concept of a contact zone, a space "where disparate cultures meet, clash, and grapple with each other, often in highly asymmetrical relations of domination and subordination—like colonialism, slavery, or their aftermaths as they are lived out across the globe today."[46]

Australia's colonial history could yield more parallels to both Cozbi and the Midianite girls, based not on colonial policy but on the opportunism exercised by colonizer men in their relations against Aboriginal communities and women. Unknowable numbers of Aboriginal women have been raped and killed by colonizer men in Australia. Recalling the gruesome violence against Cozbi, there were incidents of torture and murder involving Indigenous women being speared by colonizer men, even in their vaginas.[47] Likewise, there are recorded accounts of white men who massacred Aboriginal families and communities while sparing young girls "as sexual hostages," a clear echo of the kidnapping of Midianite girls.[48] Yet the main focus in this chapter has been the more formal and systemic violence produced by colonial ideology and policy in Australian history. I have argued that the contradictory attitudes of colonizer men to native women as found in the narratives of Cozbi and the Midianite girls can also be witnessed in colonial Australian attitudes to Indigenous women and girls. These seemingly conflicting attitudes can be accounted for when we attend to the reproductive power of indigenous women and the colonizer's need to assimilate and convert such women to the desires and visions of the colonial nation. My approach involved extending Trible's method of literary analysis of biblical texts of terror in order to consider how the patriarchal and colonial logic underlying such terrorizing of women and girls has been echoed in a particular historical reality.

While these parallels are interesting and instructive, in the case of colonial Australia (at least) the effects of this ideology are not confined to the official texts and narratives of the colonizers. The conquest and conversion that are key to understanding colonial attitudes toward Indigenous women have played out in people's lives to devastating effect. The violence, destruction, and dispossession

---

[46] Pratt, *Imperial Eyes*, 4.
[47] Janine P. Roberts, *Massacres to Mining: The Colonisation of Aboriginal Australia* (Melbourne: Dove Communications, 1981), 19.
[48] Grimshaw et al., *Creating* 132–33; Roberts, *Massacres to Mining*, 20.

supposedly legitimated by this colonial ideology are difficult to overstate. Indigenous children, including girls, continue to be removed from their families at higher rates than ever before.[49] While resistance is always ongoing, Indigenous women and children throughout Australia carry the trauma and other consequences of this colonialism and will continue to do so for generations to come.

BIBLIOGRAPHY

Anthony, Thalia. "NTER Took the Children Away," *Arena Magazine* 148 (2017): 21–25.

Bartrop, Paul R. "The Holocaust, the Aborigines, and the Bureaucracy of Destruction: An Australian Dimension of Genocide." *Journal of Genocide Research* 3 (2001): 75–87.

Bellis, Alice Ogden. *Helpmates, Harlots, and Heroes: Women's Stories in the Hebrew Bible.* 2nd ed. Louisville: Westminster John Knox, 2007.

Dor, Yonina. "From the Well in Midian to the Baal of Peor: Different Attitudes to Marriage of Israelites to Midianite Women." Pages 150–69 in *Mixed Marriages: Intermarriage and Group Identity in the Second Temple Period.* Edited by Christian Frevel. New York: T&T Clark, 2011.

Dube, Musa W. "Boundaries and Bridges: Journeys of a Postcolonial Feminist in Biblical Studies." *Journal of the European Society of Women in Theological Research* 22 (2014): 139–56.

———. "Dinah (Genesis 34) at the Contact Zone: 'Shall our Sister Become a Whore?'" Pages 39–58 in *Feminist Frameworks: Power, Ambiguity, and Intersectionality.* Edited by L. Juliana M. Claassens and Carolyn Sharp. London: Bloomsbury T&T Clark, 2017.

———. "Intercultural Biblical Interpretations." *Swedish Missiological Themes* 98 (2010): 361–88.

———. "Toward a Post-Colonial Feminist Interpretation of the Bible." *Semeia* 78 (1997): 11–26.

Ellinghaus, Katherine. "Absorbing the 'Aboriginal Problem': Controlling Interracial Marriage in Australia in the Late Nineteenth and Early Twentieth Centuries." *Aboriginal History* 27 (2003): 183–207.

Goodall, Heather. "'Saving the Children': Gender and the Colonization of Aboriginal Australian Children in NSW, 1788 to 1990." *Aboriginal Law Bulletin* 44 (1990): 6–9.

Grimshaw, Patricia, Marilyn Lake, Ann McGrath, and Marian Quartly. *Creating a Nation.* Perth: API Network, Curtin University of Technology, Australian Research Institute, 2006.

Jebb, Mary Anne, and Anna Haebich. "Across the Great Divide: Gender Relations on Australian Frontiers." Pages 20–41 in *Gender Relations in Australia: Domination and Negotiation.* Edited by Kay Saunders and Robert Evans. Sydney: Harcourt Brace Jovanovich, 1992.

---

[49] This has been facilitated by such recent policies as the Northern Territory Emergency Response; see Thalia Anthony, "NTER Took the Children Away," *Arena Magazine* 148 (2017): 21–25. While the ideologies and laws that underpin such child removals may have changed, the impact is no less devastating for Indigenous families and communities.

Korff, Jens. "A Guide to Australia's Stolen Generations." *Creative Spirits*. January 14, 2021. https://tinyurl.com/ezmztz8x.

Kwok, Pui-Lan. "Making the Connections: Postcolonial Studies and Feminist Biblical Interpretation." Pages 45–63 in *The Postcolonial Biblical Reader*. Edited by R. S. Sugirtharajah. Oxford: Blackwell, 2006.

Neville, A. O. *Australia's Coloured Minority, Its Place in the Community*. Sydney: Currawong, 1947.

Organ, Barbara E. "Pursuing Phinehas: A Synchronic Reading (Highlighting the Interaction, Composition and Purpose of Biblical Narrative)." *CBQ* 63 (2001): 203–18.

Pratt, Mary Louise, *Imperial Eyes: Travel Writing and Transculturation*. New York: Routledge, 1992.

Read, Peter. *A Hundred Years War: The Wiradjuri People and the State*. Canberra: Australian National University Press, 1988.

———. "The Myth of the Stolen Generations—A Rebuttal." *ABC Online*. October 4, 2010. https://tinyurl.com/3686wwcv.

Rees, Anthony. *[Re]reading Again: A Mosaic Reading of Numbers 25*. LHBOTS 589. Playing the Texts 19. New York: Bloomsbury T&T Clark, 2015.

Reif, S. C. "What Enraged Phinehas?: A Study of Numbers 25:8." *JBL* 90 (1971): 200–206.

Ringe, Sharon H. "Places at the Table: Feminist and Postcolonial Biblical Interpretation." Pages 136–51 in *The Postcolonial Bible*. Edited by R. S. Sugirtharajah. Sheffield: Sheffield Academic, 1998.

Robert, Hannah. "Disciplining the Female Aboriginal Body: Inter-racial Sex and the Pretence of Separation." *Australian Feminist Studies* 16 (2001): 69–81.

Roberts, Janine P. *Massacres to Mining: The Colonisation of Aboriginal Australia* Melbourne: Dove Communications, 1981.

Scholz, Susanne. *Introducing the Women's Hebrew Bible*. London: Bloomsbury, 2014.

Sivan, Helena Zlotnick. "The Rape Of Cozbi (Numbers XXV)." *VT* 51 (2001): 69–80.

Skye, Lee Miena. "Australian Aboriginal Catholic Women Seek Wholeness: Hearts Are Still Burning." *Pacifica* 19 (2006): 283–307.

———. "Australian Aboriginal Women's Christologies." Pages 162–71 in *The Strength of Her Witness: Jesus Christ in the Global Voices of Women*. Edited by Elisabeth A. Johnson. Maryknoll, NY: Orbis Books, 2016.

———. "How Australian Aboriginal Christian Womanist *Tiddas* (Sisters) Theologians Celebrate the Eucharist." Pages 54–77 in *Reinterpreting the Eucharist: Explorations in Feminist Theology and Ethics*. Edited by Anne Elvey, Carol Hogan, Kim Power, and Claire Renkin. London: Routledge, 2014.

———. "How Australian Aboriginal *Tiddas* (Sisters) Theologians Deal with the Threat of Genocide." *Feminist Theology* 23 (2015): 128–42.

Trible, Phyllis. *Texts of Terror: Literary-Feminist Readings of Biblical Narratives*. London: SCM, 2003.

Wolfe, Patrick. "Nation and MiscegeNation: Discursive Continuity in the Post-Mabo Era." *Social Analysis: The International Journal of Social and Cultural Practice* 36 (1994): 93–152.

3

Numbers 25: A Reading by a Queer Australian

Karen Eller

Terra nullius is the primary assumption of British occupation of the Australian continent for Australians of my generation (1960s third-generation English), one that indicates an unquestionable right to occupy *Terra Australis*, the land of the Holy Spirit. The indigenous inhabitants were routinely depicted as savages, hunter-gatherers at best, less evolved and therefore considered subhuman—fauna, even—and the land therefore available for occupation.[1] This occupation took place with the mindset that land is gendered feminine and therefore open to rape and exploitation, flora and fauna included. Mother Nature was invested with a fickle feminine character, to which the British colonists responded with an arrogant response aimed at total subjugation. Until very recently, even the national anthem described Australia as a country "young and free," denying the presence of continuous habitation of its indigenous custodians for over 60,000 years. Australian school curricula offered scant introduction to indigenous culture and heritage; classroom discussions about Australia's foundations were dominated by European history and narratives of white explorers. Massacres and brutal violence against Australia's indigenous people has only begun to be discussed in recent years. The rhetoric of white superiority over our indigenous sisters and brothers, established in the late eighteenth century and continued through the nineteenth and twentieth centuries, overrides established evidence to the contrary in a fantasy of hegemonic imagination designed to support and entrench the position of power the colonizers had and continue to have over the First Nations peoples of Australia.[2]

---

[1] For a full discussion of primary evidence for indigenous Australian settlement and agricultural practices, see Bruce Pascoe, *Dark Emu: Aboriginal Australia and the Birth of Agriculture* (Broome: Magabala, 2018).

[2] For further discussion about fantastic hegemonic imagination, see Emilie M. Townes, *Womanist Ethics and the Cultural Production of Evil* (New York: Palgrave Macmillan, 2006).

National foundations built on massacre and brutal violence are by no means unique to Australia. The shocking violence in Num 25 jolts the reader into an unwelcome contemplation of YHWH as a bloodthirsty warrior god. This chapter offers a critical literary analysis of Num 25 in dialogue with other texts and proposes a feminist hermeneutic for engaging with a distasteful text. Numbers 25, while unpalatable for many, is valuable for the way in which it uncovers the hidden agendas of those who seek to bolster their own power. Human fingerprints can be found all over this text and, as I shall demonstrate, helps us to see human self-interest messing with God's good intent for humanity. The text has lessons for peoples of all nations, including all Australians, regardless of ancestry.

Numbers offers an official narrative of the tribe of Israel's transition from a travelling band of released captives to a people of military might endorsed by YHWH. Numbers 25 marks a significant point of transition in the book. At the beginning of Num 25 we meet an unruly and rebellious mob, but by the end of the saga, Israel is ready to be counted and counted upon. While it might read as an historical account of events having taken place, Num 25 serves as a foundational narrative for ancient Israel, written to bolster and perpetuate self-understanding and beliefs.

THE PLOT THICKENS (WITH BLOOD)

Numbers 25 is packaged into four distinct parts, which show strong evidence of multiple layers of narration and redaction. The disjunctures in the text are striking. The first part (Num 25:1–5) locates the tribes of Israel at an acacia grove in the Transjordan and reports that "the people began to have sexual relations with the women of Moab."[3] The daughters of Moab invite the people of Israel to be their guests; some accept the Moabite hospitality, which means that they eat with the Moabites and pay homage to their god. We know that the Moabites are related to the Israelites as descendants of Lot (Gen 19:37), and we can imagine that Moabite and Israelite worship may have shared common traits despite the different names for their respective deities.[4] The text claims, "Israel yoked itself to the Baal of Peor, and the LORD's anger was kindled against Israel." We cannot be certain that the Baal of Peor is not YHWH by another name. Already we are uncomfortable with the text! Yet it gets more uncomfortable. YHWH tells Moses, in order to assuage hir[5] anger to, "Take all the chiefs … and impale them in the sun."

---

[3] NRSV is used unless otherwise indicated.
[4] Wilda Gafney, "A Queer Womanist Midrashic Reading of Numbers 25:1–18," in *Leviticus and Numbers: Texts and Contexts*, ed. Athalya Brenner and Archie Chi Chung Lee (Minneapolis: Fortress, 2013), 193.
[5] "Hir" is used here as a nonbinary pronoun for YHWH, an amalgam of "his" and "her."

Moses does not do this; instead he tells the judges to kill any of their people who had committed apostasy.

The second part (Num 25:6–9) raises the intensity by shifting from the past tense into the present tense, and tells of an Israelite who brings a Midianite into his family, perhaps in marriage; the text does not clarify further. This happens in sight of Moses and the "whole congregation" who are "weeping at the Tent of Meeting." Again, we are not given more specific information and are left to ponder whether the Israelites are weeping because of the impending killing of the idolatrous and sexually wanton Israelites or because of the deaths from the plague we have not yet been told about. Phinehas, grandson of Aaron and Levite guard of the Tent of Meeting, responds immediately to the impending interethnic sexual coupling by following the couple into their tent and thrusting his spear through the two of them, the man and the woman through her belly (or genitals). The plague that had not previously been mentioned ceases at this point, with twenty-four thousand dead.

The third part of the episode (Num 25:10–13) takes an unexpected leap to tell of YHWH commending Phinehas for his zeal and making a covenant of peace with Phinehas, which granted a perpetual priesthood to Phinehas and his descendants. The zealous action of Phinehas is labelled by YHWH as an atonement for the (idolatrous and sexually depraved) Israelites. The reader is left stunned that an act of sexual violence against a young couple is not reprimanded but is commended and rewarded in perpetuity.

The final part of the chapter (Num 25:14–18) belatedly names the Israelite man as Zimri, a leader of the Simeonite clan. The woman, Cozbi, is identified as the daughter of a Midianite chieftain. The chapter concludes with YHWH telling Moses to "harass the Midianites and defeat them; for they have harassed you and deceived you in the affair of Peor, and in the affair of Cozbi … she was killed on the day of the plague that resulted from Peor" (25:17–18). We are witness to bloodshed spawning more bloodshed and ponder with incredulity how the God of Abraham came to be depicted as a bloodthirsty, warmongering, jealous zealot for masculine dominance over indigenous families.

INSIGHTS GAINED FROM COMPARING OTHER TEXTS

To bring some context and insights into this text, it is helpful to look at other texts which can be linked to Num 25. Psalm 106:28–31 may be a precedent for the telling of the story, as the plague is directly linked to the Baal of Peor, and Phinehas is given credit for its ending. There is, however, no mention of Cozbi or Zimri.[6] It

---

[6] Anthony Rees, *[Re]Reading Again: A Mosaic Reading of Numbers 25* (London: Bloomsbury, 2015), 82.

is possible that a later editor of Num 25 has drawn on the psalm and inserted extra content to suit his purposes.

> Then they attached themselves to the Baal of Peor,
> and ate sacrifices offered to the dead;
> they provoked the LORD to anger with their deeds,
> and a plague broke out among them.
> Then Phinehas stood up and interceded,
> and the plague was stopped.
> And that has been reckoned to him as righteousness
> from generation to generation forever. (Ps 106:28–31)

The plague at Shittim recalls the plague at the base of Mount Sinai, punishment for the golden calf idolatry and rebellion of the people (Exod 32). Anthony Rees and Dennis T. Olson suggest that the golden calf and the affair of Peor provide bookends for the struggle of the old generation, and that this second plague "effectively exterminates the wilderness generation and makes way for the new generation who will step into the promised land."[7] Rees argues that the plague goes unmentioned because it was assumed knowledge.[8] The nuggets of an earlier epic tradition are thus in part discernible.

A further parallel with the golden calf incident comes to light when we consider the roles that Aaron and Phinehas are allocated in each incident. Aaron, when confronted with an agitated mob in the absence of Moses, acquiesces to their desires and leads them in smelting gold for their calf idol (Exod 32:1–6). Aaron's priestly leadership is thus exposed as weak and malleable. Phinehas, by contrast, is shown to be decisive and quick to take action (Num 25:7–8).

A further significant inconsistency lies in the portrayal of the character of Moses at these two junctures. The golden calf episode sees Moses pleading to YHWH for mercy on behalf of the congregation (Exod 32:11–14). Indeed, Moses is characterized as chief intercessor who pleads for the people at several points throughout the Pentateuch: for deliverance from slavery (Exod 7–12), from fire (Num 12:2), for protection (Exod 14), for water (Exod 15:25; 17:1–7), for food (Exod 16; Num 11:10–35), and for healing (Num 12:13). On each of these occasions, Moses pleads, and YHWH responds with mercy. In the crisis depicted in Num 25, however, Moses's response stands in stark contrast to these previous incidents. His leadership is called into question, and he listens to YHWH's punishment of the people but does not negotiate a more favorable outcome. Rather, he makes his own pronouncement, which, it seems, is never carried out. Moses is portrayed as

---

[7] Rees, *[Re]Reading*, 82 cites Dennis T. Olson, *Numbers*, Interpretation: A Bible Commentary for Preaching and Teaching (Louisville: Westminster John Knox, 1996), 156.
[8] Rees, *[Re]Reading*, 82.

both mute and immobile with the two young lovers before his eyes. This radical departure in the character of Moses in the narrative thus far is further evidence that a redactor is pushing an agenda.

In the postexilic book of Ezra, we encounter a priest being propped up in importance by an impressive genealogy that reaches back to Aaron, Eleazar, and Phinehas (Ezra 7:1–6), in comparison to the governor, Nehemiah, who is given a rudimentary introduction.[9] In Num 25, YHWH is depicted as enthusiastic in granting Phinehas a perversely ironic covenant of peace as reward for the murderous act of killing Cozbi and Nimri (Num 25:10–13). Covenants with individuals are exceedingly rare in the biblical canon, reserved for Noah and the great patriarchal figureheads of Abraham, Jacob and David. There is no further biblical narrative extolling the fine leadership of Phinehas, so this covenant seems out of place.

Baruch Levine proposes that this part of the text serves as an etiology for the authority of the Levites as priests.[10] A claim on the Israel's priesthood by the descendants of Zadok, the high priest during Solomon's reign (Ezek 40:46; 43:19; 44:15; 48:10), may have pressed the issue and inspired the redactor(s) to insert an exaggerated claim to perpetual priesthood for the descendants of Phinehas.[11] It is also possible that the Levites were in a power struggle against remnant royalty, and Num 25 demonstrates Levitical authority and status over the royal couple. At stake is the authority to interpret the law and exert editorial influence on the preserved tradition—thus, the power to wield enormous influence over the people in YHWH's name.

The narrator himself wields enormous power, more than YHWH himself, it seems.[12] The narrator presumes to have knowledge of the thoughts and emotions of YHWH and uses his words to paint an image of YHWH to suit his purposes. The image of a wildly angry YHWH in Num 25:4, who demands that heads be impaled—the Hebrew word *rosh* can refer to both bodily heads and leadership heads, is designed to strike terror into a hearer who may be considering an illicit affair or who sacrifices to a god other than YHWH. It is alarming that this passage suggests that YHWH demands human sacrifice as atonement for the sins of the people. While the heads did not get skewered, the bodies of Cozbi and Zimri did. The narrator puts the following expression on (the lips of) YHWH: "because he

---

[9] Ron L. Stanley, "Ezra-Nehemiah," in *The Queer Bible Commentary*, ed. Deryn Guest et al. (London: SCM, 2006), 268–77.
[10] Rees, *[Re]Reading*, 68 cites Baruch Levine, *Numbers 21–26: A New Translation with Introduction and Commentary*, Anchor Bible 4A (New York: Doubleday, 2000), 288.
[11] Marko Marttila, "The Figure of Phinehas from Different Perspectives: The Hero of His People in Num. 25:6–13, Ps. 106:28–31 and Sir. 45:23–26." *JAJ* 5 (2014): 14 and Rees, *[Re]Reading*, 79–80.
[12] Rees, *[Re]Reading*, 108.

(Phinehas) was zealous for his God, and made atonement for the Israelites" (Num 25:13).

The demand for human sacrifice to YHWH directly contradicts the commandments given to Moses by YHWH for Hebrew people to live peaceably in community together. "You shall not murder" (Exod 20:13; Deut 5:17). The account of Abraham taking Isaac to Moriah for sacrifice (Gen 22:1–19) can also be read as a polemic against a practice adopted among other religions in the ancient world: YHWH does not demand human sacrifice. But Zimri, the Israelite chieftain, one of their own, is brutally murdered.

It is also well worth considering other impressions of YHWH in the Bible that speak against the jealous, vengeful caricature in Num 25. A multiplicity of authors has resulted in a multiplicity of characterizations of YHWH. Numbers 11:11–15 for example, portrays Moses appealing to a maternal God, expected to suckle their defenseless child after having conceived and given birth.[13] This passage appears in the overarching narrative of YHWH as liberator and sustainer. Indeed, YHWH is depicted as a god who is just and has mercy on outsiders with hir words of inclusion: "You shall not oppress a resident alien; you know the heart of an alien, for you were aliens in the land of Egypt" (Exod 23:9).

The sum of all these inconsistencies leads the reader to consider that perhaps this particular representation of YHWH is a projection of the character of the redactor, rather than having any connection with the God of steadfast love and mercy who sides with the oppressed. In the petitions of Moses mentioned above, YHWH is depicted as a merciful God who liberates, protects, quenches thirst, feeds, and heals the people. Here, however, it seems the redactor has forgotten who YHWH is or seeks to portray hir differently.

TAKING AN HISTORICAL SIDEWAYS GLANCE (AT WOMEN)

Before we reject this text of terror in disgust, it is helpful to consider how women are portrayed in the text. The use of זנ״ה (to play the harlot) as a label for the sinfulness of Israel is a feminized and sexualized term that is derogatory toward women.[14] The daughters of Moab and Cozbi, the murdered Midianite, are portrayed as threats to Israel.[15] The trope of the foreign woman leading Israel astray from YHWH is prevalent throughout the Hebrew canon. For example, Solomon

---

[13] Katharine Doob Sakenfeld, "Numbers," in *Women's Bible Commentary*, ed. Carol A. Newsom, Sharon H. Ringe, and Jacqueline E. Lapsley, 3rd ed. (Louisville: Westminster John Knox, 2012), 83.
[14] Rees, *[Re]Reading*, 126–29.
[15] Rees, *[Re]Reading*, 88.

is subjected to critical gaze for taking up foreign wives (1 Kgs 11).[16] Foreign women come with foreign gods and Israelite men who succumb to foreign women are deemed to have succumbed to foreign gods. Sexual liaisons with foreign women result in disaster, but not always. Moses, hero of the wilderness wanderings, married a Midianite woman, Zipporah. Later, in the pogrom against Midian, Midianite virgins are spared for the Israelite men (Num 31:18), and Ruth, matriarch of David's family, is herself a Moabite, and Rahab a Canaanite. Inconsistencies abound.

Interethnic sexual relations come under heavy attack in the postexilic period, as recorded in Ezra 9–10. Ezra bemoans: "the holy seed has mixed itself with the peoples of the lands" (Ezra 9:2); in Ezra 10, Ezra and the Levites determine that the foreign wives of the returning exiles and their bastard children be banned and sent away. Given that ethnic purity was not such a consuming issue for the wilderness generation, it would appear that the issue of miscegenation has been retrojected into the text.[17] A postexilic redactor's quill has pierced the integrity of the narrative as surely as Phinehas's spear has violated the young lovers.

Further evidence of anachronistic political interference in the text is the name given to Cozbi. The root from which the name is derived is כז״ב, which Rees translates in verbal form as "to lie" or "to be a liar." Rees also offers the nouns "lie," "deception," and "falsehood" as used with this meaning in Num 23:19.[18] He adds that, in Akkadian, a cognate language, *kubzu* means "voluptuous, sexually vigorous," and is used as a euphemism for sexual organs. The Australian mind jumps directly to "cunt," a word that collapses the female sexual part with the vilest description of a deceitful person, and usually applied to a man! More than that, Cozbi is of high social status, a right royal cunt! Further related meanings of Cozbi include "luxuriant," "abundant," "charm," and "attractiveness." The character is cast as highly desirable yet deceitful.[19] Harriet C. Lutzky suggests that Cozbi's name is linked to local goddesses and thus adds a cultic element that links Cozbi to her Moabite "sisters."[20] In naming Cozbi, the redactor has placed desire and danger as collaborators in a plot to trick the Israelites.

Woman as trickster is a repeated trope in the Hebrew Bible. Genesis 27 affords Rebekah special knowledge of Jacob's destiny as YHWH's choice to be

---

[16] Sakenfeld, "Numbers," 85.
[17] Rees, *[Re]Reading*, 88.
[18] Rees, *[Re]Reading*, 130.
[19] Rees, *[Re]Reading*, 131.
[20] Rees, *[Re]Reading*, 131 cites Harriet C. Lutzky, "The Name 'Cozbi' (Numbers XXV 15,18)," *VT* 47 (1997): 547.

Isaac's heir.[21] Rebekah coaches Jacob into deceiving his father in order to carry out YHWH's program. Genesis 38 tells how Tamar tricks Judah into having sex with her by disguising herself as a prostitute in order to exact justice. Israelite women are tricksters for YHWH's purposes and for the prosperity of their kin. Foreign women, however, are cast as tricksters against YHWH and YHWH's people. Potiphar's wife (Gen 39) and Jezebel (1 Kgs 16:31–36; 21:5–16; 2 Kgs 9:30–37) are classic examples of foreign women who cannot be trusted.

The negative impression given of Cozbi, and indeed women in general, can be distilled elsewhere in the Torah. A classic example is evident in the way creation mythology is often given misogynistic interpretation. Genesis 1:27 presents simultaneous creation of male and female: "So God created humankind in his image, in the image of God he created them, male and female he created them." A second narrative presents the male, Adam, created first, from the dust of the earth, and the female created from the man's rib (Gen 2:22). Many interpreters ignore the first account to emphasize the second and suggest that, because Eve was created second, she is inferior to Adam.[22] The human encounter with the snake, in which "they want to be shrewd, but they end up nude," has a long history of blaming the woman for a decision in which the man had full command over his choice.[23] "She took of its fruit and ate; and she also gave some to her husband, who was with her, and he ate" (Gen 3:6). The pattern of blaming women for the decisions of men extends into Num 25. The final verses read:

> The LORD said to Moses, "Harass the Midianites, and defeat them; for they have harassed you by the trickery with which they deceived you in the affair of Peor, and in the affair of Cozbi, the daughter of a leader of Midian, their sister; she was killed on the day of the plague that resulted from Peor." (Num 25:16–18)

For the redactor of Num 25, it does not matter that Cozbi is Midianite; he simply lumps the foreign women together as tricksters who will resort to all sorts of cunning ploys to distract the Israelites from YHWH. The Israelite men are thus exonerated of their failures.

---

[21] Susan Niditch, "Genesis," in *Women's Bible Commentary*, ed. Carol A. Newsom, Sharon H. Ringe, and Jacqueline E. Lapsley, 3rd ed. (Louisville: Westminster John Knox, 2012), 41–42.

[22] Anne W. Stewart, "Eve and Her Interpreters," in *Women's Bible Commentary*, ed. Carol A. Newsom, Sharon H. Ringe, and Jacqueline E. Lapsley, 3rd ed. (Louisville: Westminster John Knox, 2012), 46.

[23] Brian F. Kolia, "Eve, The Serpent and a Samoan Love Story," in *Sex and the Bible*, ed. Mark Roncace (Point of View, 2020), Kindle.

In *Texts of Terror*, Phyllis Trible draws attention to four narratives in which women are subjected to extreme suffering.[24] Trible seeks to find redemptive qualities in the four narratives and thus invites us to be on alert for any angles that might redeem other female characters given harsh treatment in Scripture. While the fate of Cozbi in Num 25 underscores a pattern of male malevolence toward women, more is at play when we dig deeper into the text.

QUEER-Y-ING THE TEXT

Tales of violence and aggression are not confined to the stories of Hebrew conquest. This queer, white Australian finds herself disturbed at discovering that she is complicit in a postcolonial oppressive stance over indigenous Australians. Intergenerational trauma over stolen children, poor access to health and education, and systemic racial prejudice results in lower life expectancy and diminished quality of life for Australia's First Nations people. At the same time, I am acutely aware of the silence of LGBQTI+ folk in Australia's foundational stories. As far as I know, there are no electorates or towns named after a queer man or woman.[25] Indeed, it is within my lived memory that homosexuality was deemed illegal and, further back, a mental illness. Australia was not a safe place to be queer. Even with same-gender marriage now enshrined in legislation, discriminatory practices are still rife, particularly in religious sectors. When I look to the Bible for evidence of my kin, there is very little to be found.

Numbers 25:1 does, however, gives us a rare glimpse into biblical awareness of same-gender attracted women. The chapter begins: "While Israel was staying at Shittim, *the people* began to have sexual relations with the women of Moab." Womanist biblical scholar Wil Gafney suggests that "the people" is an inclusive term, which leaves open the possibility that Hebrew women were included alongside Hebrew men in having sexual relations with the daughters of Moab.[26]

If we look at earlier English translations, we see some ambiguity emerge. The RSV opts for "and the people began to play the harlot." Similarly, the WEB chooses "and the people began to play the prostitute." Tikva Frymer-Kensky

---

[24] Phyllis Trible, *Texts of Terror: Literary-Feminist Readings of Biblical Narratives* (London: SCM, 2002).

[25] An exception might be found in the Australian towns Drysdale and Newcomb, which are named after nineteenth-century missionary women who discreetly maintained an intimate, secret relationship.

[26] Gafney, "Queer Womanist Midrashic Reading," 191–92. The word העם, *ha'am* is translated as "the people" and does not denote a distinct gender in the way that language of "sons" or "daughters" might. Cf. the specific identification of the daughters of Moab (בנות מואב, *benot Mo'av*) in Num 25:1.

argues that this translation of זנ״ה speaks of Israelite faithlessness and ought not be translated to implicate Israelite sexual relations with the Moabite women.[27] She proposes that the sexual overtones of the text are the invention of postbiblical interpreters. This sexualized language, as Rees argues, is ambiguous; we cannot be certain if זנ״ה is intended solely as metaphor in this instance. While Rees is quick to separate the Israelite women from sexual involvement with the Moabite women, it is fair to leave open the possibility that the women as well as the Israelite men were enjoying sexual relations with the daughters of Moab.[28] I can imagine same-gender attracted women held in a patriarchal family structure finding delight in the anonymity of securing a lover or lovers among the Moabite women. Human desire, wild and unpredictable as it is, could reasonably have found expression in woman-woman sex on the plains of Moab. It is disappointing to this queer reader that some English translations, including NIV, NLT, and GNB, replace "the people" with "men," thus erasing the trace of female-female sexual liaison.

Elsewhere in Scripture, sexual encounter between women can only be read between the lines. Dinah "went out to visit the women of the region" (Gen 34:1). Could it be that Dinah was sexually interested in the Hivite women? Perhaps, but the narrator leaves the purpose of her visit to the reader's imagination. Dinah is taken by force to Shechem and is given no voice in the text. The men argue and barter over her as a possession rather than as a valued family member. Any whisper of a same-gender attraction is also summarily silenced.

Some have speculated that the love shared between Ruth and Naomi included a sexual element. Mona West draws a parallel between contemporary LGBQTI+ families and the speculative family of Naomi, Ruth, and Boaz.[29] West poses the possibility of Ruth and Naomi forming family with Boaz for seed and security and offers the following interpretation:

> When Ruth and Boaz marry, they have a son. The women of the town have some things to say about this birth and this family. They acknowledge Ruth's devotion to Naomi by claiming, "your daughter-in-law who loves you, who is more to you than seven sons, has borne him."… They proclaim, "a son has been born to Naomi." In their blessing the townswomen seem to know better than anyone the unusual and creative nature of this family of choice.[30]

---

[27] Rees, *[Re]Reading*, 124 cites Tikva Frymer-Kensky, *Reading the Women of the Bible* (New York: Schocken, 2002), 217.
[28] Rees, *[Re]Reading*, 124, 127.
[29] Mona West, "Ruth, Naomi, and Boaz as a Family of Choice," in *Sex and the Bible*, ed. Mark Roncace (Point of View, 2020), Kindle.
[30] West, "Ruth, Naomi, and Boaz," Kindle.

For West, the creativity employed by Naomi and Ruth parallels the creativity of LGBQTI+ people in forming families for themselves. Yet one has to read between the lines to discover these traces of nonconforming stories within the pages of Scripture. How many more have been erased or lost? Erasure of LGBQTI+ folk from histories, biblical and otherwise, is itself a violence against humanity.

SEXUAL VIOLENCE IN SCRIPTURE

As discussed earlier, the actions of Phinehas in Num 25 are intended to prop up the authority of the priesthood in postexilic times. The ideology of priestly leadership was exclusionary and separatist and particularly dangerous for those who did not qualify for it, both Levites and member of the community alike.

The killing of Cozbi and Zimri is a dangerous story, as it appears to condone sexual violence. The spear used by Phinehas can be understood as a phallic symbol used to penetrate and violate both the Midianite woman and the Simeonite chieftain.[31] The physical point of Cozbi's penetration has received varying translations. The Hebrew אל קבתה, *'el qovatah* is commonly translated as "through the belly" (KJV, NRSV) or "through the body" (NIV, WEB). Other translations interpret a more aggressively sexual act and translate "through her genital parts" (NWT).[32] This translation has precedent in the Babylonian Talmud and other rabbinic sources.[33] The Septuagint, Peshitta, and Vulgate translate the word as "womb," which also has a sexual implication.[34] The deaths of Cozbi and Zimri thus constitute more than an act of zeal; Phinehas's act is a textual event that officially sanctions sexual violence against a foreign woman.[35] The text not only delegitimizes the sexual union between an Israelite and foreign woman, it also legitimizes sexual violence against foreign women.

It is deeply disturbing that YHWH is depicted in Num 25 as not just applauding the sexual violence inflicted upon the young lovers but sanctioning it with a perpetual covenant with the house of the assailant. We must look elsewhere within Scripture to discover if this characterization can be validated. The story of Dinah's rape and the massacre of Hivites that follows (Gen 34) has a number of elements in common with Num 25. Both the rape of Dinah and the murder of Cozbi and Zimri are episodes of sexual violence. Dinah (an Israelite woman) is raped by

---

[31] Anthony Rees, "Numbers 25 and Beyond: Phinehas and Other Detestable Practice(r)s," in *Leviticus and Numbers: Texts and Contexts*, ed. Athalya Brenner and Archie Chi Chung Lee (Minneapolis: Fortress, 2013), 167.
[32] Rees, "Numbers 25," 168.
[33] Rees, "Numbers 25," 168.
[34] Rees, "Numbers 25," 168.
[35] Rees, "Numbers 25," 168.

Shechem, a foreigner (Hivite). While Jacob was prepared to accept a generous marriage arrangement, Dinah's defilement is avenged by her brothers, Levi and Simeon, to the extent of killing (by deceit) all the men of the city and taking the women, children, and livestock for themselves. This marked relationship between Levite and Simeonite is severed at the murder of Zimri the Simeonite, at the hand of Phinehas the Levite.

In a further parallel to the Israelite-foreigner pairing, Dinah (Israelite) is given no agency in her assault by Shechem (Hivite). She is also given no voice in the negotiations that follow. Dinah is (treated as) the property of her father and brothers, and it is her brothers' decisions and actions that determine her fate (to which we are not privy). Israelite women are not permitted to partner with foreign men, and there are dire consequences if sexual violence is perpetrated against an Israelite woman. In the case of Cozbi and Zimri, the sexual coupling appears to be by mutual consent, yet it ends in both their deaths. A further puzzlement is that, in Num 30–31, the Midianites are killed, but the Israelites are permitted to keep the Midianite virgins for themselves. The taking of foreign women as booty is permitted when one wins a war, seemingly as it has no impact on land inheritance.

The silence of Dinah and the silence of YHWH both scream a radical departure from what is good and life-giving in YHWH's creation. By the time we encounter Cozbi, we are so accustomed to the silence of defiled women, we do not expect that she would have a voice at all. Yet this very realization spurs this reader to shout about the predicament of this literary character.

Sexual violence comes under scrutiny in Gen 18–19. For LGBQTI+ folk, Gen 19 has been mistakenly used as a prooftext for condemnation of homosexual sex between men. In pre-Christian times, the sins of Sodom and Gomorrah were strongly connected with a culture of lack of hospitality and sexual violence.[36] While Lot is held up as a righteous man for providing hospitality to the two angels, the men of Sodom are depicted as a frenzied mob baying for sexual violence against the guests. Lot intervenes, but his own life becomes endangered until the angels in the power of YHWH rescue Lot and blind the would-be assailants. YHWH spares Lot and his family but destroys Sodom and Gomorrah along with it. The characterization of YHWH in this text is thus a long way from the deity who approves sexual violence in Num 25.

The wickedness of Sodom has everything to do with their lack of respect for the stranger, both human and angel. A story with a similar structure appears in Judg 19. Trible draws attention to the unnamed concubine of Judg 19, a prime example of the appalling treatment meted out against women in Hebrew

---

[36] Megan Warner, "Were the Sodomites Really Sodomites? Homosexuality in Genesis 19," in *Five Uneasy Pieces: Essays on Scripture and Sexuality*, ed. Nigel Wright (Adelaide: ATF Theology, 2012), 1.

Scripture.³⁷ The residents of Gibeah, like the Sodomites, are intent on sexual violence against the man who has sought shelter. There are no angels to intervene, and the unnamed Levite saves himself by throwing out his unnamed, runaway concubine to be violently raped. We assume she is killed as there is no sign of life from her. The Levite proceeds to take her home with him, dismember her, and distribute her body parts to the tribes of Israel. The city of Gibeah, thus demonstrated as wicked, becomes the birthplace of Saul, the first of Israel's kings. YHWH is strangely silent throughout this text, perhaps gob(d)smacked by such appalling behavior. The absence of engagement with YHWH when people take matters into their own hands inevitably leads to death and destruction, with women bearing the brunt of untamed male sexual aggression.

At the other extreme, the daughter of Jephthah (Judg 11), another subject of interest to Trible, is either killed or subjected to years of celibacy on account of her father's folly. Women, it seems, are expendable and subject to the whims of men, a dangerous precedent set for women of every century since.

Biblical texts are inconsistent in their treatment of sexualized violence, perhaps reflecting humanity's own long history of sexual violence, particularly during colonization. Marcella Althaus-Reid considers the devastating consequences to indigenous South American peoples by the Spanish conquistadors who murdered and raped their way across the continent in the fifteenth century.³⁸ Rees paints a similar picture of the colonizers of Australia.³⁹ In this vein, it makes sense that the lived experiences of Israelites, both as colonizers and colonized, might result in colonizing narratives that tell of rape and murder as methods of securing their domination over the indigenous inhabitants of the invaded lands.

Nāsili Vaka'uta takes a helpful Pacific Island perspective on sexual violence and colonization with his concept of a "Porno-tropic Tradition" in which the colonizing nation feminizes and sexualizes the foreign land. He writes:

> Men at the margins usually resort to violence. At the margins, foreign lands are feminized and destined to be inseminated with the male seeds of civilization. At the margins, feminized land is renamed—naming is an extension of the male intruders and stakes their claim to the female body. At the margins, however, male anxiety and male crisis of identity are exposed.⁴⁰

---

[37] Trible, *Texts*, 65–92.
[38] Marcella Althaus-Reid, *Indecent Theology: Theological Perversions in Sex, Gender and Politics* (London: Routledge, 2000), 11–19.
[39] Rees, "Numbers 25," 163–64.
[40] Nāsili Vaka'uta, "Indicting YHWH: Interpreting Numbers 25 in Oceania," in *Leviticus and Numbers: Texts and Contexts*, ed. Athalya Brenner and Archie Chi Chung Lee (Minneapolis: Fortress, 2013), 183.

It is no accident then, that the initial foray by spies into Canaan is a comical tale of the two spies who go sex-first, directly to the house of the prostitute, Rahab. Colonization, in the shape of land acquisition, is expected to be accompanied by sexual violence and the spoils of war—"booty" and livestock.

NOT ALL SEX IS BAD: HUMAN DESIRE AS A GIFT FROM GOD

Sexual violence is not to be confused with sexual intimacy. Song of Songs has steadfastly remained within the canon of Scripture despite its attention to desire and eroticism. Sexual desire, while feared in some texts for its wildness and uncontrollability, is celebrated and glorified in this text. Song of Songs speaks of sexual longing and desire, both inside and beyond marriage. It deems black as beautiful (Song 1:5) and delights in interracial sexual union (Song 6:13). All fear of sexual desire is swept away, in its place a wholehearted rejoicing in the fullness of humanity consummated in sexual union.

> Set me as a seal upon your heart, as a seal upon your arm;
> for love is strong as death, passion fierce as the grave.
> Its flashes are flashes of fire, a raging flame.
> Many waters cannot quench love, neither can floods drown it.
> If one offered for love all the wealth of his house,
> it would be utterly scorned. (Song 8:6–7)

If only Cozbi and Zimri were afforded this sort of treatment! Perhaps Phinehas could have been big-noted for heroic deeds in saving the nation from plague by other means.

FUCKING WITH NARRATIVE

National identity is shaped by the stories a nation tells about itself. The book of Nehemiah records an historic moment when Ezra, the scribe, delivers to the remnant peoples the newly recovered book of the law of Moses (Neh 8:1–12). This book is read to the assembled people seven months after their arrival in Jerusalem from exile in Babylon. It is read and interpreted over seven days, in which the festival of booths is recovered and reinstituted. Given his record of denouncing mixed marriages and expelling foreigners, it is possible that Ezra or someone under his direction has inserted some narrative of fantastic imagination into the tradition. The tale of Phinehas and his zealous action against Cozbi and Zimri is thus an example of the national narrative being adulterated by people in a position of power for their own benefit and at the expense of the vulnerable.

Australian national identity is likewise shaped by narratives that have been collected, collated, revised, and edited or deliberately omitted. Stories of indigenous grain stores and agricultural practices have been systemically blotted out from national memory. Stories of massacres, rapes, and theft of land have been sanitized and minimized or conveniently forgotten.

As a teenager, I rode my horse on Marida Yallock, a former squatter's station alongside the Mount Emu Creek between Terang, my hometown, and Camperdown, in Victoria's Western District. Until recently, I remained blissfully ignorant that, in 1839, all but a handful of Tamberee Gundidj, a clan of the Djargurd Wurrung people, were murdered at their campsite in a bloody massacre at what become known locally as Murdering Gully.[41] An overseer, Frederick Taylor led a sortie of shepherds and shot dead all the native men, women, and children they could see, resulting in the deaths of thirty-five people. A few survived by hiding in the long grass and later had their testimonies recorded. Taylor fled the country for a time but was never prosecuted. The indigenous name, Puuroyuup, meaning "flowing stream," vanished from use, and the official name, Mount Emu Creek, came into use to replace the unpalatable Murdering Gully. This shocking history remains seldom discussed or acknowledged. Yet snippets remain in the diary entries of landholders, as well as reports by officials of the day, buried in governmental archives.

In our current time, truth-telling is coming to be understood as a genuine path toward healing and wholeness. Truth-telling requires respectful listening. Careful listening demands critical attention to stories told, with a suspicion toward who is telling the story and for what purpose. Attention must also be given to the gaps and silences; what is not told can say as much as what is. The pastoral Arcadia of my home country was the fantasy of my early years, cultivated by a collective amnesia about the bloody occupation by white settlers. The emergence of guns, spears, and writers' quills has seen this fantasy deconstructed in favor of something closer to the truth of narrative surrounding the foundational events of my home country.

REIMAGINING COZBI

Writers' quills have, in this chapter, been shown to fabricate and fuck with traditions. They also have the capacity to deconstruct narrative and reshape it into story that is more honest and helpful in guiding our lives into the future. The narratives of Hebrew foundations have been fixed into a canon that itself can no longer be edited or revised, but Midrashic interpretation can make this reshaping

---

[41] Charles Wightman Sievwright, Protector of Aborigines, Archives Authority of New South Wales 1846, 4/1135.1.

possible. For an Australian woman who loves women, there is opportunity to reimagine Cozbi as delicious fruit that has been scorned and devoured by the ignorance and insecurity of men—to write a narrative that tells of her violation, murder, and then further violation by using Cozbi and Zimri as scapegoats to elevate the political ambitions of the priesthood. The female genitals are an exquisite source of pleasure and of progeny, of life into future generations. When treated with dignity and respect, they will produce the fullest of God's abundance. We are thus able to reimagine Cozbi given full respect and honor, a joyful welcome into the family of God's chosen people. Although Cozbi, as a literary character, is killed off, we are free to imagine her extended family, Hebrew and Midianite, giving honor to her name.

Similarly, it is encouraging that the telling of history and foundation narratives of Australia are being given more nuanced and thoughtful consideration, with increased dignity and respect given to the First Nations people. Numbers 25 and the foundation narratives of the Hebrew people also warrant more nuanced and thoughtful consideration.

CONCLUDING REMARKS

As Sharon Ringe asks, what are we to do with this text?[42] Numbers 25 is a sobering reminder of how YHWH's voice can be and has been perverted to promote an ideology that is inconsistent with a God of liberation and steadfast love for hir people. The folly of men pervades the Hebrew Scripture, and always the people are invited back into relationship with YHWH. Rather than reject Num 25 on account of its violations, we are invited to include it as a valuable text that helps us identify and understand the way editors and redactors used and abused their authority to manipulate national sentiment. Numbers 25 is a clear example of why it is reckless to read biblical text uncritically. In particular, the way Num 25 sanctions sexual violence alerts us to the dangers of taking any particular verse of Scripture as an authoritative declaration on human sexuality. Careful reading of Hebrew Scripture will reveal multiple and at times conflicting understandings about YHWH's gift of sexual desire to humanity.

Numbers 25:1 opens the door to the likelihood that same-gender sexual relationships between women were an expected component of the sexual desires and longings existent within community. Like the annihilation of the Midianites in Num 31, as directed by editorial ventriloquism of YHWH in Num 25, the erasure of LGBQTI+ folk in Scripture can never be complete. Midianites continued to

---

[42] Sharon H. Ringe, "When Women Interpret the Bible," in *Women's Bible Commentary*, ed. Carol A. Newsom, Sharon H. Ringe, and Jacqueline E. Lapsley, 3rd ed. (Louisville: Westminster John Knox, 2012), 2.

exist, as do queers and indigenous Australians. It is up to us to interrogate with suspicion the narratives we have been handed, both biblical and local, to detect remnant memories and to amplify those the tradition would silence.

BIBLIOGRAPHY

Althaus-Reid, Marcella. *Indecent Theology: Theological Perversions in Sex, Gender and Politics*. London: Routledge, 2000.
Frymer-Kensky, Tikva. *Reading the Women of the Bible*. New York: Schocken, 2002.
Gafney, Wilda. "A Queer Womanist Midrashic Reading of Numbers 25:1–18." Pages 189–98 in *Leviticus and Numbers: Texts and Contexts*. Edited by Athalya Brenner and Archie Chi Chung Lee. Minneapolis: Fortress, 2013.
Kolia, Brian F. "Eve, the Serpent and a Samoan Love Story." In *Sex and the Bible*. Edited by Mark Roncace. Point of View, 2020. Kindle.
Levine, Baruch. *Numbers 21–26: A New Translation with Introduction and Commentary*. AB 4A. New York: Doubleday, 2000.
Lutzky, Harriet C. "The Name 'Cozbi' (Numbers XXV 15,18)." *VT* 47 (1997): 546–49.
Marttila, Marko. "The Figure of Phinehas from Different Perspectives: The Hero of His People in Num. 25:6–13, Ps. 106:28–31 and Sir. 45:23–26." *JAJ* 5 (2014): 2–24.
Niditch, Susan. "Genesis." Pages 27–45 in *Women's Bible Commentary*. Edited by Carol A. Newsom, Sharon H. Ringe, and Jacqueline E. Lapsley. 3rd ed. Louisville: Westminster John Knox, 2012.
Olson, Dennis T. *Numbers*. Interpretation: A Bible Commentary for Preaching and Teaching. Louisville: Westminster John Knox, 1996.
Pascoe, Bruce. *Dark Emu: Aboriginal Australia and the Birth of Agriculture*. Broome: Magabala Books, 2018.
Rees, Anthony. "Numbers 25 and Beyond: Phinehas and Other Detestable Practice(r)s." Pages 163–78 in *Leviticus and Numbers: Texts and Contexts*. Edited by Athalya Brenner and Archie Chi Chung Lee. Minneapolis: Fortress, 2013.
———. *[Re]Reading Again: A Mosaic Reading of Numbers 25*. LHBOTS 589. New York: Bloomsbury T&T Clark, 2015.
Ringe, Sharon H. "When Women Interpret the Bible." Pages 1–10 in *Women's Bible Commentary*. Edited by Carol A. Newsom, Sharon H. Ringe, and Jacqueline E. Lapsley. 3rd ed. Louisville: Westminster John Knox, 2012.
Sakenfeld, Katharine Doob. "Numbers." Pages 79–87 in *Women's Bible Commentary*. Edited by Carol A. Newsom, Sharon H. Ringe, and Jacqueline E. Lapsley. 3rd ed. Louisville: Westminster John Knox, 2012.
Stanley, Ron L. "Ezra–Nehemiah." Pages 268–77 in *The Queer Bible Commentary*. Edited by Deryn Guest, Robert E. Goss, Mona West, and Thomas Bohache. London: SCM, 2006.
Stewart, Anne W. "Eve and Her Interpreters." Pages 46–50 in *Women's Bible Commentary*. Edited by Carol A. Newsom, Sharon H. Ringe, and Jacqueline E. Lapsley. 3rd ed. Louisville: Westminster John Knox, 2012.

Townes, Emilie M. *Womanist Ethics and the Cultural Production of Evil*. New York: Palgrave Macmillan, 2006.
Trible, Phyllis. *Texts of Terror: Literary-Feminist Readings of Biblical Narratives*. London: SCM, 2002.
Vaka'uta, Nāsili. "Indicting YHWH: Interpreting Numbers 25 in Oceania." Pages 179–88 in *Leviticus and Numbers: Texts and Contexts*. Edited by Athalya Brenner and Archie Chi Chung Lee. Minneapolis: Fortress, 2013.
Warner, Megan. "Were the Sodomites Really Sodomites? Homosexuality in Genesis 19." Pages 1–11 in *Five Uneasy Pieces: Essays on Scripture and Sexuality*. Edited by Nigel Wright. Adelaide: ATF Theology, 2012.
West, Mona. "Ruth, Naomi, and Boaz as a Family of Choice." In *Sex and the Bible*. Edited by Mark Roncace. Point of View, 2020. Kindle.

4

But He Would Not Listen to Her:
Revisiting the Story of Tamar in 2 Samuel 13

Rachelle Gilmour

Thirty-six years later, Phyllis Trible's *Texts of Terror* continues to awaken readers to the literary depths and female voices of biblical stories. In my experience, this has been the case for many students of the Bible in an Australian context, such is the illuminating and provocative influence of this work. In her introduction to *Texts of Terror*, Trible explains that the purpose of her reading is, firstly, to "recover a neglected history"—that is, to hear women's voices in the text that have otherwise been disregarded or overlooked—and, secondly, to wrestle with stories of terror, to be wounded, but to hold on, seeking a blessing.[1] It is primarily the second goal that I will address as I revisit Trible's provocative and illuminating reading of Tamar's story in 2 Sam 13, unveiling/unpacking its full terror and evaluating whether any sense of hope can be found.

I will focus on the portrayal of Absalom in the story. Is he the "good" brother and Amnon the "bad" brother in this story? Or do the narrator's poignant words in 2 Sam 13:14, "but he would not listen to her," describe Absalom as much as they do Amnon? As I revisit Trible's *Texts of Terror*, I will evaluate Absalom's actions in this story; then, using further insights from Trible's reading, I will highlight a number of parallels between Absalom and Amnon that are set up in the structure of the narrative through the identification of Tamar with wisdom.

ABSALOM AS COMPASSIONATE AVENGER?

Trible's literary analysis of 2 Sam 13 offers a charismatic and moving portrait of the terror in Tamar's story. Amnon violates his sister Tamar with brutal rape and

---

[1] Phyllis Trible, *Texts of Terror: Literary-Feminist Readings of Biblical Narratives*, OBT (Philadelphia: Fortress, 1984), 3 and 4, respectively.

rejection, and Tamar's father, King David, fails to act, neglecting his duty to protect and to do justice. Trible suggests that, after the rape, there is a ray of comfort in this story, and this is one important aspect of her interpretation that I will revisit. Trible describes Absalom as "the advocate of Tamar": he advises Tamar, he opposes Amnon, he "supports and protects" Tamar, and he counters David.[2] In 2 Sam 13:23–37, Absalom lures Amnon to a feast in Baal-hazor, and he commands his servants to murder Amnon. Trible concludes: "If we cannot sanction the violent revenge Absalom exacted, we can appropriate the compassion he shows for his sister."[3]

Many interpreters, including a number of feminist studies since Trible, have read Absalom positively in this way.[4] But *does* Absalom show compassion and exact revenge for his sister? I will address the second part of the question first, showing that Absalom's murder of Amnon is revenge for an insult to himself, not to his sister.

The literary context of other rape stories and biblical laws suggest that rape in ancient Israel was understood not primarily in terms of man's power over a woman, but in terms of a man's power over other men.[5] The violation of a woman

---

[2] Trible, *Texts*, 51–52.
[3] Trible, *Texts*, 55–56.
[4] See esp. Amy Kalmanofsky, *Dangerous Sisters of the Hebrew Bible* (Minneapolis: Fortress Press, 2014), 111; Mary Anna Bader, *Sexual Violation in the Hebrew Bible: A Multi-Methodological Study of Genesis 34 and 2 Samuel 13* (New York: Lang, 2006), 164; Johanna Stiebert, *Fathers and Daughters in the Hebrew Bible* (Oxford: Oxford University Press, 2013), 61–62; Shimon Bar Efrat, *Narrative Art in the Bible* (Sheffield: Almond Press, 1989), 271–73; J. P. Fokkelman, *King David*, vol. 1 of *Narrative Art and Poetry in the Books of Samuel*, 2 vols. (Assen: Van Gorcum, 1981), 111 and Walter Brueggemann, *First and Second Samuel*, Interpretation (Louisville: John Knox, 1990), 288–90. A positive reading of Absalom is not consensus, however. Richard G. Smith, *Fate of Justice and Righteousness during David's Reign: Narrative Ethics and Rereading the Court History according to 2 Samuel 8:15–20:26*, LHBOTS 508 (New York: T&T Clark, 2009), 153–63 sees Absalom's words to Tamar as callous but maintains that in that context incest was deserving of death, so Absalom performs an execution. Fokkelien van Dijk-Hemmes, "Tamar and the Limits of Patriarchy: Between Rape and Seduction (2 Samuel 13 and Genesis 38)," in *Anti-Covenant: Counter-Reading Women's Lives in the Hebrew Bible*, ed. Mieke Bal (Sheffield: Almond Press, 1989), 144 agrees that Absalom's words are meant as consolation and that he will take law into his own hands but suggests that they are simultaneously part of a process of concealment, silencing Tamar. Tikva Frymer-Kensky, *Reading the Women of the Bible* (New York: Schocken Books, 2002), 167–68 argues that Absalom silences Tamar for the sake of family honor and so betrays her. She notes that delayed vengeance does not vindicate Tamar in public (169).
[5] Carolyn Pressler, *The View of Women Found in the Deuteronomic Family Laws*, BZAW 216 (Berlin: de Gruyter, 1993), 31–43; Frank M. Yamada, *Configurations of Rape in the Hebrew Bible: A Literary Analysis of Three Rape Narratives* (New York: Lang, 2008), 21–25; Leah Rediger

was viewed as taking from another man's domain, either from the woman's husband in the case of adultery, or from her father if she was unmarried. Biblical laws were designed to protect the rights of men, who in turn were responsible for the welfare of dependent women. This is demonstrated in the case laws involving the violation of an unmarried woman in Deut 22, where restitution is made through marriage or financial compensation to the father:

> If a man meets a virgin who is not engaged, and seizes her and lies with her, and they are caught in the act, the man who lay with her shall give fifty shekels of silver to the young woman's father, and she shall become his wife. Because he violated her he shall not be permitted to divorce her as long as he lives. (Deut 22:28–29 [NRSV])

Consent from the woman in sexual violation is taken into consideration (see Deut 22:24–27), so women were understood as having agency and being more than just property. However, restitution in biblical laws was directed towards an unmarried woman's father because he was considered the primary injured party.[6] Furthermore, as injured party, the violation of a man's wife or daughter was viewed as undermining the performance of his own masculinity, thus affecting his own body alongside the physical violation of the woman over whom he had dominance.[7]

Given the ancient Israelite context, the rape of Tamar by Amnon is interpreted in light of the injury against David and the challenge to his authority. David's responsibility for Tamar is brought to the fore in 2 Sam 13:6, when Amnon asks David to send Tamar to him. Tamar's subordination to David is also demonstrated in the succession of events in verse 7, where David sends Tamar to Amnon, and in verse 8, where Tamar immediately obeys. Even if Amnon is motivated by lust or love for Tamar, the inevitable ramification of the rape is a challenge to David as father, because it violates his sexual domain and, by extension, his masculinity.

Schulte, *The Absence of God in Biblical Rape Narratives* (Minneapolis: Fortress, 2017), 10–15; Susan Brooks Thistlewaite, "'You May Enjoy the Spoil of Your Enemies': Rape as a Biblical Metaphor for War," *Semeia* 61 (1993): 62.

[6] See esp. T. M. Lemos, *Violence and Personhood in Ancient Israel and Comparative Contexts* (Oxford: Oxford University Press, 2017), 61–95, who argues that women in biblical texts were liable to have their personhood erased, not because they were considered property, but because they were considered subordinates. Note that the male head of the household had the means to provide for the violated woman, thus indirectly bringing restitution to her also.

[7] On the particular role of honor, shame, and masculinity, see Ken Stone, *Sex, Honor and Power in the Deuteronomistic History*, JSOTSup 234 (Sheffield: Sheffield Academic, 1996), 41–46; Hilary Lipka, "Shaved Beards and Bared Buttocks: Shame and the Undermining of Masculine Performance in Biblical Texts," in *Being a Man: Negotiating Ancient Constructs of Masculinity*, ed. Ilona Zsolnay (London: Routledge, 2017), 176–97.

This aspect of the rape's significance reveals a detail that is crucial for interpreting the story: By raping Tamar, Amnon challenges David's authority and therefore his position as king. Indeed, Tamar's appeals to Amnon in 2 Sam 13:13 escalate in terms of the status of the persons on whom the act will bring shame. Tamar's first appeal emphasizes that there will be shame upon herself: "Where could I carry my shame?" She then appeals to Amnon's own honor: "You would be as one of the scoundrels in Israel." Finally, juxtaposed with the violent use of force in verse 14, Tamar implores Amnon to speak to the king, using the term "the king" instead of "our father" or "my father." By using force in place of asking permission, Amnon violates David's authority; from an ancient perspective, this is arguably the height of the offense. Amnon challenges David's power, power that resides in his position not only as father but as king.

The books of Samuel and Kings contain a number of other examples in which taking the sexual property of the king is associated with an attempt to seize power. Absalom's rape of his father's concubines in 2 Sam 16:22 during his coup of David's kingship will be examined below. In 2 Sam 3:6–11, Ishbaal accuses Abner of taking Rizpah, the concubine of his father, Saul, and Abner responds with an affirmation of political loyalty: "Today I keep showing loyalty to the house of your father Saul … and yet you charge me now with a crime concerning this woman" (verse 8). The implication is that, by accusing Abner of seizing a former king's concubine, Ishbaal is accusing him of trying to seize power. In 1 Kgs 1:1–4, it is reported that David's masculinity is compromised by his impotence when Abishag is brought to keep him warm. This is juxtaposed with the report in verse 5 that his son Adonijah plots a coup against his kingship.

In this reading, Absalom has a motivation to react to the violation beyond compassion for his sister. Absalom has reason to murder Amnon because Amnon is making a power play against their father, the king, which threatens Absalom's potential to be his father's heir. Although Amnon is the older brother (2 Sam 3:2), in the context of the ancient Near East, including ancient Israel, the eldest son was not automatically successor to the king.[8] The king needed to appoint his heir, so Absalom had potential to succeed as king in competition with Amnon even though he was not the firstborn.

There is yet another inferred motivation for Absalom's response: the undermining of his own masculinity. Mary Anna Bader points out that in narratives, unlike laws, unmarried women are subordinate not only to their fathers, but also to their brothers.[9] For example, in the story of Dinah in Gen 34, Dinah's brothers

---

[8] Andrew Knapp, *Royal Apologetic in the Ancient Near East* (Atlanta: SBL Press, 2015), 45–72. Several commentators who read Absalom's response to Tamar as compassionate also acknowledge the underlying friction between Absalom and Amnon over succession in the story, including Trible, *Texts*, 40 and Brueggemann, *First and Second Samuel*, 290.

[9] Bader, *Sexual Violation*, 75–79.

consider the marriage of their sister to Shechem as a disgrace to themselves, saying to him in verse 14: "We cannot do this thing, to give our sister to one who is uncircumcised, for that would be a disgrace to us." Although this statement is part of their deceit, its effectiveness in convincing Hamor and Shechem (Gen 34:18) demonstrates that it reflects social custom.

Returning to 2 Sam 13, Amnon's rape of Tamar is a threat against Absalom directly, a threat to the performance of his own masculinity, not just that of his father David. After Absalom murders Amnon, and after David finally accepts Absalom's return to Jerusalem in 2 Sam 14:23–24, a note about Absalom in verses 25–27 describes his good looks, thick hair, and progeny. Each of these characteristics affirms his masculinity, suggesting that it has been restored as a result of the death of Amnon.[10] Moreover, Absalom's daughter is named Tamar (verse 27) and so he has another, undefiled, Tamar under his roof, erasing the former insult.[11] On the level of Absalom's masculinity, his revenge has been effective. Absalom thus has two reasons to murder Amnon after the rape of Tamar: Amnon has challenged King David's power and is in competition with Absalom to be David's heir, and Amnon has directly insulted Absalom by violating his sister.

The narrator does not explicitly reveal Absalom's motivation for having Amnon murdered, but the restoration of Absalom's own interests and not those of his sister strongly implies that the revenge is for himself. With the murder of Amnon, Absalom removes the threat to David's power as king (a threat he himself will renew in 2 Sam 15), the competitor to be heir to the throne, and the male who has gained dominance over his sister, undermining his own masculine performance. Nothing is achieved for Tamar, who remains desolate in Absalom's house (2 Sam 13:20) and who is not mentioned again after 2 Sam 13:32.

Absalom's compassion may still be genuine, following Trible's reading, even if his revenge is directed toward restoring his own interests rather than those of Tamar. However, there is significant evidence in the text to suggest that Absalom silences Tamar rather than comforting her and thereby prevents the primary means by which she could gain recognition that wrong was done to her. Tamar did not speak directly to Absalom after her rape but put "ashes on her head, and tore the long robe that she was wearing; she put her hand on her head, and went away, crying aloud as she went" (2 Sam 13:19). Tamar goes into mourning, making known her distress both visually and audibly. The verb used for "crying aloud," וזעקה, *veza'aqah* is a variant form of the term used in the law of Deuteronomy to describe what a woman does to proclaim that she did not give her consent

---

[10] Stone, *Sex, Honor and Power*, 122–24.
[11] There are a number of different interpretations of Absalom naming his daughter Tamar; e.g., Trible, *Texts*, 55 considers the naming a poignant memorial for Tamar rather than a replacement.

in the violation (צע״ק, "to cry out").¹² Tamar thus protests as well as grieves.¹³ Absalom does not respond to the protest but telling her (literally) "do not place the matter on her heart" (verse 20)—that is, do not pay attention or do not follow through with claiming innocence by crying out.¹⁴ Furthermore, it is not until Tamar is *in* Absalom's house in verse 20 that she is described as desolate. Absalom keeps her there to silence her so that he can exact his own revenge on Amnon, by removing Amnon as his political threat and reasserting his own masculinity.

If, contrary to Trible's reading, Absalom is yet another male character who suppresses or ignores Tamar's voice, we must wrestle with the text from a feminist perspective anew. The work of Esther Fuchs, especially her reading of 2 Sam 13 in *Sexual Politics in the Biblical Narrative*, brings another perspective to our engagement with a text of such terror.¹⁵ Firstly, she examines the story from a different perspective, radically questioning what she calls the "patriarchal investments" of the story.¹⁶ These patriarchal investments are not difficult to find. For example, Tamar, the construction of a male author, says "speak to the king; for he will not withhold me from you" (verse 13) and "No, my brother; for this wrong in sending me away is greater than the other that you did to me" (verse 16). These courses of action retrieve honor for the males of Tamar's family, not, arguably, for her own welfare. As Fuchs points out, Tamar's words reveal that "violating the law is worse

---

¹² Fokkelman, *King David*, 111. Fokkelman also argues that Absalom silences Tamar in order to spare her in his revenge on Amnon. See *HALOT* 1:277 on the variant forms of the same root, זע״ק and צע״ק.

¹³ On public shaming as a means of social control, see Victor H. Matthews, "Honor and Shame in Gender-Related Legal Situations in the Hebrew Bible," in *Gender and Law in the Hebrew Bible and the Ancient Near East*, ed. Victor H. Matthews, Bernard M. Levinson, and Tikva Frymer-Kensky, JSOT Sup 262 (Sheffield: Sheffield Academic, 1998), 97–112.

¹⁴ One argument is that Absalom silences Tamar in order to preserve the family honor; see Frymer-Kensky, *Reading*, 167. This reading is supported by Absalom's words in 2 Sam 13:20: "he is your brother"—i.e., it is an inner family scandal. There are two arguments against this, however. First, Absalom has little concern for his family honor, which becomes evident later in the narrative when he has Amnon murdered. His alternative method of dealing with the problem does not maintain family honor. Second, as demonstrated in Deut 25:5–10, a woman had the right to publicly shame a member of her own family (her dead husband's brother) before the elders if he is not willing to do his duty for her; see Matthews, "Honor and Shame," 100–101.

¹⁵ Esther Fuchs, *Sexual Politics in the Biblical Narrative*, JSOTSup 310 (London: Sheffield Academic, 2000), 200–224. See also her more recent and comprehensive critique of feminist approaches in Fuchs, *Feminist Theory and the Bible: Interrogating the Sources*, Feminist Studies and Sacred Texts (Lanham, MD: Lexington Books, 2016).

¹⁶ Fuchs, *Sexual Politics*, 26.

that violating a woman."[17] The violation of Tamar starts in her father's house, for he has the power to send or withhold her, and ends in Absalom's house, which, in Tamar's words, is worse than rape. Fuchs's methodology is compelling, showing that there is terror in the story's structure, in its legal foundation, and its cultural custom, not just in the events that take place. Fuchs thus develops Trible's feminist approach in an important way.

As part of her critique of the patriarchal structure underlying the story, Fuchs highlights that the rape of Tamar is an offense against Tamar's father and brother, as I outlined above. But this brings me to the second reason for engaging with Fuchs's reading: she argues that Absalom is nevertheless portrayed *by the story* as its hero, as an avenger for Tamar, even though he is acting in his own interests.[18] Tamar has no opportunity to take revenge into her own hands and no recourse to legal justice. In the absence of her father, she has only her brother to act for her and take her place as avenger. The difference from Trible's reading is this: Fuchs acknowledges that Absalom is not murdering Amnon *for Tamar*. But, she says, the narrative portrayal justifies Absalom murdering Amnon because of how much distress is caused to Tamar by the rape. She writes, "by validating the brother's right to protect his sister, the patriarchal ideology only perpetuates the sister's political impotence.... For the right to protect is also the right to dominate."[19]

An examination of the broader narrative context, however, suggests that Absalom is not justified in the story's portrayal and evaluation. The rape of Tamar is part of the outworking of the punishment of David prophesied by Nathan in 2 Sam 12. Nathan says, "the sword shall never depart from your house" and "I will raise up trouble against you from within your own house" (2 Sam 12:10–11). It has been noted in a number of literary readings that David's punishment and the strife in his family echo David's own sins. Amnon rapes Tamar, just as David takes Bathsheba, and Absalom murders Amnon just as David murders Uriah.[20] Absalom murdering Amnon is part of the pattern of magnifying David's sins in David's family; it is no more heroic than David's murder of Uriah. Rape and violence directed outside of David's family is now directed inward, with violent incest and fratricide. Fratricide follows rape as a continuation of tragedy, not poetic justice.

In summary, there is more terror, and irredeemable terror, in 2 Sam 13 than Trible argued. Tamar has no comforter. The whole system in which the laws and

---

[17] Fuchs, *Sexual Politics*, 216. Pamela Tamarkin Reis, "Cupidity and Stupidity: Woman's Agency and the 'Rape' of Tamar," *JANES* 25 (1997): 43–60 has proposed that Tamar is responsible for encouraging Amnon. This reading does not give due weight to Tamar's entreaties to Amnon.

[18] Fuchs, *Sexual Politics*, 219–23.

[19] Fuchs, *Sexual Politics*, 223.

[20] Rachelle Gilmour, *Representing the Past: A Literary Analysis of Narrative Historiography in the Book of Samuel*, VTSup 143 (Leiden: Brill, 2011), 200–204.

Tamar's family structure are implicated is problematic in a feminist reading, and Tamar is the victim not only of Amnon, but of the whole outworking of God's punishment of David. Just as Amnon does not listen to Tamar, neither does Absalom listen to Tamar but silences her in pursuit of his own ambition. Although a patriarchal system underlies this story, and no attempt is made within the story to dismantle that system, it is also not endorsed. The story conveys no illusions that Tamar is safe or protected in either her father's or her brother's house. Absalom is, in fact, another oppressor.

AMNON AND ABSALOM IN PARALLEL

Now that I have reevaluated the common reading that Absalom has compassion for Tamar, and that he can be considered the "good" brother, I will draw out the ways in which Absalom and Amnon are paralleled in 2 Sam 13 and beyond, further grounding this text of terror. I will extend rather than revise Trible's reading of this story, exploring the implications of her identification of Tamar with wisdom.

In 2 Sam 13, both Absalom and Amnon are repeatedly referred to as Tamar's "brother"—Amnon seven times and Absalom twice.[21] The repetition is commonly understood to emphasize that Amnon's act was incestuous, as well as point to the family conflict between brothers.[22] However, another function of this repetition is to parallel Absalom and Amnon in the story: they are both defined as the brother of Tamar (and son of David in 2 Sam 13:1).[23]

A number of other parallels unfold as the narrative progresses, which build upon their parallel designation as Tamar's brothers. Both brothers are said to hate: Amnon "hates" Tamar after the rape (2 Sam 13:15), and Absalom "hates" Amnon after he hears of the rape (2 Sam 13:22). Amnon confines Tamar in his room when he rapes her, and, conversely, forcibly removes her afterward, bolting the door (2 Sam 13:17). So, too, is Tamar confined desolate to Absalom's house (2 Sam 13:20). Finally, neither brother listens to Tamar's voice, Amnon in 2 Sam 13:13–14 and Absalom in 2 Sam 13:19–20.

---

[21] For Amnon, see 2 Sam 13:7–8, 10, 12, 16, 20 (x2). For Absalom, see 2 Sam 13:20 (x2). Note, too, that Amnon also calls Absalom his "brother" in v. 4.

[22] See, e.g., George Ridout, "The Rape of Tamar: A Rhetorical Analysis of 2 Sam 13:1–22" in *Rhetorical Criticism: Essays in Honor of James Muilenburg*, ed. Jared J. Jackson and Martin Kessler (Eugene, OR: Pickwick, 1974), 75–84. On the sibling terminology in 2 Sam 13:20, see Bar Efrat, *Narrative Art*, 272.

[23] Trible, *Texts*, 38 points out the circular arrangement of 2 Sam 13:1, where Tamar is enclosed by "Absalom, son of David" and "Amnon, son of David."

4. But He Would Not Listen to Her

As the story of David's house in 2 Samuel continues, so do parallels between Amnon and Absalom. The most egregious parallel is in 2 Sam 16:21, when Absalom's advisor Ahithophel counsels him to rape his father's concubines in a tent on the palace roof, and Absalom rapes them in verse 22. Echoes of Amnon's actions abound. As discussed earlier, the rape of Tamar is a power play by Amnon against David (and Absalom); so, too, the rape of the concubines is part of Absalom's seizure of power from David in his coup. Just as Tamar is sent to Amnon by David, so also are the concubines abandoned by David when he flees Jerusalem. Just as Tamar is silenced, nothing is told of the concubines' voices or their reactions to the violation. Finally, just as Tamar was shut up in her brother's house in 2 Sam 20:3, it is reported that David kept the concubines under guard and shut them up in his house until their deaths.

There is another, rather more complex parallel between Amnon and Absalom in 2 Sam 16–17, which requires us to revisit Trible's analysis of 2 Sam 13 in *Texts of Terror*. The chapter is entitled "Tamar: The Royal Rape of Wisdom," but the focus on the theme of wisdom has generally not been taken up in subsequent literary (or feminist) readings.[24] Trible points out that Amnon's friend, Jonadab, is "cunning/wise" in 2 Sam 13:3 and that Jonadab gives advice to Amnon using the "skills of a counsellor."[25] Crucially, in this scene Tamar's wisdom is set over against Jonadab's cunning: "wisdom opposes craftiness."[26] Tamar tells Amnon of his foolishness, saying, "do not do this *foolishness* [הנבלה, *hanevalah*].... You would be like one of the *fools* [הנבלים, *hanevalim*] in Israel" (2 Sam 13:12–13; note repetition of the root נב״ל "to be a fool"). After the rape, Tamar speaks again, asking Amnon not to eject her and offering a solution that avoids shame (but not tragedy) on them both. However, according to Trible, "the words of this wise woman he spurns a second time."[27]

Trible deliberately reads 2 Sam 13 in isolation from the context of 2 Samuel but, by expanding her reading into the surrounding literary context, a further echo of Tamar's story can be found.[28] The contest, which involves Jonadab and Tamar as counsellors in 2 Sam 13, parallels another contest of counsellors in 2 Sam 16–17. When David hears of Absalom's rebellion, he flees Jerusalem, leaving his ten concubines behind (2 Sam 15:16), and Absalom enters Jerusalem with his

---

[24] An exception is Bader, *Sexual Violation*, 146, who points out that Jonadab is portrayed with the negative connotations of being "wise" (2 Sam 13:3) but Tamar with the positive connotations, creating an implicit irony.

[25] Trible, *Texts*, 41. In 2 Sam 13:3, Jonadab is described as חכם, *hakham*, a term that usually means "wise" but can have negative connotations such that the English word "cunning" is a better translation.

[26] Trible, *Texts*, 46.

[27] Trible, *Texts*, 48.

[28] Trible, *Texts*, 37.

counsellor Ahithophel (2 Sam 16:15). Meanwhile, in 2 Sam 15:31, David prays that God might turn Ahithophel's counsel into foolishness, although the term used for foolishness (סכל) in 15:31 is different from the root (נב״ל) repeated by Tamar in 13:12–13. In the next verse, Hushai the Archite, another counsellor in Israel, comes to meet David with "his coat torn and earth on his head" expressing loyalty. His appearance echoes that of Tamar, who, in 2 Sam 13:19, "took ashes upon her head and tore the coat of sleeves that was upon her." Hushai is then sent by David back to Absalom to be Absalom's advisor in order to defeat the counsel of Ahithophel.[29]

In the ensuing scene (2 Sam 16:15–17:14), Ahithophel and Hushai give opposing counsel to Absalom, just as Jonadab and Tamar give opposing counsel to Amnon. Ahithophel is known for his good counsel (16:23), so it follows that Absalom will take his advice, as indeed he does when he rapes David's concubines. The tragic violation of these women follows from the advice of Absalom's counsellor, just as the violation of Tamar follows from the advice of Jonadab.

After the violation of the concubines, however, there is an interruption to the tragic parallels between Amnon and Absalom and their counsellors. In 2 Sam 17, God intervenes so that Absalom listens to Hushai rather than Ahithophel. This is reported explicitly in 2 Sam 17:14: "the LORD ordained to defeat the good counsel of Ahithophel so that the LORD might bring ruin on Absalom." In this battle of counsellors, Absalom listens to the military strategy of Hushai, and Hushai is able to warn David. As a result, the strife in the house of David ceases, and David regains his throne. The parallels are finally broken but only with God's intervention.

CONCLUSION

In this chapter, I have argued that the story of Tamar is a text of even more terror than Trible claimed thirty-five years ago. Tamar receives no compassion from her brother Absalom; like Amnon, who shuts Tamar out, Absalom shuts her in. Moreover, Absalom continues to act in ways that are parallel to Amnon as the tragedy in David's house compounds, including the rape of David's concubines. The parallels culminate in a scene where Absalom is given conflicting advice from two counsellors, just as Amnon is given conflicting advice from two counsellors, one of whom is Tamar.

Can this reading still find a blessing in a story of terror, as Trible sets out to do in *Texts of Terror*? On the one hand, the triumph of Hushai's counsel can be seen as a turn toward hope, which succeeds in lieu of Tamar's own wise counsel.

---

[29] Incidentally, David here is also depicted much like Tamar, "weeping as he went, with his head covered and walking barefoot" in 2 Sam 15:30; cf. 2 Sam 13:19, "She put her hands on her head and went away and cried out."

In the narrative of 2 Sam 13, God neither speaks nor explicitly acts throughout Tamar's story while the consequences of human actions play out, but this silence is not forever. It is finally broken in 17:14. On the other hand, the challenge of Tamar's tragedy for a feminist reading becomes all the more acute when we consider the timing of God's intervention in the events: it is tragically too late to prevent the violence against and violation of Tamar and the concubines. Human actions, including the abuse and consequences of the patriarchal structure, are depicted realistically rather than overturned. It is left to our role as interpreters to critique society then and now.

BIBLIOGRAPHY

Bader, Mary Anna. *Sexual Violation in the Hebrew Bible: A Multi-Methodological Study of Genesis 34 and 2 Samuel 13*. New York: Lang, 2006.
Bar Efrat, Shimon. *Narrative Art in the Bible*. Sheffield: Almond Press, 1989.
Brueggemann, Walter. *First and Second Samuel*. Interpretation. Louisville: John Knox, 1990.
Dijk-Hemmes, Fokkelien van. "Tamar and the Limits of Patriarchy: Between Rape and Seduction (2 Samuel 13 and Genesis 38)." Pages 135–56 in *Anti-Covenant: Counter-Reading Women's Lives in the Hebrew Bible*. Edited by Mieke Bal. Sheffield: Almond Press, 1989.
Fokkelman, J. P. *King David*. Vol. 1 of *Narrative Art and Poetry in the Books of Samuel*. 2 vols. Assen: Van Gorcum, 1981.
Frymer-Kensky, Tikva. *Reading the Women of the Bible*. New York: Schocken, 2002.
Fuchs, Esther. *Feminist Theory and the Bible: Interrogating the Sources*. Feminist Studies and Sacred Texts. Lanham, MD: Lexington Books, 2016.
———. *Sexual Politics in the Biblical Narrative: Reading the Hebrew Bible as a Woman*. JSOTSup. 310. London: Sheffield Academic, 2000.
Gilmour, Rachelle. *Representing the Past: A Literary Analysis of Narrative Historiography in the Book of Samuel*. VTSup 143. Leiden: Brill, 2011.
Kalmanofsky, Amy. *Dangerous Sisters of the Hebrew Bible*. Minneapolis: Fortress, 2014.
Knapp, Andrew. *Royal Apologetic in the Ancient Near East*. Atlanta: SBL Press, 2015.
Lemos, T. M. *Violence and Personhood in Ancient Israel and Comparative Contexts*. Oxford: Oxford University Press, 2017.
Lipka, Hilary B. "Shaved Beards and Bared Buttocks: Shame and the Undermining of Masculine Performance in Biblical Texts." Pages 176–97 in *Being a Man: Negotiating Ancient Constructs of Masculinity*. Edited by Ilona Zsolnay. London: Routledge, 2017.
Matthews, Victor H. "Honor and Shame in Gender-Related Legal Situations in the Hebrew Bible." Pages 97–112 in *Gender and Law in the Hebrew Bible and the Ancient Near East*. Edited by Victor H. Matthews, Bernard M. Levinson, and Tikva Frymer-Kensky. JSOTSup 262. Sheffield: Sheffield Academic, 1998.
Pressler, Carolyn. *The View of Women Found in the Deuteronomic Family Laws*. BZAW 216. Berlin: de Gruyter, 1993.
Reis, Pamela Tamarkin. "Cupidity and Stupidity: Woman's Agency and the 'Rape' of Tamar." *JANES* 25 (1997): 43–60.

Ridout, George. "The Rape of Tamar: A Rhetorical Anaysis of 2 Sam 13:1–22." Pages 75–84 in *Rhetorical Criticism: Essays in Honor of James Muilenburg*. Edited by Jared J. Jackson and Martin Kessler. Eugene, OR: Pickwick, 1974.

Schulte, Leah Rediger. *The Absence of God in Biblical Rape Narratives*. Minneapolis: Fortress, 2017.

Smith, Richard G. *Fate of Justice and Righteousness during David's Reign: Narrative Ethics and Rereading the Court History according to 2 Samuel 8:15–20:26*. LHBOTS 508. New York: T&T Clark, 2009.

Stiebert, Johanna. *Fathers and Daughters in the Hebrew Bible*. Oxford: Oxford University Press, 2013.

Stone, Ken. *Sex, Honor and Power in the Deuteronomistic History*. JSOTSup 234. Sheffield: Sheffield Academic, 1996.

Thistlewaite, Susan Brooks. "'You May Enjoy the Spoil of Your Enemies': Rape as a Biblical Metaphor for War." *Semeia* 61 (1993): 59–78.

Trible, Phyllis. *Texts of Terror: Literary-Feminist Readings of Biblical Narratives*. OBT. Philadelphia: Fortress, 1984.

Yamada, Frank M. *Configurations of Rape in the Hebrew Bible: A Literary Analysis of Three Rape Narratives*. New York: Lang, 2008.

5

Clean and Unclean: Multiple Readings of Mark 7:24–30/31

Dorothy A. Lee

Phyllis Trible, in her groundbreaking study of several narratives about women in the Hebrew Scriptures, argued that they present significant interpretive problems for contemporary readers, particularly from a feminist viewpoint.[1] She famously describes these narratives as "texts of terror"—that is, "sad stories...that yield four portraits of suffering in ancient Israel."[2] Trible's methodology is narrative-critical, but she is also well aware of the hermeneutical issues involved in translating ancient texts into new and radically different contexts. The question I wish to ask in this essay is whether the story of the Syro-Phoenician woman in the Gospel of Mark qualifies as a text of terror (Mark 7:24–30/31). To answer this question involves negotiating a path through a number of different ways of reading the narrative.

The story of Jesus's encounter with a gentile woman whose daughter is possessed by a demon is difficult and controversial. It raises issues of ritual purity and inclusion, social status, gender, and race, as well as questions of genre. Sitting at a crossroads, a meeting of diverse paths, it is a significant narrative that is subject to more than one interpretation, and therein lies the difficulty in assessing the story. This essay will explore four ways of reading the text—missional, pedagogical, paradigmatic, and christological—although there is considerable diversity of opinion within each. The four interpretative approaches in some ways complement each other, so they are not necessarily mutually exclusive, but in other respects they clash, offering opposing answers to the fundamental questions of the story's genre and purpose.

---

[1] Phyllis Trible, *Texts of Terror: Literary-Feminist Readings of Biblical Narratives*, OBT (Philadelphia: Fortress, 1984).
[2] Trible, *Texts*, 1.

The Syro-Phoenician narrative is a stylized rather than journalistic or psychological narrative and, despite its likely historical origin, is best read as a "literary creation and not as a window into a real encounter."[3] Like other Markan exorcisms, it points symbolically to the gospel's apocalyptic character (Mark 1:21–27, 34; 3:11, 5:1–20; 6:7, 13; 9:14–29).[4] At the center of the narrative stands a Markan parable, a parable (παραβολή) being a fictional, appealing, and realistic narrative that operates metaphorically.[5] Although the parable is initiated by Jesus, it is completed by the woman.[6] The formal structure is a chiasm in seven scenes, as shown in figure 1.

    A Jesus's secret arrival in gentile territory: hidden (v. 24)
        B Woman's arrival: need (vv. 25–26)
            C Woman's request for miracle (v. 26)
                D Parable of bread and table (vv. 27–28)
            C' Jesus's agreement to miracle (v. 29)
        B' Woman's departure: healing (v. 30)
    A' Jesus's departure to other gentile territory (v. 31)

Fig. 1. Chiastic structure of the parable in Mark 7:24–31

Mark describes the woman's ethnic and geographical identity carefully, giving the story its dramatic edge.[7] She is doubly unclean, because of her gender and her gentile status, while her daughter is possessed by an "unclean spirit" (πνεῦμα ἀκάθαρτον, Mark 7:25). Not only is she a gentile but she is also described as

---

[3] Sharon H. Ringe, "A Gentile Woman's Story, Revisited: Rereading Mark 7:24–31," in *A Feminist Companion to Mark*, ed. Amy-Jill Levine and Marianne Blickenstaff (Sheffield: Sheffield Academic, 2001), 96.

[4] Francis J. Moloney, *The Gospel of Mark: A Commentary* (Peabody, MA: Hendrickson, 2002), 147 points out that the pericope follows the typical form of a miracle story (with the exception of the parable): request for healing, Jesus's response, miracle performed with word, touch or gesture, and success of the miracle described.

[5] For this definition of parable, see Ruben Zimmermann, *Puzzling the Parables of Jesus: Methods and Interpretation* (Minneapolis: Fortress, 2015), 138–50; see also 100–102.

[6] On the metaphorical exchange as parable, see Kelly R. Iverson, *Gentiles in the Gospel of Mark: "Even the Dogs under the Table Eat the Children's Crumbs,"* LNTS (London: T&T Clark, 2007), 52–54 and David E. Malick, "An Examination of Jesus' View of Women through Three Intercalations in the Gospel of Mark," *Priscilla Papers*, July 31, 2013, https://tinyurl.com/rj693knk. See also David Rhoads, "Jesus and the Syrophoenician Woman in Mark: A Narrative-Critical Study," *JAAR* 62 (1994): 355–57, who interprets this and the other Markan parables as essentially allegory.

[7] Ringe, "Gentile Woman's Story," 86.

"Greek" ('Ἑλληνίς, Mark 7:26), which suggests that she belongs to a higher socio-economic and cultural class.[8] She is also associated with the city of Tyre, a wealthy and commercially dominating city, dependent for its agricultural needs on the poorer and economically deprived Jewish villages in the Galilee.[9] Despite the appropriate form of the woman's request and the subservient posture with which she enacts it (Mark 7:25c), it appears at first as if Jesus will refuse her due to his desire to remain hidden ("he did not want anyone to know him," οὐδένα ἤθελεν γνῶναι, Mark 7:24b).[10] The potential rebuff increases the narrative tension, as it seems unprecedented in the gospel (Mark 7:27).[11] Dogs (κυνάρια) are unclean animals in the Jewish context, and gentiles, who are unclean by virtue of standing outside the law, can be referred to metaphorically as "dogs" within the Jewish world.[12] In the end, Jesus assents to the miracle (Mark 7:29) thanks to the woman's agile response within the metaphorical terms of the parable (Mark 7:28).[13]

---

[8] Gerd Theissen, *The Gospels in Context: Social and Political History in the Synoptic Tradition* (London: Bloomsbury Academic, 2004), 70–72. The question of Mark's geographical origin may have relevance here, given that Syria is the main contender to Rome; see Mary Rose D'Angelo, "(Re)presentations of Women in the Gospels: John and Mark," in *Women and Christian Origins*, ed. Ross Shepard Kreamer and Mary Rose D'Angelo (New York: Oxford University Press, 1999), 129–49; Jennifer A. Glancy, "Jesus, the Syrophoenician Woman and Other First Century Bodies," *BibInt* 18 (2010): 350–51.

[9] Theissen, *Gospels*, 66–80; Hisako Kinukawa, "The Exploitation of Peasants in the Regions of Tyre and Galilee," in *Islands, Islanders, and the Bible: Ruminations*, ed. Jione Havea, Margaret Aymer, and Steed V. Davidson (Atlanta: SBL Press, 2015), 136–43; Jane E. Hicks, "Moral Agency at the Borders: Rereading the Story of the Syrophoenician Woman," *WW* 23 (2003): 80–83.

[10] On prostration here and in Mark more generally, see Glancy, "Jesus," 352–59.

[11] Rhoads, "Jesus," 354.

[12] See, e.g. 1 Sam 24:14; Isa 56:10; Matt 7:6; Phil 3:2; Rev 22:15. A qualifying voice is that of Geoffrey David Miller, "Attitudes Towards Dogs in Ancient Israel: A Reassessment," *JSNT* 32 (2008): 487–500, who argues that dogs could be kept as working animals (e.g., sheepdogs) and pets in Israel (e.g., Tob 6:2; 11:4), although in general dogs were more highly valued in the surrounding nations. See also Joel Marcus, *Mark 1–8: A New Translation with Introduction and Commentary*, AB 27 (New York: Doubleday, 2000), 464. Attempts have been made to soften the language by suggesting "puppies" to translate the diminutive form. There is no evidence that the diminutive form was used in this way; see Adela Yarbro Collins, *Mark: A Commentary* (Philadelphia: Augsburg Fortress, 2007), 367. See also Alan H. Cadwallader, *Beyond the Word of a Woman: Recovering the Bodies of the Syrophoenician Women* (Adelaide: ATF Press, 2008), 87–139 on the use of the diminutive and the Greek origins of the saying, which he regards as a proverb.

[13] The timing is slightly ambiguous, given the use of the perfect indicative rather than the present imperative ("the demon has gone out from your daughter," ἐξελήλυθεν ἐκ τῆς θυγατρός σου τὸ δαιμόνιον, Mark 7:29) and raises the question of when the girl is actually healed. Other healings and exorcisms in Mark, which are not performed at a distance,

The story is sometimes problematic for modern readers. The woman has been described as an "ambivalent figure" in the world of the text.[14] The parable seems harsh to modern ears, particularly if taken literally, with its comparison between children and dogs, insiders and outsiders, even if the woman's status is a privileged one by virtue of her ethnic identity. It is particularly striking given the immediate Markan context: the preceding controversy about clean and unclean, where Jesus sets aside the laws of ritual purity (Mark 7:1–23). Given the theological importance of geography, it is also curious that the Markan Jesus retreats in secret to gentile territory, the inhabitants of which have previously shown interest in his ministry (Mark 3:8). The secrecy motif plays a role here, as part of a recurring theme in Mark that depicts Jesus's uneasy relationship with his popularity and miraculous powers.[15] Unlike other Markan exorcisms, Jesus does not confront the demon but performs the miracle from a distance.[16]

The first interpretation of the Syro-Phoenician story is in the Gospel of Matthew (Matt 15:21–28).[17] Matthew follows Mark fairly closely, while making the story more dramatic and increasing the suspense.[18] The woman is named as "Canaanite," evoking the ancient enemies of Israel.[19] She is thus identified explicitly

---

involve a direct command or commanding gesture (e.g. Mark 1:25; 1:31; 1:41; 2:11; 3:5; 4:39; 5:8; 5:34; 5:41; 7:34; 8:23–25; 9:25). Only once is there no follow-up to the command to "go"; a perfect indicative appears here instead ("your faith has saved you," ἡ πίστις σου σέσωκέν σε, 10:52). On the woman's boldness in the story, see Mary-Ann Tolbert, "Mark," in *The Women's Bible Commentary: Expanded Edition with Apocrypha*, ed. Carol A. Newsom and Sharon H. Ringe, 2nd ed. (Louisville: Westminster John Knox/SPCK, 1998), 356–57.

[14] Collins, *Mark*, 368.

[15] Elizabeth Struthers Malbon, *Mark's Jesus: Characterization as Narrative Christology* (Waco, TX: Baylor University Press, 2009), 133–34. On the secrecy motif, see M. Eugene Boring, *Mark: A Commentary* (Louisville: Westminster John Knox, 2006), 209–10.

[16] Ringe, "Gentile Woman's Story," 87.

[17] Dorothy A. Lee, "The Faith of the Canaanite Woman (Mt 15.21–28): Narrative, Theology, Ministry," *JAS* 13 (2015): 12–29.

[18] Luke omits the narrative, which is itself a form of interpretation; this absence is surprising given the Lukan emphasis on the gentiles. Perhaps Luke dislikes the canine imagery, but it is more likely that the story is excised along with other material in this section of Mark, including the death of John the Baptist, the second feeding story, the discussion about clean and unclean, and two other healing stories. This is part of the so-called Great Omission (Mark 6:45–8:26/par.), and is occasioned by Luke's wider focus on Gentile inclusion in Acts (e.g., Acts 10). The narrative is also absent from the Gospel of John, although a loose parallel can be drawn with the story of the Samaritan woman (John 4:1–42), which has gender and ethnic elements. The story concludes with the Samaritans, who acclaim Jesus as universal Savior based on the woman's apostolic witness (John 4:42).

[19] See Jub. 20.22–24. Josephus, *C. Ap.* 1.70 (Thackeray, LCL) describes the Tyrians as "notoriously our bitterest enemies." On the depiction of Canaanites as villains in the Old

not only as "other" but also as "enemy." Jesus is silent when she first approaches him, and the disciples, who often misunderstand the real significance of events, want Jesus to dismiss her (either by granting or refusing her request) because they find the situation embarrassing and potentially shameful.[20] Yet Jesus's final words to the woman are even more astonishing and emphatic than those of the Markan Jesus: "O woman, great is your faith!" (Matt 15:28). This is consistent with Matthew's emphasis on faith throughout the miracle stories in his redaction of Mark.[21] The exclamatory ὦ γύναι, "O woman" (the "O" is often omitted in translation) carries with it a depth of emotion on Jesus's part, revealing how deeply he is touched by the woman's faith.[22]

MISSIONAL READINGS

The first major strand of interpretation relates to mission.[23] In this view, the woman represents the gentiles; her gender, while significant, is secondary to her ethnicity. Jesus can be seen as moving beyond the Jewish people toward those gentiles whose need of him and faith in him are strikingly apparent. In Eastern Orthodox readings, the gentiles "have become worthy of the children's bread, by their humility and faith."[24] For them, this is a story of opening doors, in which "humility opens the floodgates of divine grace."[25] Such a reading centers on the overcoming of barriers between Jew and gentile.[26] When read as a missional narrative, then, the pericope highlights Jesus's ministry as directed initially at Israel, confirming Israel's election by God and God's choice of the poor and insignificant. This theme may well be more explicit in Matthew's gospel (e.g., Matt 10:5–6), but

---

Testament, see Glenna S. Jackson, *"Have Mercy on Me": The Story of the Canaanite Woman in Matthew 15.21–28* (Sheffield: Sheffield Academic, 2002), 70–82.

[20] Matthew is generally less critical of the disciples than Mark.

[21] Heinz Joachim Held, "Matthew as Interpreter of the Miracle Stories," in *Tradition and Interpretation in Matthew*, ed. Guenther Bornkamm, Gerhard Barth, and Heinz Joachim Held, trans. Percy Scott, 2nd ed. (London: SCM, 1982), 275–96.

[22] Boring, *Mark*, 208. Pre-Enlightenment exegesis tends to conflate the Markan and Matthean versions.

[23] Ulrich Luz, *Matthew 8–20: A Commentary*, trans. James E. Crouch, Hermeneia (Minneapolis: Fortress, 2001), 337–38.

[24] Tadros Y. Malaty, *The Gospel according to Saint Mark* (Orange, CA: Coptic Orthodox Christian Center, 2003), 126.

[25] Antony Hughes, "Sermon on the Sunday of the Canaanite Woman," St. Mary Orthodox Church, Cambridge MA, February 10, 2008, https://tinyurl.com/aupm3b52.

[26] For a view that disputes use of the term "Gentile" in this text, cf. Hans Leander, *Discourses of Empire: The Gospel of Mark from a Postcolonial Perspective* (Atlanta: Society of Biblical Literature, 2013), 225–30, who sees her identity as specifically Greek.

it is also assumed in Mark, where the primary group of outsiders initially consists of sinners and tax collectors who, while alienated from their own traditions and identity (Mark 2:15–17), are nonetheless Jewish. The woman may be associated with powerful, elite cities, yet her status within the text is that of outsider. In sociological terms, Jesus's response to her request seems initially to reinforce that status as other, rendering her effectively invisible for his mission. In the end, however, the narrative shows that "the gospel involves neither the dissolution of ethnicity nor the rejection of one's own ethnic identity."[27]

This missional understanding of the Markan text also has a temporal aspect. Gentiles are to be included in the future but not in the primary ministry of Jesus. The key word here is "first" (πρῶτον, Mark 7:27), which implies that gentiles will be fed and outsiders included, eventually equalizing Israel's priority.[28] Viewed from this angle, the Syro-Phoenician story points to the broadening of mission beyond Israel, evident within the literary shape of the third narrative cycle, with its increasingly outward focus (Mark 6:6b–8:21).[29] Although not the first example of Jesus's ministry to gentiles, our story pushes further toward their inclusion (Mark 3:7–12; 5:1–20).[30] Based on these exemptions within the ministry of Jesus, the Markan story offers a prefiguring of the post-Easter mission, providing "the impetus for the early Church to transcend these boundaries" in its later missional goal.[31] In this mission, gentiles enter "the reign of God" (ἡ βασιλεία τοῦ θεοῦ, Mark 1:15) from their own cultural milieu. Jesus's permissive attitude toward the Torah (Mark 2:23–3:5), along with the woman's assumption that dogs belong in home and family, suggests an openness in this gospel not just to gentile presence but also to gentile customs and culture.[32] Jesus's mission, which first converges on Israel's inside-outsiders, moves beyond them to those entirely outside Israel: "Israel is now being fed with eschatological salvation in the ministry of Jesus. After Easter, under the guidance of the Spirit, this salvation will come to the Gentiles as well."[33] From this viewpoint, the woman as cultural outsider becomes "the pioneer and paradigm of all Gentile believers."[34]

---

[27] Julien C. H. Smith, "The Construction of Identity in Mark 7:24–30: The Syrophoenician Woman and the Problem of Ethnicity," *BibInt* 20 (2012): 481.

[28] T. Alec Burkill, "The Historical Development of the Story of the Syrophoenician Woman (Mark VII:24–31)," *NovT* 9 (1967): 161–77.

[29] Moloney, *Gospel of Mark*, 147–48 points out that there may well be people in the Markan community who oppose the inclusion of the gentiles—and against whom this story is aimed.

[30] Iverson, *Gentiles*, 51.

[31] Robert A. Guelich, *Mark 1–8:26*, WBC (Dallas, TX: Word, 1989), 389.

[32] Francis Dufton, "The Syrophoenician Woman and her Dogs," *ExpT* 100 (1989): 417.

[33] Boring, *Mark*, 212.

[34] Brendan Byrne, *A Costly Freedom: A Theological Reading of Mark's Gospel* (Collegeville, MN: Liturgical Press, 2008), 126.

Feminist readings support emphasis on the ethnicity of the confrontation, arguing that gender awareness should not bypass the powerful ethnic and political implications.[35] A postcolonial reading looks at the story through the lens of the Roman Empire, on the one hand, and the reign of God, on the other, which displaces it in the Markan worldview.[36] From a Korean viewpoint, Seong-Hee Kim sees the gentile woman becoming "the catalyst for moving Jesus to acknowledge his ministry to the Gentile people."[37] Postcolonial readings also critique European hermeneutics that continue to marginalize those outside the dominant culture. For example, where the Syro-Phoenician woman is seen to represent the submissive "heathen" who is meekly grateful to the Christian missionary, depriving her of cultural identity is seen as deeply problematic.[38] Such European interpretation illustrates the tendency to read the biblical text from the viewpoint of the colonizer rather than the colonized, as Hans Leander argues.[39] In this view, the Syro-Phoenician woman and her daughter can be seen as subalterns and the narrative itself subversive on their behalf.[40] The woman is poised between "Roman colonialism and Jewish patriarchalism," in the words of David Joy, while the narrative "is a pointer to new ways of breaking the boundaries of gender, race, and religion."[41]

An alternative postcolonial reading sees the story as an inversion of power on the basis of ethnicity. Writing with a Chinese outlook, Poling Sun argues that "the Syrophoenician woman does not come to Jesus as a victim oppressed by colonialism or male domination … but as Syrophoenician power, a dominant and

---

[35] According to Victoria Phillips, "The Failure of the Women Who Followed Jesus in the Gospel of Mark," in *A Feminist Companion to Mark*, ed. Amy-Jill Levine and Marianne Blickenstaff (Sheffield: Sheffield Academic, 2001), 225, "women of color, among other others, have challenged the use of gender as a category in isolation from other variables of social location, such as ethnicity, class, or status."

[36] See, e.g., Seong-Hee Kim, *Mark, Women and Empire: A Korean Postcolonial Perspective* (Sheffield: Sheffield Phoenix, 2010), 60–78; Raj Nadella, "The Two Banquets: Mark's Vision of Anti-Imperial Economics," *Int* 70 (2016): 172–83.

[37] Ranjini Wickramaratne Rebera, "The Syro-Phoenician Woman: A South African Perspective," in *A Feminist Companion to Mark*, ed. Amy-Jill Levine and Marianne Blickenstaff (Sheffield: Sheffield Academic, 2001), 107.

[38] Pui-Lan Kwok, *Discovering the Bible in the Non-Biblical World* (Maryknoll, NY: Orbis Books, 1995), 71–83.

[39] Leander, *Discourses*, 109–15.

[40] Leander, *Discourses*, 330–36. For a subaltern reading of the narrative, see further C. I. David Joy, *Mark and Its Subalterns: A Hermeneutical Paradigm for a Postcolonial Context* (London: Equinox, 2008), 143–65.

[41] Joy, *Mark and Its Subalterns*, 164–65. For a Dalit reading that questions chosenness, see Surekha Nelavala, "Smart Syrophoenician Woman: A Dalit Feminist Reading of Mark 7:24–31," *ExpT* 118 (2006): 64–69.

oppressing group."[42] In her view, the appellation "dogs" refers to that oppressive economic power rather than to the woman herself or to ethnicity in general. What the narrative calls forth in the woman, she argues, is repentance from participation in political and economic oppression. Jesus represents "the voice of the powerless to name the dog."[43] The woman's response to the parable, in this reading, implies a repentant spirit and a willingness to turn from the tyranny and dominion of her environment.

This first, missional way of reading focuses on the inclusive imperative for mission in Mark's account, where the alien outsider is given a place at the table. It also offers a much-needed critique of historical forms of mission that have shown disregard for ethnic culture and context, supporting instead the overriding ethos of the colonizer. The picture of Jesus as representing the voice of the colonized coheres more closely with Mark's theology of the cross than the image of Jesus as the insensitive colonizer. From both standpoints, the woman and her daughter embody the widening scope of salvation and the benefits of God's reign disseminated beyond insider bounds.[44]

PEDAGOGICAL READINGS

The story of the Syro-Phoenician woman has also been read as a pedagogical narrative, in which the evangelist is engaged in teaching; the first exorcism in Mark, after all, is framed by references to Jesus's authoritative teaching ("as one holding authority," ὡς ἐξουσίαν ἔχων, Mark 1:21; "a new teaching with authority," διδαχὴ καινὴ κατ' ἐξουσίαν, Mark 1:27). The controversial question here is who or what functions as teacher in the narrative. Is it Jesus himself teaching the woman about the priority of Israel and about authentic faith? Is it Mark the evangelist teaching his audience through the didactic metaphor of bread? Or is it the gentile woman teaching Jesus (not to mention the Markan audience) about the need for a wide and generous policy of inclusion? The answer will depend on the way in which the parable at the center of the narrative is viewed.[45]

---

[42] Poling Sun, "Naming the Dog: Another Asian Reading of Mark 7:24–30," *RevExp* 107 (2010): 389.

[43] Sun, "Naming," 390.

[44] R. T. France, *The Gospel of Mark: A Commentary on the Greek Text*, NIGTC (Grand Rapids: Eerdmans, 2002), 296.

[45] For Cadwallader, *Beyond the Word*, 3–52, the offence is based on the association of women with the nonrational and the bestial. An ethological reading, in his view, focuses on the comparison between human and animal in the ancient world, where animals are regarded as inferior because of their lack of reason and women are associated with them: "animals are the antithesis of *logos*" (5–6).

A number of gender readings argue that Jesus is overtly and inexcusably offensive to the woman in naming her a dog, and that he himself is the student in the narrative.[46] His negative response is seen to cohere with the repression of women across the ancient world. The story is thus read as an example of role reversal: a woman anxious over her daughter's condition teaches a man the true implications of his own teaching that he has not himself yet fully grasped.[47] This reading focuses on the specific response of the Markan Jesus to the woman's faith (διὰ τοῦτον τὸν λόγον ὕπαγε, Mark 7:29), not "For saying that, you may go" (NRSV) but "On account of this *word*, go," referring to the "word" or "words" of the gospel.[48] In this view, Jesus is "an initially sexist, but finally teachable man," who hears his message echoed back to him in new guise.[49]

A rather different example of pedagogical interpretation is to see the Markan story as ironic, testing the depth and authenticity of faith. This literary technique is found in a number of biblical narratives where the central character endures a trial of faith: Abraham's summons to sacrifice Isaac (Gen 22:1–19), the hardships faced by Ruth and Naomi (Ruth 1:1–2:13), the unmerited sufferings of Job (Job 1:1–19), and the dangers faced by Esther (Esth 3:7–4:17), as well as Jesus's own experience in the wilderness (Mark 1:12–13 pars.).[50] A miracle parallel in Mark is the story of the dying girl whose father, Jairus, seeks Jesus's urgent help only to be tested by the delay caused by the woman with a hemorrhage. Yet Jesus encourages him to "go on believing" when he hears that his daughter has died and human hope has fled (μόνον πίστευε, Mark 5:36). The overcoming of such obstacles is also

---

[46] F. W. Beare, *The Gospel according to Matthew* (Oxford: Basil Blackwell, 1981), 242 expresses his sense of outrage at Matthew's narrative: Jesus's attitude to her is brutal, representing "the worst kind of chauvinism." See also Leticia A. Guardiola-Saénz, "Borderless Women and Borderless Texts: A Cultural Reading of Matthew 15:21–28," *Semeia* 78 (1997): 69–81, who sees the woman as victimized and oppressed even by Matthew, and Ringe, "Gentile Woman's Story," 89–90.

[47] In Matthew's version, some argue that the woman plays the role that should have been taken by Jesus; see, e.g., J. Martin C. Scott, "Matthew 15.21–28: A Test-Case for Jesus' Manners," *JSNT* 63 (1996): 21–44; Anita Monro, "Alterity and the Canaanite Woman: A Postmodern Feminist Theological Reflection on Political Action," *Colloq* 26 (1994): 32–43.

[48] Cf. Mark 1:45; 4:14–20; 4:33; 7:13; 8:38; 9:10; 10:22; 13:31; 14:39. See esp. Cadwallader, *Beyond the Word*, 253–60 and Joanna Dewey, "The Gospel of Mark," in *Searching the Scriptures: A Feminist Commentary*, ed. Elisabeth Schuessler Fiorenza (New York: Crossroad, 1994), 2:484–85. Cadwallader, *Beyond the Word*, 276–82, however, sees Mark's conclusion negatively as "logocentric," rather than focused on the bodies of the two females.

[49] Ringe, "Gentile Woman's Story," 99.

[50] Jennifer L. Koosed, "Ruth as a Fairy Tale," Bible Odyssey, https://tinyurl.com/4pf5678w.

a feature of the suppliant narratives in Mark and has an important catechetical function for the Markan community.[51]

In this interpretation, the central parable operates as "peirastic irony," where the surface meaning is the opposite of the inner significance (cf. πειράζεσθαι, "to try").[52] Here the Markan Jesus employs imagery that "is a challenge to the woman to justify her request."[53] Her reaction reveals that she has succeeded in grasping the deeper meaning and has extended the parable on her own initiative, displaying steadfastness of faith as well as creative understanding through the ordeal.[54] This motif can be read as part of the wider Markan irony, which has the privileged insiders, to whom "the mystery of the kingdom" is given, standing in contrast to the ancillary outsiders, to whom "everything comes in parables" (τὸ μυστήριον τῆς βασιλείας ... ἐν παραβολαῖς τὰ πάντα γίνεται, Mark 4:11). Yet these outsiders are the very ones who ultimately understand, even without Jesus's clarification, in contrast to the uncomprehending insiders for whom everything is explained. In this reading, the Syro-Phoenician woman is an example of the outsider who, when tested, far exceeds the insiders in her capacity to grasp Jesus's meaning.[55]

The point can be taken further. The woman's active engagement with the parable, extending it to include the "dogs under the table" (τὰ κυνάρια ὑποκάτω τῆς τραπέζης, 7:28), is itself didactic. She plays an educative role within the text alongside the Markan Jesus. The parables often require an explanation from Jesus for the disciples who fail to comprehend them ("are you too thus without understanding?", οὕτως καὶ ὑμεῖς ἀσύνετοί ἐστε, Mark 7:18a), yet this parable is grasped immediately by the woman as she enlarges the metaphor to encompass her and her daughter. In this sense, the parable both fortifies Jesus's authority as teacher and incorporates the woman as an active participant in the pedagogy through the magnetic force of her wit, insight, and faith.

The pedagogical approach to the Syro-Phoenician tale thus takes two rather different forms. In the first case, the woman is seen as the educator of Jesus who fails to perceive the full meaning of his own teaching. In the second case, the pedagogical dimension comes through irony, where the woman becomes a co-teacher with Jesus, confirming the inherent perceptiveness of the outsider. Yet there are

---

[51] So Rhoads, "Jesus" 348–51, who sees the story not as a testing narrative but as an example of "A Suppliant with Faith" along with ten other such stories in Mark. See also Gerd Theissen, *Miracle Stories of the Early Christian Tradition* (Edinburgh: T&T Clark, 1983), 74–80 and Collins, *Mark*, 366.

[52] Jerry Camery-Hoggatt, *Irony in Mark's Gospel: Text and Subtext*, SNTSM (Cambridge: Cambridge University Press, 1992), 149–51; Marcus, *Mark 1–8*, 468–70; Iverson, *Gentiles*, 52.

[53] Morna D. Hooker, *The Gospel according to St Mark* (London: Black, 1991), 183.

[54] Marcus, *Mark 1–8*, 468 reads "on account of this word" as Jesus's acknowledgement that the woman has passed the text.

[55] Iverson, *Gentiles*, 48–57.

problems with the first interpretation despite its popularity in contemporary circles. In its desire to emphasize the woman's educative role within the text, the portrayal of the Markan Jesus fails to grasp the parable. It also fails to recognize the ironic imagery and the particular shape of the gospel's christology (as we will see). In either case, the story operates didactically as both warning and encouragement for the implied reader, with the woman playing an instructive role.

PARADIGMATIC READINGS

A third way of reading the Syro-Phoenician narrative is to interpret the woman as a paradigm of discipleship. There are different forms of this view, but the woman functions as a remarkable model of faith, service, and resilience in all of them. Spirituality remains the main lens of interpretation in popular reading.[56] This devotional view shows no particular concern about the use of canine imagery but emphasizes the woman's spiritual deference and humility. Patristic writers see the woman's persistence as eliciting the divine mercy of Jesus (Chrysostom, Ephrem the Syrian), while interpretations from the Eastern Orthodox traditions follow a similar line, focusing on the woman's self-abasement and pertinacity.[57] The Western tradition has likewise read it as a parenetic narrative extolling the religious virtues of humility.[58] For example, the story makes its way into the Book of Common Prayer (1662), in the Prayer of Humble Access, in which the Syro-Phoenician woman serves as a model of humility and trust for men as well as women.

> We do not presume to come to this thy table, merciful LORD,
> trusting in our own righteousness, but in thy manifold and great mercies.
> We are not worthy so much as to gather up the crumbs under thy table.
> But thou art the same LORD, whose property is always to have mercy.[59]

---

[56] For a brief historical outline of different interpretations of the Syrophoenician narrative, see Alan H. Cadwallader, "The Building of Awareness of Hermeneutics Through the History of Interpretations of the Bible," *Colloq* 33 (2001): 15–19. See also Theissen, *Gospels*, 62–65.

[57] On patristic interpretation, see Thomas C. Oden and Christopher A. Hall, eds., *Mark: Ancient Christian Commentary on Scripture* (Downers Grove, IL: IVP Academic, 1998), 95–96. Tertullian sees it as illustrating the equal moral dignity of women.

[58] Luz, *Matthew* 8–20, 337–38. Faith becomes the center of the narrative for the Protestant reformers: faith in the word of God.

[59] Cynthia B. Kittredge, "Not Worthy So Much as to Gather up the Crumbs under Thy Table: Reflection on the Sources and History of the Prayer of Humble Access," *STRev* 50 (2006) 80–92. *A Prayer Book for Australia* (Alexandria, NSW: Broughton Books, 112), 125

Yet there is more than humility in the woman's spirituality. She is also a model of dauntless courage in service to her daughter, who shows a self-awareness and tenacity that is without ego, false pride, or self-delusion. With a clear assessment of her need, she is prepared to approach Jesus with boldness as well as compliance, in the confident hope of divine compassion. In this reading, the luminous exemplar of a courageous and selfless spirituality is female, not male. The Syro-Phoenician woman is a role model whose paradoxical virtues—self-awareness and resilience, lack of pretension and audacity—are worthy of imitation.

A paradigmatic reading also interprets the narrative not as singular and exceptional but as cohering with the significant role that outsiders, particularly women, play in Mark's gospel.[60] The woman's faith is shared by others and tallies with other Markan stories, as we have already noted, where outsiders display exemplary insight denied to the insiders. This group includes those with a physical disability, such as the woman with a hemorrhage, whose paradigmatic faith, endorsed enthusiastically by Jesus, encourages Jairus in his own faith (Mark 5:34–36). Likewise blind Bartimaeus, at the climax of the journey to Jerusalem, displays an insight and depth of faith that is lacking in Jesus's closest associates (Mark 10:46–52).

Most significantly, the passion narrative begins and ends with the faithfulness of women as disciples and ministers, in contrast to the twelve, who desert, betray, or deny Jesus. With their faith and insight, the three "myrrh-bearing women"—Mary Magdalene, Mary the mother of James, and Salome ("they bought spices to come and anoint him," ἠγόρασαν ἀρώματα ἵνα ἐλθοῦσαι ἀλείψωσιν αὐτόν, Mark 16:1)—parallel yet exceed the inner three male disciples, Peter, James, and John. The latter receive privileged access to Jesus without understanding either his person or his ministry. The women disciples in effect take over the apostolic role which, as the listing of the twelve makes clear earlier in the gospel, has a dual role: to be Jesus's companions and to be sent out to proclaim his message ("to be with him and that he might send them out to proclaim," ἵνα ὦσιν μετ' αὐτοῦ καὶ ἀποστέλλῃ αὐτοὺς κηρύσσειν, Mark 3:14). The faith of these women is admittedly complicated by the ambiguous ending of the gospel ("and they said nothing to anyone for they were afraid," καὶ οὐδενὶ οὐδὲν εἶπαν· ἐφοβοῦντο γάρ, Mark 16:8). While some advocate that the female disciples abandon the tomb in disobedient fear and silence, the wider gospel suggests that they are temporarily overwhelmed by the ineffable message of the resurrection, which has little to do with

---

includes the prayer as integral to the First Order of Holy Communion and as optional in the Second Order. Many other contemporary Anglican and other denominational liturgies continue to use it, usually as an option.

[60] On the reversal of outsiders and insiders in Mark, see Kim, *Mark, Women, and Empire*, 119–20.

disobedience and everything to do with fear and silence as the appropriate response to an epiphany.[61]

Within the wider narrative framework of the gospel, the Syro-Phoenician woman's meeting with Jesus has notable ecclesial dimensions. The issue is what she represents, as woman and as ethnic outsider, within the community of faith. Once again the literary context of the story plays a key role in its interpretation. Mark sets up a series of narratives that push the significance of Jesus and the makeup of the new community beyond its Jewish bounds. These episodes reinforce the geographical movement in the gospel beyond a Jewish environment to a more diverse audience, including gentile outsiders.[62] The gentile cycle in which our story is embedded is framed on either side by the intransigence of the Markan Pharisees and the misunderstanding of the disciples. It begins with the controversy on defilement, in which Jesus radically reinterprets "clean" and "unclean" as moral rather than ritual categories (Mark 7:1–23), and it ends with the hostile questioning of the Pharisees and the dismay of the disciples, who have forgotten to bring bread (Mark 8:11–21).[63]

The implications of the controversy with the Pharisees (Mark 7:1–13) spills over into the following scenes. By the end of the Syro-Phoenician story, the uncleanness has entirely gone from both mother and daughter. The woman's irrepressible spirit has given her access to the table on behalf of her child: "The mother has won her daughter's deliverance."[64] Thereafter Jesus heals a disabled man in gentile territory, offering him the metaphorical "bread" of the children (Mark 7:31–37), and feeds a crowd of four thousand people with bread and fish, again in gentile territory (Mark 8:1–10).[65] The imagery belongs in the wider context of food/bread/eating in this section of the gospel (Mark 6:21, 30–44; 7:1–23; 8:1–10, 14–21). The Syro-Phoenician thus represents "border-crossing agency," and the story is a boundary crossing event, a key marker for the community in its identity.[66] Its representative character establishes the woman as a model of faith and

---

[61] For an overview of the two opposing views, see Kim, *Mark, Women and Empire*, 135–42, who reads the narrative through the lenses of Taoism and Buddhism and sees the women's silence as "the hallmark of the divine" (150): the appropriate response to Jesus's kenosis (149–52).

[62] Moloney, *Gospel of Mark*, 146–47.

[63] On the immediate literary context, see esp. Rhoads, "Jesus," 347–48. Smith, "Construction," 465–66 identifies a chiastic structure for this section.

[64] Cadwallader, *Beyond the Word*, 339.

[65] On the semantic field surrounding the language for children within the story, see esp. Petr Pokorny, "From a Puppy to a Child: Some Problems of Contemporary Biblical Exegesis Demonstrated from Mark 7.24–30/Matt 15,21–8," *NTS* 41 (1995): 337.

[66] Hicks, "Moral Agency," 83. See also Pheme Perkins, "The Gospel of Mark," *NIB* 8:609–11.

service, an example for the disciples with their misunderstanding and prejudice and for the implied readers of the gospel. The woman's story signifies the opening of doors, access to the table, and inclusion and belonging for those standing outside by reason of gender, ethnicity, or ritual impurity. In the end, the contemporary reader is "no less impressed by the fact that, along with this demon, the equally threatening demon of prejudice between the members of different nations and cultures was 'driven out.'"[67]

From this viewpoint, the unnamed Syro-Phoenician woman and her daughter function not only as persons in their own right, with their own complex cultural identity, but also as representatives of the overturning of clean and unclean, with its far-reaching implications for women and outsiders, for femaleness and alterity.[68] In the words of Ranjini Wickramaratne Rebera, the woman is "an icon of power to women in today's church who are prevented from claiming the right to own their power and to use it for others."[69] For Mark's community, the Syro-Phoenician also stands as the representative of the gentiles more generally, whose faith and insight enable them to follow her into the βασιλεία (kingdom) with its nourishment and privileges.[70] The gentiles are an integral part of Mark's community, their presence confirmed in the widening of boundaries in Jesus's ministry. This in itself says something about the nature of the Markan God as inclusive and the community as reflective of the boundary-crossing nature of God. In this process of opening doors and table hospitality, the Syro-Phoenician plays a leading role for the Markan community. It is her faith and persistence that go ahead of the gentiles, her educative role that draws them in. We might well expect a male to play the critical role of opening doors on outsiders within the androcentric context of the biblical world. But this role is given instead to a woman whose need stimulates a faith that is exemplary for Jew and gentile, man and woman alike.

---

[67] Theissen, *Gospels*, 80.

[68] Glancy, "Jesus," 361–62 points out that no single depiction is sufficient for the woman's complex identity, taking into account her cultural corporeality. Later tradition, at least from the fourth century, names her "Justa" and her daughter "Bernice"; see Pseudo-Clementine Homilies 2:19 and 3:73; Elaine M. Wainwright, "Not Without My Daughter: Gender and Demon Possession in Matthew 15.21–28," in *A Feminist Companion to Matthew*, ed. Amy-Jill Levine (Sheffield: Sheffield Academic, 2001), 126–29; Alan H. Cadwallader, "What's in a Name? The Tenacity of a Tradition of Interpretation," *Lutheran Theological Journal* 39 (2005): 218–34.

[69] Rebera, "Syro-Phoenician Woman," 106.

[70] The woman is not the first gentile to appear in Mark's gospel; before her, the Gerasene demoniac approaches Jesus not as a suppliant but as an aggressive challenger through the demons which inhabit him (Mark 5:1–20).

CHRISTOLOGICAL READINGS

An explicitly christological reading of the Syro-Phoenician narrative is an often neglected contribution to the debate. This fourth way of reading begins with the presupposition that, as for all theology, any reading speaks to the coherence of the gospel as well as its contingency: the text has the capacity to speak powerfully from specific contexts, yet also to reach across boundaries.[71] From this perspective, the confrontation between Jesus and the woman can be read as an encounter between God and the suppliant who stands outside the chosen people of God. Such a reading focuses on Jesus's fundamental identity and the countercultural nature of his authority in this gospel.[72] The core symbol for Jesus in Mark is "my beloved Son" (ὁ υἱός μου ὁ ἀγαπητός), confirmed in the baptism and transfiguration narratives, which launch the two major sections of Jesus's ministry (Mark 1:1–8:21; 8:22–10:52). In the first case, the declaration is an intimate one at the baptism, addressed by the divine voice to Jesus himself. In the second, the declaration is a proclamation addressed to the three disciples at the transfiguration and, by implication, the reader. It is closely tied to the injunction, "Listen to him" (ἀκούετε αὐτοῦ, Mark 9:7), indicating Jesus's paradoxical teaching and community values that will unfold on the journey to Jerusalem. Precisely in his identity as Son, Jesus "activates God's Reign on earth" and "redefines the very structure of the family, upsetting the established order."[73]

The Markan Jesus, moreover, is far from being a patriarchal figure of power but is one whose authority is substantiated through suffering, renunciation, and powerlessness (Mark 8:27; 9:30–31; 10:32–34). Indeed, his model of leadership explicitly undermines the patriarchal system of the Greco-Roman world. In challenging the classic pyramid structure, the Markan Jesus gives priority to the lowliest as the true exemplars of service and self-giving love (Mark 10:42–44). They are also models for his own role and behavior as one who came "not to be served but to serve," both in his ministry and in his self-sacrificing death (οὐκ ἦλθεν διακονηθῆναι ἀλλὰ διακονῆσαι, Mark 10:45). Suppliants such as the Syro-Phoenician woman contrast markedly with the inner group of disciples. Whereas the latter misunderstand the inverted dynamics of the reign of God, the former grasp

---

[71] The two terms, "contingency" and "coherence," are used to refer to the nature of the gospel in the authentic Pauline epistles by J. Christiaan Beker, *Paul the Apostle: The Triumph of God in Life and Thought* (Philadelphia: Fortress, 1980), 11–16.

[72] In her narrative Christology, Malbon, *Mark's Jesus*, 231–44 distinguishes between the Markan Jesus (what Jesus says and does, and what is said of him), who deflects attention away from himself to God, and the narrator of the gospel, who has a wider overview of Jesus's significance.

[73] Sharon Betsworth, *The Reign of God Is Such as These: A Socio-Literary Analysis of Daughters in the Gospel of Mark*, LNTS 422 (London: T&T Clark, 2010), 138.

them immediately. The woman names Jesus Κύριε ("Lord," Mark 7:28), not simply giving him a title of respect from a suppliant to a healer, but also, for the Markan audience, acknowledging that Jesus's subversive authority is divine in origin.[74] This authority promotes a new understanding of power as selfless service rather than dominating mandate.[75]

The same christological dimension is present in our story in the overturning of power relations between the woman and Jesus. In the battle of wits that constitutes the parable, Jesus loses the verbal contest and accedes to the woman's request. Far from attempting to claw back lost honor, Jesus willingly relinquishes the power of winning the debate. Her quickness of wit and his apparent change of heart justify her inclusion as a recipient of his ministry. Jesus "recognizes and affirms the woman's wit and self-abasement," allowing himself to be worsted in the contest and expressing his admiration for her victory.[76] The seeming disregard for his own honor and the "bare-faced assault" on his authority in a culture in which patriarchal power is built on the amassing of such tokens, leads the Markan Jesus to accept willingly the "cup" of shame and humiliation in the cross (Mark 14:36; 10:38–39).[77] Rejected by the religious authorities in Jerusalem and crucified by the Romans for sedition, Jesus himself becomes the ultimate outsider whose rejection is transformed as the catalyst for new life and belonging. In Mark's gospel he is "the wounded one, the one who bore the scars," enabling new life through identification with the suffering.[78]

The Syro-Phoenician daughter is also significant in a salvific understanding of the story, as a girl whom we never meet but for whom the mother successfully intercedes. According to Sharon Betsworth, in her study of daughters in Mark's gospel, daughters are among the most vulnerable in a patriarchal society and beset with social and personal dangers as a consequence. The mother and daughter in

---

[74] Boring, *Mark*, 208, 214 and Iverson, *Gentiles*, 55–56. The title κύριος occurs on twelve other occasions in Mark's gospel, always in reference to God or Jesus (see Mark 12:36) and always with the meaning "LORD." See also the verbal cognate, κατακθριεύουσιν, which has the distinctly negative connotation of dominating power ("to lord it over," Mark 10:42), the antithesis of that exercised by Jesus.

[75] A further potential reading of the narrative that has been suggested is that of interreligious dialogue, but this reading depends on how we interpret the nature of the woman's faith; see Rebera, "Syro-Phoenician Woman," 108–9.

[76] Collins, *Mark*, 368.

[77] Glancy, "Jesus," 361.

[78] Phuc Phan Thi Kim, the so-called napalm girl in the famous photograph from the Vietnam War, discovered Christ in these terms after years of ongoing pain and suffering; see Kim, "These Bombs Led Me to Christ," *Christianity Today*, April 20, 2018, https://tinyurl.com/3snm5skz. See also Kim, *Fire Road: The Napalm Girl's Journey through the Horrors of War to Faith, Forgiveness, and Peace* (Carol Stream, IL: Tyndale House, 2017).

this narrative, she argues, contrast favorably with Herodias and her daughter in the story of John the Baptist's murder (Mark 6:21–29). Both adolescent girls are dependent on adult protection; unlike the latter story, the Syro-Phoenician narrative "highlights positively the mother-daughter bond."[79] Like Jairus's daughter, the Syro-Phoenician girl is "the emotional focus of the story" and belongs among the "little ones" of the gospel (Mark 9:37).[80] Mark's focus on daughters embraces them within the orbit of salvation because they, too, belong to the radically reconstructed family of Jesus and the reign of God. Salvation has a vital place in this narrative, because Jesus acts precisely as the "divine guardian and protector" of the Syro-Phoenician daughter and indeed of all who are socially and culturally vulnerable.[81]

A further christological dimension in the story is found in its sacramental overtones, which arise from the symbolism of the table (τραπέζα) and bread (ἄρτος) lying at the heart of the narrative. This symbolic trope runs through the Gospel of Mark, explicit in Jesus's subversive table practice of eating with tax collectors and sinners (Mark 2:15–17) and bypassing ritual laws of handwashing before meals (Mark 7:1–23). The two feeding stories continue the theme of Jesus's table sharing, first in a Jewish and then a gentile context (Mark 6:34–44; 8:1–10), indicating the eschatological banquet. The climax of this trope is the Last Supper, a Passover meal, where Jesus is the host at the table (Mark 14:12–25). Astonishingly, Jesus identifies himself in this scene, in the light of his impending death, as the bread to be eaten ("take, this is my body," λάβετε, τοῦτό ἐστιν τὸ σῶμά μου, Mark 14:22). Now bread is a key symbol not only of hospitality, communion, and inclusion but also of his own body, broken and distributed, given as food to his followers and anticipating the future realization of God's reign (Mark 14:25). The eucharistic symbolism of bread and table involves also a "destabilisation of gender categories" within the gospel that is profoundly inclusive, one in which "the body of Jesus opens a space for Mark's audience that is characterised by différance and transcendence of boundaries—ethnic boundaries, gender boundaries, socioeconomic boundaries, perhaps even religious boundaries."[82]

CONCLUSION

While there is overlap at some points and conflict of interpretation at other points, the various interpretations of the Syro-Phoenician narrative find unity in their desire to seek an inclusive vision beyond literal or metaphorical divisions of clean

---

[79] Betsworth, *Reign*, 129.
[80] Betsworth, *Reign*, 130–31.
[81] Betsworth, *Reign*, 138.
[82] Leander, *Discourses*, 237–38.

and unclean, whether cultic, cultural, or ethnic. Each has a point of view that cannot be summarily dismissed. They each bring their own insights to the table of interpretation, speaking from different contexts and perspectives. If the table of biblical interpretation is to be inclusive, gender readings need to embrace not univocity but diversity; they need to impose not a monolithic reading but be open to a multiplicity of interpretation that listens to women's readings from different angles. Invitation to the table involves neither a competitive spirit nor unanimity but participation in dialogue, including the capacity to listen with respect and grace where opinions differ.[83]

We are left with the question of whether the Syro-Phoenician narrative is itself a text of terror, as defined by Trible, and whether an inclusive vision is achieved by reading with or against the grain—either by drawing out the strengths of the text or by exposing its limitations. The view of this writer is that, when interpreted with all four approaches, including the christological, the text cannot be so described because it has a happy rather than a sad ending, and it is not essentially misogynistic. A reading that takes seriously the ironic and christological features of the story releases it from the kind of "Christian chauvinism" that demeans, diminishes and abuses women.[84]

This discussion of various readings has included East and West, past and present, catholic and evangelical, spiritual and political, salvific and christological, each with a voice to be heard. It points to the shape of the Christian community as one that "cleanses" the artificial barriers human beings erect against each another. In the end, for Mark and his community, the Syro-Phoenician woman plays a decisive role, exemplifying the true nature of authority and discipleship. She assists in expanding the bounds of the community around Jesus beyond barriers of clean and unclean which, in the words of the Markan Jesus, consists of those who do the will of God and so become "my brother and sister and mother" (ἀδελφός μου καὶ ἀδελφή καὶ μήτηρ, Mark 3:35).

BIBLIOGRAPHY

Beare, Francis Wright. *The Gospel according to Matthew*. Oxford: Basil Blackwell, 1981.
Beker, J. Christiaan. *Paul the Apostle: The Triumph of God in Life and Thought*. Philadelphia: Fortress, 1980.
Betsworth, Sharon. *The Reign of God Is Such as These: A Socio-Literary Analysis of Daughters in the Gospel of Mark*. LNTS. London: T&T Clark, 2010.

---

[83] For an example of this model within the context of interreligious engagement, using the methods developed in "scriptural reasoning," see esp. the collection of essays in David F. Ford and C. C. Pecknold, eds., *The Promise of Scriptural Reasoning* (Malden, MA: Blackwell, 2006).

[84] Trible, *Texts*, 1–7, esp. 2.

Boring, M. Eugene. *Mark: A Commentary*. Louisville: Westminster John Knox, 2006.
Burkill, T. Alec. "The Historical Development of the Story of the Syrophoenician Woman (Mark VII: 24–31)." *NovT* 9 (1967): 161–77.
Byrne, Brendan. *A Costly Freedom: A Theological Reading of Mark's Gospel*. Collegeville, MN: Liturgical Press, 2008.
Cadwallader, Alan H. *Beyond the Word of a Woman: Recovering the Bodies of the Syrophoenician Women*. Adelaide: ATF Press, 2008.
———. "The Building of Awareness of Hermeneutics Through the History of Interpretations of the Bible." *Colloq* 33 (2001): 3–21.
———. "What's in a Name? The Tenacity of a Tradition of Interpretation." *Lutheran Theological Journal* 39 (2005): 218–34.
Camery-Hoggatt, Jerry. *Irony in Mark's Gospel: Text and Subtext*. SNTSMS. Cambridge: Cambridge University Press, 1992.
Collins, Adela Yarbro. *Mark: A Commentary*. Philadelphia: Augsburg Fortress, 2007.
D'Angelo, Mary Rose. "(Re)presentations of Women in the Gospels: John and Mark." Pages 129–49 in *Women and Christian Origins*. Edited by Ross Shepard Kreamer and Mary Rose D'Angelo. New York: Oxford University Press, 1999.
Dewey, Joanna. "The Gospel of Mark." Pages 470–509 in *Searching the Scriptures: A Feminist Commentary*. Edited by Elisabeth Schuessler Fiorenza. New York: Crossroad, 1994.
Dufton, Francis. "The Syrophoenician Woman and her Dogs." *ExpT* 100 (1989): 417.
Ford, David F., and C. C. Pecknold, eds. *The Promise of Scriptural Reasoning*. Malden, MA: Blackwell, 2006.
France, R. T. *The Gospel of Mark: A Commentary on the Greek Text*. NIGTC. Grand Rapids: Eerdmans, 2002.
Glancy, Jennifer A. "Jesus, the Syrophoenician Woman and Other First Century Bodies." *BibInt* 18 (2010): 342–63.
Guardiola-Saénz, Leticia A. "Borderless Women and Borderless Texts: A Cultural Reading of Matthew 15:21–28." *Semeia* 78 (1997): 69–81.
Guelich, Robert A. *Mark 1–8:26*. WBC. Dallas, TX: Word, 1989.
Held, Heinz Joachim. "Matthew as Interpreter of the Miracle Stories." Pages 165–299 in *Tradition and Interpretation in Matthew*. Edited by Guenther Bornkamm, Gerhard Barth, and Heinz Joachim Held. Translated by Percy Scott. 2nd ed. London: SCM, 1982.
Hicks, Jane E. "Moral Agency at the Borders: Rereading the Story of the Syrophoenician Woman." *WW* 23 (2003): 76–84.
Hooker, Morna D. *The Gospel according to St Mark*. London: A & C Black, 1991.
Hughes, Antony. "Sermon on the Sunday of the Canaanite Woman." St. Mary Orthodox Church, Cambridge, MA. February 10, 2008. https://tinyurl.com/aupm3b52.
Iverson, Kelly R. *Gentiles in the Gospel of Mark: "Even the Dogs Under the Table Eat the Children's Crumbs"*. LNTS. London: T&T Clark, 2007.
Jackson, Glenna S. *"Have Mercy on Me": The Story of the Canaanite Woman in Matthew 15.21–28*. Sheffield: Sheffield Academic, 2002.
Thackeray, J., trans. *Josephus, in Nine Volumes*. LCL. Cambridge: Harvard University Press, 1986.
Joy, C. I. David. *Mark and Its Subalterns: A Hermeneutical Paradigm for a Postcolonial Context*. London: Equinox, 2008.

Kim, Seong Hee. *Mark, Women and Empire: A Korean Postcolonial Perspective*. Sheffield: Sheffield Phoenix, 2010.

Kim Phuc, Phan Thi. "These Bombs Led Me to Christ." Christianity Today. April 20, 2018. https://tinyurl.com/3snm5skz.

———. *Fire Road: The Napalm Girl's Journey through the Horrors of War to Faith, Forgiveness, and Peace*. Carol Stream, IL: Tyndale House, 2017.

Kinukawa, Hisako. "The Exploitation of Peasants in the Regions of Tyre and Galilee." Pages 136–43 in *Islands, Islanders, and the Bible: Ruminations* Edited by Jione Havea, Margaret Aymer, and Steed V. Davidson. Atlanta: SBL Press, 2015.

Kittredge, Cynthia B. "Not Worthy So Much as to Gather up the Crumbs Under Thy Table: Reflection on the Sources and History of the Prayer of Humble Access." *STRev* 50 (2006): 80–92.

Koosed, Jennifer L. "Ruth as a Fairy Tale." Bible Odyssey. https://tinyurl.com/4pf5678w.

Kwok, Pui-Lan. *Discovering the Bible in the Non-Biblical World*. Maryknoll, NY: Orbis Books, 1995.

Leander, Hans. *Discourses of Empire: The Gospel of Mark from a Postcolonial Perspective*. Atlanta: Society of Biblical Literature, 2013.

Lee, Dorothy A. "The Faith of the Canaanite Woman (Mt 15.21–28): Narrative, Theology, Ministry." *JAS* 13 (2015): 12–29.

Luz, Ulrich. *Matthew 8–20: A Commentary*. Translated by James E. Crouch. Hermeneia. Minneapolis: Fortress, 2001.

Malaty, Tadros Y. *The Gospel According to Saint Mark*. Orange, CA: Coptic Orthodox Christian Center, 2003.

Malbon, Elizabeth Struthers. *Mark's Jesus: Characterization as Narrative Christology*. Waco, TX: Baylor University Press, 2009.

Malick, David E. "An Examination of Jesus' View of Women Through Three Intercalations in the Gospel of Mark." *Priscilla Papers*. July 31, 2013. https://tinyurl.com/rj693knk.

Marcus, Joel. *Mark 1–8: A New Translation with Introduction and Commentary*. AB 27. New York: Doubleday, 2000.

Miller, Geoffrey David. "Attitudes Towards Dogs in Ancient Israel: A Reassessment." *JSNT* 32 (2008): 487–500.

Moloney, Francis J. *The Gospel of Mark: A Commentary*. Peabody, MA: Hendrickson, 2002.

Monro, Anita. "Alterity and the Canaanite Woman: A Postmodern Feminist Theological Reflection on Political Action." *Colloq* 26 (1994): 32–43.

Nadella, Raj. "The Two Banquets: Mark's Vision of Anti-Imperial Economics." *Int* 70 (2016): 172–83.

Nelavala, Surekha. "Smart Syrophoenician Woman: A Dalit Feminist Reading of Mark 7:24–31." *ExpT* 118 (2006): 64–69.

Oden, Thomas C., and Christopher A. Hall, eds. *Mark: Ancient Christian Commentary on Scripture*. Downers Grove, IL: IVP Academic, 1998.

Perkins, Pheme. "The Gospel of Mark." *NIB* 8:509–733.

Phillips, Victoria. "The Failure of the Women Who Followed Jesus in the Gospel of Mark." Pages 222–34 in *A Feminist Companion to Mark*. Edited by Amy-Jill Levine and Marianne Blickenstaff. Sheffield: Sheffield Academic, 2001.

Pokorny, Petr. "From a Puppy to a Child: Some Problems of Contemporary Biblical Exegesis Demonstrated from Mark 7.24–30/Matt 15,21–8." NTS 41 (1995): 321–37.

A Prayer Book for Australia. Alexandria, NSW: Broughton, 1995.

Rebera, Ranjini Wickramaratne. "The Syro-Phoenician Woman: A South African Perspective." Pages 100–110 in *A Feminist Companion to Mark*. Edited by Amy-Jill Levine and Marianne Blickenstaff. Sheffield: Sheffield Academic, 2001.

Rhoads, David. "Jesus and the Syrophoenician Woman in Mark: A Narrative-Critical Study." *JAAR* 62 (1994): 343–76.

Ringe, Sharon H. "A Gentile Woman's Story, Revisited: Rereading Mark 7:24–31." Pages 79–100 in *A Feminist Companion to* Mark. Edited by Amy-Jill Levine and Marianne Blickenstaff. Sheffield: Sheffield Academic, 2001.

Scott, J. Martin C. "Matthew 15.21–28: A Test-Case for Jesus' Manners." *JSNT* 63 (1996): 21–44.

Smith, Julien C. H. "The Construction of Identity in Mark 7:24–30: The Syrophoenician Woman and the Problem of Ethnicity." *BibInt* 20 (2012): 458–81.

Sun, Poling. "Naming the Dog: Another Asian Reading of Mark 7:24–30." *RevExp* 107 (2010): 381–94.

Theissen, Gerd. *The Gospels in Context: Social and Political History in the Synoptic Tradition*. London: Bloomsbury Academic, 2004.

———. Miracle Stories of the Early Christian Tradition. Edinburgh: T&T Clark, 1983.

Tolbert, Mary-Ann. "Mark." Pages 350–62 in *The Women's Bible Commentary: Expanded Edition with Apocrypha*. Edited by Carol A. Newsom and Sharon H. Ringe. 2nd ed. Louisville: Westminster John Knox/SPCK, 1998.

Trible, Phyllis. *Texts of Terror: Literary-Feminist Readings of Biblical Narratives*. OBT. Philadelphia: Fortress, 1984.

Wainwright, Elaine M. "Not Without My Daughter: Gender and Demon Possession in Matthew 15.21–28." Pages 126–37 in A Feminist Companion to Matthew. Edited by Amy-Jill Levine. Sheffield: Sheffield Academic, 2001.

Zimmermann, Ruben. *Puzzling the Parables of Jesus: Methods and Interpretation*. Minneapolis: Fortress, 2015.

6

Desolate, Devastated, Redeemed, Restored: Feminist Visions of Daughter Zion in the Australian Context

Angela Sawyer

A prior student of the Hebrew Bible said to me recently: "I don't remember much about what I learned, but I do remember reading Trible." Phyllis Trible's *Texts of Terror* and *God and the Rhetoric of Sexuality* were groundbreaking for their content but even more so for the possibilities they presented.[1] Trible exposed passages that had been previously overlooked because they were considered too violent, dark, or troubling. Her work put the spotlight on characters regularly ignored or trivialized, such as the unnamed woman, the daughter of Jephthah, and Tamar.

Trible's work has been so effective and has remained important not only because it highlighted these ancient texts and contexts of terror through careful and considerate literary rhetorical analysis, but also, and perhaps more importantly, because it resonated deeply with the disturbing realities of contemporary contexts of terror such as sexual abuse, gender discrimination, and domestic violence. We reappraise the texts of violence as we reappraise the situations of violence today. As we challenge traditional readings, we find that situations of violence ancient and modern are also problematized.

It is toward these categories of violence and recovery—reading ancient texts and navigating modern contexts—that I turn in my analysis. I begin by exploring the issue of domestic violence in Australia. Traditional readings of the metaphor of relationship between YHWH and the people of Israel in Deutero-Isaiah tend to highlight a restorative tone. I suggest that this metaphor is more complex when read in light of situations of domestic violence. I note from the outset that difficult

---

[1] Phyllis Trible, *God and the Rhetoric of Sexuality* (Philadelphia: Fortress, 1978); Trible, *Texts of Terror: Literary-Feminist Readings of Biblical Narratives*, OBT (Philadelphia: Fortress, 1984).

and disturbing topics, personal to many, will be raised, and I argue that these are important and worth engaging.[2]

DOMESTIC VIOLENCE

In 2015, Rosie Batty was given the title of "Australian of the Year" due to her public campaigning against domestic violence.[3] The previous year, Rosie's eleven-year-old son, Luke, had been murdered by his father, her ex-husband. There have been too many other public murders of partners and children in Australia, bringing the often privatized crime of domestic violence into a public arena.[4] Batty's particular contribution was that she talked about this issue openly and continuously, raising awareness of it. Such public campaigning led to the Royal Commission into Family Violence in Victoria.[5] The findings of this commission are grueling but important reading. I will touch on only those aspects of this exhaustive report that are relevant to my own research on depictions of violent relationships in Deutero-Isaiah. The major features of the report include the effect of family violence, both on the victims and perpetrators; the potential cycle of violence in following generations; and systemic problems with reporting and getting help when in situations of domestic violence. Although the Commission defines family violence broadly, it states that "the most common manifestation of family violence is intimate partner violence committed by men against their current or former female partners. This violence can also affect children. It is the form of

---

[2] Gerlinde Baumann, *Love and Violence: Marriage as Metaphor for the Relationship between YHWH and Israel in the Prophetic Books* (Collegeville, MN: Liturgical Press, 2003), ix–xi observes the personal impact of studying topics related to violence and gender as well as the reality of her own context as a woman in modern Germany. I likewise acknowledge my own challenge dealing with topics of physical and sexual violence and gender discrimination both personally and societally.

[3] I note that in the Australian context domestic violence has received a strong focus in the media, legal, and political spheres; see Rosie Batty and Bryce Corbett, *A Mother's Story* (Sydney: Harper Collins, 2015).

[4] There are many organizations involved in campaigning against violence against women and domestic violence. I note in particular the White Ribbon Foundation. A key part of this organization's task is education, resourcing, and particularly (in their own words) "engaging men and boys to end men's violence against women and girls"; see "Our Vision," White Ribbon Australia, https://tinyurl.com/wuccxmz6. Regarding the different definitions and statistics around domestic violence, see "Fact File: Domestic Violence in Australia," *ABC News*, April 14, 2016, https://tinyurl.com/42k39mrp.

[5] State of Victoria, *Royal Commission into Family Violence: Summary and Recommendations*, Parl Paper No 132 (2014–2016), https://tinyurl.com/ra7bs3sm. The report and its recommendations was handed down to the Victorian Government on March 29, 2016.

family violence that we know most about, and it is the key focus of most services and programs."[6]

This gendered relational violence is where my focus will be. However, I would say that the issues of violence that we are dealing with in Deutero-Isaiah, although they have a gendered element, also represent generalized violence.[7] The Royal Commission summarizes:

> The causes of family violence are complex and include gender inequality and community attitudes towards women. Contributing factors may include financial pressures, alcohol and drug abuse, mental illness and social and economic exclusion.... There is no doubt that violence against women and children is deeply rooted in power imbalances that are reinforced by gender norms and stereotypes.[8]

This statement implies a responsibility on the part of those of us in the community who are involved in education around these issues to be aware not only of gender inequality and attitudes in the community toward women, but also of how we contribute to supporting or dismantling power imbalances, norms, and stereotypes.

If we were at all lulled into thinking that crimes of family violence do not occur in the church, the work of Julia Baird and Hayley Gleeson has engaged relentlessly with this topic and disavowed us of that false notion.[9] In a series of articles published by the Australian Broadcasting Corporation, Baird interviewed both partners of people in church roles and members of congregations who have experienced domestic abuse. The distortion of Scripture and theological justifications for violence used by priests/pastors or congregants who have participated in abuse run through these harrowing accounts as common threads. Baird and Gleeson observe a strong connection between the use of "texts of abuse" in the

---

[6] State of Victoria, *Royal Commission into Family Violence: Summary and Recommendations*, 2. See also State of Victoria, *Royal Commission into Family Violence: Report and Recommendations*, 4 vols., Parl Paper No. 132 (2014–2016), 1:17, https://tinyurl.com/22nrjm45, which includes an excursus titled "Why do people say family violence is gendered?" that states: "In Victoria three-quarters of victims in family violence incidents attended by police are female and 77 percent of perpetrators recorded by police are male."
[7] The events surrounding the Babylonian exile.
[8] State of Victoria, *Royal Commission into Family Violence: Summary and Recommendations*, 2.
[9] Julia Baird and Hayley Gleeson, "'Submit to Your Husbands': Women Told to Endure Domestic Violence in the Name of God," *ABC News*, October 21, 2018, https://tinyurl.com/3xsuykh2; Baird and Gleeson, "Raped, Tracked, Humiliated: Clergy Wives Speak Out About Domestic Violence," *ABC News*, November 23, 2017, https://tinyurl.com/bbhj77yp. Note that this series of works also investigates abuse in religions other than Christianity.

Bible and the legitimation of abuse of women and children. Distorted notions regarding family relationships, a woman's role, and patriarchal hierarchies that perpetuate power imbalances appear again and again in the stories of domestic violence in the church. When working with my students, I often refer to this as the problem of "The Bible says..." and discuss how it taps into basic issues of biblical interpretation. Baird calls attention to repeating themes in the stories of domestic violence around church and theological institutional teaching on male authority, divorce, and submission, and she identifies the overall issue as "biblical literalism."[10] Biblical teaching can have liberating or potentially violent effects on real life situations. This makes it imperative that we engage with texts of violence and texts of healing, which can sometimes be the very same texts.

The depiction of women in the Bible as punishable or evil is highly problematic and well explored in biblical scholarship.[11] The effect of violent sexual metaphors in both ancient and contemporary contexts has been a focus of feminist studies that have sought to understand, reinterpret, reframe, or reject these in contemporary use.[12] As Renita Weems suggests, "the correlation drawn repeatedly in prophetic literature between divine judgment and husbands battering their wives is daunting and telling. It suggests that as far back as the days of biblical writings women in love were women in trouble."[13] I seek to engage various depictions of Zion in Deutero-Isaiah as a story of restoration useful to contemporary conversations around domestic violence because they have a redemptive focus. These academic investigations can be brought into mainstream church and community conversations. I will consider the potential of Contextual Bible Study as one mechanism for a community-based approach. However, although my reading of these

---

[10] Baird and Gleeson, "'Submit.'"
[11] Gale A. Yee, *Poor Banished Children of Eve: Woman as Evil in the Hebrew Bible* (Minneapolis: Fortress, 2003).
[12] Renita J. Weems, *Battered Love: Marriage, Sex, and Violence in the Hebrew Prophets*, OBT (Minneapolis: Fortress, 1995); Gerlinde Baumann, "Prophetic Objections to YHWH as the Violent Husband of Israel: Reinterpretations of the Prophetic Marriage Metaphor in Second Isaiah (Isaiah 40–55)," in *Prophets and Daniel*, A Feminist Companion to the Bible (Second Series), ed. Athalya Brenner (London: Sheffield Academic, 2001), 88–120; Baumann, *Love and Violence*; Carleen Mandolfo, *Daughter Zion Talks Back to the Prophets: A Dialogic Theology of the Book of Lamentations*, SemeiaSt 58 (Atlanta: Society of Biblical Literature, 2007); Sharon Moughtin-Mumby, *Sexual and Marital Metaphors in Hosea, Jeremiah, Isaiah and Ezekiel*, Oxford Theological Monographs (Oxford: Oxford University Press, 2008); Julia M. O'Brien, *Challenging Prophetic Metaphor: Theology and Ideology in the Prophets* (Louisville: Westminster John Knox, 2008); and Brittany Kim, "YHWH as Jealous Husband: Abusive Authoritarian or Passionate Protector? A Reexamination of a Prophetic Image," in *Daughter Zion: Her Portrait, Her Response*, ed. Mark J. Boda, Carol J. Dempsey, and Leann Snow Flesher, AIL (Atlanta: Society of Biblical Literature, 2012), 127–47.
[13] Weems, *Battered Love*, 3.

texts has a restorative angle, I admit to deep suspicion of Deutero-Isaiah's hopeful reputation.

DAUGHTER ZION

Deutero-Isaiah reframes Daughter Zion's journey from desolate woman to restored bride in a way that rhetorically resists stereotyped categorizations of mother and child, husband and wife. I am interested here in the possible meanings and implications created for the reader today, cognizant of situations of domestic violence. The representation of Zion's development in Deutero-Isaiah is not without problems, which I shall identify along the way, but I take the position that the journey with her is worth the effort. I will deal with passages such as Isa 49:14–26; 50:1–3; 51:17–52:6; and 54, in which Zion is characteristically identified using the literary device of personification and figures of speech such as synecdoche and metonymy.[14] These devices allow many traumatized people to be represented in the one figure (Isa 40:1–2). Zion is depicted in the multiple guises of daughter (Isa 52:2), mother (Isa 49:15–26; 50:1; 51:17–20; 54:1–3), and/or wife (Isa 49:18; 54:5–8), sometimes within the same passage: mother and daughter appear together in Isaiah 51:17–52:3, mother and implied wife in Isa 50:1, and mother and wife in Isa 54. Her identity is often in relation to someone else, such as a husband (Isa 50:1) or children (Isa 49:15–23), or a position that she has generally lost or thought she has lost, such as that of former bride (Isa 54:6) or barren 'mother' (Isa 54:1).

Zion enters the stage of Deutero-Isaiah in 49:14 with an explosive accusation: "YHWH has forgotten me, my LORD has forsaken me." These are the only words attributed to Zion in Deutero-Isaiah as direct speech.[15] The context of the accusation is the violence, loss, and devastation related to the exile. The passage is framed with Zion depicted as the bereaved mother of dead children. Trible notes the chiasm of Isa 49:13 and 49:15, which "encircles the suffering people with divine comfort and compassion."[16] The response from YHWH in verse 15 alludes

---

[14] Metonymy is a figure of speech in which smaller part or attribute substitutes for the larger; e.g., "the Crown" represents the power of the monarchy, or the name "Zion" represents the people of Judah, the inhabitants of the city, or the people in exile. In synecdoche, the part represents the whole; e.g., "the White House" represents the governing power of the United States. See Janet Martin Soskice, *Metaphor and Religious Language* (Oxford: Clarendon, 1985), 57.

[15] In Isa 49:20–21, Zion is double-voiced (to use a Bakhtinian concept). She is commanded to "Sing" in Isa 54:1. On the concept of double-voicing, see Barbara Green, *Mikhail Bakhtin and Biblical Scholarship: An Introduction*, SemeiaSt (Atlanta: Society of Biblical Literature, 2000), 35–43, 47–53.

[16] Trible, *God*, 51.

to Zion's own neglect, entailing possible violence to her own children. Trible's significant work on God's "womb-love" includes an exploration of Isa 49:15.[17] The imagery depicts Zion wearing replacement children as ornaments like a bride. Images of violence are paralleled with images of restoration. The passage ends as Isa 49:26 portrays retaliatory violence against Zion's enemies.

A particular issue for those who are escaping domestic violence is safe housing. Isaiah 49 looks at the possibility of space or a new home for Zion and her children, and Isa 54:2 talks about enlarging the place of her tent. How might this rhetoric be received by those for whom loss of security and safety is a reality? Isaiah 50:1–3 challenges the assumptions of the children of Zion that their mother has been divorced, and there are strong implications of blame, as YHWH asserts his strength. Isaiah 51:17–52:6 portrays a drunken, bereaved, captive Daughter Zion, raped and abused, left on the street, encouraged to free herself from her chains of slavery and move toward enthronement, like a queen. Isaiah 54 completes the picture with barren Zion, an abandoned wife, being received by her redeemer, who has confessed, finally, to the abandonment. Here we are heading toward resolution of the violence. As we can see from this brief overview, the passages richly intertwine images of familial loss, violence, and restoration and frame them with relational metaphors.

There is great potential for reading Zion's journey in Deutero-Isaiah as restorative, but this reading also has some disturbing outcomes. It is not universally accepted that these texts need to be read in relation to one another or demonstrate a positive voice for Zion.[18] Alternative views suggest that Deutero-Isaiah defends only YHWH's dominant position.[19] Deutero-Isaiah's Zion takes on the complaints of Lamentations but without the vehemence that Lamentations demonstrates.[20] I consider that Zion's personification in Deutero-Isaiah invites us to read her more hopefully, but critically, with eyes open to the rhetorical resistance in the text. To read Zion in Deutero-Isaiah as a layered representation is far more interesting

---

[17] Trible, *God*, 51–52.

[18] See Mandolfo, *Daughter Zion*, 103–20 on "God 'speaks tenderly' to Jerusalem?" and Weems, *Battered Love*, 45.

[19] Mandolfo, *Daughter of Zion*, 113. In relation to the point on Zion's development, Lena-Sofia Tiemeyer, "Isaiah 40–55: A Judahite Reading Drama," in *Daughter Zion: Her Portrait, Her Response*, ed. Mark J. Boda, Carol J. Dempsey, and Leann Snow Flesher (Atlanta: Society of Biblical Literature, 2012), 55–75 offers a dramatic presentation of Zion as a counter voice and treats her more optimistically than Mandolfo, with an understanding that the emphasis is less on her sin and more on her bright future. See also Richtsje Abma, *Bonds of Love: Methodic Studies of Prophetic Texts with Marriage Imagery (Isaiah 50:1–3 and 54:1–10, Hosea 1–3, Jeremiah 2–3)* (Assen: Van Gorcum, 1999).

[20] Mandolfo, *Daughter Zion*, 108 suggests that the cry of Isa 49:14 is "pathetic, in every sense," particularly when compared to the length and tone of the Servant Song.

than taking the binary position that she is portrayed negatively in Ezekiel and Jeremiah and positively in Deutero-Isaiah.

A rhetorical approach can consider the impact of speech on its hearers not only historically but in contemporary contexts.[21] We need to acknowledge the danger in accepting metaphors as justifications for perpetuating violence against women and instead critically engage them.[22] Problematic depictions of sexual and physical violence within a metaphorical marriage relationship between YHWH and the people of Israel/Judah/the city of Zion have been explored extensively by feminist scholars including not only Weems, but also Gerlinde Baumann, Katheryn Pfisterer Darr, and Kathleen M. O'Connor.[23] Sharon Moughtin-Mumby carefully differentiates the use of "the" metaphor into different portrayals of "a" metaphor.[24] Each text that uses a marriage or a sexual metaphor represents different parties. Even with these necessary distinctions, there is value in reading Zion's presentation in Deutero-Isaiah using a comparative approach, which allows us to see it as influenced by previous uses of marriage and sexual metaphors yet sometimes challenging these other uses and ultimately having a different message.[25] In Deutero-Isaiah, Zion is not being punished by her husband but accepted back into a relationship (Isa 40:2; 49:15–26; 50:1; 54:5–8), and her enemies are promised punishment (Isa 47; 49:23, 26; 51:22–23).[26] However, Zion's restoration

---

[21] Kim, "YHWH," 147 presents the perspective that the original hearers of prophetic marriage metaphors (the focus of her argument) "would not have viewed these passages as providing justification for men to abuse their wives. Indeed, both male and female hearers would have been compelled to identify with the adulterous wife, not the faithful divine husband who is at the same time supreme God and judge."

[22] Moughtin-Mumby, *Sexual and Marital Metaphors*, 5; Baumann, *Love and Violence*, 24–25, 116–18.

[23] Katheryn Pfisterer Darr, *Isaiah's Vision and the Family of God*, Literary Currents in Biblical Interpretation (Louisville: Westminster John Knox, 1994); Weems, *Battered Love*; Kathleen M. O'Connor, "'Speak Tenderly to Jerusalem': Second Isaiah's Reception and Use of Daughter Zion," *PSB* 20 (1999): 281–94; Baumann, "Prophetic Objections"; and Baumann, *Love and Violence*.

[24] Moughtin-Mumby, *Sexual and Marital Metaphors*, 23–48.

[25] See the exploration of how Deutero-Isaiah borrows a form of a marriage metaphor used variously in Jeremiah (wife Judah) and Lamentations in O'Connor, "Speak Tenderly." I also note here the work of Patricia Tull Willey, *Remember the Former Things: The Recollection of Previous Texts in Second Isaiah*, SBLDS 161 (Atlanta: Scholars Press, 1997), who argues convincingly for Deutero-Isaiah's reuse of other texts for its purposes.

[26] Baumann, "Prophetic Objections," 116.

can be read as a wife's reliance on her husband, which could reinforce negative aspects of remaining with an abusive partner.[27]

The representations of Zion in Deutero-Isaiah give us opportunities to encounter rhetorical resistance and countervoices to dominant patriarchal ideologies, such as Zion's voice in Isa 49:14, the questioning of (implied) Zion's divorce in Isa 50:1, and the rejection of the shame motif in Isa 52:1–2.[28] The positive feminine depiction of Zion in Deutero-Isaiah contrasts with her depiction in other prophetic texts, but I would suggest there are still seams of trauma.[29] As Baumann points out, passages in Deutero-Isaiah that employ the marriage metaphor do so with prophetic oracles of salvation, not judgement, in contrast to the various literary forms used to employ marriage metaphors found in Hosea, Ezekiel, and Jeremiah.[30] Deutero-Isaiah contains multiple representations of Zion that destabilize how we read these metaphors. She is a daughter in Isa 52:2, yet also enthroned (as a queen?). YHWH is the implied father, husband, and king. Yet, even as YHWH plays the father role, we might note that YHWH is depicted as a mother in Isa 49:15, which speaks about Zion's own motherhood. Zion is barren and single, yet mother, widow, and wife in Isa 54. We also read contrasting depictions of YHWH. I think it is precisely this rhetorical resistance that is useful for our studies today. Zion is not straightforward. Daughter Zion represents resilience. She speaks in Isa 49:14, with a voice that is limited and muted but nonetheless present. The presence of Zion's voice in the text challenges the assertion that YHWH's voice takes precedence. She rises from the dust in Isa 52:2. There is a future for her in Isa 52:1–2 and in Isa 54.

Deutero-Isaiah depicts the kind of damaged relationships that affect whole families—a reality for exiles and a reality for many people today.[31] A people who suffered needed to be persuaded that an alternative potential future was possible.

---

[27] Walter Brueggemann, *Isaiah 40–66*, Westminster Bible Companion (Louisville: Westminster John Knox, 1998), 150; John F. A. Sawyer, "Daughter of Zion and Servant of the Lord in Isaiah: A Comparison," *JSOT* 44 (1989): 89–107, esp. 95.

[28] On the use of countervoices in Deutero-Isaiah, see also Bebb Wheeler Stone, "Second Isaiah: Prophet to Patriarchy," *JSOT* 56 (1992): 85–99, who picks up the work on this in Trible, *God*, 7, 202.

[29] Kathryn L. Roberts, "Isaiah 49:14–18," *Interpretation* 57 (2003): 58–60; Martien A. Halvorson-Taylor, *Enduring Exile: The Metaphorization of Exile in the Hebrew Bible*, VTSup (Leiden: Brill, 2011), 117. The changed circumstances of female societal roles in exile is noted by Darr, *Isaiah's Vision*, 85–87. The loss of male leaders, the destruction of many family structures, and other factors related to exile may have led to Zion's different presentation in Deutero-Isaiah.

[30] Baumann, "Prophetic Objections," 116 notes that Isa 47's portrayal of the punishment of Daughter Babylon is the exception, but she is not married to YHWH.

[31] O'Connor, "Speak Tenderly," 282.

O'Connor emphasizes the rhetorical task of the prophet/poet to reinterpret the received imagery of Zion as the divorcée:

> Second Isaiah now needs her story to get the people out of exile.... Second Isaiah received a symbolic story of complex rhetorical power wherein a treacherous wife brought punishment upon herself and hence, deserved exile. But Second Isaiah diminishes, even discounts, Zion's culpability. Instead of stressing depictions of the adulterous wife, he draws heavily on Lamentations portrayal of the abused female and bereft mother who furiously resists her abuser. God, not she, is on the defensive. Second Isaiah reconfigures the understanding of the exile when he diminishes Zion's culpability and lays it at her divine husband's door.[32]

Honor and shame in the context of exile are both present within Deutero-Isaiah. Attitudes toward female sexuality, roles in society, submission, and authority all play into what we are reading here, where sociohistorical contexts need to be taken into account. The use of relational terms and roles such as daughter, young girl, widow, and wife to depict Zion connote a power imbalance. Gale Yee has argued that use of marriage metaphor in prophetic texts depicting a personified wife as unfaithful works rhetorically by shaming the male leadership audience, as well as the people in general, by feminizing them.[33] In contrast, the rhetorical aim of Deutero-Isaiah's Zion seems to move beyond blame of Zion. In her shadow may lurk the real trauma of real women, and the feminizing aspect of these chapters is overtly positive.[34] O'Connor's view of YHWH's culpability in Deutero-Isaiah may be correct, but the relationships used to depict YHWH are still powerful roles such as militant husband, judge, and redeemer God. It is also possible that societal understandings and misunderstandings of YHWH's character and YHWH's roles are being transformed, just as the text seems to be shifting Zion's portrayal. This alternate view of YHWH is demonstrated in Isa 49:15 with distinctive mothering imagery, as well as in Isa 50:1 where the bill of divorce is contested, questioning the assumption that YHWH has rejected the people via covenantal imagery.

Deutero-Isaiah is steeped in references to the impact of war and exile: death, desolation of the land, destroyed walls, sexual assault, cannibalism, captives and warriors, plunder, displacement, famine, sword, enemies, and chains. These graphic references to violence are remarkably present in a text of hope and demonstrate its potential as to both represent and mask trauma, to reframe but also to repeat damaging ideas.

---

[32] O'Connor, "Speak Tenderly," 293–94.
[33] Yee, *Poor Banished Children*, 98.
[34] John F. A. Sawyer, *The Fifth Gospel: Isaiah in the History of Christianity* (Cambridge: Cambridge University Press, 1996), 198–219.

COMMUNITY RESPONSES

Raising the profile of a poetic character such as Zion, in line with Trible's literary-feminist and rhetorical approach, provides a useful literary and pastoral resource that can be used in the conversation about domestic violence issues in Australia today. Combining understandings of metaphor theory, particularly cognitive approaches, with trauma theories, I advocate the use of such texts as potentially beneficial for those who have experienced violence and trauma. One of the challenges in feminist theological studies in Australia today is making the connections between what are generally thought to be obscure, rarely addressed biblical texts and ordinary readers who are suffering.

Weaving one's way through complex metaphors takes time and careful study. Daughter Zion is not a celebrated figure, and it is easier to be drawn to narrative rather than poetic presentations of women in the Bible in a "text of terror" approach. Yet, one issue we have with problematic ideas around leadership and marital relationships is that they are often based on distorted or simplistic readings of figurative models and metaphors. For example, if Jesus is the groom, the church is the bride, and if Jesus is the head, the church is the body; men end up representing Jesus, and women the submissive church. Our reliance on these metaphors, particularly if they underpin abusive notions about women and their roles, needs to be interrogated.[35]

Trauma study offers helpful insights for our interpretation of Zion's personification in Deutero-Isaiah. Christopher Frechette argues that the portrayal of Daughter Babylon's violation in Isa 47 is a contrast to Daughter Zion's restoration that allows the audience to express rage against the cause of the trauma by providing a symbolic representation of it.[36] Daughter Babylon appears in the context of Deutero-Isaiah's effort to reinterpret Zion's situation as "one in which YHWH indeed desired to comfort Daughter Zion and to renew a relationship with her, affirming both her dignity and her safety."[37] I contend that Zion also bares trauma upon her symbolic representation, which likewise becomes a narrative mechanism for expressing that brokenness. William Morrow convincingly argues that the Servant represents vicarious atonement in Deutero-Isaiah (particularly Isa 53)

---

[35] See the stories regarding the misuse of passages (such as Eph 5:22–23) covered by Baird and Gleeson, "'Submit.'"

[36] Christopher G. Frechette, "Daughter Babylon Raped and Bereaved (Isaiah 47): Symbolic Violence and Meaning Making in Recovery From Trauma," in *Bible through the Lens of Trauma*, ed. Elizabeth Boase and Christopher G. Frechette, SemSt (Atlanta: SBL Press, 2016), 77.

[37] Frechette, "Daughter Babylon," 79.

where the exiles' adversity is experienced on behalf of future generations.³⁸ He proposes that "the exiles' sense of excess suffering is taken seriously but reframed as an asset instead of a liability."³⁹ Taking this lead, I consider Zion to be a representation of communal trauma as well as possible recovery. Interestingly, these two characters alternate in Deutero-Isaiah as different representations of trauma and recovery.⁴⁰

Zion's statement, "The LORD has forsaken me, my LORD has forgotten me" in Isa 49:14 is short, and the questions directed to her—"can a woman forget her nursing child, or show no compassion for the child of her womb?" (Isa 49:15)—appear to remain unanswered in the immediate literary context. This may represent the silencing caused by trauma.⁴¹ Survival literature, which employs literary devices such as metaphor and personification, can be a means of giving voice to a disaster or traumatic situation. It can also demonstrate how a community loses language—the ability to clearly describe events—and may use characters (such as Zion) to bear the tragedy on their behalf. As Judith Herman explains, "the conflict between the will to deny horrible events and the will to proclaim them aloud is the central dialectic of psychological trauma."⁴² We see this tension in the Daughter Zion story.⁴³ Both the voice of Zion and the gaps in the story can provide opportunities to speak into, reinterpret, and reframe. This is not to say that Deutero-Isaiah has all the answers, just that it has not been considered thoroughly enough in the conversation on violence and the Bible.

Speaking out about offensive views takes courage in the modern climate of the #MeToo movement, the online world of Incel, and the horrific realities of trolling. People who speak up can often be vilified, and encouragement may be necessary through group solidarity. Space is needed to bring voice to traumatic situations and to denounce offensive views. According to the Royal Commission into Family Violence, "confronting the factors that make perpetrators violent, including attitudes to women and community tolerance for violence, is crucial."⁴⁴

---

³⁸ William Morrow, "Post-Traumatic Stress Disorder and Vicarious Atonement in Second Isaiah," in *Psychology and the Bible: A New Way to Read the Scriptures*, ed. J. Harold Ellens and Wayne G. Rollins (Westport, CT: Praeger, 2004), 177.
³⁹ Morrow, "Post-Traumatic Stress Disorder," 180.
⁴⁰ An observation clearly made by Sawyer, "Daughter."
⁴¹ Kathleen M. O'Connor, *Jeremiah: Pain and Promise* (Minneapolis: Fortress, 2011), 24 talks about the effect of trauma to cause a "breakdown of language."
⁴² Judith Herman, *Trauma and Recovery: The Aftermath of Violence—From Domestic Abuse to Political Terror* (New York: Basic Books, 1997), 1.
⁴³ David M. Carr, *Holy Resilience: The Bible's Traumatic Origins* (New Haven: Yale University Press, 2014), 84, 89 suggests that Daughter Zion's voice represents the voice of the exiled people, giving them a mechanism for dealing with their trauma.
⁴⁴ State of Victoria, *Royal Commission into Family Violence: Summary and Recommendations*, 28.

Transparent conversation about gender and relationship issues is vital in marriage preparation and parenting courses, the pulpit, and theology classrooms, as well as the media. Female representation is necessary from church councils to university and school boards. We have much work to do, given that some still view feminist biblical studies as either optional in the curriculum, specialist, or too volatile. Even having female voices in a bibliography or set readings can be perceived as controversial rather than normative.

The biblical text does not need to be abandoned because of its abusive use, even if handling stories of violence proves challenging. As Julia O'Brien asserts, "I believe it is important, even ethically mandatory, to recognize and resist dangerous thinking whenever it occurs, including and perhaps especially in the Bible."[45] This includes exposing violent texts as well as the violent *use* of texts. As O'Brien argues, "these books should be read, that they have value for the life well lived ... wrestling with these books led me into deep reflection on intimate relationships, parenting, anger, violence, politics, the power of language and the responsibility that Christians have for the way that they think and talk about the divine."[46] Both the Royal Commission into Family Violence and the work of Baird and Gleeson advocate for the place of faith communities in proactively dealing with family violence, advice, and healing.[47] The Bible continues to play an important role in these communities as a valued resource. Yet, in some cases, we need to acknowledge and address the way it has been distorted in damaging ways.

---

[45] O'Brien, *Challenging*, xxi.
[46] O'Brien, *Challenging*, xxi.
[47] The section of the report that deals specifically with faith communities is State of Victoria, *Royal Commission into Family Violence: Report and Recommendations*, vol. 5. The report advocates for education in faith communities on the topic of family violence, suggesting that they are well placed to serve the community in this way. The report addresses the barriers to seeking help that people may face in faith communities, with reasons such as male dominated leadership, ill-informed responses to domestic violence, collusion with abusers, problematic and moralistic views around marriage and divorce that encourage women and children to remain in contexts of violence, and failure to report to secular authorities such as police in cases of abuse. As this report notes, there were cases where "The commission heard that some men use faith to excuse their behaviour" (136). Despite these issues, the Commission observes that "faith settings are an integral part of the community response to family violence" (137). This Commission provides recommendations (163-165) for the resourcing and training (professional development) of faith-based leaders and communities in responding to domestic violence as well as communication across multifaith representatives and the Department of Health and Human Services. See also Julia Baird and Hayley Gleeson, "Australian Church Leaders Call for Urgent Respond to Domestic Violence," *ABC News*, July 21, 2017, https://tinyurl.com/ymxmasyp.

The Commission recommends the involvement of women, as well as experts in the field of family violence, in training and education around these issues, and that further work be done in this area.

> The Commission heard that some attitudes and practices, and inadequate or ill-informed responses by faith leaders, risk exposing victims to further and sustained abuse by family members. Women experiencing family violence can face barriers to seeking help in their faith community because of particular religious beliefs—for example, about divorce or gender roles.[48]

Religious institutions need to assess how much the current processes and procedures allow reporting or provide hurdles that get in the way of it, and consider how difficult they are to navigate. How impenetrable or accessible is the teaching around these topics?

CONTEXTUAL BIBLE STUDY

One approach to biblical studies that has proven fruitful within the context of dealing with difficult biblical passages alongside marginalized and vulnerable communities is Contextual Bible Study. It was initially developed in South Africa under the political regime of apartheid by biblical scholars, such as Gerald West, whose work is informed by liberation theology.[49] This community-based process has now over thirty years of practice in many locations globally. I advocate for the value of engaging with the imagery of Zion in Deutero-Isaiah in Contextual Bible Study alongside those who have experienced the trauma of domestic violence. This approach offers a reflective space to see oneself within the text, to inform, to educate, and to be among potential support in the context of the ordinary reader. According to the Royal Commission into Family Violence in Victoria the evidence "highlighted the importance of trauma-sensitive therapeutic interventions in assisting in victims' recovery"[50] A tool such as CBS could be a potentially

---

[48] State of Victoria, *Royal Commission into Family Violence: Summary and Recommendations*, 35.
[49] Gerald O. West, *Contextual Bible Study* (Dorpspruit: Cluster, 1993). See the following for examples of how Contextual Bible Study uses academic investigations of texts and links with marginalized communities: West, *Biblical Hermeneutics of Liberation: Modes of Reading the Bible in the South African Context*, Bible and Liberation Series (Pietermaritzburg: Cluster, 1991); West, "Articulating, Owning and Mainstreaming Local Theologies: The Contribution of Contextual Bible Study," *Journal of Theology for Southern Africa* 122 (2005–2007): 23–35; West, "Do Two Walk Together? Walking With the Other Through Contextual Bible Study," *AThR* 93 (2011): 431–49; and West, ed., *Reading Other-Wise: Socially Engaged Biblical Scholars Reading with Their Local Communities* (Leiden: Brill, 2007).
[50] State of Victoria, *Royal Commission into Family Violence: Summary and Recommendations*, 30.

valuable resource to unpack Zion's presentation in Deutero-Isaiah in an accessible manner.[51] As an approach that encourages growth and gender equality, and that openly deals with challenging texts, CBS has been used to study many narrative biblical texts. It has also benefited considerably from resources such as Trible's *Texts of Terror*.[52] A careful consideration when CBS is used in the context of those who have experienced domestic violence is the power of the facilitator.[53] It is also important to provide a safe place to explore biblical texts and maintain the confidentiality of shared experiences in group work.[54]

Exploring a poetic text such as Zion's portrayal in Deutero-Isaiah is promising, particularly for those who have experienced trauma, and because it enhances CBS, which usually explores narrative forms. The See-Judge-Act process of CBS begins with acknowledgement of one's context and proceeds to connect with the biblical voice, with the ultimate aim of transformation.[55] Poetic depictions of a traumatized individual can be fragmented, just like the individual or the community represented, and may provide space for multiple readings.[56] Engaging with Deutero-Isaiah's Zion passages through CBS can allow for creative expression: participants can draw Zion, sing, sculpt, or create something physical, such as a dance, in response to these passages. This practice may lead us to draw or express our own trauma, sadness, or brokenness and not just Zion's. It may create the opportunity to communicate disappointment with Zion for not speaking more, or

---

[51] Deutero-Isaiah's Zion passages have currently been unexplored in published contextual bible studies.

[52] Gerald O. West, "Exegesis Seeking Appropriation; Appropriation Seeking Exegesis: Re-Reading 2 Samuel 13:1–22 in Search of Redemptive Masculinities." *Verbum et Ecclesia* 34 (2013): 1–6, who outlines the development of Contextual Bible Study on 2 Samuel 13:1–22 around the topic of masculinity. This study focused on the rape of Tamar, triggered by Trible's work on this passage. This study takes into account the African context and localized questions.

[53] The place of power in the CBS facilitator relationship has been considered by Tiffany Webster, "The Problem of Power in Contextual Bible Study," *Track Changes* 6 (Winter 2014): 109–33; Webster, "'A Miner Knows Better Than Anybody You Have Little Power over Mother Nature': Exploring Genesis 1:26–31 and the Concepts of Control and Power With South Derbyshire Coal Miners," *JBRec* 2 (2015): 145–74.

[54] A consideration of using Contextual Bible Study alongside traumatized people as "a therapeutic praxis" is found in Gerald O. West, "Between Text and Trauma: Reading Job With People Living With HIV," in *Bible through the Lens of Trauma*, edited by Elizabeth Boase and Christopher G. Frechette (Atlanta: SBL Press, 2016), 209–30.

[55] West, "Between Text and Trauma," 211.

[56] Samuel E. Balentine, "The Prose and Poetry of Exile," in *Interpreting Exile: Displacement and Deportation in Biblical and Modern Contexts*, ed. Brad E Kelle, Frank Ritchel Ames, and Jacob L. Wright, AIL (Atlanta: Society of Biblical Literature, 2011), 345–64 explains why poetry is useful in providing language to trauma.

compassion toward her and ultimately toward ourselves. The expression is not just about dealing with the past but also about engaging in peacemaking efforts that may change the future and enable growth.[57]

Zion's voice in Isa 49:14 might be a muted, downplayed voice, but her claim that YHWH has forgotten and forsaken her is highly charged. A woman's voice that asserts a truthful claim about her poor treatment is significant in a relationship where violence is perpetuated but speaking up can also be a dangerous act. The dominating figure of God in the Zion passages of Deutero-Isaiah portray an overwhelming power imbalance. With Zion as wife and mother to YHWH, we need to ask whether YHWH is depicted as an abusive husband.[58] Zion's subversive message of her forsaken forgotten status, although challenged, gets through by remaining in the text. Trible's work has shown us that by liberating women from the pages of the text we bring their stories into current conversations, where we can demystify them and the violence perpetrated against them. Secrets and silencing do not end violence.

BIBLIOGRAPHY

Abma, Richtsje. *Bonds of Love: Methodic Studies of Prophetic Texts with Marriage Imagery (Isaiah 50:1–3 and 54:1–10, Hosea 1–3, Jeremiah 2–3)*. SSN. Assen: Van Gorcum, 1999.
Baird, Julia, and Hayley Gleeson. "Australian Church Leaders Call for Urgent Respond to Domestic Violence." *ABC News*. July 21, 2017. https://tinyurl.com/ymxmasyp.
———. "Raped, Tracked, Humiliated: Clergy Wives Speak Out About Domestic Violence." *ABC News*. November 23, 2017. https://tinyurl.com/bbhj77yp.
———. "'Submit to Your Husbands': Women Told to Endure Domestic Violence in the Name of God." *ABC News*. October 21, 2018. https://tinyurl.com/3xsuykh2.
Balentine, Samuel E. "The Prose and Poetry of Exile." Pages 345–64 in *Interpreting Exile: Displacement and Deportation in Biblical and Modern Contexts*. Edited by Brad E Kelle, Frank Ritchel Ames, and Jacob L. Wright. Atlanta: Society of Biblical Literature, 2011.
Batty, Rosie, and Bryce Corbett. *A Mother's Story*. Sydney: Harper Collins, 2015.
Baumann, Gerlinde. *Love and Violence: Marriage as Metaphor for the Relationship between YHWH and Israel in the Prophetic Books*. Collegeville, MN: Liturgical Press, 2003.
———. "Prophetic Objections to YHWH as the Violent Husband of Israel: Reinterpretations of the Prophetic Marriage Metaphor in Second Isaiah (Isaiah 40–55)." Pages 88–120 in *Prophets and Daniel*. A Feminist Companion to the Bible. Second Series. Edited by Athalya Brenner. London: Sheffield Academic, 2001.

---

[57] See, e.g., Pauline Kollontai, "Healing the Heart in Bosnia-Herzegovina: Art, Children and Peacemaking," *International Journal of Children's Spirituality* 15 (2010): 261–71.
[58] O'Brien, *Challenging*, ch. 4 explores the use of a marriage metaphor in Hosea as a basis for discussing YHWH depicted as an abusing husband. She asks a question relevant to Deutero-Isaiah's presentation of YHWH: "Is God's power, even when couched in terms of love, ultimately inescapable?" (74).

Brueggemann, Walter. *Isaiah 40–66*. Westminster Bible Companion. Louisville: Westminster John Knox, 1998.
Carr, David M. *Holy Resilience: The Bible's Traumatic Origins*. New Haven: Yale University Press, 2014.
Darr, Katheryn Pfisterer. *Isaiah's Vision and the Family of God*. Literary Currents in Biblical Interpretation. Louisville: Westminster John Knox, 1994.
"Fact File: Domestic Violence in Australia." *ABC News*. April 14, 2016. https://tinyurl.com/42k39mrp.
Frechette, Christopher G. "Daughter Babylon Raped and Bereaved (Isaiah 47): Symbolic Violence and Meaning Making in Recovery From Trauma." Pages 67–83 in *Bible through the Lens of Trauma*. Edited by Elizabeth Boase and Christopher G. Frechette. SemeiaSt. Atlanta: SBL Press, 2016.
Green, Barbara. *Mikhail Bakhtin and Biblical Scholarship: An Introduction*. SemeiaSt. Atlanta: Society of Biblical Literature, 2000.
Halvorson-Taylor, Martien A. *Enduring Exile: The Metaphorization of Exile in the Hebrew Bible*. VTSup. Leiden: Brill, 2011.
Herman, Judith. *Trauma and Recovery: The Aftermath of Violence—From Domestic Abuse to Political Terror*. New York: Basic Books, 1997.
Kim, Brittany. "YHWH as Jealous Husband: Abusive Authoritarian or Passionate Protector? A Reexamination of a Prophetic Image." Pages 127–47 in *Daughter Zion: Her Portrait, Her Response*. Edited by Mark J. Boda, Carol J. Dempsey, and Leann Snow Flesher. AIL. Atlanta: Society of Biblical Literature, 2012.
Kollontai, Pauline. "Healing the Heart in Bosnia-Herzegovina: Art, Children and Peacemaking." *International Journal of Children's Spirituality* 15 (2010): 261–71.
Mandolfo, Carleen. *Daughter Zion Talks Back to the Prophets: A Dialogic Theology of the Book of Lamentations*. SemeiaSt 58. Atlanta: Society of Biblical Literature, 2007.
Morrow, William. "Post-Traumatic Stress Disorder and Vicarious Atonement in Second Isaiah." Pages 167–84 in *Psychology and the Bible: A New Way to Read the Scriptures*. Edited by J. Harold Ellens and Wayne G. Rollins. Westport, CT: Praeger, 2004.
Moughtin-Mumby, Sharon. *Sexual and Marital Metaphors in Hosea, Jeremiah, Isaiah and Ezekiel*. Oxford Theological Monographs. Oxford: Oxford University Press, 2008.
O'Brien, Julia M. *Challenging Prophetic Metaphor: Theology and Ideology in the Prophets*. Louisville: Westminster John Knox, 2008.
O'Connor, Kathleen M. *Jeremiah: Pain and Promise*. Minneapolis: Fortress, 2011.
———. "'Speak Tenderly to Jerusalem': Second Isaiah's Reception and Use of Daughter Zion." *PSB* 20 (1999): 281–94.
"Our Vision." White Ribbon Australia. https://tinyurl.com/wuccxmz6.
Roberts, Kathryn L. "Isaiah 49:14–18." *Int* 57 (2003): 58–60.
Sawyer, John F. A. "Daughter of Zion and Servant of the LORD in Isaiah: A Comparison." *JSOT* 44 (1989): 89–107.
———. *The Fifth Gospel: Isaiah in the History of Christianity*. Cambridge: Cambridge University Press, 1996.
Soskice, Janet Martin. *Metaphor and Religious Language*. Oxford: Clarendon, 1985.
State of Victoria. *Royal Commission into Family Violence: Report and Recommendations*. 4 vols. Parl Paper 132 (2014–2016). https://tinyurl.com/22nrjm45.

———. *Royal Commission into Family Violence: Summary and Recommendations*, Parl Paper 132 (2014–2016). https://tinyurl.com/ra7bs3sm.
Stone, Bebb Wheeler. "Second Isaiah: Prophet to Patriarchy." *JSOT* 56 (1992): 85–99.
Tiemeyer, Lena-Sofia. "Isaiah 40–55: A Judahite Reading Drama." Pages 55–75 in *Daughter Zion: Her Portrait, Her Response*. Edited by Mark J. Boda, Carol J. Dempsey, and Leann Snow Flesher. Atlanta: Society of Biblical Literature, 2012.
Trible, Phyllis. *God and the Rhetoric of Sexuality*. Philadelphia: Fortress, 1978.
———. *Texts of Terror: Literary-Feminist Readings of Biblical Narratives*. OBT. Philadelphia: Fortress, 1984.
Webster, Tiffany. "'A Miner Knows Better Than Anybody You Have Little Power over Mother Nature': Exploring Genesis 1:26–31 and the Concepts of Control and Power With South Derbyshire Coal Miners." *JBRec* 2 (2015): 145–74.
———. "The Problem of Power in Contextual Bible Study." *Track Changes* 6 (Winter 2014): 109–33.
Weems, Renita J. *Battered Love: Marriage, Sex, and Violence in the Hebrew Prophets*. OBT. Minneapolis: Fortress, 1995.
West, Gerald O. "Articulating, Owning and Mainstreaming Local Theologies: The Contribution of Contextual Bible Study." *JTSA* 122 (2005–2007): 23–35.
———. "Between Text and Trauma: Reading Job with People Living With HIV." Pages 209–30 in *Bible Through the Lens of Trauma*. Edited by Elizabeth Boase and Christopher G. Frechette. Atlanta: SBL Press, 2016.
———. *Biblical Hermeneutics of Liberation: Modes of Reading the Bible in the South African Context*. Bible and Liberation Series. Pietermaritzburg: Cluster, 1991.
———. *Contextual Bible Study*. Dorpspruit: Cluster, 1993.
———. "Do Two Walk Together? Walking With the Other Through Contextual Bible Study." *AThR* 93 (2011): 431–49.
———. "Exegesis Seeking Appropriation; Appropriation Seeking Exegesis: Re-Reading 2 Samuel 13:1–22 in Search of Redemptive Masculinities." *Verbum et Ecclesia* 34 (2013): 1–6.
West, Gerald O., ed. *Reading Other-Wise: Socially Engaged Biblical Scholars Reading with Their Local Communities*. Leiden: Brill, 2007.
Willey, Patricia Tull. *Remember the Former Things: The Recollection of Previous Texts in Second Isaiah*. SBLDS 161. Atlanta: Scholars Press, 1997.
Yee, Gale A. *Poor Banished Children of Eve: Woman as Evil in the Hebrew Bible*. Minneapolis: Fortress, 2003.

7

Invoking Jezebel, Invoking Terror: The Threat of Sexual Violence in the Apocalypse to John

Robyn J. Whitaker

John's Apocalypse is well known for its sexualized violence and extreme use of female stereotypes. These include the whore of Babylon, who is "mother of all whores," the bride who is the bride of Christ, the heavenly goddess over whom the angels of heaven fight, and Jezebel—the topic of this chapter. What sets Jezebel apart from these others is that she is a real person, not a symbol for something else. The rest of the female characters or feminized images in the Apocalypse, such as the bride of Christ, are symbolic beings who represent cities, God's people, or the church.

Jezebel, I will argue, is John's moniker for an actual female prophetic leader of an early Christian community who is his rival for leadership of the community in Thyatira. Yet the tradition remembers her differently because John's forceful rhetoric has worked on us. Using a feminist-literary method of reading in the tradition of Phyllis Trible's *Texts of Terror*, I will demonstrate that John's use of one of the Hebrew Bible's texts of terror—the gruesome death of Queen Jezebel—serves to silence, threaten, other, and ultimately dehumanize and dismiss his prophetic rival. This chapter will unfold in four parts. I will begin with Queen Jezebel as she is described in the narratives of 1 and 2 Kings, arguing that the report of her death is a text of terror in Trible's terms. We will then move on to the passage in John's Apocalypse where the name "Jezebel" is invoked, where I will analyze the rhetoric John uses to diminish his opponent's power and influence. I will then compare John's treatment of another rival, Balaam, with Jezebel to further scrutinize John's rhetorical strategies in dealing with a female opponent. Lastly, I will look at the implications of John's conflict rhetoric for the Christian tradition, arguing that it serves to extend an ancient text of terror and thereby justify threats of sexualized violence as a means to control women.

JEZEBEL IN THE HEBREW BIBLE

The biblical Jezebel, the original Jezebel, first appears in 1 Kgs 16. She is introduced as the foreign wife of King Ahab (v. 31), the more evil son of an evil father (v. 30). The narrative frames her from the very beginning as inextricably associated with Ahab's sinfulness, the daughter of a foreign king and follower of Baal who will be blamed for the king's idolatry (v. 31).

The Hebrew verbs make clear that Baal worship and the idolatrous construction of a sacred pole are Ahab's actions alone. In a few short verses, the narrator relates that Ahab *takes* (a wife), *goes*, *serves* Baal, *worships* Baal, *erects* an altar, *makes* the sacred pole, and *acts to provoke* the anger of the God of Israel (1 Kgs 16:31b–33). Jezebel is passive and silent. Yet the inference is that this foreign woman is at least partially responsible for the unfaithfulness of the king of Israel toward his own God.[1]

Jezebel appears at several other points in the narratives of Kings, each of which I will touch on only briefly. Jezebel's agency within the text grows as she becomes embroiled in a battle with the prophets of YHWH. The first action accredited to her is almost an aside. The narrative of 1 Kgs 18 begins with a focus on the prophet Elijah. He is the main character. Yet, in telling Elijah's story, the biblical narrator introduces the time period as "when Jezebel was destroying the prophets of YHWH" (v. 4). Her power cannot be hidden. This action is restated as a known truth about Jezebel in verse 13: she is a killer of God's prophets. Again, the focus is not on Jezebel *per se*, but on the actions of Elijah, who saves God's prophets. Jezebel neither speaks nor acts directly. Rather, she serves as the silent villain to the Bible's hero, Elijah.[2]

Jezebel speaks for the first time in 1 Kgs 19:2. Her message to Elijah damns her: she threatens to take his life as he took the life of the prophets of Baal. She promises violence as an answer to violence, yet the story is still not hers. Elijah remains the main character, and Jezebel's threat acts as a narrative prompt to explain his flight to Judah and ultimately his divinely mandated allegiance to Jehu as the future king (v. 16). Jezebel is a foil in the story of male power struggles over prophetic and royal leadership.

Perhaps the most well-known story about Jezebel is that of the conflict with Naboth over a vineyard. When Ahab responds to Naboth's refusal to sell his land

---

[1] A long tradition of suspicion toward foreign wives is woven throughout Scripture, mostly because of the concern that worship and allegiance to YHWH alone will wane. See, e.g., Deut 7:3; Neh 10:30.

[2] Phyllis Trible, "Exegesis for Storytellers and Other Strangers," *JBL* 114 (1995): 4–5. Indeed, the prophetic battle that occurs in 1 Kgs 18 is between Elijah and the prophets of Baal. Jezebel is absent.

with sulking and inaction (1 Kgs 21:4), Jezebel takes charge.[3] The story portrays her as a manipulative, murderous, and fraudulent wife (not queen) who writes letters in King Ahab's name and uses his seal to plot the unjust murder of Naboth (1 Kgs 21:5–16).[4] The text, however, holds Ahab mutually responsible. It is his blood that the dogs will lick up and he is the one whom Elijah declares to have done evil in God's sight (1 Kgs 21:19–20). Elijah prophesies the demise of Ahab's household: all will be destroyed and eaten by the dogs, not only Jezebel but the household (1 Kgs 21:23–24). Yet again, Jezebel's agency as a woman is minimized. Her husband is responsible for her, and, as part of his household, she will suffer for his crimes as much as for her own, which was to "incite" him in his evildoing (1 Kgs 21:25).

While violence has an assiduous and unrelenting presence throughout these narratives in 1 Kings, it is the narration of Jezebel's death in 2 Kgs 9 that is the real text of terror. Her demise, foretold in 1 Kgs 21:23, is delayed in the narrative while the machinations of male power demand attention. The prophets of YHWH, however, do not forget her. The retributive violence afforded her now comes at the behest of Elisha, who, after anointing Jehu as king, commands him immediately to kill Jezebel (2 Kgs 9:7). Her murder is his first royal activity. The vindictive nature of Elisha's command is captured in the first person verb, that "I may take vengeance" for the death of the prophets of YHWH.[5] What was a general threat against the household of Ahab now (re)focuses on Jezebel, a foreign wife who dared challenge the religious power and traditions of Israel. Her death will be cathartic.

When Jehu comes to kill Jezebel, she, having been forewarned of his visit, prepares to receive him officially by applying makeup to her eyes, adorning her head, and sitting by the window (2 Kgs 9:30). While some male commentators have speculated that she intended to seduce Jehu—what other earthly reason could a woman have for applying makeup?—she is a queen, arguably dressing to officially receive a king, even one who might kill her.[6] The text nowhere hints at seduction, nor does it introduce a sexual tone here. While we can only speculate

---

[3] Makhosazana Nzimande, "Reconfiguring Jezebel: A Postcolonial Imbokodo Reading of the Story of Naboth's Vineyard (1 Kings 21:1–16)," in *African and European Readers of the Bible in Dialogue: In Quest of a Shared Meaning*, ed. H. de Wit and G. West (Leiden: Brill, 2008), 249 describes her as bringing a "colonizing legacy" to Israel in her conquest of Naboth's vineyard and religious zeal.
[4] For the point that she is not a queen, see Trible, "Exegesis," 10.
[5] From Jehu's perspective, the act is revenge for the unjust death of Naboth, his kinsman (2 Kgs 9:26). Both Elisha and Jehu are therefore portrayed as acting in vengeance, although their reasons differ.
[6] See, e.g., Marvin Sweeney, *I and II Kings: A Commentary*, OTL (Louisville: Westminster John Knox, 2007), 335.

about her motives, it is more plausible that her actions are those of a queen preparing to receive a royal visitor or "heroically" face her death, than those of a woman seeking to seduce.[7]

The fear that this foreign woman and her foreign god invoke in the tradition is evident in the graphic violence in the narration of her death. The text of 2 Kgs 9:30–37 is one of the most gruesome death scenes in the Hebrew Bible. Jehu comes to Jezebel (9:30), who greets him, asking if he comes in peace. He does not bother to answer her and arguably does not even look at her. Looking at "the window" and addressing the eunuchs who serve her instead, Jehu asks whose side they are on. The narrator triangulates the action: Jezebel looks at and addresses Jehu, while he looks at and addresses the eunuchs. She is ignored, diminished, and dismissed; her fate is already sealed. Yet again, the text presents Jezebel surrounded by the activity of men who will determine her future. She is rendered silent, passive, victim.

When the eunuchs throw her down from the window at Jehu's command, the narrator comments that "some blood splattered on the wall" and upon the horses who trampled on her (2 Kgs 9:33). In these few brief words the narrator vividly communicates that her body is broken open and battered. Her makeup and head adornment are no longer able to preserve her dignity or her life.

At this point, Jehu somewhat callously enters Jezebel's home, eats her food, and drinks her wine. Trible describes him as having "satisfied himself."[8] Violence has not diminished his appetite. His entry and eating signifies the demise of Ahab's household. Jehu is now master and does not need a host to invite him in. He claims the space as his own.

But the narrator is not finished. In a subtle twist, Jehu orders her buried, for she is "a king's daughter" (2 Kgs 9:34). His command could be an attempt to portray him as a man concerned to do the right thing in death. Yet it is undoubtedly a narrative device to mark the fulfillment of Elijah's prophecy, for, when the servants are sent to bury her, they find nothing but her skull, her feet, and the palms of her hands. There is nothing left to bury. Jezebel is denied proper burial, and Elijah's prophecy that the "dogs shall eat her flesh" is reiterated at her end (2 Kgs 9:36).

While the Hebrew Bible paints Jezebel as an evil woman who misused her power, her story could equally be construed as that of a foreign princess, raised to rule, who remained faithful to her own religious tradition even after being sent to be married in a foreign land. From a different perspective, she would be an exemplar of faith. Certainly she abused her power, killing many, but this is nothing that

---

[7] Nzimande, "Reconfiguring Jezebel," 236.
[8] Trible, "Exegesis," 16.

male kings of Israel such as Saul (1 Sam 19) and David (2 Sam 11) did not do, yet they maintain their hero status and retain their lives.

The story of Queen Jezebel in 2 Kings is indeed a text of terror. It serves as a reminder of what the powerful can do to someone who is a threat to the religious or political status quo. It is also a timeless story of the vulnerability of the outsider or foreigner in the land and the threat of violence that hovers over women's lives wherever they find themselves. Trible does not address this particular story in *Texts of Terror*, but what she writes about another biblical woman who suffered horrendous violence—the unnamed woman of Judg 19—applies equally well here too: "Violence and vengeance are not just characteristics of a distant, pre-Christian past; they infect the community of the elect to this day. Woman as object is still captured, betrayed, raped, tortured, murdered, dismembered, and scattered. To take to heart this ancient story, then, is to confess its present reality."[9]

REVELATION 2:18–29

When John calls his prophetic rival in Thyatira "Jezebel," he conjures all the violence, threat, and condemnation associated with the story from the Hebrew Bible. Who is the Jezebel named in Rev 2:20? While it is possible that John is calling a male opponent by a female name or inventing a fictional character to combat certain theological ideas, the level of vitriol and the continuing feminine noun forms (e.g., προφῆτις, *prophetis*) suggest that a human woman is being attacked here.[10] After all, insults and name-calling work best if there is a hint of truth, of plausibility, to them, and the name "Jezebel" works best for a female rival. Assuming she is a real woman, which the majority of scholars do, the first thing John has done is to give his prophetic rival a pseudonym, a name from the biblical tradition that does an awful lot of work for him.

Once we acknowledge that John's Jezebel is a human woman, we enter interesting territory. John's name-calling unwittingly reveals an influential, even powerful female rival who is teaching and leading the Thyatiran community. Paul Brooks Duff describes Jezebel as a "rival Christian prophet" and "leader" of the

---

[9] Phyllis Trible, *Texts of Terror: Literary-Feminist Readings of Biblical Narratives* (Philadelphia: Fortress, 1984), 87.
[10] Here I agree with David Aune, *Revelation*, 3 vols., WBC (Dallas, TX: Word, 1997), 203; David Barr, ed., *The Reality of the Apocalypse: Rhetoric and Politics in the Book of Revelation* (Atlanta: Society of Biblical Literature, 2006), 61; Jennifer Knust, *Abandoned to Lust: Sexual Slander and Ancient Christianity* (New York: Columbia University Press, 2006), 130; Craig Koester, *Revelation: A New Translation with Introduction and Commentary*, Anchor Bible (New Haven: Yale University Press, 2014), 298; and Pamela Thimmes, "Teaching and Beguiling My Servants: The Letter to Thyatira (Rev 2:18–29)" in *A Feminist Companion to the Apocalypse of John*, ed. Amy-Jill Levine (London: T&T Clark, 2009), 72.

community, or at least of a faction within it that teaches a more tolerant approach to eating meat sacrificed to idols (εἰδωλόθυτα).[11] Her teaching appears to be the central issue. It is also an issue in the Pergamum community, where it is associated with the teaching of Balaam (Rev 2:14), an issue to which we will return.

The message to Thyatira (Rev 2:18-29) is the fourth of seven messages directed to seven communities in Asia Minor. They are all presented as divine messages, voiced by the risen Christ using images from the opening vision (Rev 1:9–20). The "son of God" who addresses the community in Thyatira commends them for their works of love, faith, and service (Rev 2:19). But this compliment of their Christian discipleship is immediately followed by John's (or Christ's) main complaint: they "tolerate (ἀφίημι) the woman Jezebel" (Rev 2:20). The precise accusation is that Jezebel calls herself a prophet and is teaching and deceiving John's servants (Rev 2:20)—that is, her teaching is itself deceptive.[12] The nature of this deceptive teaching is that Christ's followers are practicing πορνεία (*porneia*), a generic term for sexual immorality, by eating meat sacrificed to idols.

The average person in first-century CE Asia Minor would have encountered meat sacrificed to idols (εἰδωλόθυτος) in a variety of settings. Idol meat could be found at the temple of a deity, a public festival, a neighbor's home, or the market.[13] Prominent citizens were expected to participate in these public cultic events, and numerous social and business interactions took place over meals. In the case of community celebrations and key festivals, idol meat may have been distributed freely, offering poor people a rare opportunity to eat meat.[14] Whether or not a Christ-believer could ethically eat such meat was a contentious issue in earliest Christianity.

The Apostle Paul's advice on the matter is that eating meat sacrificed to idols did not matter because idols themselves were not gods and therefore had no power (1 Cor 8:7–8). He acknowledges that not everyone will understand this distinction and cautions against leading others astray. But Paul ultimately concedes that eating idol meat is acceptable when receiving hospitality from others (1 Cor 10:27). The Apocalypse's Jezebel and Balaam would seem to be in accord with this type of approach to the matter.

---

[11] Paul Brooks Duff, *Who Rides the Beast? Prophetic Rivalry and the Rhetoric of Crisis in the Churches of the Apocalypse* (Oxford: Oxford University Press, 2001), 40, 59. Duff considers intra-Christian conflict as the main community issue in the Apocalypse.

[12] The verb here is πλανάω, "to deceive," one that associates her with other symbolic characters who oppose God in the Apocalypse such as the dragon, beasts, Babylon, and the false prophets (see Rev 12:9; 13:14; 18:23; 19:20). Note that several English translators have sexualized πλανάω, translating it as "beguiling" (NRSV) or "seducing" (ESV).

[13] Duff, *Who Rides?*, 52.

[14] Plutarch, *Demetr.* 11; Suetonius, *Jul.* 38.

By associating the matter of idol meat with *porneia*, John increases the seriousness of the charge. It is unlikely, however, that his Jezebel was promoting or practicing sexually immoral behavior. The same combination of charges is found in the message to Pergamum in reference to the teaching of Balaam (Rev 2:14), who is not sexualized, which suggests that these activities are interrelated for John: to eat meat sacrificed to idols is to commit religious infidelity. The grammar likewise supports this interpretation: to "eat food sacrificed to idols and to practice *porneia*" might best be translated as "to eat food sacrificed to idols—*that is*, to practice *porneia*."[15]

Jezebel is therefore not accused of two separate activities. Rather, eating food that has been offered to a foreign deity or the emperor in cultic worship is akin to participating in that cult and is therefore a form of idolatry—in John's view. By invoking the Hebrew Bible's association of idolatry with adultery, John frames this practice of cultural assimilation as unfaithfulness to God and religious infidelity, symbolized as adulterous or sexually immoral behavior.

We should note, first and foremost, that, as horrendous as John's hypersexualized attack on her will be shown to be, Jezebel is not attacked simply for being female. If that were the case, there are a number of rhetorical arguments John might have made simply to establish that women cannot teach or lead the church. But he does not go down that path. The issue here is not that a woman is teaching, but the *content* of her teaching. There is a doctrinal difference at stake that goes to the heart of how John believes Christians should behave, and this is what offends him so greatly.[16] Additionally, he may be concerned that he is about to lose this theological battle or indeed any influence over this community—hence the level of conflict.

While John's criticism of his Jezebel is not a criticism of her gender, the manner of it is entirely gendered. This female leader in Thyatira is neither a queen nor foreign, but what she has in common with the biblical Jezebel is that she is a threat to power and cult. By robbing her of her real name, John dehumanizes her. What better way to ruin a woman's reputation than to give her a joke name? She becomes a stereotype and not a person.

Not only does the name-calling turn her into a stereotype, but John also distances her in two other ways by choosing this name. Firstly, because Jezebel is the quintessential foreigner and Baal worshipper in the Hebrew Bible, John aligns his opponent with a foreign woman who worships foreign gods. In the world in which the Apocalypse was written and into which it speaks, she is the insider, the one *in*

---

[15] Reading the καὶ in Rev 2:20 as epexegetical or explanatory in its usage. Other epexegetical uses occur in Rev 1:9; 2:2; 3:14; 12:17; see Brian Blount, *Revelation: A Commentary*, NTL (Louisville: Westminster John Knox, 2009), 27–28, 33.
[16] M. Eugene Boring, *Revelation* (Louisville: Westminster John Knox, 1989), 92–93; Thimmes, "Teaching and Beguiling," 74.

situ in Thyatira, and it is reasonable to assume that she is a respected member and leader in that community if many are following her teaching. John seeks to make the insider the outsider by making her foreign and metaphorically placing her outside the community of faith.[17]

The second way John others her is to make her idolatrous and sexually promiscuous. There is no hint in the original Queen Jezebel story that she was sexually promiscuous, physically beautiful, or particularly alluring. (Her physical appearance is not described anywhere in Kings, although later artists depict her as seductive and beautiful.) By describing his Jezebel's teaching as *porneia*, John fights a doctrinal dispute through sexual slander. In doing so, he employs a well-known technique in Greco-Roman rhetoric.

Jennifer Knust's work on sexual slander outlines how elite males diminished and undercut their opponents by appealing to known techniques of sexual slander.[18] The epitome of masculinity was self-control, and any man positioning himself as an orator, philosopher, or teacher would be expected to model chaste, controlled behavior. For example, Aeschines writes that "the words of a shameless man, who has treated his own body with scorn could never benefit the hearer."[19] Christians adopted this rhetoric, presenting false teachers as sexually promiscuous or as pleasure seekers, in contrast to the sexually virtuous true followers of Christ.[20]

While part of John's milieu, the Greco-Roman sources do not adequately account for John's rhetoric here or the complexity of the threat against her. As a Hellenistic Jewish Christ-follower, John inhabits a hybrid world, and the biblical tradition he evokes with the name "Jezebel" accounts more fully for his approach to this prophetic rival.

To mitigate the teaching of rival prophets and leaders, John draws on a wider prophetic tradition in which worship of other deities is framed as adultery because it involves breaking the marriage-like covenant with YHWH.[21] Idolatry becomes adultery, a symbolism most famously used in Hos 1:2, where the prophet is told to "take a wife of whoredom" so he will know how God feels, a wife later described

---

[17] Thimmes, "Teaching and Beguiling," 75–77. Womanist scholars have pointed out that John's ethnic othering taps into ancient and modern stereotypes about foreign women as exotic and sexually promiscuous, and thus able to be treated as less human.

[18] Knust, *Abandoned*, 3.

[19] Aeschines, *Tim.* 1.32.

[20] Knust, *Abandoned*, 9–10. New Testament examples include Phil 4:18–19; Eph 5:6–18; 2 Tim 3:1–9; Heb 6:4–8, 2 Pet 1:4–9; 2:1–22; 3:3–4; 1 John 2:18–19, 4:1–4; Jude 3–18; Rev 2:14, 20.

[21] The LXX translates the Hebrew root זנ״ה (the root used for "adultery" and associated words) as *porneia/o*, which is a Greek term with a wider frame of reference than זנ״ה. Words derived from זנ״ה are frequently used as metaphors for religious unfaithfulness in the Hebrew Bible.

as "whoring" herself, committing adultery (Hos 2:2), and decking herself with jewels as she pursues Baal (Hos 2:13). John uses all of these images in describing the Whore of Babylon (Rev 17) but he introduces some of them here in Rev 2 when he describes the activities of Jezebel as teaching her followers to act in sexually immoral ways (πορνεύω).

Another biblical antecedent to John's gendered critique of Jezebel can be found in Ezek 16 and 23.[22] In Ezek 23, a well-known text of terror, Samaria and Jerusalem are recast as the sisters Oholah and Oholibah. Both are accused of promiscuous behavior, adultery, whoring themselves—the Septuagint translates *porneia*—an activity defined in the text as making and serving idols. Similar to the manner in which John threatens his Jezebel, the prophet Ezekiel portrays Oholah and Oholibah as destroyed by their lovers, who pollute their beds and are used against them in their downfall.

One aspect of these symbolic women in the prophetic texts of Hosea and Ezekiel is that the imagery associated with them is used mostly to describe the behavior of men. They stand as metaphors or symbols for Israel, or groups of God's people. When John uses similar images and punishments for the Whore of Babylon (Rev 17–18), he is participating in this wider prophetic rhetorical convention. However, in Rev 2, all this invective is aimed at a real human woman—an individual opponent who is apparently so threatening that John has to go to such extremes to negate her influence and teaching.

John extends the metaphor of sexual promiscuity in the punishment he imagines for Jezebel and her different ethical teaching. She is condemned to the bed (κλίνη) and to distress along with those who have committed adultery with her. Use of the specific word for adultery (μοιχεύω) in 2:22 does not indicate that literal adultery has occurred.[23] John uses a prophetic *topos* to denote religious infidelity or idolatry. Her offspring are also threatened with death so that all the churches will know that God is in control (Rev 2:23). The threat of "throwing her on a bed" introduces a sexual tone and the potential of sexualized violence.[24] Similarly, the

---

[22] The Apocalypse shows a high level of awareness and use of Ezekiel, so it would be likely that John was aware of these famous passages; see Jean-Pierre Ruiz, *Ezekiel in the Apocalypse: The Transformation of Prophetic Language in Revelation 16,17–19,10* (Frankfurt am Main: Lang, 1989); Gregory Beale, *John's Use of the Old Testament in Revelation* (Sheffield: Sheffield Academic, 1998).

[23] Aune, *Revelation*, 204, points out that nearly all the *porn-* cognates are figurative, not literal, in Revelation.

[24] Βάλλω used as an active verb denotes something that is done to her, possibly with force. κλίνη can be translated as "couch," "sickbed," or "bed" and has resonances of where one reclines to eat as well as where one lies ill or engages in sexual activity; see Koester, *Revelation*, 299. Several scholars have noted that in this context κλίνη introduces a sexual element and the threat of rape; see Thimmes, "Teaching and Beguiling," 74; Olivia Stewart Lester,

threat to kill her children is one that strikes at her sexual productivity even while serving as a metaphor for her followers.

What makes these threats against Jezebel striking in their force is that they are voiced by the son of God (Rev 2:18), the risen Christ from the opening vision (Rev 1:9–20). God (or Jesus) rarely speaks directly in the Apocalypse, although a myriad of angelic intermediaries communicates for him. It is therefore conspicuous that these messages to the seven churches are depicted as direct speech from the risen Christ. This technique allows John to appeal to divine authority. It is not his message, it is Christ's. John draws upon the highest authority—namely, God—to condemn this woman.

In adopting this approach, John locates the violence, indeed the sexualized violence, that is being threatened against Jezebel as coming directly from the deity. While divine violence is a threat that hovers over any biblical prophet (for example, Ezekiel is bound and muted by God in Ezek 3:25–26 and 4:7–8), evidence suggests that female prophets are more likely to be recipients of divine violence, and that the violence is often more graphically described.[25] However, nowhere in the biblical tradition is a female prophet divinely threatened with rape. John has invented a new rhetorical threat to silence and beat his female opponent. The contrast to his treatment of Balaam only further highlights the gendered nature of his attack here, and we turn to that text now.

THE COUNTEREXAMPLE OF BALAAM

Jezebel is not the only opponent to whom John gives a false name. Name-calling is one of John's key strategies for vilifying his opponents.[26] He particularly likes to use figures from the Hebrew Bible—Jezebel, Balaam, Babylon, and that "ancient serpent," Satan. However, a comparison with John's treatment of Balaam highlights the misogyny and sexualized violence aimed at his female opponent in particular.

In the message to Pergamum, there is a group following the teaching of someone called "Balaam" (Rev 2:12–17). Like Jezebel, Balaam is not an actual name. John writes that Balaam is the one who taught Balak to put a stumbling block before the sons of Israel (Rev 2:14), a clear reference to Num 22–25. In the biblical tradition, Balaam is a prophet who worships foreign gods and convinces Israelite

---

"Jezebel: A Study in Prophecy, Divine Violence, and Gender," in *New Perspectives on the Book of Revelation*, ed. Adela Yarbro Collins (Leuven: Peeters, 2017), 520.

[25] Lester, "Jezebel," 510.

[26] Jean-Pierre Ruiz, "Betwixt and Between on the LORD's Day: Liturgy and the Apocalypse," in *The Reality of the Apocalypse: Rhetoric and Politics in the Book of Revelation*, ed. D. Barr (Atlanta: Society of Biblical Literature, 2006), 238.

men to have relations with Moabite women. John's charge against the group he accuses of holding to the "teaching of Balaam" is that they likewise allow people to eat food sacrificed to idols and practice *porneia* (Rev 2:14)—the exact same crime committed by Jezebel. The difference is that the Balaam group is not sexualized, despite the use of prophetic metaphor of adultery to describe idolatry. No precise punishment is issued, but there is a threat to come and make war if members of this group do not repent.

Male opponents in the Apocalypse receive threats of "manly" violence: a sword fight (Rev 2:16). While still violent and potentially fatal, a sword fight is a meeting of equals: two men, equally armed. This sword fight is obviously metaphorical, although still ominous. It is the "sword of my mouth," the sharp, double-edged one from the opening vision of Christ (Rev 1:16) that is figuratively brandished here. While a symbol of violence, the double-edged sword also serves as a metaphor for rhetorical discourse and the menacing power of the word of God. Female opponents like Jezebel, on the other hand, are terrorized with rape-like punishment and the death of their offspring (Rev 2:22–23). The gendered nature of this latter threat adds a personal tone to the attack. There is no real equivalence.

In one last rhetorical move, John attempts to divide the Thyatiran community into two groups and issues them with an implicit threat: those who side with Jezebel will suffer her fate. "The rest" are promised authority over the nations and a rod of iron with which to rule (Rev 2:24–26). If his slander and depersonalizing of the female leader has not worked, then the threat of violence to the community themselves might.

A LEGACY OF SEXUAL VIOLENCE

In this chapter, I have suggested that John is doing something new in using the biblical tradition in this way—namely, taking metaphors from the Hebrew Bible and applying them in an intensely personal, sexualized, and gendered way to one female opponent. Within the Apocalypse, the Whore of Babylon is threatened with a similar fate, but she is an image for Rome and the predominantly male, patriarchal power that is the Roman Empire. John's Jezebel, by contrast, is a human woman, a rival and fellow Christian. When we move beyond the text of the Apocalypse, there is similarly an absence of this kind of rhetoric in the rest of New Testament or in Greco-Roman rhetorical texts.[27]

---

[27] One explanation for the lack of examples in Greco-Roman texts is the scarcity of female orators in the ancient world. So, while there are numerous examples of indirect accusation, sexual slander, and name-calling from elite men to their male opponents, there is no male-to-female equivalent.

My desire to return to the Jezebel of Revelation and look at her afresh is driven in part by a desire to understand John's sources, influences, and rhetorical strategies. What we have uncovered is an unprecedented level of rhetorical vitriol and the weaponization of the Hebrew Bible that seeks to undermine and destroy an opponent and her views. And, while this appears to be a somewhat isolated incident in the ancient world, John's rhetoric has unfortunately survived as a strategy to dismiss women's leadership.

The Christian tradition has done as much damage to Jezebel as John did in making her a stereotype of all that is frightening about female leadership that cannot be controlled. These biblical Jezebels have become conflated in a tradition that now associates the name "Jezebel" with a seductress and femme fatale, a dangerous beauty who is sexually promiscuous, and an immoral religious outsider. A few examples from the tradition demonstrate the point. In the fourth century, Ephrem the Syrian mentions Jezebel at least three times in his *Nisibene Hymns*, always as a negative figure associated with Satan and death. He writes: "Sheol was not indeed Sheol but its semblance: Jezebel was the true Sheol, who devoured the just" (*Hymn* 67). In the sixteenth century, a friar wrote to warn Henry VIII that his love for Anne Boleyn would destroy him. The friar compares Anne Boleyn to Jezebel, writing: "A King who is besotted with his own Jezebel, a woman who is bringing about his ruin and that of the church, I say unto you as Elijah said to Ahab 'the dogs shall lick your blood'."[28] In doing so, this friar continues the rhetoric of violence and the othering of a female opponent of whom he disapproves. Even though he is alluding to the story in 1 Kings, the friar is rendering it through the lens of Rev 2 and later Christian interpretation. Janet Gaines has documented the numerous references to Jezebel in sermons and theological writings throughout history. She gives the example of the reformer John Knox, who referred to Queen Mary and similar female leaders as "the Jezebels" and, in doing so, framed himself as the Elijah of his day.[29] "Jezebel" became a label used to discredit Catholics, female leaders, female preachers, and theological opponents.

In addition to countless historical novels and artists' depictions, Jezebel enters the fictional world in more subtle ways. Novelist Tom Robbins uses her in a way that is typical of the Christian church and aforementioned sermons but also somewhat sympathetic to her. In *Skinny Legs and All*, Robbins narrates the adventures of Ellen Cherry, a newly wed artist from Virginia, who drives across the United States in an Airstream with her husband, Boomer. Early in the book, we learn that, despite her conservative southern upbringing, Ellen dreams of being an artist and moving to New York. Her conservative Christian family eventually allows her

---

[28] Cited in Janet Gaines, *Music in the Old Bones: Jezebel through the Ages* (Carbondale: Southern Illinois University Press, 1999), 99.
[29] Gaines, *Music*, 101.

to enroll in art school, in Virginia, not too far away. All that comes to an abrupt end, however, when her father and uncle Buddy, the local apocalyptic minister, hear that this art college uses live naked models for life drawing. Naked men and women, walking around in a classroom!—nothing could be more offensive to the LORD. So they burst into class one day and pull Ellen away from such evil. Her uncle stays to preach *at* the female nude model while her father hustles Ellen out. As they forcibly pack up Ellen's college dorm room Robbins writes;

> the two men seized dry washcloths and scrubbed the lipstick, rouge, and eyeshadow from her face. So harsh was the scrubbing that it peeled the skin from her cheeks...
> All the while, as the men scrubbed at her, they uttered one word, over and over,
> "Jezebel," they chanted.
> "Jezebel."[30]

CONCLUSION

Jezebel in our Western tradition, grounded in the Bible, has become shorthand for a wanton woman: a hybrid character formed from these two biblical women, who emerges with painted face, dangerous sexual power, and an entourage of men who follow. Most of those stereotypes are simply bad biblical exegesis, but they persist and are hard to subdue. The first steps to recovering and honoring these biblical Jezebels lies in feminist techniques of retelling and reimagining the original stories as well as simultaneously challenging the othering and dehumanizing tactics of name-calling and rhetorical sexualized violence in our own time, even or precisely when that occurs in the biblical tradition and in the church.

A reexamination of the biblical narrative reveals two Jezebels who were arguably both strong, powerful women capable of persuading others of their views and loyal to their own religious beliefs and practices. Yet "Jezebel" has become a moniker far removed from a Phoenecian queen or first-century Christian leader whose Christian views were perhaps a bit too Pauline and accommodating for John. Their stories have come to us solely through the words of their opponents. John of Patmos, however, might be surprised to know that the female rival he sought to dismiss and silence continues to be as well-known as he is.

Drawing on the biblical tradition of Queen Jezebel, John's rhetoric works in a threefold manner to dehumanize this first-century Christian leader, portray her as an outsider or foreigner, and cast her as an immoral woman. Her real name has been lost to history. John's rhetoric was arguably highly successful in that

---

[30] Tom Robbins, *Skinny Legs and All* (New York: Bantam Dell, 1991), Kindle.

sense. She was silenced and turned into a caricature in order for him to win a prophetic power battle. But at what cost? Arguably, the cost has been too high, not just for the real woman hidden behind John's Jezebel, but for every woman since who has been silenced, othered, robbed of her identity, sexualized, disempowered, and demonized.

BIBLIOGRAPHY

Aune, David Edward. *Revelation*. 3 vols. WBC 52A–C. Dallas, TX: Word, 1997.
Barr, David, ed. *The Reality of the Apocalypse: Rhetoric and Politics in the Book of Revelation*. Atlanta: Society of Biblical Literature, 2006.
Beale, Gregory K. *John's Use of the Old Testament in Revelation*. Sheffield: Sheffield Academic, 1998.
Blount, Brian K. *Revelation: A Commentary*. NTL. Louisville: Westminster John Knox, 2009.
Boring, M. Eugene. *Revelation*. Louisville: Westminster John Knox, 1989.
Duff, Paul Brooks. *Who Rides the Beast? Prophetic Rivalry and the Rhetoric of Crisis in the Churches of the Apocalypse*. Oxford: Oxford University Press, 2001.
Gaines, Janet Howe. *Music in the Old Bones: Jezebel through the Ages*. Carbondale, IL: Southern Illinois University Press, 1999.
Knust, Jennifer Wright. *Abandoned to Lust: Sexual Slander and Ancient Christianity*. New York: Columbia University Press, 2006.
Koester, Craig R. *Revelation: A New Translation with Introduction and Commentary*. AB 38A. New Haven: Yale University Press, 2014.
Lester, Olivia Stewart. "Jezebel: A Study in Prophecy, Divine Violence, and Gender." Pages 509–22 in *New Perspectives on the Book of Revelation*. BETL 291. Edited by Adela Yarbro Collins. Leuven: Peeters, 2017.
Nzimande, Makhosazana K. "Reconfiguring Jezebel: A Postcolonial Imbokodo Reading of the Story of Naboth's Vineyard (1 Kings 21:1–16)." Pages 223–58 in *African and European Readers of the Bible in Dialogue: In Quest of a Shared Meaning*. Edited by H. de Wit and G. West. Leiden: Brill, 2008.
Robbins, Tom. *Skinny Legs and All*. New York: Bantam Dell, 1991.
Ruiz, Jean-Pierre. *Ezekiel in the Apocalypse: The Transformation of Prophetic Language in Revelation 16,17–19,10*. Europäische Hochschulschriften 376. Frankfurt am Main: Lang, 1989.
———. "Betwixt and Between on the LORD's Day: Liturgy and the Apocalypse." Pages 221–42 in *The Reality of the Apocalypse: Rhetoric and Politics in the Book of Revelation*. Edited by D. Barr. Atlanta: Society of Biblical Literature, 2006.
Sweeney, Marvin A. *I and II Kings: A Commentary*. OTL. Louisville: Westminster John Knox, 2007.
Thimmes, Pamela. "Teaching and Beguiling My Servants: The Letter to Thyatira (Rev 2:18–29)." Pages 69–87 in *A Feminist Companion to the Apocalypse of John*. Edited by A. J. Levine. London: T&T Clark, 2009.
Trible, Phyllis. "Exegesis for Storytellers and Other Strangers." *JBL* 114 (1995): 3–19.
———. *Texts of Terror: Literary-Feminist Readings of Biblical Narratives*. OBT. Philadelphia: Fortress Press, 1984.

8

The Leadership of Women in Early Christianity

Adela Yarbro Collins

In her book *Texts of Terror*, Phyllis Trible lifts up and tells the stories of Hagar, Tamar, the unnamed concubine from Bethlehem murdered in Gibeah, and the daughter of Jephthah.[1] She describes this book as calling for a time to weep and mourn. This volume followed her *God and the Rhetoric of Sexuality*, which calls for a time to laugh and dance.[2] Most of the texts discussed here in this chapter call for a time to remember women leaders in the early church and thus to laugh and dance. Along the way, however, we will meet texts of oppression written by those who tried to suppress the leadership of women, such as the first letter to Timothy and some of Epiphanius's writings. Trible's example encourages us to mourn those traditions that oppress and silence women's leadership and to celebrate the evidence for women leaders and the women and men who supported them.

INTRODUCTION

In the earliest Christian communities, forms of leadership were fluid and diverse. So I will speak about "functions" or "positions" when addressing the situation reflected in Paul's letters and reserve the term "office" for the period in which some early Christian writers began to foster the development of institutions.[3]

---

[1] Phyllis Trible, *Texts of Terror: Literary-Feminist Readings of Biblical Narratives*, OBT (Philadelphia: Fortress, 1984).
[2] Trible, *Texts*, xiii; Phyllis Trible, *God and the Rhetoric of Sexuality* (London: SCM, 1978).
[3] The term "functions" is used by Marlis Gielen, "Die Wahrnehmung gemeindlicher Leitungsfunktionen durch Frauen im Spiegel der Pastoralbriefe," in *Neutestamentliche Ämtermodelle im Kontext*, ed. Thomas Schmeller, Martin Ebner, and Rudolf Hoppe, QD 239 (Freiburg: Herder, 2010), 129–65; the term "roles" is used in Margaret Y. MacDonald, *The Pauline Churches: A Socio-Historical Study of Institutionalization in the Pauline and Deutero-Pauline Writings*, SNTSMS 60 (New York: Cambridge University Press, 1988), 59–60.

With regard to office, I agree with Hans von Campenhausen that there is "no need to assume that office as such, even if it is of natural origin and thus by definition cannot be termed 'spiritual' in the sense of being a direct divine endowment, must therefore be set in diametric opposition to the Spirit."[4]

John Reumann pointed out in the early 1990s that some scholars have looked to Jewish or Semitic practices and others to Greco-Roman materials for the question of origins. I agree with him that it is an outdated attitude, one which asserts or assumes that an argument for a Jewish or Semitic source is intrinsically better than one for a Greek or Roman source.[5] It is striking that the names of the functions or positions in Paul's community vary in his letters.[6] This suggests that Paul did not impose a system or structure of ministerial roles; rather, they emerged in each community according to the respective cultural contexts and affinities.

Because there was diversity in forms of leadership from one Pauline congregation to another, the diversity among congregations with a different origin and among those from different parts of the empire is likely to be even greater. As Ute Eisen has observed, evidence for a particular office or practice in one locality does not mean that it was characteristic of all Christian communities throughout the Mediterranean world.[7]

HOUSE CHURCHES AS THE CONTEXT FOR MINISTRY

There is widespread agreement that ministry in Paul's time was carried out in the context of local households.[8] Along with this setting came the social practices of

---

[4] Hans von Campenhausen, *Ecclesiastical Authority and Spiritual Power in the Church of the First Three Centuries*, trans. J. A. Baker (Stanford, CA: Stanford University Press, 1969), 80.

[5] John Reumann, "Church Office in Paul, Especially in Philippians," in *Origins and Method: Towards a New Understanding of Judaism and Christianity*, ed. B. H. McLean, JSNTSS 86 (Sheffield: JSOT Press, 1993), 86, 88; Reumann, "Contributions of the Philippian Community to Paul and to Earliest Christianity," *NTS* 39 (1993): 446–47.

[6] Tobias Nicklas, "Offices? Roles, Functions: Authorities and Ethos in Earliest Christianity—A Look into the World of Pauline Communities," in *Rabbi—Pastor—Priest: Their Roles and Profiles through the Ages*, ed. Walter Homolka and Heinz-Günther Schöttler, SJ 64 (Berlin: de Gruyter, 2013), 35–36.

[7] Ute E. Eisen, *Women Officeholders in Early Christianity: Epigraphical and Literary Studies*, trans. Linda Maloney (Collegeville, MN: Liturgical Press, 2000), 6. See also Paul F. Bradshaw, *The Search for the Origins of Christian Worship: Sources and Methods for the Study of Early Liturgy*, 2nd ed. (New York: Oxford University Press, 2002), 193–95; MacDonald, *Pauline Churches*, 59–60.

[8] Floyd V. Filson, "The Significance of the Early House Churches," *JBL* 58 (1939): 106; Hans-Josef Klauck, *Hausgemeinde und Hauskirche im frühen Christentum*, SBS 103 (Stuttgart: Katholisches Bibelwerk, 1981), 21–44; Reumann, "Church Office," 86–87; Reumann, "Contributions," 447 (c); and Bradshaw, *Search*, 194.

patronage. Some of these households were under the authority of men, the heads of extended families and their slaves. Such men were wealthy and powerful *patres familias*, who could offer hospitality and administrative expertise. Such a leader could also have other roles in the community, such as prophet or teacher, depending on the individual case.[9] As host, the head of the household probably presided over the thanksgiving meal unless an honored guest was present.[10] In some of the house churches referred to by Paul, the heads of the household were women. Given their wealth, status, and expertise, these women were probably also leaders of the communities that met in their homes. Because Prisca is mentioned along with her husband Aquila, it is likely that they both exercised leadership of the community that met in their homes in Corinth, Ephesus, and Rome.[11] The letter to the Colossians, which is probably not by Paul but stands in the Pauline tradition, mentions a woman, Nympha, who was the head of a household and in whose house a community met. Later scribes did not accept the existence of such a woman, who likely exercised leadership in that community, and modified the text to make her a man (Nymphas).[12]

APOSTLES

The first function or position I would like to discuss is apostleship. In the texts that eventually became the New Testament, two kinds of apostles appear. Those of one type are commissioned by the risen Christ, those of the other by a local community.[13] Paul presents himself as an apostle commissioned by the risen LORD and refers to Epaphroditus as "your apostle," implying that the community in Philippi had commissioned him to travel to take him their financial gift.[14] Paul

---

[9] Harry O. Maier, *The Social Setting of the Ministry as Reflected in the Writings of Hermas, Clement, and Ignatius* (Waterloo, ON: Wilfrid Laurier University Press, 1991), 4, 39; Bradshaw, *Search*, 194; and Teresa Berger, *Gender Differences and the Making of Liturgical History* (Farnham, Surrey, UK: Ashgate, 2011), 132. See also Reumann, "Church Office," 87.

[10] Klauck, *Hausgemeinde und Hauskirche*, 43.

[11] 1 Cor 16:19; Rom 16:3–5; cf. Acts 18:1–3, 18–19; Christoph G. Müller, *Frühchristliche Ehepaare und paulinische Mission*, SBS 215 (Stuttgart: Katholisches Bibelwerk, 2008) 27–29, 31; and Klauck, *Hausgemeinde und Hauskirche*, 21–26. It is not clear whether Chloe, mentioned in 1 Cor 1:11, was Christian or not; "those of Chloe" may refer to slaves in her household who were "in Christ"; see Klauck, *Hausgemeinde und Hauskirche*, 28–29.

[12] Col 4:15 and Klauck, *Hausgemeinde und Hauskirche*, 44–45. Scribes read the accusative *Nymphan* (Νύμφαν) as having a circumflex accent on the last syllable rather than an acute on the first. They also changed the feminine genitive singular possessive pronoun to the masculine; see Klauck, *Hausgemeinde und Hauskirche*, 44.

[13] Reumann, "Church Office," 84.

[14] For Paul's self-presentation, see Gal 1:1; cf. 1 Cor 1:1; 9:1; 2 Cor 1:1; Rom 1:1; 11:13.

also refers to "those who were apostles before me" in Jerusalem.[15] This group included Cephas, also known as Peter, and James, the brother of the LORD. In 1 Cor 9, Paul refers to these two men and also to "the other apostles." The fact that he asks "Have I not seen the LORD?" in the same context suggests that he considered all of these apostles to have been commissioned by the risen LORD.[16] This inference fits with Paul's statement later in the same letter that Christ "appeared to James and then to all the apostles."[17] Just before that, he says that Christ appeared first to Cephas and then to the twelve. It is likely that Paul considered the twelve, including Peter, to be apostles commissioned by the risen LORD. It is noteworthy, however, that some itinerant teachers who called themselves apostles were not recognized by Paul as such.[18]

This discussion provides a context for considering the apostles of Rom 16:7. Paul asks his Roman addressees to greet two people who are his "kin." He probably uses the Greek word in question to mean "fellow Jews," because he uses it that way in Rom 9:3. They have also been fellow prisoners with him. Finally, he describes them as "prominent" or "outstanding" among the apostles and as having become "in Christ" before him.[19] Because they had been in prison, they were likely apostles of the first type, those commissioned by the risen Christ to travel from place to place proclaiming him. Their being imprisoned *with* Paul suggests that, like him, they were proclaiming Christ to *gentiles*. Because they were apostles so early, they may have been among those apostles Paul mentions in 1 Corinthians 15 to whom the LORD appeared. Because their names are Greek, they may have belonged to the Greek-speaking community in Jerusalem.

One of these two apostles in Rom 16:7 is Andronicus, a name that appears in the Maccabean literature.[20] For the first millennium at least, the second name, Ἰουνίαν (Iounian), was taken as equivalent to the Latin name Junia and to represent a female apostle. John Chrysostom praised her as follows: "Indeed, how great the wisdom of this woman must have been that she was deemed worthy of the title of apostle."[21] Beginning in the late Middle Ages, however, the name was taken to be that of a man, Junias, even though such a name is unattested in antiquity. Prejudice against the idea of a female apostle played a significant role. The Revised Standard Version of 1946 is an egregious example, which describes "Andronicus and Junias" as "men of note among the apostles."[22] It is probable that, like Prisca

---

[15] Gal 1:17.
[16] 1 Cor 9:1, 5.
[17] 1 Cor 15:7.
[18] 2 Cor 11:5, 13; 12:11.
[19] Nicklas, "Offices?," 35 and n. 40.
[20] Peter Lampe, "Andronicus 3," *ABD* 1:247.
[21] Cited by Eldon Jay Epp, *Junia: The First Woman Apostle* (Minneapolis: Fortress), 32.
[22] Epp, *Junia*, 39; see his n. 30 for more examples of English translations of this type.

and Aquila, they were a married couple, who traveled, proclaimed, and taught together.[23]

Today many scholars accept that Junia was a female apostle. Paul's acceptance of her authority is impressive, especially in light of what he says in 1 Corinthians: "God appointed in the church first apostles, then prophets, etc."[24] His use of the word "first" has a temporal sense but also the sense of most authoritative. This authority was not that of a fixed office but one that had to be acknowledged to be effective.[25]

OVERSEERS AND BISHOPS

Paul addresses his letter to the Philippians also to the *episkopoi* (ἐπισκόποι) and *diakonoi* (διακόνοι) of that community. Some scholars have argued that the function called *episkopos* here derived from the Jewish Scriptures, the synagogue, or the office of the *mebaqqer* described in the Dead Sea Scrolls.[26] Because both terms may be translated "overseer" or "inspector," the office in the Dead Sea Scrolls is a striking analogy. As we have seen, however, Paul did not establish a regular set of functions in each community, so it is likely that the members of the Philippian community established such functions on the basis of practices familiar to them in their city.[27] This means that the term probably came from Greek usage for supervisors in city governments or officials of voluntary associations. Such officers often had a variety of responsibilities, and the term was not yet a technical one.[28]

It is inappropriate to translate the term *episkopos* in Phil 1:1 with "bishop" because the use of the plural indicates that the position is not yet an office involving oversight of all the believers in a particular city as a whole. It may be that the use of the term originated in the context of a house church in Philippi. If the head of the household performed a variety of tasks, including financial stewardship and administrative leadership, the term *episkopos* would be appropriate for such a

---

[23] Müller, *Frühchristliche Ehepaare*, 37–40.
[24] 1 Cor 12:28.
[25] Nicklas, "Offices?," 27.
[26] Reumann, "Contributions," 447 (e) and Reumann, "Church Office," 88.
[27] Reumann, "Contributions," 449 (g).
[28] Reumann, "Contributions," 447-48 (e); Reumann, "Church Office," 88; and Hans Lietzmann, "Zur altchristlichen Vefassungsgeschichte," *ZWT* 55 (1914): 97–153, repr. in Lietzmann, *Kleine Schriften 1*, TU 67 (Berlin: Akademie, 1958) 141–85; K. Kertelge, ed., *Das kirchliche Amt im Neuen Testament* (Wege der Forschung 189; Darmstadt: Wissenschaftliche Buchgesellschaft, 1977), 96–101; Martin Dibelius, "'Bischöfe' und 'Diakonen' in Philippi," in *Das kirchliche Amt im Neuen Testament*, ed. Karl Kertelge, Wege der Forschung 189 (Darmstadt: Wissenschaftliche Buchgesellschaft, 1977), 414.

leader, whether male or female, whether *pater* or *mater familias*, aided by *diakonoi*.[29] In addition to the functions of apostle, prophet, and teacher, which are mentioned in 1 Corinthians, the author of the *Didache* urges the communities:

> to elect for yourselves *episkopoi* and *diakonoi* who are worthy of the LORD, gentle men who are not fond of money, who are true and approved. For these also conduct the ministry (*leitourgian*) of the prophets and teachers among you. And so, do not disregard them. For these are the ones who have found honor among you, along with the prophets and teachers.[30]

The author may urge election to such positions in order to fill any gaps left by the itinerant leaders. When, for example, there is no prophet present to lead the eucharist, one of these elected leaders can do so, using the prayers given in chapters 9–10. They may also have taken over other types of leadership exercised by teachers, apostles, and prophets.[31]

When introducing the two functions that are less recognized, the author seems to assume that men (*andres*, ἄνδρες) will exercise them. While women are not explicitly excluded, it seems more likely that they would be accepted in the functions of teacher, apostle, and prophet, from the point of view of the author at least, than in these newer, although less respected, positions. As Karen King has pointed out, however, women in the early church who had the gift of prophecy were more likely to exercise other kinds of power than those without it.[32]

The offices of bishop, deacon, and elder constitute a major topic in the Pastoral Epistles, which were probably written in the first half of the second century.[33] Unlike the *Didache* and the Shepherd of Hermas, 1 Timothy and Titus speak of the bishop only in the singular.[34] This practice fits with the use of the feminine abstract noun, as in 1 Clement, to refer to the office (*episkope*): "If someone aspires to the office of bishop, he (or she) desires a good work."[35]

---

[29] Reumann, "Contributions," 449–50.
[30] *Didache* 15.1–2.
[31] Von Campenhausen, *Ecclesiastical Authority*, 73–74; Lietzmann, "Zur altchristlichen Vefassungsgeschichte," 95 emphasized their likely administrative and practical duties, such as care for the poor.
[32] Karen L. King, "Prophetic Power and Women's Authority," in *Women Preachers and Prophets through Two Millennia of Christianity*, ed. Beverly Mayne Kienzle and Pamela J. Walker (Berkeley: University of California Press, 1998), 21–41.
[33] At least 1 Tim was composed well into the second century; see Jens Herzer, "Juden—Christen—Gnostiker. Zur Gegnerproblematik der Pastoralbriefe," in *Die Entstehung des Christentums aus dem Judentum = Berliner Theologische Zeitschrift* 25 (2008): 161, 165, 167.
[34] 1 Tim 3:2; Titus 1:7.
[35] 1 Tim 3:1.

It is noteworthy that, according to 1 Timothy, the bishop must manage his own household well because his duty is to take care of the church of God. It is implied that each local community is an instance of the household of God. This metaphor supports the idea that the function of *episkopoi* in the church probably originated in the house churches of Philippi. As we have seen, the head of the household likely exercised such a function, including women who headed their own households. The association of the bishop with the elders, however, moved the function of the *episkopos* in a patriarchal direction.[36]

Given that the author of 1 Timothy forbids women to teach and to have authority over men, he would be unlikely to approve of a female bishop.[37] His elaborate prohibition and defense, however, suggest that he in fact knows of women who are teaching, and that some men recognized their authority. From this point of view, his speaking of bishops and elders as men may only hide the fact that there were women bishops and elders in the area where he was active.

The letters of Ignatius provide evidence that there were still house churches headed by women in the second century.[38] In his letter to the Smyrneans, Ignatius greets the household of Tavia. The widow of a certain Epitropus led another house church in Smyrna; Ignatius greets her and her children at the end of his letter to Polycarp.[39]

Eisen's book on *Women Officeholders in Early Christianity* includes a chapter on women as bishops. Here she presents evidence for two female bishops in Italy. The first case involves an inscription from Umbria that mentions a "venerable Lady Bishop" (*uenerabilis fem[ina] episkopa*), whose name unfortunately is not included in the surviving part of the inscription.[40] The inscription dates to around 500. Scholars have regularly interpreted this inscription to mean that the woman was the wife of a bishop. Enough of the inscription has been preserved, however, to make clear that no husband is mentioned. In any case, the wives of bishops were normally called *coniux*, referring to one who is united in marriage and usually a wife because it is usually feminine.[41]

---

[36] von Campenhausen, *Ecclesiastical Authority*, 116–17.

[37] He assumes that bishops will be men, because he lists as one qualification that the bishop should be "the husband of one wife" (1 Tim 3:2).

[38] Some scholars date his letters to the time of the emperor Trajan, others to the mid-second century.

[39] Ignatius, *To the Smyrnaeans* 13.2; *To Polycarp* 8.2; these passages are cited by Eisen, *Women Officeholders*, 206.

[40] Eisen, *Women Officeholders*, 199–200.

[41] Eisen, *Women Officeholders*, 200; Lewis and Short, *A Latin Dictionary: Founded on Andrews' Edition of Freund's Latin Dictionary, Revised, Enlarged, and in Great Part Rewritten* (Oxford: Clarendon, 1959), s.v. conjunx/conjux.

The second case is even more striking. Two Latin inscriptions dating to the early ninth century were found in the Chapel of Saint Zeno in the basilica of Santa Prassede in Rome. A mosaic depicts the bust of a woman with the label *Theodora episkopa*. She was the mother of Paschal I, who was pope from 817 to 824. It is clear that she was not a bishop's wife because her husband, Bonosus, is listed in the *Liber Pontificalis* as the father of this pope, without any official title.[42] Theodora's son dedicated the second inscription. The relevant part refers to the entrance to the basilica where "the body of his most gracious mother, the Lady Theodora, the bishop, rests." Since the word *episkopa* follows her name, it is likely that this term indicates an office she held. Because the evidence for female bishops is so rare, scholars have come up with a variety of theories to explain how and why Theodora came to be called a bishop. The simplest explanation is that she was consecrated or ordained as a Roman bishop.[43]

No Greek inscription has as yet been published testifying to a female bishop. Hans Achelis, however, has argued credibly that, in the church order called the *Didascalia Apostolorum* (*Teaching of the Apostles*), "the enrolled widows exercised episcopal functions and thus represented competition for the male bishop." This church order dates to the first half of the third century and probably originated in Syria.[44] Epiphanius, bishop of Salamis on Cyprus in the fourth century, testifies that the Montanists ordained women as bishops.[45] Epiphanius is against such a practice. If such women were prophets as well as bishops, Epiphanius provides evidence that women prophets may sometimes exercise other forms of power as well.

DIAKONOI, DEACONS, AND DEACONESSES

When many readers of the New Testament think of the terms *diakonos*, *diakonia*, and *diakonein*, they think of passages like Mark 1:31, which tells how the mother-in-law of Peter served Jesus and four disciples after Jesus had healed her of a fever. Here the term "served" seems to be connected with providing food and waiting on them at table. Or they may think of Acts 6, according to which the twelve chose seven Hellenists to wait on tables, thus serving their widows and others in need. A clue that the word group should not be defined entirely by table service or other service to the poor may be found in the fact that the author of Acts does not call the seven *diakonoi*. He describes them instead as men full of spirit and wisdom and

---

[42] Eisen, *Women Officeholders*, 202–3.
[43] Eisen, *Women Officeholders*, 203–4.
[44] Eisen, *Women Officeholders*, 207; cf. 150–51.
[45] Epiphanius, *Panarion* 49.2.5; Eisen, *Women Officeholders*, 207; cf. 118.

depicts them as performing signs and wonders and teaching (Stephen in Acts 6 and 7), and as proclaiming the word (Philip in Acts 8).

A major shift in the understanding of this word group began with Dieter Georgi's treatment of the rivals of Paul in 2 Corinthians, who seem to have described themselves individually as *diakonos theou* (ὡς θεοῦ διάκονοι, messengers/envoys of God). He argued on the basis of Greek texts outside the New Testament that *diakonos* can mean "messenger" and considered it a small step from that usage to the meaning "envoy." He saw an analogy between the usage in the New Testament and that in Epictetus, when he describes the true cynic and his divine mission. Georgi concluded that more New Testament passages refer to a *diakonos* as proclaimer than as one waiting tables.[46]

The need for a change was thoroughly argued by John Neil Collins, who made a broad study of the word group in non-Christian, non-Jewish Greek texts.[47] In his review of the book, Jerome Neyrey helpfully summarized Collins's conclusions and how they affect the understanding of "service" in a variety of passages in early Christian texts:

> (1) [*diakonoi* can be] spokesmen for God (1 Cor 3:5; 2 Cor 3:6; 11:23), who have rights and duties and act as mouthpieces, agents, and go-betweens for God; (2) [or they may be] travelling emissaries (Rom 15:25), who act as delegates or legations from one church to another, sometimes carrying letters or collections; Collins argues that such "servants" embody loyalty to those who commission them rather than menial service to others. He notes how Paul himself was "servant" of certain churches and how others served as his "servants" or emissaries who went out on his errands and acted as his delegates. Finally, Collins traces the gradual development of the specific role of "deacon" from the simple assistant to the overseer (Phil 1:1; 1 Tim) to the emerging cultic roles noted in *Did*. 15:1 and the non-presbyteral liturgical assistants described in *1 Clem*. 42:4.[48]

Thus the *diakonoi* of Phil 1:1 are well understood as assistants to the *episkopoi*, not necessarily their household slaves.

In the case of this function, we have a woman explicitly named a *diakonos* by Paul, namely Phoebe, whom he commends to his Roman addressees for hospitality and whatever else she needs.[49] There is widespread agreement that Phoebe was

---

[46] Dieter Georgi, *The Opponents of Paul in Second Corinthians* (Philadelphia: Fortress, 1986), 27–32.

[47] John Neil Collins, *Diakonia: Re-Interpreting the Ancient Sources* (New York: Oxford University Press, 1990).

[48] Jerome H. Neyrey, review of John N. Collins, *Diakonia: Re-Interpreting the Ancient Sources*, in *BTB* 21 (1991): 167 (slightly modified). See also the positive review of K. Grayston in *Theological Studies* n.s. 43 (1992): 198–200.

[49] Rom 16:1–2.

the person to whom Paul entrusted his letter to the Romans and that she delivered it. Given the ancient practices involved in sending and delivering letters, it is clear that Phoebe must have been able to clarify the contents of the letter and to answer questions about it posed by the addressees. Because Paul had not met most of the members of the communities in Rome, and because they had received negative reports about his theology, she must have possessed both theological competence and diplomatic skill.[50]

There is no consensus concerning the further interpretation of the passage. In addition to saying that she is a *diakonos*, Paul also describes her as *prostatis* (προστάτις, patron). The most important questions for grasping the sense of this passage as a whole are what each of these functions entails and how the two relate to each other. With regard to *prostatis*, the most persuasive interpretation begins with the observation that, where Roman influence is present, this term is equivalent to the Latin *patrona* and thus evokes the practices related to the social institution of patronage.[51] In the context of the early Christian mission, the meaning would be that Phoebe provided material and legal assistance for Paul and others. If Phoebe was in a position to offer hospitality and protection from ill-disposed political authorities, she must have had a rather high social standing and most likely her own house. Thus the term *prostatis* suggests that she was the head of a house church in the eastern port of Corinth. This picture is supported by the fact that she is traveling alone and independently. She would, however, have had an entourage of slaves, servants, and perhaps clients traveling with her.[52]

Some scholars have argued that, in the phrase "*diakonos* of the church in Cenchreae," *diakonos* signifies a function within the community that met in her house.[53] If Phoebe were the head of a house church, however, it would make more sense for her to take the role of an *episkopos* with *diakonoi* as her assistants within the community. The other interpretation that fits the context in Romans is that she was a delegate or emissary of the community in Cenchreae, sent to Rome with a particular task to fulfill.[54]

---

[50] Gielen, "Die Wahrnehmung," 139–40.

[51] Wayne A. Meeks, *The First Urban Christians: The Social World of the Apostle Paul*, 2nd ed. (New Haven: Yale University Press, 2003), 13, 27, 60, 217 n. 62; Annette Merz, "Phöbe. Diakon(in) der Gemeinde von Kenchreä—eine wichtige Mitstreiterin des Paulus neu entdeckt," in *Frauen gestalten Diakonie I. Von der biblischen Zeit bis zum Pietismus*, ed. Adelheid M. von Hauff (Stuttgart: Kohlhammer, 2007), 131–32 and 131 n. 8.

[52] Merz, "Phöbe," 132.

[53] See, e.g., Gielen, "Die Wahrnehmung," 141, 157. See also the critical discussion of this kind of hypothesis by Merz, "Phöbe," 132–36.

[54] Compare the second major kind of "service" a *diakonos* may have fulfilled in Neyrey, review of Collins, *Diakonia*.

Annette Merz has proposed a credible explanation of what that task was.[55] In light of the way Paul speaks about other coworkers and their relations with their communities and with himself, she concludes that Phoebe, as *diakonos* of Cenchreae, was given by her community a specific task to fulfill in the context of Paul's missionary work. Bringing the letter to the Romans must have been only a part of that task. Given the overall situation implied by Rom 15, the other part of Phoebe's task was to prepare the logistics for Paul's mission to Spain and perhaps to take part in it. The greetings to old friends of Paul in the rest of Rom 16 and perhaps to Roman Christians Paul did not know personally seem to constitute a strategy to bring his former coworkers together with his potentially new coworkers for the purpose of putting the Romans' minds at rest about Paul's theology and to encourage them all to plan for the mission to Spain. Perhaps Paul hoped some of his old coworkers would go with him. Because some of the persons mentioned in Rom 16:21–23 are among those who accompany Paul to Jerusalem with the collection, he may be introducing them in order to prepare for the possibility that they would go with him, first to Rome and then to Spain.[56]

The idea that a community would send its leader to Rome as their emissary is not a problem for this interpretation. Because the role of leader of a house church was a function, not a highly exalted office, the congregation still had agency and could very well have responded to Paul's request, with her permission, by issuing such a commission.

As the function of *episkopos* or overseer becomes the office of bishop in the Pastoral Epistles, the function of *diakonos* or emissary becomes the office of deacon in 1 Timothy. As we have seen, the *episkopoi* and *diakonoi* are mentioned together in Phil 1:1, where the *diakonoi* are probably the assistants of the overseer. In 1 Timothy, the deacons are also closely connected with the bishop. The discussion of the qualifications of the deacons follows immediately upon that of the bishop.[57]

In 1 Tim 3:8–13 the qualifications for the office of deacon are listed but not the duties. Qualifications for "women" are given in verse 11. Some scholars have argued that these women are the wives of the male deacons. There is, however, no possessive pronoun to indicate that the women are the deacons' wives. Furthermore, there is no discussion of what is expected of the bishop's wife, so it would be strange to give such a discussion for the deacons' wives. Later church orders from the mid-third and fourth centuries clearly speak about an office of female

---

[55] In contrast, Anni Hentschel, *Diakonia im Neuen Testament*, WUNT 2/226 (Tübingen: Mohr Siebeck, 2007), 172 leaves open whether *diakonos* here refers to the fulfillment of a task beyond the community or a function within the community.

[56] Merz, "Phöbe," 136–40.

[57] 1 Tim 3:8–13 (deacons) follows 3:1–7 (bishop). On the association of the bishop and the deacons, see von Campenhausen, *Ecclesiastical Authority*, 107.

diakonoi (using the grammatically masculine plural ending) and allude to this passage as the precedent for such an office.[58]

Later on, the office of female deacon or deaconess was much more common in the eastern Mediterranean region than in the western.[59] In the earliest church, both men and women such as Phoebe exercised the function of *diakonos*. The new, separate office of female deacon first appears in literature in the third century in the church order called *Didascalia Apostolorum* (*Teaching of the Apostles*), which I have already mentioned in connection with women bishops. Inscriptions attesting to this office begin to appear only in the fourth century.[60] In the literature and inscriptions, they appear in a variety of contexts: guardians of shrines, persons of influence in ecclesiastical conflicts, female monks and superiors in monasteries, and choir leaders.

In the church orders, the deacons are the personal agents of the bishop, analogous to Phil 1:1 and 1 Tim 3.[61] The bishop is like God, the male deacon like Christ, and the female deacon like the Holy Spirit. The female deacons, as part of the clergy, had a higher status than the official widows and virgins.[62] The female deacons had considerable mobility and responsibility for the women of the community.[63]

ELDERS, PRESBYTERS, AND PRIESTS

The last function, and later office, that I would like to discuss is that of elder. This office evolved over time. The group or council of elders probably originated in the early Christian community in Jerusalem. This group was an eschatological adaptation of the elders who participated in the revelation of the law to Moses and who saw the glory of the Lord on Mount Sinai.[64] After the crisis in Jerusalem involving the death of James and the destruction of the city by the Romans, the function or office of a group of elders spread to the diaspora, probably in the main centers

---

[58] Korinna Zamfir, *Men and Women in the Household of God: A Contextual Approach to Roles and Ministries in the Pastoral Epistles*, Novum Testamentum et orbis antiquus/Studien zur Umwelt des Neuen Testaments 103 (Göttingen: Vandenhoeck & Ruprecht, 2013), 350–51.

[59] Kevin Madigan and Carolyn Osiek, eds., *Ordained Women in the Early Church: A Documentary History* (Baltimore: Johns Hopkins University Press, 2005), 25; Eisen, *Women Officeholders*, 158–98.

[60] Madigan and Osiek, *Ordained Women*, 25; Eisen, *Women Officeholders*, 158–85.

[61] Madigan and Osiek, *Ordained Women*, 107.

[62] Madigan and Osiek, *Ordained Women*, 111.

[63] Madigan and Osiek, *Ordained Women*, 112.

[64] Martin Karrer, "Das urchristliche Ältestenamt," *NovT* 32 (1990): 168.

such as Ephesus.[65] From these centers it eventually spread to other cities, perhaps as early as the beginning of the second century.[66]

The feminine form of the word for elder, *presbytera*, can refer simply to an older woman; the wife of a male elder, a *presbyteros*; or a woman who functioned as an elder or presbyter in her own right. Kevin Madigan and Carolyn Osiek, as well as Eisen, have collected the ancient evidence for women who exercised the function or held the office of a presbyter.[67]

There is evidence for such women in both the eastern and the western Mediterranean regions, and the evidence is more abundant for the west. Councils and synods of both the east and the west denounced the practice of women presbyters, but the inscriptional and literary evidence suggests that the practice continued at least until the sixth century.

In the east, the Council of Laodicea, which met in the fourth century, and the antiheretical work by Epiphanius from the same period condemn the practice of women presbyters. It should be recalled that councils and synods were generally reactive; their condemnation of women presbyters therefore indicates that there were women recognized as such in some areas. The same probably holds for the work of Epiphanius.[68] In contrast, the Acts of Philip, from the late fourth or early fifth century, simply assumes the activity of women presbyters.[69]

Four inscriptions from the east commemorate individual women who were presbyters during their lifetime. These are Ammion, from the first half of the third century in Asia Minor, Artemidora, from the second or third century in Egypt, Epikto, from the second to the fourth century on the island of Thera, and Kale, from the fourth or fifth century in Sicily.

In the west, Tertullian, who wrote in the late second and early third century, recognized the utterances of female prophets as authoritative. He placed the authority of an oracle spoken by a certain Prisca alongside the Hebrew Scriptures and the writings of Paul.[70] Yet he forbade women to teach, baptize, and celebrate the eucharist, apparently on the basis of 1 Cor 14:34–35 and 1 Tim 2:11–12. He inferred from those passages that sacerdotal—that is, priestly—tasks are proper to men alone.[71]

---

[65] Karrer, "Das urchristliche Ältestenamt," 171, 175, 187.
[66] Karrer, "Das urchristliche Ältestenamt," 187.
[67] Madigan and Osiek, *Ordained Women*, 163–202 and Eisen, *Women Officeholders*, 116–42.
[68] See Madigan and Osiek, *Ordained Women*, 163–64 for the Council of Laodicea and 164–66 on Epiphanius.
[69] Madigan and Osiek, *Ordained Women*, 166–67.
[70] Tertullian, *Exhortation to Chastity* 10.5; *The Soul* 9.4; Madigan and Osiek, *Ordained Women*, 179.
[71] Tertullian, *The Veiling of Virgins* 9.1; Madigan and Osiek, *Ordained Women*, 178.

The most striking literary evidence comes from the correspondence of Cyprian, bishop of Carthage. Firmilian, bishop of Caesarea in Cappadocia, was Cyprian's ally in his controversy with Stephen, bishop of Rome. In around 256, Firmilian wrote Cyprian a letter that included the following remarks:

> There rose up suddenly then a certain woman who, in a state of ecstasy, presented herself as a prophet (propheten) and acted as if filled with the Holy Spirit... But that woman, who previously through the illusions and treacheries of the Demon in order to deceive the faithful ... had also often dared this ... to sanctify the bread and to pretend to confect the eucharist and make the sacrifice to the LORD ... and she also baptized many, usurping the usual and legitimate mode of questioning, so that nothing might seem to deviate from ecclesiastical rule.[72]

It is noteworthy that Firmilian does not label this woman as a member of a deviant group but as deviant within the church itself.[73] This is a prime example of the power of a woman with the gift of prophecy to extend her ministry, in this case, to presbyteral or priestly functions. Furthermore, the letter shows that those to whom she ministered recognized her presbyteral or priestly ministry.

Canons and personal letters from the west attest to a movement beginning in the late fourth century that called for greater leadership on the part of women. This movement seems to have been inspired by followers of Priscillian, bishop of Avila in Spain, who exemplified and called for an ascetic way of life. Canon 2 of the Synod of Nîmes, which took place around 394, condemned the ordination of women to "levitical service." Because "levitical" and "sacerdotal" were used synonymously at this time, the issue in question is women priests or presbyters who celebrated the eucharist.[74]

Pope Gelasius I wrote a letter to bishops in southern Italy in about 494, objecting to the encouragement given to women "to serve at the sacred altars and to perform all the other tasks that are assigned only to the service of men." Madigan and Osiek conclude that this text implies that:

> the functions exercised by women at the altars, therefore, can refer only to the administration of the sacraments, to the liturgical service, and to the public and official announcement of the [gospel] message, all of which comprise the duties of ministerial priesthood... Hence ... Gelasius intended to stigmatize and

---

[72] Quoted from Madigan and Osiek, *Ordained Women*, 182.
[73] As noted in Madigan and Osiek, *Ordained Women*, 182.
[74] Madigan and Osiek, *Ordained Women*, 184–85.

condemn ... [the service of] true and proper presbyters who were performing all the duties traditionally reserved for men alone.[75]

An inscription from southern Italy may provide supporting evidence that women presbyters were active around the same time and in the same place. In other words, the condemnation by Gelasius was a response to actual practices approved by some male bishops and priests. In this inscription "Leta the presbyter[ess]" is commemorated by her husband, who apparently had no ecclesiastical office.[76]

Another inscription testifies that Flavia Vitalia was a presbyter in about 425 in the Roman province of Dalmatia on the Adriatic Sea, in modern Croatia. The only activity mentioned is her right to sell church property. Because her town was relatively near and similar to those addressed by Gelasius, she may be one of the women functioning as a full presbyter or priest.[77]

CONCLUSION

I have tried to show in this chapter that women in the early church ministered in a variety of functions, including the role of apostle, which was for Paul the most authoritative form of activity in the service of God. Furthermore, the condemnations and prohibitions of the official, sometimes ordained ministry of women by councils and synods and in the writings of early Christian male leaders are not absolute. Rather, they are evidence for the existence of practices they attempt to suppress. Finally, the surviving inscriptions provide confirming evidence that these practices were not only going on but that they were approved and recognized by some male leaders and by the people that women served. Opposing the leadership of women in the church today, therefore, goes against Scripture and tradition. It can no longer be said that women cannot be ordained to priestly ministry because the church has never ordained women as priests.

BIBLIOGRAPHY

Berger, Teresa. *Gender Differences and the Making of Liturgical History*. Farnham, Surrey, UK: Ashgate, 2011.

---

[75] Madigan and Osiek, *Ordained Women*, 186–87, following, in part, Giorgio Otranto.
[76] Madigan and Osiek, *Ordained Women*, 193–95. Although Madigan and Osiek connect another inscription, which is from Sicily, with the east because it is in Greek (171), Eisen, *Women Officeholders*, 128–29 connects it with the west and the letter of Gelasius.
[77] Madigan and Osiek, *Ordained Women*, 196. Another inscription from same place mentions a "priestess." Since the inscription includes a cross, it is clearly Christian (197).

Bradshaw, Paul F. *The Search for the Origins of Christian Worship: Sources and Methods for the Study of Early Liturgy*. 2nd ed. Oxford: Oxford University Press, 2002.

Campenhausen, Hans von. *Ecclesiastical Authority and Spiritual Power in the Church of the First Three Centuries*. Translated by J. A. Baker. Stanford: Stanford University Press, 1969.

Collins, John Neil. *Diakonia: Re-Interpreting the Ancient Sources*. Oxford: Oxford University Press, 1990.

Dibelius, Martin. "'Bischöfe' und 'Diakonen' in Philippi." Pages 413–17 in *Das kirchliche Amt im Neuen Testament*. Edited by Karl Kertelge. Wege der Forschung 189. Darmstadt: Wissenschaftliche Buchgesellschaft, 1977.

Eisen, Ute E. *Women Officeholders in Early Christianity: Epigraphical and Literary Studies*. Translated by Linda Maloney. Collegeville, MN: Liturgical Press, 2000.

Epp, Eldon Jay. *Junia: The First Woman Apostle*. Minneapolis: Fortress, 2005.

Filson, Floyd V. "The Significance of the Early House Churches." *JBL* 58 (1939): 105–12.

Georgi, Dieter. *The Opponents of Paul in Second Corinthians*. Philadelphia: Fortress, 1986.

Gielen, Marlis. "Die Wahrnehmung gemeindlicher Leitungsfunktionen durch Frauen im Spiegel der Pastoralbriefe." Pages 129–65 in *Neutestamentliche Ämtermodelle im Kontext*. Edited by Thomas Schmeller, Martin Ebner, and Rudolf Hoppe. QD 239. Freiburg: Herder, 2010.

Grayston, Kenneth. Review of *Diakonia: Re-Interpreting the Ancient Sources* by John N. Collins. *TS* n.s. 43 (1992): 198–200.

Hentschel, Anni. *Diakonia im Neuen Testament*. WUNT 2/226. Tübingen: Mohr Siebeck, 2007.

Herzer, Jens. "Juden—Christen—Gnostiker. Zur Gegnerproblematik der Pastoralbriefe." Pages 143–68 in *Die Entstehung des Christentums aus dem Judentum = Berliner Theologische Zeitschrift* 25 (2008).

Karrer, Martin. "Das urchristliche Ältestenamt." *NovT* 32 (1990): 152–88.

King, Karen L. "Prophetic Power and Women's Authority." Pages 21–41 in *Women Preachers and Prophets through Two Millennia of Christianity*. Edited by Beverly Mayne Kienzle and Pamela J. Walker. Berkeley: University of California Press, 1998.

Klauck, Hans-Josef. *Hausgemeinde und Hauskirche im frühen Christentum*. SBS 103. Stuttgart: Katholisches Bibelwerk, 1981.

Lewis, Charlton T., and Charles Short. *A Latin Dictionary*. Oxford: Clarendon, 1879.

Lietzmann, Hans. "Zur altchristlichen Verfassungsgeschichte." Pages 93–143 in *Das kirchliche Amt im Neuen Testament*. Edited by Karl Kertelge. Wege der Forschung 189. Darmstadt: Wissenschaftliche Buchgesellschaft, 1977.

MacDonald, Margaret Y. *The Pauline Churches: A Socio-Rhetorical Study of Institutionalization in the Pauline and Deutero-Pauline Writings*. SNTSMS 60. Cambridge: Cambridge University Press, 1988.

Madigan, Kevin, and Carolyn Osiek, eds. *Ordained Women in the Early Church: A Documentary History*. Baltimore: Johns Hopkins University Press, 2005.

Maier, Harry O. *The Social Setting of the Ministry as Reflected in the Writings of Hermas, Clement, and Ignatius*. Waterloo, ON: Wilfrid Laurier University Press, 1991.

Meeks, Wayne A. *The First Urban Christians: The Social World of the Apostle Paul*. 2nd ed. New Haven: Yale University Press, 2003.

Merz, Annette. "Phöbe. Diakon(in) der Gemeinde von Kenchreä—eine wichtige Mitstreiterin des Paulus neu entdeckt." Pages 125–40 in *Frauen gestalten Diakonie I. Von der biblischen Zeit bis zum Pietismus*. Edited by Adelheid M. von Hauff. Stuttgart: Kohlhammer, 2007.

Müller, Christoph G. *Frühchristliche Ehepaare und paulinische Mission*. SBS 215. Stuttgart: Katholisches Bibelwerk, 2008.

Neyrey, Jerome H. Review of *Diakonia: Re-Interpreting the Ancient Sources* by John N. Collins. *BTB* 21 (1991): 166–67.

Nicklas, Tobias. "Offices? Roles, Functions: Authorities and Ethos in Earliest Christianity—A Look into the World of Pauline Communities." Pages 23–40 in *Rabbi—Pastor—Priest: Their Roles and Profiles through the Ages*. Edited by Walter Homolka and Heinz-Günther Schöttler. SJ 64. Berlin: de Gruyter, 2013.

Reumann, John. "Church Office in Paul, Especially in Philippians." Pages 82–91 in *Origins and Method: Towards a New Understanding of Judaism and Christianity*. JSNTSup 86. Sheffield: JSOT Press, 1993.

———. "Contributions of the Philippian Community to Paul and to Earliest Christianity." *NTS* 39 (1993): 438–57.

Trible, Phyllis. *God and the Rhetoric of Sexuality*. Philadelphia: Fortress, 1978.

———. *Texts of Terror: Literary-Feminist Readings of Biblical Narratives*. OBT. Philadelphia: Fortress, 1984.

Zamfir, Korinna. *Men and Women in the Household of God: A Contextual Approach to Roles and Ministries in the Pastoral Epistles*. NTOA/SUNT 103. Göttingen: Vandenhoeck & Ruprecht, 2013.

9
Reading Crucifixion Narratives as Texts of Terror

David Tombs

Chapter 3 in Phyllis Trible's *Texts of Terror*—titled "The Unnamed Woman: The Extravagance of Violence"—is a landmark text in feminist biblical scholarship on Judges 19.[1] Trible offers an unflinching discussion of the betrayal, rape, torture, murder, and dismemberment of an unnamed woman. Her term "extravagance" captures the horrifying level of violence unleashed against an innocent victim. Cheryl Exum speaks of the violence as "brutally excessive and offensive."[2]

This chapter starts with Trible's compelling feminist reading of how the text presents the narrative. It then turns to a more recent act of extravagant violence against an unnamed woman, witnessed in the execution of a woman in El Salvador in the early 1980s. Drawing on these two stories of unnamed women, the third section explores the stripping and mocking of Jesus in Matt 27:27–31 as a text of terror. It argues that an approach similar to Trible's reading of Judg 19 in its attention to text, attention to silence, and attention to a possible echo may offer a further perspective on the state terror and sexual violence in the crucifixion.[3] The reading of Matt 27:27–31 explored in the third section is part of a wider attempt to draw upon Latin American liberation theologies and feminist theologies to better understand the crucifixion narratives as accounts of torture and state terror.[4]

---

[1] Phyllis Trible, *Texts of Terror: Literary-Feminist Readings of Biblical Narratives*, OBT (Philadelphia: Fortress, 1984), 65–91.
[2] Cheryl Exum, *Fragmented Women: Feminist (Sub)versions of Biblical Narratives*, JSOTSup 163 (Sheffield: Sheffield Academic, 1993), 170–201, esp. 171.
[3] I am indebted to many colleagues for suggestions and comments on earlier versions, especially to James Harding and Gerald West, who looked at earlier drafts. All errors and omissions are, of course, entirely my own.
[4] David Tombs, "Crucifixion, State Terror, and Sexual Abuse," *USQR* 53 (1999): 89–109; Tombs, "Prisoner Abuse: From Abu Ghraib to The Passion of The Christ," in *Religions and the Politics of Peace and Conflict*, ed. Linda Hogan and Dylan Lehrke, PTMS (Eugene, OR: Wipf and Stock, 2009), 179–205; Tombs, "Silent No More: Sexual Violence in Conflict as

THE EXTRAVAGANCE OF VIOLENCE AGAINST THE UNNAMED WOMAN IN JUDGES 19

Trible describes Judg 19 as "a story we want to forget but are commanded to speak."[5] It "depicts the horrors of male power, brutality, and triumphalism; of female helplessness, abuse, and annihilation."[6] The story itself is quite brief.[7] A Levite, his male assistant, and his concubine (פילגש, *pilegesh*) stop for a night in the town of Gibeah (Judg 19:1).[8] They have left Bethlehem and are travelling north, back to the hill country of Ephraim.[9] Because their departure from

---

a Challenge to the Worldwide Church," *AcT* 3 (2014): 142–60; Tombs, "Lived Religion and the Intolerance of the Cross," in *Lived Religion and Politics of (In)tolerance*, ed. Ruard Ganzevoort and Srdjan Sremac, Palgrave Studies in Lived Religion and Societal Changes (London: Palgrave Macmillan, 2017), 63–83.

[5] Trible, *Texts*, 65.

[6] Trible, *Texts*, 65.

[7] For commentary and analysis since *Texts of Terror*, see esp. Koala Jones-Warsaw, "Toward a Womanist Hermeneutic: A Reading of Judges 19–21" (172–86), Peggy Kamuf, "Author of a Crime" (187–207), and Mieke Bal, "A Body of Writing: Judges 19" (208–30), all in Athalya Brenner, ed., *Feminist Companion to Judges*, Feminist Companion to the Bible 4 (Sheffield: Sheffield Academic, 1993). See also Alice A. Keefe, "Rapes of Women/Wars of Men," *Semeia* 61 (1993): 79–97; Ken Stone, *Sex, Honor and Power in the Deuteronomistic History*, JSOTSup 234 (Sheffield: Sheffield Academic, 1996); Frank M. Yamada, *Configurations of Rape in the Hebrew Bible: A Literary Analysis of Three Rape Narratives* (New York: Lang, 2008); Susan Niditch, *Judges: A Commentary*, OTL (Louisville: Westminster John Knox, 2008); Susanne Scholz, *Sacred Witness: Rape in the Hebrew Bible* (Minneapolis: Fortress, 2010); Kjell Renato Lings, *Love Lost in Translation: Homosexuality and the Bible* (Bloomington, IN: Trafford, 2013), 445–85; James Harding, "Homophobia and Masculine Domination in Judges 19–21," *The Bible and Critical Theory* 12 (2016): 41–71.

[8] Trible, *Texts*, 65 notes the marked contrast between the high-status Levite and the low-status concubine. The woman is doubly disadvantaged as a woman in a patriarchal society, and as a concubine rather than a wife. As a concubine, she "is not the equivalent of a wife but is virtually a slave, secured by a man for his own Purposes." Most commentators speak of the "Levite's concubine" or just "the concubine," which might be taken as uncritically accepting her social situation and its patriarchal values. Subsequent work has also questioned how the woman's status as *pilegesh* is to be understood; see Bal, "Body." Exum, *Fragmented Women*, 177 describes her as "a legal wife of secondary rank." Trible's decision to refer to the *pilegesh* primarily as the "unnamed woman" resists both reducing the woman to her position in relation to the Levite and the social conventions on the inferior worth of a concubine. Exum, *Fragmented Women*, 176 takes an alternative approach and gives the woman the imagined name of Bath-sheber "the daughter of breaking."

[9] The woman was from Bethlehem (Judg 19:1) and had been in Bethlehem for four months visiting her father (19:2). The Levite had come to take her home and had received hospitality from his father-in-law for three days. On the fourth day, the Levite planned for

Bethlehem was delayed, they are unable to complete the journey in one day. They know they must find a safe place to stay the night. The Levite decides not to stop at Jebus (Jerusalem) because he does not want to stay in a city of foreigners. They press on to the Benjaminite city of Gibeah and reach it at sunset. They do not initially find anyone who offers to take them in for the night, but they are eventually given shelter by an old man who is returning from his fields at the end of the day. Like the Levite, the old man is an Ephraimite and thus an outsider in Gibeah. He welcomes them with words of peace, but there is also a hint of foreboding in his message: "And the old man said, 'Peace be to you; I will care for all your wants; only, do not spend the night in the square'" (19:20).

After the host and the Levite take bread and wine, a crowd of men from the city surround the house and pound on the door. They demand that the Levite be brought out and handed over to them so that they can "know" him. The host, the old man, refuses their demand and implores them not to treat a guest in this vile way. He offers to bring out instead his own virgin daughter and the Levite's concubine, and tells the men: "Ravish them and do with them what seems good to you; but against this man do not do so vile a thing." (Judg 19:24, RSV).[10] The men of Gibeah do not listen, so the Levite seizes his concubine and "put her out to them; and they knew her, and abused her all night until the morning. And as the dawn began to break, they let her go" (Judg 19:25c). When the Levite gets up to leave the next morning, he finds her lying at the threshold of the house. He tells her to get up so they can go, but she gives no response. He puts her on his donkey and takes her back to his house in Ephraim. When he gets home, he takes a knife and divides her limb by limb. He then sends her body throughout Israel as a summons to the tribes (Judg 19:29).

---

them to leave, but his father-in-law sucessfully pressed him to stay (19:5–6). On the fifth day, the Levite got up early, but once again his father-in-law encouraged him to stay. However, in the afternoon the Levite decided to leave, despite his father-in-law pointing to the late hour (19:8–10).

[10] This is the first mention of the daughter. Like the unnamed woman, the host's daughter is also unnamed and is not recorded as speaking at any point. It is usually assumed that the actions of the Levite mean that she escapes being handed over to the crowd. It is true that there is no mention of her being handed over or of what happens to her. It is not impossible, however, that, just as the Levite hands over the unnamed woman, the host also hands over his unnamed daughter. This is, after all, what he has offered to do. There is no mention of this, but the narrative is focused on the Levite and the unnamed woman, and the unnamed daughter is largely marginal to this. The text does not rule out the possibility that the unnamed daughter suffers a similar fate, but the narrator shows so little interest in this that it is not included in the narrative.

Mieke Bal describes Judg 19 as "the most horrible story of the Hebrew Bible."[11] There are other passages in which sexual violence and bloodshed are more widespread, but none in which they are depicted in such graphic and confronting detail. In addition to the extravagant violence of the passage itself, it precipitates a much wider sequence of violence and rape. In the remaining two chapters of Judges (20–21), the violence spreads.

Trible points out that, despite the extravagance of the violence in Judg 19 and the bloodshed and violence that follow it, the story was largely ignored and typically met with an "overwhelming silence" prior to her work.[12] Commentaries included the passage but did not problematize the story. They passed by "on the other side" when faced by the rape and dismemberment. In the years since, an extensive feminist literature on Judg 19 has developed. In retrospect, *Texts of Terror* and other feminist work of this period contributed to a decisive shift in the willingness to confront sexual and gender-based violence. Even so, there is still considerable work to be done in exposing the ways in which biblical interpretation can normalize and sustain rape culture.[13]

The intention of this chapter is to identify three important strands of Trible's close reading that might be extended to other biblical texts, starting with her detailed attention to text, in both its content and its form. Second, we will examine Trible's attention to the silences within the text and the gaps to which these silences might point. Third, we will consider Trible's ear for textual echoes and resonances that might serve as subtle signs and witness to deeper layers beneath the surface. Trible's ground-breaking work in each of these strands in Judg 19 will serve in the third section of this chapter as a model for addressing sexual violence in Matt 27:27–31.

ATTENTION TO THE TEXT

Trible's reading of Judg 19 seeks to recover as much as possible from all the characters involved in the narrative. It is especially attentive to the experiences of the unnamed woman. She is marginalized and obscured by the narrator, and this exclusion can be further compounded in subsequent readings that fail to recognize it. Trible gives particular attention to the agency of the woman and the ways in

---

[11] Bal, "Body," 209.
[12] Trible, *Texts*, 86.
[13] For a wider discussion of issues in reading rape and sexual violence in biblical texts, see esp. the recent collection by Caroline Blyth, Emily Colgan, and Katie Edwards, eds., *Rape Culture, Gender Violence and Religion: Biblical Perspectives* (London: Palgrave Macmillan, 2018), as well as the accompanying volumes Blyth, Colgan, and Edwards, eds., *Rape Culture, Gender Violence and Religion: Christian Perspectives* (London: Palgrave Macmillan, 2018) and Blyth, Colgan, and Edwards, eds., *Rape Culture, Gender Violence and Religion: Interdisciplinary Perspectives* (London: Palgrave Macmillan, 2018).

which her agency is taken from her. Trible's eye for literary features opens up the density and layers of the story.[14] Her careful reading takes the time to investigate and spell out the significance of textual details. Many of these are missed or unnoticed in a more hurried reading. For example, Trible notes the implication in the Levite's ingratiating speech to the old man: the Levite's words "your maidservant" refer to the woman in a way that suggests she is not just property, but that she will become the old man's property for the night, as his maidservant rather than the servant of the Levite (Judg 19:19).[15] This might simply be a mark of a guest's respect and appreciation of hospitality. But it could also be read as a troubling offer of the woman's sexual service, and a sign of how readily this is normalized in the narrative as a transaction between the two men.

Trible's close examination of Judg 19:25c is particularly significant in her attention to the language of violence. She notes:

> Reporting the crime, the narrator appropriates the vocabulary of the wicked men of the city who wished to know the male guest. "And they knew [יד״ע] her" (19:25c). In this context "to know" loses all ambiguity. It means rape, and it parallels a verb connoting ruthless abuse. "And they raped [יד״ע] her and tortured [על״ל] her all night until the morning" (19:25d). These third-person plural verbs and the time reference guarantee that the crime was not a single deed but rather multiple acts of violence.[16]

As Trible notes, there is no question that the root יד״ע is sexual in this context, even though the RSV uses the term "knew." The combination of "raped and tortured" presents the rapes within a prolonged, intentional, and brutal mistreatment of her body. It fits with a feminist analysis of rape as about power rather than just sex. The root על״ל is usually translated into English as abused (NRSV, RSV, KJV, NIV). In the Septuagint, it is translated by the Greek *enepaixan* (ἐνέπαιξαν), which is typically translated as "mocked" or "made fun of." Trible's translation of על״ל as "tortured" rather than "abused" or "mocked" is unusual but appropriate. The choice of "torture" underscores the severity of the abuse, the extravagance of the violence as multiple acts. "Raped and abused" might be read as nearly synonymous words for the men's actions in raping her, and this might in turn encourage a focus on the men's sexual gratification, but Trible's use of "tortured" points to the disturbing truth. The key to the passage is the display of terror, which communicates male power through extravagant violence.

The connection between rape and torture implied here deserves more attention and has been a focus of my own research for many years. Rape and torture

---

[14] Phyllis Trible, *God and the Rhetoric of Sexuality* (Philadelphia: Fortress, 1978).
[15] Trible, *Texts*, 72.
[16] Trible, *Texts*, 76.

are intimately connected in Judg 19 and in many other contexts.[17] The emphasis is not on sexual pleasure but on power, subjugation, and humiliation. The implication of יד״ע and על״ל is that, regardless of any gratification the men of Gibeah derive from the rape, their actions have to be understood in terms of violence, not passion. The rapes serve to torture the unnamed woman throughout the night—to mock and humiliate. In the process, the men of Gibeah also mocked and humiliated the old man and the Levite. The men of Gibeah rape the woman because they have been prevented from raping the Levite. One reading of Judg 19 is that the conflict is between the men, and the men of Gibeah wish to signal that the Ephraimite and the Levite do not belong in Benjamin.[18] When they are frustrated in their designs on the Levite, they turn to the woman instead. The intertribal conflict that follows (Judg 19–21) suggests this wider dimension of tribal hostility in Judg 19.[19] However, recognition of sexual violence as part of male tribal conflict should not detract from or displace the sense of horror evoked by the violence against the woman.

Research on torture reports, truth commissions, and human rights documentation from many different parts of the world makes clear that torture has a devastating and long-standing impact on the individual victim.[20] Just as importantly, torture impacts a wider audience because it sends a wider public message of terror, threat, and fear.[21] Sexual violence is common in torture, and it communicates the public message in an especially powerful way. The frequency of sexual violence in torture and its use to terrorize may at first seem so obvious that they barely deserve to be remarked upon. Even so, the way in which Trible brings sexual violence and torture together so clearly and explicitly in her translation of Judg 19:25 is an important reminder of their close connection and common purpose, and this will be discussed later in relation to crucifixion.

---

[17] There is no need to think that Judg 19:25 is suggesting that the woman was first raped (יד״ע) and then tortured (על״ל), as if she might have been tortured after the rape in some other way. It is more appropriate to see the narrator as presenting the rape and the torture as one activity. The rape is the torture, and the torture is the rape.

[18] As Exum, *Fragmented Women*, 182 points out, this does not mean that the men of Gibeah are homosexuals. The rape of the Levite would have forced him into the passive role and into the position of the woman.

[19] Stone, *Sex, Honor and Power*; Harding, "Homophobia."

[20] Elaine Scarry, *The Body in Pain: The Making and Unmaking of the World* (Oxford: Oxford University Press, 1985) explores the pyschological impact of torture and how it works to unmake the world of the victim. Sexual violence can be an especially effective instrument to do this.

[21] Tombs, "Crucifixion," 90–92.

NOTICING THE SILENCES

Trible devotes as much care to what the text does not say, where it remains silent, as she does to the structure of the text and its language. She looks for what is missing or unspoken in the text and offers insight into the gaps and their importance. In particular, she recognizes that the men speak throughout the story, but the woman does not.[22] Trible recalls that the intention of the Levite in going to Bethlehem is "to speak to the heart of his concubine" (Judg 19:3). Yet he has not spoken to her when he arrives in Gibeah. Instead, he has directed his attention to the other men, including his father-in-law, his male attendant, and now the old man.[23] When the Levite and the old man agree on staying the night, the men speak to each other but ignore the woman. They do not ask her opinion or whether she agrees. Trible notices that her exclusion from the table can be seen as a harbinger of the even greater lack of concern for her later in the narrative; their failure to consider her wishes in where to stop is also a telling indication of their outlook. When faced by a hostile crowd, the men will sacrifice her without much thought for the consequences.

Trible likewise notices that the unnamed woman appears to be excluded from the hospitality when the two men sit down to eat (Judg 19:6, 8).[24] This is another clear sign that the woman is marginalized and less important than the male characters. Without stating it explicitly, the silence in the text underlines the relationships between her and the men. At this stage in the narrative, the reader might not notice this silent reminder of her inferior standing, but a few verses later the significance of her lower status will become obvious and all-important.

Noticing the silences in the text as well as what is explicit also involves being attentive to what is foregrounded and what is minimized or ignored. For example, Trible contrasts the relatively detailed accounts of the Levite's time with the woman's father, even the evening in Gibeah before the crowd arrive, compared to the very short space given to the attack on the woman. In contrast to the extended description of male carousing and conversation, the description of the all-night rape of the woman is highly compressed and reported with minimal detail.[25]

Perhaps the most disturbing silence is the lack of certainty in the text about whether the Levite finds the woman already dead at the doorway the next morning, whether he finds her alive but she dies on the journey, or whether she makes it home alive but then dies at his hands when he dismembers her with the knife. No matter which reading one might favor, his betrayal of her has led to her death. Even so, Trible's attention to detail shows how the text might work to cover the

---

[22] Trible, *Texts*, 66.
[23] Trible, *Texts*, 73.
[24] Trible, *Texts*, 68–69.
[25] Trible, *Texts*, 76.

possibility that she is alive when he takes the knife. The Septuagint and the Vulgate make clear that the woman is already dead, whereas the Hebrew wording is more ambiguous. When the tribes gather at Mizpah, the Levite says: "They meant to kill me, and they ravished my concubine, and she is dead" (Judg 20:5b RSV). As Trible notes, he omits his own role in the violence against the woman. She suggests that "his carefully phrased admission, 'she is dead,' rather than, 'they killed her,' reinforces the suspicion that he is murderer as well as betrayer."[26]

In either case, the silence of the Levite when he finds the woman at the door is a truly shocking silence. He does not ask her what she needs, or how he might help. Nor does he ask anything at all about what has happened. He only tells her to get up. The Levite is the first in a long line of people who will say nothing and ask nothing about her experience.

LISTENING FOR TEXTUAL ECHOES

Trible's work on the unnamed woman not only pays close attention to presences and silences in the text, it also shows how echoes of other texts may be heard and prove relevant to reading Judg 19. Some echoes might be obvious to anyone who is familiar with biblical narrative. Others may be less obvious to the general reader but clear to an exegete. Still other possible echoes may be faint and uncertain even to a trained and experienced reader, who can do no more than ask if they might be present.

When the host responds to the men beating on the door by offering his daughter and the unnamed woman, there is a clear and obvious parallel to the men of Sodom in Gen 19:1–29. Any reader who is familiar with Gen 19 is likely to immediately sense the threat and menace. As Trible puts it: "To those familiar with the traditions of Ancient Israel, terrible memories surface."[27] When the Levite returns to his house in Ephraim and takes the knife, an echo with the earlier sacrifice of Isaac (Gen 22:10) may be less obvious. Yet, as Trible notes, Judg 19:29 and Gen 22:10 are the only texts within the Hebrew Bible that share this precise vocabulary.[28] This verbal echo has further importance because, when Abraham takes the knife, he intends to slay his son until an angel stops him. It is possible that, when the Levite "took the knife," he not only intended to slay the concubine but went through with his plan. As noted above, Trible points out that the Greek of the Septuagint rules out such a possibility, but the Hebrew text keeps it open.[29] For Trible, the unique parallel to the action of Abraham encourages this reading

---

[26] Trible, *Texts*, 82.
[27] Trible, *Texts*, 74.
[28] Trible, *Texts*, 80. The phrase is ויקח את המאכלת.
[29] Trible, *Texts*, 80.

of the Hebrew.[30] She concludes: "Perhaps the purpose in taking the knife, to slay the victim, is not specified here because indeed it does happen. The narrator, however, protects his protagonist through ambiguity."[31]

These echoes and resonances are particularly important because they are not straightforward or explicit, yet they can dramatically change how the passage is understood. Even though an echo may be quiet, the interpretation of a passage can hinge decisively on whether an echo is heard and how it is then interpreted. Viewed alongside the other two techniques of close reading, pausing to listen for possible echoes is important because echoes occupy the gap between what is said and what is not said. They offer a third alternative for the reader to consider, which links what is explicit with what is left unspoken.

EXTRAVAGANT VIOLENCE AGAINST A HEALTH WORKER IN EL SALVADOR

Sexual violence can intimidate and terrorize, and it can be used in armed conflicts to send a powerful public message to a much wider audience. To this end, sexual violence may be enacted in public as an intentional spectacle. This "spectacular violence" involves both extravagance and the spectacle of a public performance. The specific act of spectacular violence that prompted the reading of crucifixion discussed in the next section took place in El Salvador during its twelve-year conflict (1980–1991). However, it is not hard to find tales of similarly extravagant sexual violence in other recent conflicts.[32] In 2004, photos of the abuses at Abu Ghraib were seen around the world.[33] Reports from other conflicts make clear that sexual violence is a common experience in conflict and is often inflicted on an extravagant scale. Recent examples include Bosnia, Rwanda, the Democratic Republic of Congo, Syria, Sri Lanka, Burma, and many other countries.[34]

---

[30] The sacrifice of Jephthah's daughter in Judg 11 comes to mind and is the subject of the following chapter of Trible, *Texts*, 93–106.
[31] Trible, *Texts*, 80.
[32] On the prevalence of rape in First and Second World Wars, the conflict in Bangladesh (1971), and US involvement in Vietnam (1965–1975), see esp. Susan Brownmiller, *Against Our Will: Men, Women and Rape* (New York: Simon and Schuster, 1975), 31–113.
[33] Tombs, "Prisoner Abuse."
[34] Helsinki Watch, *War Crimes in the Bosnia-Herzegovina: A Helsinki Watch Report*, 2 vols. (New York: Human Rights Watch, 1992–1993); Human Rights Watch, *Shattered Lives: Sexual Violence during the Rwandan Genocide and Its Aftermath* (New York: Human Rights Watch, 1996); Human Rights Watch, *Soldiers Who Rape, Commanders Who Condone: Sexual Violence and Military Reform in the Democratic Republic of Congo* (New York: Human Rights Watch, 2009); Human Rights Watch, *Syria: Sexual Assault in Detention* (New York: Human Rights Watch, 2012); Human Rights Watch, *"We Will Teach You a Lesson": Sexual Violence against Tamils by Sri Lankan*

The Salvadoran teenager Brenda Sánchez-Galan testifies to a horrific execution she witnessed during El Salvador's conflict.[35] She worked as an assistant in a medical center for refugees near the capital, San Salvador. During the war, the Salvadoran military committed widespread human rights abuses against civilians. The medical center was supported by the Lutheran church, and the military accused the church of supporting political reforms. At one point, the military arrested the medical center's doctor and tortured him for six months. He was eventually released, following pressure from the Swiss embassy. The security forces then targeted his assistants. One night, soldiers abducted one of Sánchez-Galan's coworkers. They tortured and raped her at the national guard headquarters. The next morning, the soldiers brought her out into the town square. A soldier placed his machine gun into her rectum and shot her in front of the assembled group.

After the execution, Sánchez-Galan and her daughter sought refuge with the Lutheran church, which helped them move to safety in Mexico City, and then to Texas, where she was able to tell her story. She was one of the first Salvadoran refugees on a modern form of the Underground Railroad to be arrested in the United States in 1984. The name of the murdered health worker is not preserved in these accounts. As in Judg 19, she is an unnamed woman who endured extravagant violence.

I first read this story in 1997, when I was doing doctoral research on Latin American liberation theology in El Salvador.[36] Reading the story made a strong impression.[37] During the 1990s, conflict-related sexual violence was receiving greater international media attention following the ethnic cleansing in Bosnia and genocide in Rwanda. Even though sexual violence was widespread and well known in El Salvador, it seemed that the story told by Sánchez-Galan did not received the attention it merited. In particular, it was strangely absent from

---

Security Forces (New York: Human Rights Watch, 2013); and Human Rights Watch, *"All of My Body Was Pain": Sexual Violence against Rohingya Women and Girls in Burma* (New York: Human Rights Watch, 2017).

[35] The account here is based on Renny Golden and Michael McConnell, *Sanctuary: The New Underground Railway* (Maryknoll, NY: Orbis Books, 1986), 64–65.

[36] The story is quoted in Christian Smith, *Resisting Reagan: The U.S. Central America Peace Movement* (Chicago: University of Chicago Press, 1996), 53.

[37] I first visited El Salvador in 1988, following a graduate year studying liberation theologies at Union Theological Seminary. During the year at Union, I was a member of the Seminary's Taskforce on Central America and took a keen interest in US support for the military regimes. While working at the University of Roehampton and studying part-time on my PhD at Heythrop College, University of London, I made further visits to El Salvador in 1996 and 1999. See David Tombs, "Jesus as a Victim of Sexual Abuse," interview with Rosie Dawson, The Shiloh Podcast, March 24, 2021, https://tinyurl.com/pajzmht8.

theological reflections, even from the otherwise powerful and inspiring work of liberation theologians in Latin America.[38]

This prompted me to take a research detour and investigate the role of sexual violence in state terror in more depth. I hoped to understand both what motivated such an act of sexual violence and why it did not receive more attention in theological works. What I thought would be a relatively short tangent soon became a long-term interest.[39] To understand the story, I was drawn into reading torture reports and truth commission publications documenting a wide range of abuses during military dictatorships and repressive regimes in Brazil, Chile, Uruguay, Argentina, El Salvador, and Guatemala during the 1970s and 1980s.

My first opportunity to present what I had found was at the Society of Biblical Literature International Meeting in Kraków in 1998.[40] I was presenting in the section on biblical hermeneutics, and I originally intended to extend work I had done a few years earlier on general principles of liberationist hermeneutics in Latin America.[41] The paper I had proposed was a study of how Latin American liberationist biblical hermeneutics evolved in a sequential process from 1968 to 1998 in response to the changing social context of each decade. However, I decided instead to offer an example of liberationist biblical hermeneutics by reading a text in light of a specific context. I spoke about how a liberationist reading of the crucifixion might be informed by a contextual awareness of Latin American state terror and torture practices. The paper was well received and subsequently published in the *Union Seminary Quarterly Review* in 1999.[42]

My central contention was that there is clear and explicit biblical evidence for the repeated stripping and exposure of Jesus before a cohort of soldiers in the *praetorium*, followed by naked exposure before the crowd at crucifixion. This punitive stripping and forced nudity deserve to be recognized as sexual abuse. Roman practice comes into clearer focus when read alongside contemporary testimonies

---

[38] David Tombs, *Latin American Liberation Theology*, Religion in the Americas Series 1 (Leiden: Brill, 2002).
[39] David Tombs, "Honour, Shame and Conquest: Male Identity, Sexual Violence and the Body Politic," *Journal of Hispanic/Latino Theology* 9 (2002): 21–40.
[40] The influence of liberation theology in shaping the insights behind the chapter is discussed in David Tombs, "The Ongoing Legacy of Liberation Theology," Inaugural Professorial Lecture, University of Otago, September 8, 2015, https://tinyurl.com/7mv4v5z4.
[41] David Tombs, "The Hermeneutics of Liberation," in *Approaches to New Testament Study*, ed. Stanley E. Porter and David Tombs, JSNTSup 120 (Sheffield: Sheffield Academic, 1995), 310–55.
[42] Tombs, "Crucifixion." For a retrospective response and reflection on the paper, see Fernando F. Segovia, "Jesus as Victim of State Terror: A Critical Reflection Twenty Years Later," in *Crucifixion, State Terror, and Sexual Abuse: Text and Context*, ed. David Tombs (Dunedin: University of Otago, Centre for Theology and Public Issues, 2018), 22–31.

of stripping and forced nudity during torture. The chapter draws on examples from Latin America in the 1970s and 1980s, but these torture practices are global and in no way limited either to Latin America or to the past. Revelations from Abu Ghraib and ongoing torture reports from many other countries have underlined this in the twenty years since the chapter was published.[43]

The chapter not only names Jesus as a victim of sexual abuse on account of the stripping but also considers the possibility that Jesus may have experienced rape or sexual assault. Because this possibility is not explicitly attested in the text, it lacks the evidence that one can more easily marshall for the stripping. Nonetheless, we should acknowledge the possibility, and the question deserves to be asked even if it cannot be answered with certainty. Yet biblical scholarship has largely avoided the issue and kept silent about what else might have followed from it.

MATTHEW 27:27–31: THE MOCKING OF JESUS IN THE *PRAETORIUM*

Texts of Terror might be read in a number of places as inviting a christological perspective on the unnamed woman. Trible uses phrases to describe the unnamed woman that clearly echo christological language. For example, she writes: "Truly, the hour is at hand, and the woman is betrayed into the hands of sinners," which recalls Mark 14:41. "No one within comes to her aid. They have fallen away in the darkness of night" likewise references Mark 14:26–42.[44] Trible adds: "Of all the characters in scripture, she is the least" and, like a eucharist, "her body has been broken and given to many."[45] However, Trible also explicitly cautions against a christological reading of Judg 19 and warns of the dangers this poses to the text.[46] Taking this warning to heart, it should be emphasized that what follows is not intended in the first instance as an attempt to read Christology into the violence against the unnamed woman.[47] Instead, it explores reading in the other direction. How might Trible's approach to Judg 19 shed light on ways to

---

[43] The original version of the chapter, Tombs, "Crucifixion, State Terror, and Sexual Abuse," did not include the disturbing story from Sánchez-Galan that initially prompted the research. At the time, the details seemed too graphic, so I drew my examples of state terror and sexual violence from other sources.

[44] Trible, *Texts*, 76.

[45] Trible, *Texts*, 80 and 81.

[46] Trible is particularly concerned that resurrection is not offered as a cheap resolution of the problems raised by the text. How resurrection is to be understood in relation to the account of crucifixion offered below is a critical question but beyond the scope of the present chapter.

[47] Drawing on Matt 25, it might be possible to make a christological reading that seeks to avoid the risks that Trible identifies, but this would be a separate task.

understand the crucifixion of Jesus as an act of terror? There is an inevitable risk that this hermeneutical approach may compound the woman's erasure by eliding her suffering into the suffering of Jesus, but acknowledging this danger and recognizing Trible's concerns at least serves as a warning. Our goal is not to turn attention away from the unnamed woman, but to explore whether elements in her story might also be found in a different text of terror.

READING THE TEXTS ON STRIPPING

Sexual violence in the stripping of Jesus is an element of the crucifixion that is strangely hidden in plain sight.[48] The stripping is explicitly recorded in the text, especially in Mark 15:16–24 and Matt 27:27–31.[49] Yet Christian memory tends to be so sanitized that the stripping is rarely named in ways that make the sexual violence clear.[50] Matthew 27:27–31 presents a brief but dense summary of the mockery in the *praetorium*:

> [27] Then the soldiers of the governor took Jesus into the governor's headquarters, and they gathered the whole cohort around him. [28] They stripped him and put a scarlet robe on him, [29] and after twisting some thorns into a crown, they put it on his head. They put a reed in his right hand and knelt before him and mocked him, saying, "Hail, King of the Jews!" [30] They spat on him, and took the reed and struck him on the head. [31] After mocking him, they stripped him of the robe and put his own clothes on him. Then they led him away to crucify him.

It is easy to read this and either not notice or not focus on the way Jesus is stripped in verse 28, mocked in verse 29, and stripped again in verse 31a. Because the Roman practice was to strip victims and crucify them naked, verse 31b also points

---

[48] It is still very unusual for the stripping to be named as sexual abuse. One important exception to this silence is Michael Trainor, *The Body of Jesus and Sexual Abuse: How the Gospel Passion Narrative Informs a Pastoral Approach* (Melbourne: Morning Star Publishing; Eugene, OR: Wipf & Stock, 2014).

[49] The traditional stages in the Stations of the Cross include the stripping of Jesus (at the cross rather than in the *praetorium*) as the tenth station. If a station were devoted to the stripping in the *praetorium* (rather than at the cross) it would come as the second station. The alternative sequence, the Scriptural Way of the Cross, introduced by Pope John Paul II on Good Friday 1991, omits the stripping and has the tenth station as "Jesus is crucified." The revised sequence seeks to align the stations with what is attested in Scripture, because the third, fourth, sixth, seventh, and ninth stations of the traditional sequence are not specifically attested. It is unclear why the stripping at the cross is not preserved as the tenth station, nor the stripping at the *praetorium* included as an earlier station.

[50] For a brief overview on seeing a sexual dimension to the stripping, see Katie B. Edwards and David Tombs, "#HimToo: Why Jesus Should Be Recognised as a Victim of Sexual Violence," *The Conversation*, March 23, 2018, https://tinyurl.com/kz2mmsjt.

to a third stripping to come. This is indicated in Matt 27:35, when Jesus's clothes are divided at the cross. This amounts to Jesus being stripped three times in Matt 27:27–35. In addition, because Jesus is flogged in verse 26, and Roman practice was to strip a victim for flogging, it is quite possible that Jesus was stripped for flogging and then stripped again for the scarlet robe. Matthew 27:26–31 can therefore be read as recording four separate acts of stripping in quick succession. Two of these are explicitly recorded (Matt 27:28 and 31a), and the other two are strongly implied in the flogging (Matt 27:26) and crucifixion (Matt 27:31).[51] It is not explicitly stated whether the stripping involved full nakedness. One or more of the earlier acts of stripping might not have left him fully naked, but there is little reason to think that Jesus was not fully naked on the cross. Most scholars see full nakedness as the standard Roman custom.[52] Because the purpose of crucifixion was to humiliate and shame a victim, as well as to end their life, it is unlikely that the Romans would have preserved the modesty of this prisoner.[53]

Roman torturers used sexual violence to demonstrate power. The Romans were highly sensitive about bodily integrity and inviolability as essential marks of masculinity.[54] A Roman man was expected to have control over his own body, as well as the bodies of all in his household, at all times. This meant it was permissible for a Roman man to breach the bodies of his female or male slaves if he saw fit, either through physical punishment or in sexual service. Such violence upheld and reinforced Roman notions of the power and control of a true Roman citizen. It was deeply shameful for a Roman man to have his body violated or penetrated. Because stripping involved the exposure of vulnerability, it was a serious violation of bodily integrity. Regardless of what might happen next, stripping a man against his wishes was viewed as a shameful violation in its own right.[55]

Control of the body was of central importance. There was nothing exceptional or shameful in a man disrobing himself in an appropriate place and by his own volition. Roman men regularly went naked in the public baths and might also

---

[51] Mark 15:16–24 suggests three strippings.
[52] For a consideration of the evidence, see Raymond E. Brown, *Death of the Messiah*, 2 vols, ABRL (New York: Doubleday, 1994), 953.
[53] Tombs, "Lived Religion," 63–83.
[54] Kenneth J. Dover, *Greek Homosexuality* (Cambridge: Harvard University Press, 1978); Eva Cantarella, *Bisexuality in the Ancient World*, trans. Cormac Ó Cuilleanáin (New Haven: Yale University Press, 1992); Judith P. Hallett and Marilyn. B. Skinner, eds., *Roman Sexualities* (Princeton: Princeton University Press, 1997); Craig A. Williams, *Roman Homosexuality: Ideologies of Masculinity in Classical Antiquity* (New York and Oxford: Oxford University Press, 1999). See also Richard C. Trexler, *Sex and Conquest: Gendered Violence, Political Order and the European Conquest of the Americas* (Ithaca, NY: Cornell University Press, 1995), 14–15.
[55] For further discussion, see Jayme R. Reaves, David Tombs, and Rocio Figueroa, eds., *"When Did We See You Naked?": Jesus as a Victim of Sexual Abuse* (London: SCM, 2021).

be naked for some sports. As long as his nakedness was his own choice—and took place in a socially appropriate context—it was not shameful. For a man to be naked and to be seen naked by others was okay as long as he was still clearly in control of his own body and its boundaries. He had to maintain the decorum appropriate to the inviolable male body. However, for one's body to be under the control of another man (or of a woman) was a sign of truly shameful servility. Precisely because of the significance and symbolism of physical inviolability in Roman eyes, stripping another man in public and exposing him as naked was a hugely significant act. Stripping and exposure demonstrated his sexual vulnerability and his lack of power and status. Stripping can also, of course, prepare the way for further physical violation.[56] But, even if further violation did not actually follow, forced nakedness was still deeply humiliating and a degrading attack on male identity.

In historical context, the repeated stripping and forced nudity of Jesus in Matt 27:27–31 cannot be dismissed as an incidental detail. It ought to be named as sexual abuse or sexual violence. This is not just a matter of using the appropriate contemporary term. The naming is necessary if we are to understand how both the Romans and Jews would have understood what was happening and what is clearly presented in the text. Having this understanding in mind is important because it raises further questions about where the text may be silent, and whether there might be further clues about sexual violence in crucifixion, which are easy to miss.

READING THE SILENCE

Stripping is often mentioned in contemporary torture reports as a distinct stage in the torture process.[57] It frequently marks a crucial transition from more generic beating and physical violence to more specifically sexual forms of violence. The significance of stripping during torture is twofold. First, it is a form of sexual abuse in and of itself. Second, it commonly serves as an initial step that is followed by other physical forms of sexual abuse. The mention of stripping in a torture report thus often serves as a clue that subsequent torture may have taken a sexual form, even when these are not explicitly mentioned. This is true for both male and female prisoners.

Public humiliation through sexual violence against political prisoners is an appropriate vantage point from which to view the crucifixion narrative. When Jesus is mocked by the soldiers in the privacy of the *praetorium* in Matt 27, the soldiers are said to put a scarlet robe on him (verse 28), twist thorns into a crown and put it on his head (verse 29a), put a reed in his right hand and kneel before

---

[56] Trexler, *Sex and Conquest*.
[57] See, e.g., Human Rights Watch, *"We Will Teach You a Lesson."*

him, and mock him as "King of the Jews!" (verse 29b). After that, they spit on him and strike him on the head with the reed (verse 30), before they finally lead him away (verse 31).

Beyond the obvious abuse of the stripping, nothing in the passage explicitly suggests that the abuse involved further sexual assault. However, it is hard to avoid the impression that something may be missing. With the "whole cohort" of soldiers assembled, it sounds like something dramatic is expected (Matt 27:27). Whole (ὅλην, *holen*) is emphatic and implies that everyone was gathered. A cohort (σπεῖραν, *speiran*) is at least five hundred soldiers. The mockery in the *praetorium* is not the spontaneous actions of a few soldiers but an organized spectacle in front of a powerful and hostile force.

Read in the context of Roman practice, Matthew's account of the *praetorium* invites a hermeneutic of suspicion. It is possible that the mockery involved more mistreatment than the text records. Given the reticence in biblical passages to describe sexual violence against male victims, it is quite possible that something more happened but is left unstated. The pressure to be silent and self-censor would presumably have been particularly strong when writing about Jesus. If Jesus was raped or experienced some other form of sexual assault after being stripped, it is not very surprising that this is not explicitly recorded in the text.

One of the challenges in reading a silence responsibly is to avoid circular argument. The silence cannot be read as evidence that something more took place, but neither should it be seen as definitive evidence that nothing happened. One way to judge how probable or improbable a particular interpretation of the silence might be is to consider the indirect evidence offered by the wider context. Although there is no direct evidence within the text, the experiences of other prisoners and their stories of mistreatment and abuse offer a form of indirect evidence from the ancient world.

The Romans, Greeks, Persians, and Assyrians all used sexual violence to punish their enemies. In the *Gorgias*, Plato alludes to the punishment of a man who sought to make himself a despot. It includes castration and having his eyes burnt out, along with other torments, prior to crucifixion or burning in a coat of pitch.[58] Plato's example is for the sake of argument, but his account of these grievous torments is so brief that he did not need to explain it. Prisoners in contemporary conflicts likewise testify to a wide range of sexual abuses that typically follow being stripped. These are not strange or unusual; they are common practice, and they are commonly silenced or underreported. If they are reported at all, it is often only euphemistically or indirectly.

---

[58] Plato, *Gorgias* 473c. See also the mention of crucifixion in Plato, *Republic* 362a, which mentions branding irons on the eyes and other extreme suffering before crucifixion.

Any assessment of whether Jesus experienced sexual assault or rape in addition to stripping is inevitably tentative.[59] It must be based on what is possible, or perhaps what is reasonably probable. We do not have the same direct evidence in the gospels that we have for the stripping, but this does not mean there is no evidence at all. The experiences of other prisoners, past and present, might serve as indirect evidence that demonstrates at least the possibility. Part of an appropriate response to the question should therefore be to explicitly register the silence, as well as the questions the silence might raise. For example, what may be missing in Matt 27:27–31 if it is read as a text of terror? Once this question is raised, it is appropriate to consider whether or not there might be textual echoes that could offer further support for this.

A POSSIBLE ECHO?

Might Matthew's account of the mockery in the *praetorium* invite someone with an attuned ear for Scripture to detect references to other passages on sexual violence, in the same way that Judg 19 invites reading with Gen 19? Matthew's passion narrative may indeed echo aspects of Judg 19.[60] Both texts involve a last meal with bread and wine (Judg 19:19–21; Matt 26:26–29). The meal is followed in Judges by a confrontation between a hostile crowd and the host (19:22–26) and in Matthew (albeit a bit later in the narrative) by a confrontation between a hostile crowd and Pilate (Matt 27:1–26). In Judges, the crowd demands that the host bring out the Levite (19:22) so he can be "known," and this is met with a counteroffer as the host offers his own daughter and the unnamed woman instead (19:23–24). The townsmen reject this and do not listen to him (19:25). In Matthew, Pilate also confronts the crowd and tries to deflect the demands for Jesus's death with a counteroffer. He offers to release either Jesus or Barabbas (27:17). However, the crowd asks for Barabbas to be freed and calls for Jesus to be condemned. Pilate tries again and asks the crowd a second time (27:21), but the crowd again calls for Barabbas to be freed and Jesus to be crucified. The confrontation with the crowd and the insistence of the crowd is a crucial turning point in both stories. An innocent person is betrayed and handed over to violence. The unnamed woman is put out to the crowd (Judg 19:25), and Jesus is handed over to the soldiers (Matt 27:26). Both are then subjected to mockery and eventually death.

---

[59] For different perspectives on whether or not it is plausible, see the blog responses to Michael Iafrate, "Was Jesus Raped? David Tombs on Sexual Violence and the Crucifixion," *VoxNova*, April 2, 2010, https://tinyurl.com/5c7y4jau.
[60] In a similar way, Tammi J. Schneider, "Achsah, the Raped Pilegesh, and the Book of Judges," in *Women in the Biblical World: A Survey of Old and New Testament Perspectives*, ed. Elizabeth A. McCabe (Lanham, MD: University Press of America, 2009), 43–58 offers a thought-provoking argument for seeing a connection between Judg 19 and the story of Achsah in Judg 1.

The two sequences clearly involve differences and contrasts as well as similarities. It is the crowd of townsmen themselves who do violence to the unnamed woman, whereas it is the Roman soldiers, not the crowd, who mock and crucify Jesus. In Judges, the sexual assault is explicitly stated in the text, but it is less clear whether the townsfolk also murder the woman. In Matthew, the execution by the Roman soldiers is clear, but the text leaves opaque whether or not sexual assault beyond stripping took place in the *praetorium*. Some readers might see Judg 19 and Matt 27 as having enough in common to think of a connection and feel an echo is plausible.[61] Other readers are likely to view the texts as having very little in common and see any connection or echo as a stretch.

In addition to the similarities already noted, a detail in the language of *enepaixan* (ἐνέπαιξαν) used in Matt 27:29 and 31 might carry particular significance as an echo of *enepaizan* (ἐνέπαιζαν) from Judg 19:25 (LXX). When the mockery of Jesus is mentioned in Matt 27:29 and 31, it is unclear how *enepaixan* should be read.[62] The Septuagint translates עָלַל in Judg 19:25 as *enepaizan* ("mocked"). Trible, however, uses the stronger term "tortured" to translate עָלַל, while the RSV and NRSV translate it as "abused." The English term "abuse" can be used for a wide spectrum of mistreatment, from fairly moderate to very severe. In view of Judges 19:25 (LXX), the Greek term *enepaixan* and the English term "mockery" seem likewise to cover a wide range of mistreatment. In some verses, the mockery is verbal and does not appear to be severe. For example, in Luke 14:29— "Otherwise, when he has laid a foundation and is not able to finish, all who see it will begin to ridicule him"—it seems primarily jocular.[63] In Matt 27:41, the mockery refers to harsh verbal abuse but without the suggestion of physical acts. Jesus is mocked on the cross by the chief priests, the scribes, and elders (Matt 27:42–43) and taunted by those crucified on either side of him (Matt 27:44). However, *empaizo* (ἐμπαίζω) and its derivatives can also be used to cover torture and extreme physical violence, as suffered by the seven sons in 2 Macc 7.[64] There is no mention of explicitly sexual violence in 2 Macc 7, but the mockery in Judg 19:25 clearly takes both a severe and a sexual form. There may also be a similar

---

[61] Arguably, the similarities in the exchange with the crowd in Gen 19 are even stronger, but there may be an additional connection in Judg 19 between Jesus and the unnamed woman. The woman's father is from Bethlehem, which suggests that she, like Jesus, would have been born there.

[62] See also "They will condemn him to death and will hand him over to the Gentiles to be mocked and flogged and crucified" (Matt 20:19; Mark 10:34; Luke 18:32).

[63] Likewise, in Matt 2:16 it might be translated as "tricked": "When Herod saw that he had been tricked by the wise men, he was infuriated, and he sent and killed all the children in and around Bethlehem who were two years old or under."

[64] The seven sons are tortured and put to death by Antiochus; the mother is also put to death, but the text does not record if she was also tortured.

connection in 1 Sam 31:4, where the same word occurs when Saul fears that the uncircumcised Philistines will make sport of him or mock him. Read in this more severe way, *enepaixan* may offer a verbal echo that serves as a quiet but important clue for how the passage is to be read. Read alongside the other possible similarities between Matt 27 and Judg 19, *enepaixan* may be a discrete invitation to see the mockery of Jesus in light of the mockery of the unnamed woman.

The possible echo of sexual assault from Judg 19 in Matt 27 should not be overstated. Whereas the attestation of stripping is clear and direct, the evidence for sexual assault in the *praetorium* is faint and indirect. It is no more than a possibility, an invitation to further work on the mocking. That said, the possibility becomes more plausible in light of two factors. First, if the stripping of Jesus is named as a form of sexual violence, or sexual abuse, in its own right, the possibility of subsequent sexual assault becomes more plausible. It shifts the context in which the rest of the narrative should be read and shapes a better sense of what is likely or unlikely. Second, in the Bible and in many other contexts, sexual violence against male victims is often disclosed indirectly or referenced euphemistically. The echo that might be present may be no more than a whisper. It amounts at best to an ambiguous fragment of evidence. In the absence of stronger evidence, however, even an ambiguous fragment deserves careful attention when it might speak to such an important issue.

CONCLUSION

Sexual violence is sometimes described as "unspeakable violence," and torture testimonies often make only understated, cryptic, or euphemistic references to what was involved. Trible's analysis of Judg 19 in *Texts of Terror* shows how the text itself, as well as the silences and the possible echoes, can be read to bring out aspects of violence that might otherwise be missed. A similar approach can be extended to reading the crucifixion narratives. The stripping and forced nudity of Jesus is clearly attested in Matt 27:27–31 and should be named as sexual violence, but there is no direct evidence of further sexual assault in the *praetorium*. However, the language of "mockery" in the *praetorium* in Matt 27:29 and 31 might be taken as a quiet hint that there was more to what happened than is explicitly revealed. Although the possible echo of Judg 19:25 is no more than a whisper, it raises an unavoidable question and invites us to give more attention to what might have happened.

BIBLIOGRAPHY

Bal, Mieke. "A Body of Writing: Judges 19." Pages 208–30 in *Feminist Companion to Judges*. Edited by Athalya Brenner. Sheffield: Sheffield Academic, 1993.

Blyth, Caroline, Emily Colgan, and Katie Edwards, eds. *Rape Culture, Gender Violence and Religion: Biblical Perspectives*. London: Palgrave Macmillan, 2018.
———. *Rape Culture, Gender Violence and Religion: Christian Perspectives*. London: Palgrave Macmillan, 2018.
———. *Rape Culture, Gender Violence and Religion: Interdisciplinary Perspectives*. London: Palgrave Macmillan, 2018.
Brown, Raymond E. *Death of the Messiah*. 2 vols. ABRL. New York: Doubleday, 1994.
Brownmiller, Susan. *Against Our Will: Men, Women and Rape*. New York: Simon & Schuster, 1975.
Cantarella, Eva. *Bisexuality in the Ancient World*. Translated by Cormac Ó Cuilleanáin. New Haven: Yale University Press, 1992.
Dover, Kenneth J. *Greek Homosexuality*. Cambridge: Harvard University Press, 1978.
Edwards, Katie B. and David Tombs, "#HimToo: Why Jesus Should Be Recognised as a Victim of Sexual Violence." *The Conversation*. March 23, 2018. https://tinyurl.com/kz2mmsjt.
Exum, J. Cheryl. *Fragmented Women: Feminist (Sub)versions of Biblical Narratives*. JSOTSup 163. Sheffield: Sheffield Academic, 1993.
Golden, Renny, and Michael McConnell. *Sanctuary: The New Underground Railway*. Maryknoll, NY: Orbis Books, 1986.
Hallett, Judith P., and Marilyn B. Skinner, eds. *Roman Sexualities*. Princeton: Princeton University Press, 1997.
Harding, James E.. "Homophobia and Masculine Domination in Judges 19–21." *Bible and Critical Theory* 12 (2016): 41–71.
Helsinki Watch. *War Crimes in the Bosnia-Herzegovina: A Helsinki Watch Report*. New York: Human Rights Watch, 1992–1993.
Human Rights Watch. *"All of My Body Was Pain": Sexual Violence against Rohingya Women and Girls in Burma*. New York: Human Rights Watch, 2017.
———. *Shattered Lives: Sexual Violence during the Rwandan Genocide and its Aftermath*. New York: Human Rights Watch, 1996.
———. *Soldiers Who Rape, Commanders Who Condone: Sexual Violence and Military Reform in the Democratic Republic of Congo*. New York: Human Rights Watch, 2009.
———. *Syria: Sexual Assault in Detention*. New York: Human Rights Watch, 2012.
———. *"We Will Teach You a Lesson": Sexual Violence against Tamils by Sri Lankan Security Forces*. New York: Human Rights Watch, 2013.
Iafrate, Michael. "Was Jesus Raped?: David Tombs on Sexual Violence and the Crucifixion." *VoxNova*. April 2, 2010. https://tinyurl.com/5c7y4jau.
Jones-Warsaw, Koala. "Toward a Womanist Hermeneutic: A Reading of Judges 19–21." Pages 172–86 in *Feminist Companion to Judges*. Edited by Athalya Brenner. Sheffield: Sheffield Academic, 1993.
Kamuf, Peggy. "Author of a Crime." Pages 187–207 in *Feminist Companion to Judges*. Edited by Athalya Brenner. Sheffield: Sheffield Academic, 1993.
Keefe, Alice A. "Rapes of Women/Wars of Men." Pages 79–97 in *Women, War, and Metaphor: Language and Society in the Study of the Hebrew Bible*. Edited by Claudia V. Camp and Carole R. Fontaine. Semeia 61. Atlanta: Scholars Press, 1993.

Lings, Kjell Renato. *Love Lost in Translation: Homosexuality and the Bible.* Bloomington, IN: Trafford, 2013.
Niditch, Susan. *Judges: A Commentary.* OTL. Louisville: Westminster John Knox, 2008.
Reaves, Jayme R. David Tombs, and Rocio Figueroa, eds. *"When Did We See You Naked?": Jesus as a Victim of Sexual Abuse.* London: SCM, 2021.
Scarry, Elaine. *The Body in Pain: The Making and Unmaking of the World.* Oxford: Oxford University Press, 1985.
Schneider, Tammi J. "Achsah, the Raped Pilegesh, and the Book of Judges." Pages 43–58 in *Women in the Biblical World: A Survey of Old and New Testament Perspectives.* Edited by Elizabeth A. McCabe. Lanham, MD: University Press of America, 2009.
Scholz, Susanne. *Sacred Witness: Rape in the Hebrew Bible.* Minneapolis: Fortress, 2010.
Segovia, Fernando F. "Jesus as Victim of State Terror: A Critical Reflection Twenty Years Later." Pages 22–31 in *Crucifixion, State Terror, and Sexual Abuse: Text and Context.* Edited by David Tombs. Dunedin: University of Otago, Centre for Theology and Public Issues, 2018.
Smith, Christian. *Resisting Reagan: The U.S. Central America Peace Movement.* Chicago: University of Chicago Press, 1996.
Stone, Ken. *Sex, Honor and Power in the Deuteronomistic History.* JSOTSup 234. Sheffield: Sheffield Academic, 1996.
Tombs, David. "Crucifixion, State Terror, and Sexual Abuse." *USQR* 53 (1999): 89–109.
———. *Crucifixion, State Terror, and Sexual Abuse: Text and Context.* Dunedin: University of Otago, Centre for Theology and Public Issues, 2018.
———. "The Hermeneutics of Liberation." Pages 310–55 in *Approaches to New Testament Study.* Edited by Stanley E. Porter and David Tombs. JSNTSup 120. Sheffield: Sheffield Academic, 1995.
———. "Honour, Shame and Conquest: Male Identity, Sexual Violence and the Body Politic." *Journal of Hispanic/Latino Theology* 9 (2002): 21–40.
———. "Jesus as a Victim of Sexual Abuse." Interview with Rosie Dawson. The Shiloh Podcast. March 24, 2021. https://tinyurl.com/pajzmht8.
———. *Latin American Liberation Theology.* Religion in the Americas 1. Leiden: Brill, 2002.
———. "Lived Religion and the Intolerance of the Cross." Pages 63–83 in *Lived Religion and Politics of (In)tolerance.* Edited by Ruard Ganzevoort and Srdjan Sremac. Palgrave Studies in Lived Religion and Societal Changes. London: Palgrave Macmillan, 2017.
———. "The Ongoing Legacy of Liberation Theology." Inaugural Professorial Lecture, University of Otago. September 8, 2015. https://tinyurl.com/7mv4v5z4.
———. "Prisoner Abuse: From Abu Ghraib to The Passion of The Christ." Pages 179–205 in *Religions and the Politics of Peace and Conflict.* Edited by Linda Hogan and Dylan Lehrke. PTMS. Eugene, OR: Wipf and Stock, 2009.
———. "Silent No More: Sexual Violence in Conflict as a Challenge to the Worldwide Church." *AcT* 34 (2014): 142–60.
Trainor, Michael. *The Body of Jesus and Sexual Abuse: How the Gospel Passion Narrative Informs a Pastoral Approach.* Melbourne: Morning Star; Eugene, OR: Wipf & Stock, 2014.
Trexler, Richard C. *Sex and Conquest: Gendered Violence, Political Order and the European Conquest of the Americas.* Ithaca, NY: Cornell University Press, 1995.
Trible, Phyllis. *God and the Rhetoric of Sexuality.* Philadelphia: Fortress, 1978.

———. *Texts of Terror: Literary-Feminist Readings of Biblical Narratives.* OBT. Philadelphia: Fortress, 1984.

Williams, Craig A. *Roman Homosexuality: Ideologies of Masculinity in Classical Antiquity.* Oxford: Oxford University Press, 1999.

Yamada, Frank M. *Configurations of Rape in the Hebrew Bible: A Literary Analysis of Three Rape Narratives.* New York: Lang. 2008.

10

The Fruit of Others' Labor: How Judges 19 Stands with Dehumanized Migrant Workers

Brent Pelton

Scripture intertwines revelatory theology with historical accounts of a people's journey alongside their faith. The messages contained within the Hebrew Bible communicate ideas that are "timeless and supracultural ... [yet] spoke[n] through and to human beings within history (i.e., within a particular chronological, linguistic, sociological, and religious context)."[1] Hearing these historical voices and the revelation they contain is a difficult balancing act, particularly in light of passages in Judges that "report various kinds of war crimes, acts of ethnic cleansing, and sexual violence, as well as statements of political chauvinism and explicit preferences for authoritarian rule."[2] Judges 19 used this form of "preached history," as did other parts of the Deuteronomistic History, to speak to the heart of the community's covenant with God and highlight when this covenant was not at the forefront of their minds.[3] The manner in which a community chooses to preserve and respond to revelatory history shapes how community members hear it and speak from a particular theological vantage point today. Using this passage of Judges as preached history, it is important to hear the contemporary examples of society turning its back on God's people. Hearing the marginality in the accounts of Judg 19 in light of the contemporary abuse of migrant workers, for example, can help to push back on the othering of marginal voices in the Hebrew Bible as simply antiquarian feature of the text that are no longer relevant to our current time and place. These voices from the past can, on the contrary, highlight cries from people

---

[1] George Eldon Ladd, *The New Testament and Criticism* (Grand Rapids: Eerdmans, 1991), as referenced by J. G. Harris, Cheryl A. Brown, and Michael S. Moore, *Joshua, Judges, Ruth* (Grand Rapids: Baker Books, 2012), 178.
[2] Susanne Scholz, "Judges," in *Women's Bible Commentary*, ed. Carol A. Newsom, Sharon H. Ringe, and Jacquiline E. Lapsley, 3rd ed. (Louisville: Westminster John Knox, 2012), 330.
[3] Harris, Brown, and Moore, *Joshua, Judges, Ruth*, 180.

society chooses to persecute, exclude, and shame in our own contemporary time and place as well.

Judges 19 tells of the denegration, sexual violence, and murder of an unnamed woman. The narrator of her story continually highlights her roles as both a wife and a concubine. From a contemporary, Western, and middle-class perspective, this seems like a paradox of identity, because it involves two different images of women—as loving partner and as supposed transgressor of sexual boundaries. This complex label, which is imposed on this protagonist, affects how we might read such a painful and powerful text. But this complex and seemingly contradictory depiction of women is not new; Judges was composed orally and later "written down only during the Babylonian exile of the sixth century BCE," and chapter 19 bears some similarities with another text that was also composed over the same approximate time period: Proverbs.[4] Many sections within Proverbs advise the young, wealthy male readers in a manner that "sounds bizarre, sexist, and, epistemologically speaking, just plain wrong," yet were designed as a means to enable these young men to understand Wisdom, a female hypostasis from the one God of Israel.[5] Proverbs and Judg 19, taken together, discuss approximations of contemporaneous teachings that explore gender and faith in ways that traverse moral boundaries. These two texts, read side-by-side, demand that current readers unpack the revelation that sits within a historical context rather than merely dismissing them as being of no contemporary value, given their gendered narratives and violence.

The book of Proverbs is framed by an *inclusio* that uses the imagery of wives to guide the reader in understanding the correct moral framework that leads toward individual, familial, and communal life in abundance.[6] Proverbs 1–9 describes Wisdom as an intimate partner, a wife who builds her house, prepares a feast, keeps the house in an ordered manner, and guides those who are lost into her home.[7] Conversely, Folly, the antithesis of Wisdom, is never at home, cannot offer food to sustain men but only fleeting sex, and lacks any kind of loyalty to her partner.[8] The reader is urged by the writer to follow Wisdom, who will give life and prosperity, whereas Folly will only lead to ruin and death. The ending of Proverbs similarly uses this spousal imagery as a "human incarnation of what Woman Wisdom teaches through her instructions about moral existence, the

---

[4] Leo G. Perdue, *Proverbs*, Interpretation (Louisville: Westminster John Knox, 2012), 16. See Trent C. Butler, *Judges*, WBC 8 (Nashville: Thomas Nelson, 2008), 830 for the idea that chapter 19 is a late element in the book of Judges, and Scholz, "Judges," 330 for the composition and date of the book.
[5] Perdue, *Proverbs*, 25.
[6] Perdue, *Proverbs*, 82, 115.
[7] Prov 9:1–6 (NRSV). Translations are from the NRSV unless otherwise noted.
[8] Prov 7:10–13, 7:18–20.

bounties of insight, and the fullness of life."[9] As a result, this *inclusio* frames the positive female presence in men's lives as a signpost for Israel's covenant with God.

It is possible that the author of Judg 19 is highlighting the unravelling moral character of Israel with this interplay of Wisdom and Folly in mind. When the Levite man says that his wife is also his concubine, he is doubting her agency and personhood. His doubt enables him to increasingly disregard her safety and well-being, and his disregard leads to the inhumane and horrific events of the narrative. The interplay between the husband framing her as a loving wife and wanting to speak kindly to her (Judg 19:3) and her eventual death and dismemberment as a concubine (Judg 19:29) speaks to the fact that Israel was in complete disarray and lost sight of its covenant with God. The Levite, who would be "entrusted in Israel with teaching the provisions of the covenant," was failing in his duty to Israel.[10] Despite his knowledge, he "was capable of the horrendous acts described. Every host[, thus,] was potentially helpless against the mistreatment of his guests, and every woman could become a victim of rape until death."[11] Israel had in fact rejected divine Wisdom and turned her into Folly, and, "without wisdom, humans were bound to lose their way and face an untimely end."[12] This end becomes apparent by the conclusion of Judges, which ends with a civil war, the near-complete genocide of fellow Israelites, and further sexual violence against Israelite women.

The narrative of Judges is an account of cyclical decline: leaders rise up only to fail in their duty to restore the covenant within the heart of the community. This path of seeking the support of God leads to the use of authority for personal gain, ambition, and power. In the end,

> Israel fails until no tribes are acting together except to annihilate another tribe, worship is directed to the gods of all Israel's enemies, Israel's armies comprise only worthless fellows, vows to God become insignificant and violent, personal lifestyle bears no resemblance to divine commands, and one tribe of Israel virtually vanishes from sight.[13]

It is dark days for the covenantal community and communion with God and God's people. This disconnect between the supposedly intended outcome and the actual results of ego and greed among a people's political leadership should not be perceived as a distant reality; it is one that many are facing here in Australia.

---

[9] Perdue, *Proverbs*, 115.
[10] J. Clinton McCann, *Judges*, Interpretation (Louisville: Westminister John Knox, 2011), 241.
[11] Havilah Dharamraj, "Judges," in *South Asian Bible Commentary* (Udaipur, Rajasthan: Open Door, 2015), 1112.
[12] Leo G. Perdue, *Proverbs*, Interpretation (Louisville: Westminster John Knox, 2012), 78.
[13] Butler, *Judges*, 120.

Former prime minister Julia Gillard said that Australia is the land of "mateship and the fair go"; former prime minister Malcolm Turnbull stated that Australians are unique in having a "culture of fair go, of looking after each other."[14] Yet it seems that our unofficial motto of fairness, equality, and safety goes only so far for our workers. Australia, far from being the land of a fair go, is a land where a single corporation can steal three hundred million dollars from its workers, a land with the sixth highest rate of workplace bullying, and a land where one in five children grow up in poverty.[15] Recent Australian prime ministers, such as Tony Abbott and Scott Morrison, express their Christian faith as an integral part of their identity, ethos, and character—yet, instead of being a time of prosperity, community, and justice, is it possible that Australia has entered its own kind of period of the judges? If our community is to empathetically and actively listen to the marginalized voices in Judg 19, one must recognize that this text "is a powerful witness against any institution… that fosters idolatry and disobedience and thus contributes to the injustice and brokenness of the human community… [It] demonstrate[s] graphically what happens when people are bent upon self-assertion and idolatry rather than submission to God and God's purposes."[16]

The following reinterpretation of Judg 19, broken into three sections, is inspired by the hardship and struggles that face fruit pickers and farm laborers in Australia. This version of Judg 19 is a means to heighten our awareness of the ways in which this passage can dialogue with the current context and draws on combined accounts and undercover journalism in this area.

PRIME MINISTERS 19:1–8

> 1 In those days, when there was no leader in Australia, a certain Prime Minister, residing in a wealthy Coalition seat of Sydney, took to himself a young farm laborer from Yogyakarta in Indonesia. 2 A young student on a working holiday visa, named Budi, whose name means "wisdom," wanted a chance at the Australian dream; however, the Prime Minister told them that they must work in

---

[14] As cited by Nicholas Barry, "In Australia, Land of the "Fair Go', Not Everyone Gets an Equal Slice of the Pie," *The Conversation*, January 26, 2017, https://tinyurl.com/89t8bdf9.
[15] Peter Ryan and David Chau, "Woolworths Investigated after Admitting It Underpaid Staff up to $300 Million," *ABC News*, October 29, 2019, https://tinyurl.com/4u5k27ce; Rachael E. Potter, Maureen F. Dollard, and Michelle R. Tuckey, *Bullying and Harassment in Australian Workplaces: Results from the Australian Workplace Barometer Project 2014/2015* (Canberra: Safe Work Australia, 2016), https://tinyurl.com/btufncdh; and Jennifer Duke, "One in Five Young Children Living in Poverty in Australia: Curtin University," *The Sydney Morning Herald*, August 28, 2020, https://tinyurl.com/5yymdj64.
[16] McCann, *Judges*, 237.

"fruit picking and packing, trimming vines, [or] working in tree farming."[17] Budi, having no knowledge of farming, angrily went off to work in the fields near Mildura in Victoria for the "88-day rule."[18] 3 Then the Prime Minister set out after them, to speak tenderly of attractive apps, great partnerships with neighbors, and how "95 percent of farmers are doing the right thing."[19] He had with him the local Nationals MP and a press bus in tow. When he reached the hostel, the other migrant workers from Afghanistan, Thailand, and Malaysia saw him and came with joy to meet him. 4 The migrant workers, the fellow farm laborers of Budi, made him stay and he remained with them for three days, so they ate and drank, and he stayed there for photo ops in his hi-vis vest. 5 On the fourth day, they got up early in the morning, and the Prime Minister prepared to go, but the migrant workers said to the Prime Minister, "fortify yourself with a bit of the fruit we pick, and, after that, you may go." 6 So the migrant workers and the Prime Minister sat and ate and drank together, and the migrant workers said to the Prime Minister, "Why not spend the night and enjoy the fruits of our labor more?" 7 When he got up (after another photo op) to go, the migrant workers kept urging him until he spent the night there again. 8 On the fifth day he got up early in the morning to leave; and the migrant workers said, "Fortify yourself with the fruits of our labor." So they lingered until the day declined, and the group of them ate and drank.

At the beginning of this chapter of Judges, the reader can anticipate the ensuing communal breakdown and atrocities that accompany it; the *inclusio* that "there was no king" prepares the reader for the fact that what is about to happen should not have happened. Yet, under the ad hoc leadership of the time, it still took place. The narrator thus gives the reader space and an open invitation to question the role that leadership of wealth, privilege, and status has in allowing such atrocities to happen to innocent people.[20] The narrator begs the reader, as the story unfolds, to ask how God's people—as individuals, communities, and governing bodies—broke down to the point that they cannot seem to see the disintegration of the covenantal bonds of the Israelite faith.

---

[17] Anne Davies, "Death in the Sun: Australia's 88-Day Law Leaves Backpackers Exploited and Exposed," *The Guardian*, May 20, 2018, https://tinyurl.com/3k8m4mjj.
[18] Davies, "Death."
[19] My translation of "95 persen dari semua petani melakukan hal yang benar" in "Petani Di Victoria Krisis Pekerja Pemetik Buah," *Tempo*, March 5, 2019, https://tinyurl.com/rmczsray. For attractive apps, see "Aplikasi Backpicker Memudahkan Pemetik Buah Mendapatkan Kerja Di Australia," *Tempo*, June 3, 2020, https://tinyurl.com/374ujjcz. And for partnerships with neighbors, see Aneeta Bhole, "Despite Travel Bans, Fruit Pickers from the Pacific Will Arrive in the NT This Month," *SBS News*, September 1, 2020, https://tinyurl.com/bmn4auwe.
[20] Mary J. Evans, *Judges and Ruth*, TOTC 7 (Downers Grove, IL: Inter-Varsity Press, 2017), 286–87.

Within this world of chaotic sociopolitical tension, the reader is introduced to the Levite man who "took a concubine."[21] This unnamed woman, if she were a concubine, would have had some legal rights as a secondary wife, yet no other partner is mentioned within the text.[22] From the outset, the author appears to be signaling that this Levite man does not realize or value the worth and dignity of this woman. Instead, the author uses the wording "took a concubine" rather than "married a wife" in order to emphasize that, right from the beginning, the Levite viewed her in terms of property rather than relationship."[23] This unnamed woman is an outsider in two other means as well: her sexuality and her geography.[24] She is characterized as a transgressor of the male-dominated society, which results in her rape, mutilation, and murder. Likewise, she must travel north in order to return home, far from where she lives with the Levite man. Instead of being a beloved wife, the Levite's characterization of her transforms her into a concubine and, later, an object of violent fantasy for the men of Gibeah.

The author, if they had knowledge of Proverbs, may be using the imagery of the beloved wife and the concubine in this preached history to illustrate how far the Israelites had fallen from their covenantal promise. The female character appears to be the capable wife of Prov 31, as she is cited as having familial and not solely sexual relationship with this wealthy Levite man.[25] Wisdom is, according to Proverbs, "a most desirable bride who bestows a garland and crown ... on her beloved.... She empowers all who govern rightly."[26] She represents Wisdom's invitation to those who are open to her. But, as the capable wife is transformed into a concubine, she becomes a symbol for the covenantal relationship the Israelites have with God. Wisdom, God's invitation into a path of freedom and liberation, becomes, in the mind's eye of the community, Folly, a path toward ruin and destruction. Wisdom, charged as an adultress and foreigner, becomes Folly, who is "outside socially accepted categories, whether ethnic, legal, social, or sexual.... She represents many different 'strange' women, all of whom ... will threaten the [Israelite] youth's wellbeing."[27]

Yet this capable wife, an incarnation of wisdom as described in Prov 31, is rejected, her character denigrated, and her worth as a human being destroyed

---

[21] Judg 19:1.
[22] Harris, Brown, and Moore, *Joshua, Judges, Ruth*, 384
[23] Evans, *Judges and Ruth*, 288.
[24] Scholz, "Judges," 364.
[25] In Judg 19:9, the host is described as a "father-in-law." In Judg 20:4, the Levite man is her "husband."
[26] Christine Roy Yoder, "Proverbs," in *Women's Bible Commentary*, Carol A. Newsom, Sharon H. Ringe, and Jacquiline E. Lapsley, 3rd ed. (Louisville: Westminster John Knox, 2012), 644.
[27] Yoder, "Proverbs," 642.

before she can even demonstrate otherwise in the story. This account removes what wisdom and persona this unnamed woman brings to the narrative. Instead, it becomes a story about the (abusive) power, authority, and wealth of a Levite man. Her work, knowledge, and experience, like that of many women throughout the world, must be funnelled through the powerful males in their family. Her narrative becomes the archetype of the incarnational work of female wisdom throughout the world that is cast aside as worthless. Their work

> is devalued, so that they receive little or no pay for their work in the home or in the community. Additionally, some women do not have the right to their own income or to money and property given them by their parents. It all goes to the husband and his family.[28]

The treatment of a devoted wife as a concubine without agency, value, or even human dignity is the story of migrant farm workers in Australia today. They are lured by a contractor, "who [is] dripping in gold jewellery [and] who produced his personal bank statement to show ... the riches that could be earned."[29] Like the Levite, all the wealth, power, and personal safety is gained by the labor of those whom he abused. The sweet words of the riches to be had, like the Levite "speak[ing] tenderly to" his wife (Judg 19:3), are half-hearted and manipulative. For the often ten hours of daily laborious work in the thirty-five-degree sun, "some [migrants] are paid as little as a few dollars an hour—some even end up owing money—to work on Australian farms" due to fees and charges.[30]

The sense of who these migrant workers are, and of their humanity, is intentionally lost in the process of hiring. Mohammad Rowi, for example, became unemployed in Malaysia and left his wife and soon-to-be-born daughter in the hope of supporting his family.[31] Yet these migrants not only experience serf-like conditions, they are also dehumanized for their efforts. The farmers echo the Levite's treatment of his devoted wife: they systematically exploit these workers and turn a blind eye to the "racism, homophobia, threats, intimidation, and bullying."[32] They encourage Australian managers to devalue and dehumanize them: "Don't

---

[28] Dharamraj, "Judges," 1116.
[29] Nick McKenzie, Richard Baker, and Saiful Hasam, "Fruits of Their Labour: Investigation into Exploitation of Migrant Fruit Picking Workers in Australia," *The Sydney Morning Herald*, accessed September 16, 2020, https://tinyurl.com/4uce25wm.
[30] Quote from McKenzie, Baker, and Hasam, "Fruits of Their Labour." For the work conditions, see Davies, "Death."
[31] McKenzie, Baker, and Hasam, "Fruits of Their Labour."
[32] James McGee, "Why I Lasted Just Five Weeks Working in the Apple Industry," *The Age*, March 3, 2019, https://tinyurl.com/vmpp8nct. On the systematic exploitation, see McKenzie, Baker, and Hasam, "Fruits of Their Labour."

make friends with them." "Don't talk to them." "Don't be nice to them."[33] Instead of honoring the backbreaking and grueling work that these migrants do for so little pay in the hope of staying in Australia, they are treated with disregard and contempt for their existence. Yet the farmers and the corporations involved knowingly turn a blind eye to the abusive nature of the fruit picking industry.[34] Coupled with slow and reluctant government intervention, it is clear that migrant laborers are turned into a dehumanized and othered labor workforce for personal gain.[35]

PRIME MINISTERS 19:9–21

[9] When he, with his laborer and Nationals MP got up to leave, the migrant workers—the ones picking the fruit he eats—said to him, "Oy, it's been a long day and it's almost evening. Spend the night. See, the daylight has almost finished. Spend the night here and enjoy the fruit. Tomorrow you can get up early in the morning, have another press conference, and go home." [10] But the man would not spend the night; he got up and departed, and arrived opposite the ACT (that is, Canberra). He had with him a press bus in tow, and his farm laborer was with him. [11] When they were near the ACT, the day was spent, and the Nationals MP said to his Prime Minister, "Come now, let us turn aside to this city of the Parliamentarians, and spend the night in it." [12] But his Prime Minister said to him, "We will not turn aside into a city with foreigners, who do not belong to the people of the Coalition; however, we will continue on to Batlow." [13] Then he said to his Nationals MP, "Come, let us try to reach one of these places, and spend the night at Batlow or beyond." [14] So they passed on and went their way, and the sun went down on them near Batlow, which belongs to the Nationals. [15] They turned aside there to go in and spend the night at Batlow. The Prime Minister went in and sat down in the open square of the city, but no one wanted a photo op or took them in to spend the night. [16] Then, in the evening, there was an old man coming from his work in the field. The man was from the harbor country of Sydney, and he was residing in Batlow. (The people of the place were Nationals members). [17] When the old man looked up and saw the wayfarer in the open square of the city, he said, "Where are you going and where do you come from?" [18] The Prime Minister answered him: "We are passing from Mildura in Victoria to the part of the harbor country in Sydney from which I come. I went to Mildura in Victoria, and I am going to my home. Nobody has offered to take me in. [19] We, your politicians, have petrol for our press bus, with fruit and wine for me and my farm laborer and the young Nationals MP along with us. We need nothing more." [20] The old man said, "Good-oh. I will take care of anything you need;

---

[33] McGee, "Why I Lasted."
[34] McKenzie, Baker, and Hasam. "Fruits of Their Labour."
[35] Davies, "Death."

only don't spend the night in the square." [21] So the old man brought him into his house and filled the press bus's tank; they washed their face, and ate and drank.

When the Levite arrived at the house in which his wife was staying, his "father-in-law" "came with joy to meet him" (Judg 19:3). Although, "the father's generosity may appear exaggerated or overbearing ... hospitality was and still is a most important cultural value, and any deficiency in fulfilling one's obligations was/is looked upon as grossly shameful, even sinful."[36] This lavish outpouring of hospitality would be performed not by the father or the Levite but by their wives. Yet, during these days of overflowing generosity and hospitality, "It is possible that the father was concerned for the wellbeing of his daughter" and the relationship she has with his son-in-law.[37] If the author is alluding to Proverbs, this overflowing bounty may signify the "joy-filled, love-inspiring, playful relationship with knowledge, God, and the world"; "to love her (Wisdom) and to accept the invitation to wisdom's table is to awaken to the interconnectedness of God's creation, to align with and participate in God's ongoing work in the world, and, as a result, to flourish."[38] This sense of abundant flourishing is seen in the fact that the father, even after days of festivities, can still provide in excess, giving his son-in-law enough supplies that, when they arrive in Gibeah, they do not need any food or provisions; they simply need a place to sleep in peace.[39]

But any hope that the reader may have concerning the relationship between the Levite and his wife is dashed with the Levite's irrational and hasty thinking.[40] As Phyllis Trible points out in *Texts of Terror*, the Levite ignores the generous hospitality and continued invitation into the home of the father-in-law. He chooses, instead, to see this invitation as a power struggle, which results in the silencing of and violence toward the unnamed woman.[41] He and his party leave his father-in-law's house regardless of the costs, and they arrive at Jebus well into the evening. The narrator seems to indicate that the Levite man takes stock of his possessions: his saddled donkeys, which would contain all of his wealth and provisions, and then his wife, who is labelled as his concubine. The fact that she is described after the loaded donkeys seems to imply that she is merely cargo to haul across the desert; the text abandons all possible pretense of valuing her human dignity and worth as a person at her father's house. She is now simply property to be seized from the north and brought back to the south, where she is to serve the Levite.

---

[36] Harris, Brown, and Moore, *Joshua, Judges, Ruth*, 378.
[37] Evans, *Judges and Ruth*, 291.
[38] Yoder, "Proverbs," 646. For the invitation to wisdom's table, see Prov 9:1–6.
[39] Harris, Brown, and Moore, *Joshua, Judges, Ruth*, 380.
[40] Harris, Brown, and Moore, *Joshua, Judges, Ruth*, 379.
[41] Phyllis Trible, *Texts of Terror: Literary-Feminist Readings of Biblical Narratives* (Philadelphia: Fortress, 1984), 82.

This scene at Jebus, later identified as Jerusalem, is both ironic and tragic. The Levite, in refusing to spend the night in a "city of foreigners" (Judg 19:12), "would rather go on to Gibeah ... or Ramah in the dark than to risk the danger of lodging among foreigners."[42] The implication is that foreigners will not provide the hospitality or safety that can be offered by fellow Israelites; yet, upon their arrival in the Israelite city of Gibeah, "no one took them in to spend the night."[43] In an ironic twist of fate, a man who is in charge of educating his people in the covenant suddenly finds that "there was no one in the city who took seriously his covenant obligations."[44] He rashly leaves the safety of his father-in-law's house and arrives in a city of Israelites only to find that the generosity of spirit had run out among his own people.

Finally, an old man from the same region as the Levite greets them and inquires how they arrived in Gibeah. He agrees to take them in, ominously foreshadowing the events to come: "only do not spend the night in the square." The welcome that he gives is *shalom* which, "semantically ... has a wide range of connotations ... peace, security, health, and order."[45] All of these attributes were provided by the father, who continually wanted to lavish his Levite son-in-law with them. However, the Levite chooses to turn away from such abundance of hospitality and risks setting out on his own path, following his own ways. Another elder, who represents those who remember the covenant, takes him in, knowing how foolishly this Levite man has acted such that he inadvertently arrives in an unforgiving environment at night.

Recklessly disregarding safety and dehumanizing people as if they were property can be seen in the dialogue surrounding the farm labor shortage due to COVID-19. With few working-holiday visa holders and migrants arriving, the Australian government has sought to shift the labor market to some of the most vulnerable in our community." One proposal is to employ the "17,000 refugees who came by boat to Australia years ago on ... Temporary Protection Visas, which last three years and do not have a direct path to permanent residency."[46] In exchange for this grueling and unforgiving work, they would be granted Australian residency, giving them a level of rights and security that they are currently being denied. Another proposal comes from the "National Farmers Federation ... [which] was encouraging the federal government to develop new programs to

---

[42] Harris, Brown, and Moore, *Joshua, Judges, Ruth*, 379 (without the bold font).
[43] Judg 9:15.
[44] Harris, Brown, and Moore, *Joshua, Judges, Ruth*, 379.
[45] Harris, Brown, and Moore, *Joshua, Judges, Ruth*, 386.
[46] Nick Bonyhady, "MPs Back Proposal to Give Refugees Residency for Fruit Picking," *The Age*, September 14, 2020, https://tinyurl.com/5a7n2yc5.

encourage unemployed Australians into farm work."⁴⁷ Yet even MP David Littleproud, the agriculture minister, admitted that this would be a difficult task to accomplish, presumably knowing that few Australians would be willing to uproot their families and lives to work on the "56 per cent of the 8000 horticulture farms…[that] had underpaid workers."⁴⁸ Preying on the most marginalized and disadvantaged, who are trapped in the socioeconomic and sociopolitical minefield that is the Australian "fair go" culture, appears to be the next rung on the ladder in abusive and dehumanizing farming practices.

Like the old man in Gibeah, those who know of the toxic culture on these farms sadly know that they can only be a stone in the way of a tidal wave of problematic practices. Supervisors such as James McGee speak of living "conditions … [that] were squalid, with stories of vermin infestations, faulty showers and flooded toilets."⁴⁹ Those supervisors who speak out about the offensive and dehumanizing characterization of the workers and their working conditions are demoted and eventually pushed out the door in the process. With haphazard, ill-equipped, and lackadaisical government regulation, "the shonky operators and the complainants have moved on before Fair Work can get involved." Empathetic supervisors simply have few options against the tide; they can try to offer as much *shalom* as they can muster in an unforgiving and hostile city, or join in the calls to rape and pillage the marginalized in the town square.⁵⁰

PRIME MINISTERS 19:22–30

> ²² While they were enjoying themselves, the farmers of the town, a perverse lot, surrounded the house and started pounding on the door. They said to the old man, the owner of the house, "Bring out the man who came into your house, so that we may fuck him over." ²³ And the man, the owner of the house, went out to them and said to them, "No, my brothers, don't be so feral. Since the Prime Minister is my guest, don't do this vile thing. ²⁴ Here are my young daughter and his farm laborer; let me bring them out now. Fuck them over and do whatever you want to them, but against this man, do not do such a feral thing." ²⁵ But the men would not listen to him. So the Prime Minister seized his farm laborer and put them out to the farmers. They "sexual[ly] harass[ed]," "sexual[ly] exploit[ed]," and eventually "rape[d]" the laborer all through the night until the morning.⁵¹ And, as the dawn began to break, they let the laborer go. ²⁶ As

---

⁴⁷ Mike Foley, "Unemployed Australians Won't Fill Gaps in Agriculture Workforce: Farmers," *The Age*, August 3, 2020, https://tinyurl.com/3wsd3uy5.
⁴⁸ Foley, "Unemployed Australians."
⁴⁹ McGee, "Why I Lasted." James McGee is a pseudonym.
⁵⁰ Davies, "Death."
⁵¹ Davies, "Death."

morning appeared, the Indonesian migrant came and fell down at the door of the old man's house where the Prime Minister was, until it was light. 27 In the morning, the Prime Minister got up, opened the doors of the house, and, when he went out to go on his way, there was his farm laborer, lying at the door of the house, with their hands on the threshold. 28 "Get up," he said, "we are going!" But there was no answer. Then he put the laborer on the press bus, and the Prime Minister set out for his home. 29 When he had entered Kirribilli House, he took his shears, and, grasping his farm laborer's passport, he cut Budi's visa into twelve pieces. He sent the pieces, along with the shell of a laborer, throughout all the territory of the Asia-Pacific. 30 Then he commanded the ambassadors whom he sent, saying, "Thus shall you say to all the Asia-Pacific, 'Has such a thing ever happened since the day that the Australians came down from the land of the British Isles until this day? Consider it, take counsel, and speak out.'"

The old man, who takes in and looks after the Israelites on their journey, represents a commitment to the covenant that is unparalleled by his younger contemporaries. The Levite, as well as the men of Gibeah, seem to represent a new age of greed, abuse, and power, disregarding the covenantal commitments and obligations to the marginalized. Far from remembering the dehumanization of their cultural narrative, which depicts them as slaves coming out of Egypt (e.g., Deut 24:13), they have become those who enslave and mistreat the weak, vulnerable, and guests within their lands. When the host of Gibeah offers his daughter and the concubine to these men who seek abusive displays of power, he says, "do to them what is good *in your own eyes*."[52] In doing so, he is offering a test and a chance at redemption; he is pointing out the absurdity of their request by offering the most vulnerable in order to open their eyes. He perhaps hopes that, in doing so, they will see what atrocity they are asking for because "violence against women serves to communicate in the Old Testament the degradation and disarray of the larger social structure."[53] Yet, before the reader can see if the men of Gibeah past their elder's test, the Levite fails it miserably. In that moment, he becomes her master (Judg 19:26–27), throwing his wife to the mob to be brutally raped by these men and proving that his years of educating his community on the wisdom of the covenant were a fraudulent act of hypocrisy.

The next morning, the reader discovers that the wife has crawled back "with her hands on the threshold" (Judg 19:27). Like the master-slave relationship that this narrative turns out to be, the Levite "responded not by 'speaking to her heart' (Judg 19:3) but by barking a command: 'Get up; let's go.'"[54] Yet, "there was no

---

[52] McCann, *Judges*, 243.
[53] McCann, *Judges*, 245 in general reference to Alice A. Keefe, "Rapes of Women/Wars of Men," in *Women, War, and Metaphor: Language and Society in the Study of the Hebrew Bible* (Atlanta: Scholars Press, 1993), 82.
[54] Harris, Brown, and Moore, *Joshua, Judges, Ruth*, 383 (emphasis removed).

answer" (Judg 19:28); his disowned and neglected partner is dead. Like the *inclusio* "there was no king," this narrative is "the end result of all the 'there was no' in the story": no king, no answer, and, thus, no hope for Israel.[55] It begs the reader to ask the question, "But what if...." The author created an opportunity for the reader to respond to the painful perspective of this woman and the breakdown of society and ask: "What could I/we/they have done to stop such brutality and violence?" The text, in a sense, begs the reader to wonder if this story speaks the truths of their own society. In doing so, it requires the reader not simply to sympathize with the inhumanity that unfolds but to respond with a commitment to ending contemporary inhumanity from taking root in the greed, authority, and power plays that are persistent in human institutions and cultures.

Judges 19, when read in light of other biblical texts, demonstrates that, "through the whirlwind of political chaos and the fire of moral depravity, God repeatedly saves Israel from itself."[56] If the author of this text is using the wife as an allegory for the teachings of Wisdom, her struggling attempt to reconnect with her husband may speak of God's commitment to God's people, even when society debases its moral and covenantal imperative to God and God's community. Wisdom, in the book of Proverbs, does not greet those who are already at her table but "stand[s] in the busiest places of the city in the thick of everyday bustle and calling out to the naive, scoffers, and fools to heed her instruction, lest disaster befall them."[57] She calls to humanity in the chaos, uncertainty, and distractions of life with an open and ceaseless invitation to liberation and life. Wisdom, even when neglected, victimized, and cast aside as Folly, continually seeks a relationship that can heal the denigration and debauchery that result from fixating on the authority and greed systematically embedded in societal institutions and cultures. Judges 19, when paired with Wisdom in Proverbs, asks the readers to empathize deeply with the marginalized and hear their voices. It demands that readers listen for Wisdom, who is calling out above all of the chaos and distractions of life and continually offering an invitation to humanity, in order to overcome the idols that transfix us and distract us from the path with God.

As we listen to the voices of the marginalized in Judges 19, we must recognize that they are not limited to a particular perspective, culture, or time. Preached history speaks across cultures, times, places, classes and experiences to a variety of marginal voices in any context. For Koala Jones-Warsaw, reducing this biblical passage to that of gendered violence, "does not adequately account for the complexity of the problems in that society. It was a society in chaos. By reducing the problem of victimization to gender," other marginal voices are reduced in the

---

[55] Harris, Brown, and Moore, *Joshua, Judges, Ruth*, 383.
[56] Dharamraj, "Judges," 1017.
[57] Yoder, "Proverbs," 644.

process.⁵⁸ Voices that speak of civil war, genocide, and the like would not be considered revelatory in contemporary society. Likewise, how a community chooses to listen and respond to preached history can engender the call for contemporary justice that this passage demands—not just for the voices heard within the text, but also in the insight the text provides into problematic constructs of culture and power.

The farm laborers who are forced into inhumane and demoralizing working conditions can empathize with the brokenness of the unnamed woman of this passage. The thousands of unnamed men and women who are forced to subsist on illegal wages and deal with illegal work practices with little if any recourse because of the corrupt and lackadaisical practices of successive governments, companies, and farmers have been pained, broken, and even killed. Mohammad Rowi, who gave up everything to try to support his family from abroad, ended with nothing to show for his time in Australia.⁵⁹ The family and friends of twenty-seven-year-old Olivier Caramin, who died due to appalling working conditions, will never know what could have been had he never worked the fields. The trauma of sexual harassment and predatory behavior, like that experience by eighteen-year-old Katherine Stoner when farmers suggested that she strip naked and pick peaches in the heat, leaves people mentally and emotionally broken.⁶⁰ These broken bodies and broken lives only begin to illustrate the "racism, homophobia, threats, intimidation, and bullying," as well as "rapes, sexual harassment, substandard living conditions, breaches of workplace safety laws and financial exploitation."⁶¹ Australia, in the process of achieving its quest for an ever-cheaper labor force, has broken not only its covenant of being a "fair go" culture but the bodies and minds of migrants as well.

CONCLUSION

When a community turns Wisdom's invitation and path into Folly's game, it turns aside from an ongoing process of liberation and flourishing. Judges and Proverbs together speak of the imperative to examine our attitudes, systems, and cultures in order to seek, nurture, and offer the *shalom* of God. Yet, when society allows power, authority, and wealth to dictate who is allowed the peace of *shalom*, human control and greed prioritize the privileged few over the broken bodies and lives of those whom society marginalizes. Judges 19 "call[s] people in every time and place

---

[58] Koala Jones-Warsaw, "Toward a Womanist Hermeneutic: A Reading of Judges 19–21," *Journal of the Interdenominational Theological Center* 22 (1994): 28–29.
[59] McKenzie, Baker, and Hasam. "Fruits of their Labour."
[60] Davies, "Death."
[61] McGee, "Why I Lasted"; Davies, "Death."

to set self-centeredness aside, to embrace God's purpose for the world, and so to contribute to the wholeness of the human community—a condition that may be summarized by the words 'justice' and 'righteousness'."[62] It demands that readers respond to all the instances of "there was no" that echo throughout this story by acting to create the *shalom* that was not offered to the unnamed woman and continues to be withheld from people of contemporary times, both named and unnamed. The voices of the migrant farm laborers echo the pained voice of this woman who was disempowered and dehumanized; it is important that we hear her voice so that her injustice does not continue on in their stories. Judges 19 continues to ask contemporary audiences how they speak into all of those cases of "there was no" in order to bring about a faith-filled reflex action for healing, justice, and *shalom* for the world and the people of God.

BIBLIOGRAPHY

"Aplikasi Backpicker Memudahkan Pemetik Buah Mendapatkan Kerja Di Australia." *Tempo*. June 3, 2020. https://tinyurl.com/374ujjcz.

Barry, Nicholas. "In Australia, Land of the 'Fair Go', Not Everyone Gets an Equal Slice of the Pie." *The Conversation*. January 26, 2017. https://tinyurl.com/89t8bdf9.

Bhole, Aneeta. "Despite Travel Bans, Fruit Pickers from the Pacific Will Arrive in the NT This Month." *SBS News*. September 1, 2020. https://tinyurl.com/bmn4auwe.

Bonyhady, Nick. "MPs Back Proposal to Give Refugees Residency for Fruit Picking." *The Age*. September 14, 2020. https://tinyurl.com/5a7n2yc5.

Butler, Trent C. *Judges*. WBC 8. Nashville: Thomas Nelson, 2008.

Davies, Anne. "Death in the Sun: Australia's 88-Day Law Leaves Backpackers Exploited and Exposed." *The Guardian*. May 20, 2018. https://tinyurl.com/3k8m4mjj.

Dharamraj, Havilah. "Judges." Pages 1011–128 in *South Asian Bible Commentary*. Udaipur, Rajasthan: Open Door, 2015.

Duke, Jennifer. "One in Five Young Children Living in Poverty in Australia: Curtin University." *The Sydney Morning Herald*. August 28, 2020. https://tinyurl.com/5yymdj64.

Evans, Mary J. *Judges and Ruth*. TOTC 7. Downers Grove, IL: Inter-Varsity Press, 2017.

Foley, Mike. "Unemployed Australians Won't Fill Gaps in Agriculture Workforce: Farmers." *The Age*. August 3, 2020. https://tinyurl.com/3wsd3uy5.

Harris, J. G., Cheryl A. Brown, and Michael S. Moore. *Joshua, Judges, Ruth*. Grand Rapids: Baker Books, 2012.

Jones-Warsaw, Koala. "Toward a Womanist Hermeneutic: A Reading of Judges 19–21." *Journal of the Interdenominational Theological Center* 22 (1994): 18–35.

Keefe, Alice A. "Rapes of Women/Wars of Men." Pages 79–97 in *Women, War, and Metaphor: Language and Society in the Study of the Hebrew Bible*. Edited by Claudia V. Camp and Carole R. Fontaine. Semeia 61. Atlanta: Scholars Press, 1993.

Ladd, George Eldon. *The New Testament and Criticism*. Grand Rapids: Eerdmans, 1991.

---

[62] McCann, *Judges*, 238.

McCann, J. Clinton. *Judges*. Interpretation. Louisville: Westminster John Knox, 2011.
McGee, James. "Why I Lasted Just Five Weeks Working in the Apple Industry." *The Age*. March 3, 2019. https://tinyurl.com/vmpp8nct.
McKenzie, Nick, Richard Baker, and Saiful Hasam. "Fruits of Their Labour: Investigation into Exploitation of Migrant Fruit Picking Workers in Australia." *The Sydney Morning Herald*. Accessed September 16, 2020. https://tinyurl.com/4uce25wm.
Perdue, Leo G. *Proverbs*. Interpretation. Louisville: Westminster John Knox, 2012.
"Petani Di Victoria Krisis Pekerja Pemetik Buah." *Tempo*. March 5, 2019. https://tinyurl.com/rmczsray.
Potter, Rachael E., Maureen F. Dollard, and Michelle R. Tuckey. *Bullying and Harassment in Australian Workplaces: Results from the Australian Workplace Barometer Project 2014/2015*. Canberra: Safe Work Australia, 2016, https://tinyurl.com/btufncdh.
Ryan, Peter, and David Chau. "Woolworths Investigated after Admitting It Underpaid Staff up to $300 Million." *ABC News*. October 29, 2019. https://tinyurl.com/4u5k27ce.
Scholz, Susanne. "Judges." Pages 330–70 in *Women's Bible Commentary*. Edited by Carol A. Newsom, Sharon H. Ringe, and Jacqueline E. Lapsley. 3rd ed. Louisville: Westminster John Knox, 2012.
Trible, Phyllis. *Texts of Terror: Literary-Feminist Readings of Biblical Narratives*. OBT. Philadelphia: Fortress, 1984.
Yoder, Christine Roy. "Proverbs." Pages 633–61 in *Womens Bible Commentary*. Edited by Carol A. Newsom, Sharon H. Ringe, and Jacqueline E. Lapsley. 3rd ed. Louisville: Westminster John Knox, 2012.

11

Interrogating Ahithophel: Intersecting Gender and Class in Biblical Text and South African Context

Gerald O. West

This essay emerges from three related strands of feminist work: the work of a biblical studies feminist ancestor, Phyllis Trible, the work of African feminist biblical studies, and the embodied work of the ordinary African women with whom I have worked through the Contextual Bible Study work of the Ujamaa Centre.[1]

African feminist theologies draw directly on the lived realities of African women, but they emerged somewhat stridently in the 1980s from a range of earlier African liberation theologies. These include African theology, South African Black theology, Tanzanian Ujamaa theology, and South African Contextual theology. Significant intersections were already recognized within these parent, "father" theologies, between ethnicity/culture and economics/class (Ujamaa theology), and between race/coloniality and economics/class (South African Black theology).[2] But African women have had to struggle to get people to recognize the

---

[1] I gratefully acknowledge the contribution of the De Carle Distinguished Lectureship at the University of Otago, Dunedin, New Zealand, toward this work. I am also grateful to the hospitality of Pilgrim Theological College, Melbourne, Australia, which enabled me to present a paper at the conference "The State of Feminist Biblical Scholarship: Where Are We Now?"

[2] Sergio Torres and Virginia Fabella, eds., *The Emergent Gospel: Theology from the Underside of History* (Maryknoll, NY: Orbis Books, 1978); Virginia Fabella and Sergio Torres, eds., *Irruption of the Third World: Challenge to Theology; Papers from the Fifth International Conference of the Ecumenical Association of Third World Theologians, August 17–29, 1981, New Delhi, India* (Maryknoll, NY: Orbis Books, 1983); Kofi Appiah-Kobi and Sergio Torres, eds., *African Theology en Route: Papers from the Pan-African Conference of Third World Theologians, December 17–23, 1977, Accra, Ghana* (Maryknoll, NY: Orbis Books, 1983); Virginia Fabella and Sergio Torres, eds., *Doing Theology in a Divided World* (Maryknoll, NY: Orbis Books, 1985); Virginia

intersection between gender and each of these other fundamental systems, whether economics/class, ethnicity/culture, or race/coloniality. Within each of these father liberation theologies, the patriarchal system was bracketed, at least for a time.

The African women's theologian Mercy Amba Oduyoye tells, for example, of how third world women had to fight to achieve recognition of their gender-systemic struggle within the Ecumenical Association of Third World Theologians (EATWOT).[3] EATWOT in the late 1970s and early 1980s had foregrounded economics/class, culture/ethnicity, and race/coloniality as the root systemic realities of struggle in the so-called Third World.[4] African women not only added patriarchy to this systemic analysis, they also insisted that it intersected each of the other systems—culture/ethnicity, race/coloniality, and economics/class, speaking of the threefold oppression of African women based on their sex/gender, their race, and their class.[5] What this formulation—sex/gender, race, class—makes clear is that culture and/as patriarchy are entangled.[6] Sex/gender are cultural and/as patriarchal. So it is not surprising that this entanglement has been the primary site of African feminist biblical and theological work.

African feminist theology—or, African "women's" theology, as they prefer—has a significant presence within African theologies. The Circle of Concerned African Women Theologians (the Circle) has been a catalyst in this process, establishing mentoring and writing circles of African women across the African continent.[7] Although the Circle has tended to focus on intersections of gender and

---

Fabella and Mercy Amba Oduyoye, eds., *With Passion and Compassion: Third World Women Doing Theology* (Maryknoll, NY: Orbis Books, 1988).

[3] Mercy Amba Oduyoye, "Reflections from a Third World Woman's Perspective: Women's Experience and Liberation Theologies," in *Irruption of the Third World: Challenge to Theology*, ed. Virginia Fabella and Sergio Torres (Maryknoll, NY: Orbis Books, 1983); Fabella and Oduyoye, *With Passion*. For a historical overview and analysis within EATWOT, see Rosemary Radford Ruether, "Feminist Theologies in Latin America," *Feminist Theology* 9 (2000): 18–32. For an African reflection, see Musa W. Dube, *Postcolonial Feminist Interpretation of the Bible* (Saint Louis, MO: Chalice, 2000), 112.

[4] For a detailed analysis of EATWOT literature in this regard, see Per Frostin, *Liberation Theology in Tanzania and South Africa: A First World Interpretation* (Lund: Lund University Press, 1988).

[5] "Women Resist Triple Oppression," South African History Archive, accessed February 5, 2021, https://tinyurl.com/rnkhxxme. This analysis uses "sex" rather than "gender." The more common term used by African women's theology, which emphasizes cultural constructions, is "gender."

[6] I use "entangled" in the way it is used by Achille Mbembe, *On the Postcolony* (Berkeley: University of California Press, 2001), 16.

[7] Mercy Amba Oduyoye and Musimbi Kanyoro, eds., *Talitha, Qumi! Proceedings of the Convocation of African Women Theologians 1989* (Ibadan: Daystar, 1990); Rachel NyaGondwe

culture and/as patriarchy, some African women biblical scholars have included race and/as class as systems that must be intersected with gender.[8]

South African feminist biblical scholar Makhosazana Nzimande, for example, stands in the tradition of South African Black theology, supplementing its resources with the work of African women's biblical hermeneutics and postcolonial biblical hermeneutics. Her *imbokodo* (grinding stone) hermeneutics draws deeply on the work of Black theology's Itumeleng Mosala.[9] Nzimande seeks to locate the struggles of "the oppressed and exploited" within a Bible that is intrinsically a site of struggle and takes up Mosala's challenge of what it means to use a Bible that was brought by missionaries and colonial powers but is now African in order to get stolen African land back.[10] She also draws on the southern African postcolonial feminist work of Musa Dube, for whom land is a central question, and who, like Mosala, recognizes the importance of the economic domain.[11]

The imperial powers and their apartheid beneficiaries must be held to account for the land they seized and the proceeds of this plunder, insists Nzimande. But, she continues, "for black African women in post-apartheid South Africa and in related postcolonial contexts where patriarchy reigns supreme, land restitution would not be beneficial unless there is a radical change in the patriarchal family structures"; what she calls "neo-tribal" patriarchal family structures are part of the problem.[12]

Nzimande's contribution to the post-apartheid land restitution project is to bring her South African context into dialogue with kindred struggles "over stolen

---

Fiedler, *A History of the Circle of Concerned African Women Theologians 1989–2007* (Zomba, Malawi: Mzuni Press, 2017).

[8] Musa W. Dube, "Toward a Postcolonial Feminist Interpretation of the Bible," *Semeia* 78 (1997): 11–26; Dube, *Postcolonial Feminist Interpretation*; Dube, "Divining Ruth for International Relations," in *Other Ways of Reading: African Women and the Bible*, ed. Musa W. Dube (Atlanta: Society of Biblical Literature and Geneva: WCC Publications, 2001); Dube, "Looking Back and Forward: Postcolonialism, Globalization, God and Gender," *Scriptura* 92 (2006): 178–93; Dube, "African Biblical Interpretation," in *The Oxford Encyclopedia of Biblical Interpretation*, ed. Steven L. McKenzie (Oxford: Oxford University Press, 2013), 8–17; Makhosazana K. Nzimande, "Postcolonial Biblical Interpretation in Post-Apartheid South Africa: The *Gebirah* in the Hebrew Bible in the Light of Queen Jezebel and the Queen Mother of Lemuel" (PhD diss., Texas Christian University, 2005); Nzimande, "Reconfiguring Jezebel: A Postcolonial *Imbokodo* Reading of the Story of Naboth's Vineyard (1 Kings 21:1–16)," in *African and European Readers of the Bible in Dialogue: In Quest of a Shared Meaning*, ed. Hans de Wit and Gerald O. West (Leiden: Brill, 2008), 223–58.

[9] *Wathint' abafazi, wathint' imbokodo* ("You strike a woman, you strike a grinding stone").

[10] Nzimande, "Reconfiguring," 230. See also Itumeleng J. Mosala, *Biblical Hermeneutics and Black Theology in South Africa* (Grand Rapids: Eerdmans, 1989), 153.

[11] Nzimande, "Reconfiguring," 233.

[12] Nzimande, "Reconfiguring," 234.

lands" in the biblical text.[13] Her first interpretive move follows Mosala, using historical-critical resources to locate the biblical text (1 Kgs 21:1–16) historically. But her next move is not a materialist sociological analysis of this period, as would be Mosala's next step; instead, she draws on feminist literary analysis in order to provide a detailed characterization of the leading female character (Queen Jezebel). The sociological contribution comes in her next move, in which she locates the text within its imperial setting (Phoenician imperialism), giving attention to both the literary imperial setting and the ancient sociohistorical imperial setting. Her final interpretive move is to delineate the class relations within this imperial context (including Jezebel as part of a royal household).[14]

She then brings this text, read through her set of (*imbokodo*) interpretive resources, into dialogue with the South African context, recovering the identity and roles of African queen mothers in their governance of African land. The recovery of African culture and/as religion, as envisaged by (the third phase of) Black theology, is apparent.[15] But she does not conclude her work with this religiocultural recovery. She pushes the boundaries of feminist postcolonial criticism to include matters of class, recovering the voices of "those at the receiving end of the Queens' and Queen Mothers' policies."[16] She uses her *imbokodo* hermeneutics "to read with sensitivity towards the marginalised and dispossessed," the South African equivalents of Naboth's wife, recognizing that "the beneficiaries" of such indigenous female elites "are themselves and their sons, rather than the general grassroots populace they are expected to represent by virtue of their royal privileges."[17] "While a postcolonial *imbokodo* hermeneutics acknowledges black female presence and activity [including female governance of African geographical territories] in African historiography, it also notes with regret the pervasive injustice that reigned supreme in African political systems of governance."[18] Remembering these powerful African women is a postcolonial imperative, insists Nzimande, but so is de-ideologizing them economically, for, in so doing, we also remember those women from the lower classes over whom these elite women had power.[19]

In this essay, I want to build on Nzimande's set of intersections, probing in particular the intersections between economic struggles and gender struggles, between economic systems and gender systems. My starting point is the absence of

---

[13] Nzimande, "Reconfiguring Jezebel," 234.
[14] Nzimande, "Reconfiguring Jezebel," 234–37.
[15] For an analysis of the different but overlapping phases of South African Black theology, see Gerald O. West, *The Stolen Bible: From Tool of Imperialism to African Icon* (Leiden: Brill and Pietermaritzburg: Cluster, 2016), 318–48.
[16] Nzimande, "Reconfiguring," 243.
[17] Nzimande, "Reconfiguring," 246–48 and 243, respectively.
[18] Nzimande, "Reconfiguring," 242–43.
[19] Nzimande, "Reconfiguring," 244, 52–54.

11. Interrogating Ahithophel

this intersection in the resistance theology of the Judean עם הארץ (*'am ha'arets*), exemplified in Ahithophel the Gilonite. My way into recovering this intersection is to follow the example of Dube, who imagined letters from Orpah to Ruth.[20] For Dube, such imaginings are required as part of a postcolonial hermeneutic, as a strategy by postcolonial African subjects to "read for" decolonization.[21] Reading for decolonization requires both rereading and rewriting the Bible, telling untold stories.[22] I imagine letters as a way of rereading and rewriting for postcolonial intersections, drawing, as Dube does, on the ways in which ordinary African women have heard and read these texts.[23]

I also follow the collection of imaginary letters between biblical characters edited by Philip Davies. Such letters, he indicates, "try to represent the implied views of their supposed writers, most of whom have not had the opportunity of expressing these before," so filling intertextual "lacunae."[24] Interestingly, he includes two letters from Ahithophel, which he characterizes as "suicide notes," one

---

[20] Musa W. Dube, "The Unpublished Letters of Orpah to Ruth," in *Ruth and Esther: A Feminist Companion to the Bible*, ed. Athalya Brenner (Sheffield: Sheffield Academic, 1999), 145–50.

[21] Dube, *Postcolonial Feminist Interpretation*, 49, 116, 22–23. "Given the centrality of cultural texts to imperialist projects," she argues in Musa W. Dube, "Reading for Decolonization (John 4:1–42)," *Semeia* 75 (1996): 42–43, "the struggle for liberation is not limited to military, economic, and political arenas. It necessarily requires and includes a cultural battle of reader-writers who attempt to arrest the violence of imperializing texts."

[22] Dube, "Unpublished Letters," 146. On rereading and rewriting, Dube, "Reading," 43 says: "The colonized reread the imperializing texts and write new narratives that assert the adequacy of their humanity, the reality of global diversity, and their right to independence." Among the rewritings that postcolonial subjects do is a rewriting of the Bible, a rewriting that "recognizes and makes attempts to arrest the imperializing aspects of the story"; see Dube, "Reading," 54. For similar African discussions about rewriting the Bible, see Isabel Mukonyora, James L. Cox, and Frans J. Verstraelen, eds., *Re-Writing the Bible: The Real Issues* (Gweru: Mambo, 1993).

[23] On the value of letters, see Dube, *Postcolonial Feminist Interpretation*, 197–98. Dube, "Unpublished Letters," 145–47 draws on her grandmother and other Batswana women. I draw on the many women who have participated in the contextual bible studies of the Ujamaa Centre for Community Development and Research over many years; see Gerald O. West and Phumzile Zondi-Mabizela, "The Bible Story That Became a Campaign: The Tamar Campaign in South Africa (and Beyond)," *Ministerial Formation* 103 (2004): 4–12. It is vital for me to locate my work, given my white male South African identity, within Black African women's experience and work. This work has partially (both "in part" and in a manner that is partial, or biased) reconstituted who I am; see Sharon D. Welch, *A Feminist Ethic of Risk* (Minneapolis: Fortress, 1990), 151.

[24] Philip R. Davies, ed., *Yours Faithfully: Virtual Letters from the Bible* (London: Equinox, 2004), vii and x, respectively. See also Georg Retzlaff, *The Other Side: Hitherto Unpublished Letters by Biblical Heroes* (Bloomington, IN: AuthorHouse, 2009).

to Absalom and one to Eliam, his son.²⁵ My letters are rather brief, limiting the liberties I have taken in my search for intersections. And I could not resist adding some biblical graffiti.²⁶ Finally, I follow the biblical letters within the 2 Samuel narratives written by David to Joab (2 Sam 11:14) and by Bathsheba to David (2 Sam 11:5), imagining further similar letters.²⁷ Trible's literary-narrative work, a significant influence on my activism and scholarship since the early 1980s, guides my literary-narrative analysis and imagination.²⁸

LETTERS LONGING FOR INTERSECTION

FROM BATHSHEBA TO AHITHOPHEL

A letter from Bathsheba:
To her grandfather, Ahithophel:
Well-being to my grandfather.
May the god Yahweh ordain well-being and health for my grandfather.²⁹

I am confused, for I sent you a letter as soon as David took me.³⁰ I was worried, for I heard, too late, that David had not gone out to battle as was the custom of kings.³¹ If I had known that David remained in Jerusalem, I never would have decided to bathe outdoors, but it was a beautiful day, and I believed the king was not in his quarters.³²

I wrote immediately, asking you to intervene, hoping that by the time I appeared before David, you would be there at his side protecting me. But you were not there. David took me.³³ While his army was ravishing the sons of Ammon, David was ravishing your granddaughter.³⁴

---

²⁵ Davies, *Yours Faithfully*, x; for the letters, see 65–68 and 69–73, respectively.
²⁶ Jennifer Baird and Claire Taylor, *Ancient Graffiti in Context* (London: Routledge, 2010).
²⁷ My thanks to Monica Melanchthon for reminding me of these letters within the narrative itself.
²⁸ Gerald O. West, *Biblical Hermeneutics of Liberation: Modes of Reading the Bible in the South African Context*, 2nd ed. (Maryknoll, NY: Orbis Books and Pietermaritzburg: Cluster, 1995 [1991]).
²⁹ The format of these letters loosely follows similar private letters from Babylonia; see A. Leo Oppenheim, ed. *Letters from Mesopotamia: Official, Business, and Private Letters on Clay Tablets from Two Millenia* (Chicago: University of Chicago Press), 193–95. Ahithophel is the father of Eliam, who is Bathsheba's father (compare 2 Sam 23:34 with 2 Sam 11:3).
³⁰ 2 Sam 11:4, where "took" is rendered with the root לקח in Hebrew.
³¹ 2 Sam 11:1.
³² 2 Sam 11:2.
³³ 2 Sam 11:4.
³⁴ 2 Sam 11:1, 4.

Did you believe that by raping me David would be bound more deeply to our family? Did you hope that David would make me his principal wife? Did you hope that your influence in the royal court would increase?

David keeps me away from the affairs of men, but I have heard rumors among the servants that David has had my husband, your son-in-law, a loyal member of Joab's army, killed. Uriah has not come to redeem me. Neither have you.

I am now pregnant and fear for my child, your great-grandson (for the women who attend me have assured me, in the name of Asherah, that I will bear a son). I remember your misgiving about the monarchy, when the prophet Samuel warned you and the other elders how a king would "take" and "take" and "take."[35] What kind of world will my son be born into? What will you do?

Grandfather, why are you silent? You told me tales of how you tried to use our law to constrain the power of the king. You believed in justice for our people, the 'am ha'arets. Am I not one of the people of the land? What is happening to our land at the hand of David? The king continues to take, and take, and take.

And so do his sons. I heard today, which is why I have found the courage to write to you once again, that Amnon has raped his sister Tamar. Even women from the royal household are not safe. I have written to Tamar. She is now in the household of Absalom. The servant who takes the letter to Tamar bears this letter to you, for I know you are fond of Absalom. I hope Tamar will be able to find a way to pass this letter on to you.

Send me a sign of hope. Intervene to stop the rape of our land and its daughters.

From Tamar to Ahithophel

A letter from Tamar:[36]
To her uncle, Ahithophel:
Now I am praying to Yahweh and the goddess Asherah to keep my uncle in good health.[37]

---

[35] 1 Sam 8:11, 13, 14, (15), 16, 17, which also use the Hebrew root לק״ח.

[36] Here and in the narrative analysis that follows I am indebted to the pioneering work of Phyllis Trible, particularly Trible, "Depatriarchalization in Biblical Interpretation," *JAAR* 41 (1973): 30–49; Trible, *Texts of Terror: Literary-Feminist Readings of Biblical Narratives* (Philadelphia: Fortress, 1984). Her work has been deeply significant for my own work; see, e.g., West, *Biblical Hermeneutics* and Gerald O. West, "Deploying the Literary Detail of a Biblical Text (2 Samuel 13:1–22) in Search of Redemptive Masculinities," in *Interested Readers: Essays on the Hebrew Bible in Honor of David J. A. Clines*, ed. James K. Aitken, Jeremy M. S. Clines, and Christl M. Maier (Atlanta: Society of Biblical Literature, 2013), 297–312.

[37] The format of these letters loosely follows similar private letters from Babylonia; see Oppenheim, *Letters*, 193–95.

I take courage from the letters of Mother Bathsheba, which a servant has brought to Absalom's house. So I send you a letter of my own.

I do not know of what she has written to you, but she has written words of wisdom and empathy to me. When my father took her, I feared for the future of my brothers. My father was obsessed by Mother Bathsheba, replacing our mothers in his heart and bed with her. But I see now that she is truly a granddaughter of yours.

She spoke to me, as I now am, a desolate woman, shut up in my brother's house.[38] She counselled me. The female servants told her how Amnon had raped me, and she heard from David that Absalom has taken me into his household. She heard, too, how I had resisted Amnon in word and deed.[39] She tells me the women are composing a story to remember me.

I write to you, wise Uncle Ahithophel, asking that you tell our story among the men. The king, my father, has said and done nothing. Brother Absalom has provided me with protection and honors me by giving my name to his own daughter.[40] But he has silenced me, limiting my resistance by restricting me to his household.

I write this letter to break my silence, asking you to rupture the silence that screams within these royal walls.[41] You are renowned for your wisdom and your commitment to justice. You spoke, Mother Bathsheba tells me, against the economic excesses of a king who would take and take and take.

But what about those who take the daughters of the people of the land?[42]

Forgive me for being so bold. I am told boldness does not become a woman. But there are rumors of change in Israel. There is a fierce light in Brother Absalom's eyes. Does it burn for justice for me? I trust you will guide him in the paths of Yahweh's justice.

FROM THE *PILAGSHIM* TO AHITHOPHEL

A letter from the *Pilagshim*:
To Elder Ahithophel:
May the gods Asherah and Yahweh "bless" (בר״ך) our elder.[43]

---

[38] 2 Sam 13:20.
[39] 2 Sam 13:12–13, 16, 19.
[40] 2 Sam 14:27.
[41] Davies, *Yours Faithfully*, 71.
[42] 1 Sam 8:13.
[43] The format of these letters loosely follows similar private letters from Babylonia; see Oppenheim, *Letters*, 193–95. For this use of בר״ך, which usually means "to bless" to mean "curse" or "blaspheme," see Job 2:9.

We are your daughters. We were taken by David from our families to serve him. Our families were told that we would be used as perfumers and cooks and bakers.[44] But the king has used us in other ways.

We have hidden our shame from our families. We have been silent. But our shame has now been exposed in public.[45] Absalom has raped us before the eyes of our families.

As for us, where will we get rid of our shame?[46] And as for you, you who has been considered wise by your people, will you not be like one of the fools in Judah?[47]

We, your daughters, testify against you. Our cries and the cries of our mother, Asherah, mount to Yahweh who hears the cries of the oppressed, even ordinary women.[48] May the god Yahweh ordain retribution for you our elder, Ahithophel the Gilonite.

GRAFFITI ON THE JERUSALEM PALACE WALL

David has taken,
Amnon has taken,
Ahithophel has taken,
Absalom has taken…
your daughters!
Vuka![49]

LOCATING AHITHOPHEL (SOCIOHISTORICALLY)

Letters such as these, voices such as these, bear witness to an unbearable gap in the biblical narrative. Ahithophel, in working for political and economic justice, chooses not to work for gender justice. He is silent about the rape of his granddaughter, his grand-niece, and the daughters of the land, the *'am ha'arets*.

Gunther Wittenberg, a South African Contextual liberation theologian and biblical scholar, makes the argument that an enduring trajectory of resistance theology is located within the *'am ha'arets*, the people of the land. Although the resistance theology of the *'am ha'arets* takes form with the rise of the monarchy, Wittenberg is careful to demonstrate the political and economic significance of

---

[44] 1 Sam 8:13.
[45] 2 Sam 16:21–22.
[46] 2 Sam 13:13.
[47] 2 Sam 13:13, reframing Tamar's words to Amnon.
[48] 2 Sam 21:10–14. For the cries of the oppressed, see Exod 3:7.
[49] *Vuka* is is Zulu for "awake" or "arise"; scholars remain puzzled by the mixture of languages used in this inscription.

this sector prior to the changes wrought by monarchy. The "men of Judah," in Wittenberg's analysis, are Judah's relatively stable, relatively prosperous, and relatively educated "traditional leadership," who represent the rural agricultural community of the 'am ha'arets.[50] Wittenberg sees this sector as the repository of an early Judean agriculture-based wisdom tradition, which drew on the Egyptian wisdom traditions that characterized "Judean towns which had long been under direct Egyptian control."[51] Importantly, the 'am ha'arets retained a substantial independence, rooted in their ownership of rural land, their memory of "a period in their history when they were not ruled by kings," their "segmentary...[relatively democratic] acephalous society," and the leadership of clan-based "elders" and/or "judges."[52]

The resistance theology of this sector takes shape, Wittenberg argues, "within the context of historical struggles and conflicts."[53] It is a theology of struggle, the locus of which is monarchy. The resistance theology of the 'am ha'arets is forged in opposition to Egyptian colonial control of the towns of Judea—for, although they "shared in the great tradition of the ancient Near East.... They no longer shared the royal-urban imperial values"—and the attempts of David and Solomon "to establish an empire according to the Egyptian model."[54] Wittenberg's analysis is nuanced, and he is careful to point out that, although the 'am ha'arets are clearly apprehensive about monarchy, they supported David's kingship due to their memory of the Egyptian model (and their experience of the Canaanite city-states).[55] Within the "stable world" of an agricultural community, "where wealth came from the land," "everybody had a place, the rich and the poor, even the king, all of whom the 'am ha'arets of Judah had come to accept as part of the just order of creation."[56]

Wittenberg discerns a division emerging among the 'am ha'arets as the monarchic system under David incrementally developed ominous exploitative systemic features. The stable world on which so much of the agricultural life and wisdom was based became unstable. As Wittenberg shows, wisdom literature captures the emergence of a systemic relationship between wealth and poverty. Proverbs 22:2—"The rich and the poor have a common bond, the LORD is the maker of them all"—seems to reflect a nonsystemic relationship between "the rich" and "the poor" when compared to Prov 29:13—"The poor and the oppressor have a

---

[50] Gunther H. Wittenberg, *Resistance Theology in the Old Testament: Collected Essays* (Pietermaritzburg: Cluster, 2007), 56–57.
[51] Wittenberg, *Resistance Theology*, 57.
[52] Wittenberg, *Resistance Theology*, 98–99.
[53] Wittenberg, *Resistance Theology*, 137.
[54] Wittenberg, *Resistance Theology*, 57.
[55] Wittenberg, *Resistance Theology*, 12, 70.
[56] Wittenberg, *Resistance Theology*, 74.

common bond, the LORD gives light to the eyes of both."[57] "The two sayings are almost identical," Wittenberg notes, "but there is a major shift in meaning in the second one—from the neutral 'rich' to the pejorative 'oppressor'." "This shift in emphasis," he continues, "from wealth as a desirable asset and a blessing of God … typical of old wisdom, to wealth as a means of oppression, can best be understood … as a reaction of the old economy to the dynamics of a growing urban-based monetary economy," and to the introduction of "Canaanite [city-temple state] business practices, especially interest on loans," systems that "could be seen as being primarily responsible for the exploitation of the rural population."[58]

This systemic shift prompted a division within the 'am ha'arets, for a certain sector of the 'am ha'arets not only benefited from it but contributed to the exploitation of "the poorer Judahite fellow citizens who were sinking even deeper into debt and serfdom."[59] A sector of the 'am ha'arets "in the latter part of the monarchy" "became a rich, land-owning class who participated in the oppression of the poorer sections of the people, together with the merchants and other feudatories in the city of Jerusalem."[60] However, rediscovering "their own ancient sacred traditions," especially the exodus tradition, there remained "a counter-movement" within the 'am ha'arets.[61] This counter-movement and its resistance theology are the focus of Wittenberg's scholarship.

Given Wittenberg's analysis, where would we locate Ahithophel? Monarchy, it would seem, was reluctantly accepted (1 Sam 8:11–17) and carefully scrutinized, particularly its tendency toward a cultic-economic system, from David's establishment and naming of his own city, "the city of David" (2 Sam 5:9), to the transfer of the ark from Shiloh to Jerusalem (2 Sam 6:12), to David's desire to build a temple (2 Sam 7:2).[62] When David became distant from his people, failing to lead them into battle (1 Sam 8:20 // 2 Sam 11:1) and to govern them (1 Sam 8:5, 20

---

[57] These are my translations.
[58] Wittenberg, *Resistance Theology*, 75.
[59] Wittenberg, *Resistance Theology*, 71.
[60] Wittenberg *Resistance Theology*, 71, 133.
[61] Wittenberg, *Resistance Theology*, 14, 71.
[62] Wittenberg, *Resistance Theology*, 100–101. Wittenberg, *Resistance Theology*, 13 locates 1 Sam 8:11–17 within "the Shilonite resistance" to Solomon's "socio-economic and religious policies." It is not clear whether Abiathar the Shilonite priest "was involved in the resistance movement after Solomon had banished him," but it is clear that the prophet Ahijah, "who played a major part in the rebellion as a supporter of Jeroboam, came from Shiloh, the ancient cultic centre of the confederation of northern tribes." So Samuel, "the last great judge at Shiloh, who was instrumental in establishing the monarchy, here [1 Sam 8:11–17] interprets the wish of the people to have a king as rebellion against Yahweh." See also Mark G. Brett, "Narrative Deliberation in Biblical Politics," in *The Oxford Handbook to Biblical Narrative*, ed. Danna Nolan Fewell (New York: Oxford University Press, 2016), 541–42.

// 2 Sam 15:3), the *'am ha'arets* "played a major role" in Absalom's rebellion: "Absalom was proclaimed king in Hebron, the sacred city of Judah. His commander-in-chief Amasa was from Judah, as was Ahithophel who came from Gilo, one of the country towns" in 2 Sam 17:23.[63] Having initially supported David, the *'am ha'arets* "changed sides and supported the rebellion of Absalom" because of the increasingly "autocratic tendencies of the state."[64] Ahithophel, it would seem, stands within the sector of the *'am ha'arets* that accepts a constrained monarchy but rejects an exploitative monarchy, particularly a monarchy in which religion is used to legitimate economic exploitation.

LOCATING AHITHOPHEL (NARRATIVELY)

Ahithophel's story is told only in part. But even though partial, his role as a central character in the rebellion of Absalom is nevertheless clearly signalled in the narrative. When Absalom is "(re)called" by David (2 Sam 14:33) it is clear that David is the king: Absalom "came to the king and prostrated himself on his face to the ground before the king, and the king kissed Absalom" (2 Sam 14:33). No sooner is Absalom—who has been in exile in Jerusalem within his own house (within which Tamar too is exiles)—recalled by David than he begins to behave like a king. He travels around Jerusalem in a chariot, accompanied by a military guard of fifty men (2 Sam 15:1), and he rises early and stands in the gate of the city, offering himself instead of the absent king, replacing David in the gate, as a would-be "judge" offering "justice," and so "stealing" "away the hearts of the men of Israel" (2 Sam 15:6).

The opening paragraph of this part of the narrative (2 Sam 15:1–6) conveys a tension within the narrative point of view. The narrator concludes the paragraph with a negative assessment of Absalom's king-like actions: "Absalom stole away the hearts of the men of Israel" (2 Sam 15:6b).[65] But, in the first part of this sentence, there is a recognition that Absalom is doing what a king, *the* king, ought to be doing: "In this manner Absalom dealt with all Israel who came to the king for judgment" (2 Sam 15:6a).

The next paragraph of the narrative shifts from Absalom as would be judge to Absalom as self-proclaimed king (2 Sam 15: 7–11). Here the narrative point of view is less ambiguous. Absalom deceives David, the king, who gives Absalom permission to travel to Hebron, the site of David's power prior to Jerusalem, where Absalom promptly declares himself "king in Hebron" (2 Sam 15:10; cf. 2 Sam

---

[63] Wittenberg, *Resistance Theology*, 69.
[64] Wittenberg, *Resistance Theology*, 56.
[65] I am using the New American Standard Bible (1995) as a base translation, but I adapt it with my own translation in places.

2:11, where David is "king in Hebron"). Although accompanied by "two hundred men from Jerusalem," the narrator is at pains to point out that they "were invited and went innocently, and they did not know anything" (2 Sam 15:11). The narrator also makes it clear that the proclamation of Absalom as king is put into the mouths of "the tribes of Israel" by "spies" (2 Sam 15:10). It is a self-proclamation: "But Absalom sent spies throughout all the tribes of Israel, saying, 'As soon as you hear the sound of the trumpet, then you shall say, "Absalom is king in Hebron"'" (2 Sam 15:10).

In the next paragraph, which consists of two significant sentences (2 Sam 15:12), Ahithophel makes his entrance into the narrative for the first time: "And Absalom sent for Ahithophel the Gilonite, David's counsellor, from his city, Giloh, while he was offering the sacrifices. And the alliance was strong, for the people increased continually with Absalom" (2 Sam 15:12). The narrative point of view of this paragraph seems to be almost positive to Absalom's rebellion. The presence of this new character seems to shift the narrative point of view, almost as if the narrator is perplexed by this development in the narrator's own story. Again, the agency is Absalom's: Absalom sent, but this time it is not spies who are sent but "David's counsellor" who is sent "for." The juxtaposition of the grammatical components of this sentence make it clear that Ahithophel is a knowing subject. The obliqueness and ambiguity of the grammar indicate the narrator's conflicted point of view. "And Absalom sent for Ahithophel the Gilonite, a/the counsellor of David, from his city (David's or Ahithophel's) while he (Ahithophel or Absalom) was offering the sacrifices" (2 Sam 15:12a). Ahithophel is a/the "counsellor of David"; he is from "his," David's city of Giloh (in Judah), and Ahithophel (in one of the readings of the ambiguous phase) is engaged in "offering the sacrifices" when he is sent for. The first sentence in this paragraph is grudgingly, ambiguously positive about Ahithophel. The second sentence is quite clear about the effect of Ahithophel's introduction into the narrative: "And the alliance was mighty, for the people were walking *en masse* with Absalom" (2 Sam 15:12b). The implied narrative logic is that Ahithophel's presence gave legitimacy to the rebellion.

The focus in the next section (2 Sam 15:13–30) is solely on David. The setting shifts from Absalom's alliance in Hebron to David's Jerusalem. There is no ambiguity in what is communicated to David here: "Then a messenger came to David, saying, 'The hearts of the men of Israel are with Absalom'" (2 Sam 15:13). David, located in the court, directly instructs his household to flee the city (2 Sam 15:14); David, having stopped on the outskirts of the city, directly urges Ittai the Gittite, a foreigner, to "return and remain with the king [Absalom]" (2 Sam 15:19); David, having passed over the brook of Kidron, directly instructs Zadok the priest and the Levites to return the ark of the covenant of God to the city, indicating that he, David, is not sure whether he has the favor of God (2 Sam 15:25–26).

As David reaches the summit of the Mount of Olives, his direct speeches are interrupted by the direct speech of an anonymous voice: "And someone told David, saying, 'Ahithophel is among the alliance with Absalom'" (2 Sam 15:31a). The implied reader assumes that David already knew that Ahithophel had consolidated Absalom's rebellion by joining it, which is why David abandons Jerusalem so readily. Perhaps the reader and David are reminded of Ahithophel's presence at the apex (in terms of setting) of the narrative to emphasize that Ahithophel is the fulcrum character. What he advises and how his advice is taken will be decisive for the outcome of this monarchy. David, the narrator tells us, recognizes this. David once again takes up the direct speech: "And David said, 'O LORD, I pray, make the counsel of Ahithophel foolishness'" (2 Sam 15:31b). Having invoked God, David then conspires with Hushai the Archite (2 Sam 15: 32–37), David's friend (2 Sam 15:37), to "thwart the counsel of Ahithophel for me" (2 Sam 15:34). Ahithophel's counsel is key.

But before we come to Ahithophel's counsel, the tension in the narrative is deepened as the reader is required to recognize that there is now a new narrative complication. The small signs of support for David as he flees Jerusalem have gradually generated some self-belief in David, who sends Hushai to intervene on his behalf. Who will prevail, Hushai or Ahithophel? As Hushai leaves David on the summit, the reader watches as Hushai arrives in Jerusalem at the same narrative moment as Absalom, in a syntactically balanced sentence: "So Hushai, David's friend, came into the city, and Absalom came into Jerusalem" (2 Sam 15:37).

Then the reader waits while two other, briefer, related rebellions are narrated, the rebellions of Mephibosheth, as narrated by Ziba (2 Sam 16:1–4), and of Shimei, as narrated by the narrator (2 Sam 16:5–14); both represent the house of Saul. David is surrounded by rebellion, both from the north (Mephibosheth and Shimei) and the south (Absalom) (2 Sam 16:11).[66]

After Shimei cries out against David's injustice, David journeys to his destination, probably the "fords of the wilderness" (2 Sam 15:28), although at this moment in the narrative it is an unspecified destination (2 Sam 16:14). But it is here in this narratively uncertain place that the narrator specifically refers to David as "the king," making it clear that David is not alone but has support, and that, although weary, David "refreshed himself there" (2 Sam 16:14).

The conflict within the narrative's point of view is clearly evident in the very next paragraph, for, no sooner have we heard that David "refreshed himself there" (16:14), than we are told in the next sentence: "Then Absalom and all the people, the men of Israel, entered Jerusalem, and Ahithophel with him" (2 Sam 16:15). Again, Ahithophel is foregrounded. Again, Ahithophel has yet to speak. But there is a clear shift in setting, from David's undisclosed place in the wilderness

---

[66] Wittenberg, *Resistance Theology*, 13.

to the Jerusalem royal court. It is here, in Jerusalem, where Ahithophel will give his counsel. The narrative tension has brought us as readers to this point. The patient reader must endure one more delay, as we hear first from Hushai, as he attempts to ingratiate himself with Absalom (2 Sam 16:16–19).

At last we do hear from Ahithophel. Like the reader, Absalom is impatient, turning from Hushai to Ahithophel: "Then Absalom said to Ahithophel, 'Give your advice. What shall we do?'" (2 Sam 16:20). What do we as readers expect at this point in the narrative? What words will warrant this amount of narrative tension, this degree of narrative preparation for the words of Ahithophel?

The larger narrative offers us plenty of clues concerning political tendencies that would worry Ahithophel and the *'am ha'arets*: David's naming of the Jebusite city of Jerusalem after himself, "the city of David" (2 Sam 5:9); the building of a palace for David (2 Sam 5:11); David "taking" more and more women as his wives (2 Sam 5:13); David's determination to move the ark of God to his city (2 Sam 6:2); David's desire to build a temple for God adjacent to his palace (2 Sam 7:2); David's decision not to lead the army out to battle as was his duty (2 Sam 11:1); David's rape of Ahitophel's granddaughter, Bathsheba, and the brutal murder of her husband, Uriah, a loyal soldier (2 Sam 11:4, 15); David's refusal to take any action against his eldest son, Amnon, when he raped his daughter, Tamar (2 Sam 13:21); and David's absence from the gates of the city, failing to govern and provide justice to the *'am ha'arets* (2 Sam 5:3–4).[67]

Ahithophel is clearly a significant and complex character within the narrative. So what will Ahithophel say?

AHITHOPHEL'S ADVICE

When Ahithophel finally speaks, this is what he says: "Go in to your father's (secondary) wives, whom he has left to keep the house" (2 Sam 16:21a). The counsel of Ahithophel is to rape the *Pilagshim*.

What kind of justice is this? In resisting the emerging exploitation of David's monarchy, Ahithophel counsels violence against women so that, he continues, "'all Israel will hear that you have made yourself odious to your father. The hands of all who are with you will also be strengthened'" (2 Sam 16:21b–c). Rape is a tactic to differentiate Absalom from his father. The heteropatriarchal logic is that by abusing his father's women he is abusing his father's property and so abusing his father.

---

[67] A textual variant offers a reason why David does nothing: "but he would not punish his son Amnon, because he loved him, for he was his firstborn" (2 Sam 13:21). See also the letters from Ahithophel in Davies, *Yours Faithfully*, 66–67, 70.

But how can Ahithophel give such counsel? Surely "all Israel" has already heard the cry of his granddaughter Bathsheba and of Tamar?[68] "Hear O Israel" that the elders of the *'am ha'arets* call for the rape or your daughters! Perhaps at this moment Ahithophel is driven by a desire to avenge his granddaughter, Bathsheba—a rape for a rape, with the bodies of women being used as sites for male revenge (against males).[69]

Absalom goes beyond the counsel of Ahithophel, forgetting the cries of his sister Tamar and her words to Amnon, "'No, my brother, do not violate them, for such a thing is not done in Israel; do not do this disgraceful thing! As for these women, where could they get rid of their reproach? And as for you, you will be like one of the fools in Israel'" (2 Sam 13:12–13). He makes sure not only that "all Israel will hear" of the rape of the *Pilagshim*, but that all Israel will see the rape of the *Pilagshim*, for, we read: "So they pitched a tent for Absalom on the roof, and Absalom went in to his father's concubines in the sight of all Israel" (2 Sam 16:22). Perhaps Absalom, like Ahithophel, is driven by revenge, avenging his sister Tamar. Perhaps Absalom and Ahithophel conspire to use the precise site at which David stood when he saw Bathsheba bathing and decided to take her, choosing this same site to (gang) rape the *Pilagshim*.

It is here, at this horrific moment, that the narrator tell us: "The advice of Ahithophel, which he gave in those days, was as if one inquired of the word of God; so was all the advice of Ahithophel regarded by both David and Absalom" (2 Sam 16: 23). As the reader is about to find out, Absalom may follow Ahithophel's counsel with respect to the first part (2 Sam 16:21), but he does not do so with respect to the second part (2 Sam 17:1–3). The narrator has separated his counsel into two parts, foregrounding the former in all its terror. Perhaps the narrator is giving readers who are positively disposed to regime change pause to consider if this rebellion has the right to replace David. Perhaps this narrator, too, is appalled by this violence against women. The domestic violence of David against Bathsheba and Amnon against Tamar has been outed here as public violence against the *Pilagshim*. Narrative time stops.

When the narrative does continue—after a chapter break, in most Bibles, which disrupts the narrative but offers the appalled reader a moment of pause—we come to the second component of Ahithophel's counsel, which is about military strategy:

---

[68] Davies, *Yours Faithfully*, 70–71.

[69] This may be a form of "homophobic violence"; see James E. Harding, "Homophobia and Rape Culture in the Narratives of Early Israel," in *Rape Culture, Gender Violence, and Religion: Biblical Perspectives*, ed. Caroline Blyth, Emily Colgan, and Katie B. Edwards (Cham: Palgrave Macmillan, 2018), 168–69.

Furthermore, Ahithophel said to Absalom, 'Please let me choose 12,000 men that I may arise and pursue David tonight. I will come upon him while he is weary and exhausted and terrify him, so that all the people who are with him will flee. Then I will strike down the king alone, and I will bring back all the people to you. The return of everyone depends on the man you seek; then all the people will be at peace. (2 Sam 17:1–3)

The logic of the two components seems to be that, having alienated himself from David, Absalom must now move quickly to annihilate a dejected David.

Strangely, although "the plan pleased Absalom and all the elders of Israel" (2 Sam 17: 4), Absalom does not simply implement Ahithophel's advice as he did earlier. Instead, he summons Hushai to see what he thinks of this military plan. Hushai counters the counsel of Ahithophel and advises against a swift attack on David. Appealing to both Absalom's fear of his father and his vanity, Hushai counsels that Absalom rather than Ahithophel lead the attack on David, but only once the entire army has been gathered and readied (2 Sam 17:7–13).[70] Rather oddly, given the godly character of Ahithophel's counsel, Absalom rejects his military counsel and delays, giving David time to regroup. The coup loses its momentum, and Absalom is eventually defeated by David.

The narrator comments, saying: "For the LORD had ordained to thwart the good counsel of Ahithophel, so that the LORD might bring calamity on Absalom" (2 Sam 17:14). This is a strange formulation, as if the narrator both wants to affirm Ahithophel and see his counsel thwarted. More strange and disturbing is why God does not intervene earlier, thwarting the rape of David's wives. It would seem that the God of this narrator is not that interested either in political injustice or in gender injustice.

INTERSECTING INJUSTICES

Following Wittenberg's identification of a resistance theology among the *'am ha 'arets*, represented by figures like Ahithophel, I had hoped for intersecting resistances. While the narrator might be ideologically aligned with David despite recognizing an array of worrying autocratic and exploitative tendencies, he is remarkably blind and deaf to violence against women, whether Bathsheba, Tamar, or the *Pilagshim*. For no sooner has David returned to Jerusalem than we read:

> Then David came to his house at Jerusalem, and the king took the ten women, the concubines whom he had left to keep the house, and placed them under

---

[70] Davies, *Yours Faithfully*, 67.

guard and provided them with sustenance, but did not go in to them. So they were shut up until the day of their death, living as widows. (2 Sam 20:3)

I am not sure the *Pilagshim* minded too much that David did not "go in to them," but the cruelty of isolating them from potential support resources for their trauma among the wider *'am ha'arets*, including hopefully their families, is beyond belief.[71] They have been taken by David, they have been taken by Ahithophel, they have been taken by Absalom, and now they have been isolated and silenced, "shut up" as was Tamar (2 Sam 20:3). Desolate women all.[72]

But what of Ahithophel? "Now when Ahithophel saw that his counsel was not followed, he saddled his donkey and arose and went to his home, to his city, and set his house in order, and strangled himself; thus he died and was buried in the grave of his father" (2 Sam 17:23). Davies imagines, in letters from Ahithophel to Absalom and from Ahithophel to Eliam, his son, that Ahithophel does this to protect his family from David's vengeance.[73] We must hope that Ahithophel's suicide did protect the women in his family from another cycle of revenge rape.[74]

There is one more letter that I want to share. This letter, composed some years later, also searches for intersections between economics and gender.

---

[71] Gerald O. West, "Between Text and Trauma: Reading Job with People Living with HIV," in *Bible through the Lens of Trauma*, ed. Elizabeth C. Boase and Christopher G. Frechette (Atlanta: SBL Press, 2016), 209–30.

[72] 2 Sam 13:20. David Tombs, "Abdonment, Rape, and Second Abandonment: Hannah Baker in *13 Reasons Why* and the Royal Concubines in 2 Samuel 15–20," in *Rape Culture, Gender Violence, and Religion*, ed. Caroline Blyth, Emily Colgan, and Katie B. Edwards (Cham: Palgrave Macmillan, 2018), 126 identifies this as a "second abandonment" by David of the *Pilagshim*, and locates David's actions within an honour-shame culture, in which the "shame associated with their defilement would have transferred to David—the 'owner' of their sexuality." He argues that, in cases like this, the "initial trauma caused by sexual violence is thereby reinforced afterwards through the secondary vicitimization at the hands of people who could offer their support" (27). The recognition of serial abandonments is crucial in the contexts of gender-based violence, including the cases of Bathsheba and Tamar. In the case of the *Pilagshim*, the abandonments are multiple, for not only has David abandoned them twice, having "taken" them in the first instance (the initial abandonment), but they are also abandoned by Ahithophel and Absalom. While the abadonment of Bathsheba is different, because it involves a forced marriage to her rapist, it remains a form of abandonment, but see Monica Melanchthon, "Bathsheba Reconfigured: Sexual Violation and After," in *Gender, Religion und Kultur*, ed. Renata Jost (Stuttgart: Kohlhammer, 2010), 77–100.

[73] Davies, *Yours Faithfully*, 68, 69. For the two letters, see 65–68, 69–73.

[74] Harding, "Homophobia" analyzes in detail the rape culture of Judges 19–21, which includes both the rape of women and the threat of the rape of a man.

FROM THE WOMEN AND MEN OF THE *MAS* TO BATHSHEBA, THE QUEEN MOTHER OF KING SOLOMON

A letter from the Women and Men of the *Mas*:[75]
To the queen mother, Bathsheba:
Well-being to our mother.
May the god Yahweh ordain well-being and health for our mother.[76]

    We, the women and men of the *Mas*, do not know how to write letters, so we have asked our father, Jeroboam, to translate our song for you.[77] We sing this song each day as we begin our work, building an empire for your son on our broken bodies.

The king has taken
oh please awaken
our mother, his mother.

We are slaves,
slaves of your son,
of Solomon.

The king has taken
we are forsaken
your daughters, your sons.

We are slaves,
slaves of your son,
of Solomon.

The king has taken
the land has been broken,
we are broken, broken.

We are slaves,
slaves of your son,
of Solomon.

The king has taken
our hope is shaken
for our mother has made him.[78]

---

[75] *Mas* (מס) is the Hebrew term for forced labor; see 2 Sam 20:24; 1 Kings 4:6; 5:13, 14; 9:15, 21; 11:28; 12:4, 18.
[76] The format of these letters loosely follows similar private letters from Babylonia; Oppenheim, *Letters*, 193–95.
[77] 1 Kgs 11:26–28; 12:2.
[78] 1 Kgs 1:11–40.

We are slaves,
slaves of your son,
of Solomon.

We are slaves,
slaves of your son,
of Solomon.

INTERSECTING STORIES

Absalom's rebellion is swiftly followed by Sheba's rebellion (2 Sam 20:1–22), as the Davidic monarchy acquires a more systemic form, taking on the mechanisms of a city-temple state with its tributary mode of production.[79] The final form of the text includes elements of the Davidic state immediately after the account of Sheba's rebellion, outlining David's administration of the state and offering fragments of David's emerging tributary economic system using a census (2 Sam 24:1–9) and forced labour (*mas*) (2 Sam 20:24) as primary means of extraction and the temple-priesthood as the primary means of legitimation (2 Sam 20:25–26). David's economic oppression, and indeed that of all monarchic systems (as Samuel warns in 1 Sam 8:10–18), is evident, albeit in fragments, in the narratives of 2 Samuel. Economic oppression becomes even clearer in the rebellion of the northern clans, united as Israel, against David's successor, his son Solomon (1 Kgs 12:1–19). But in 2 Samuel we have to discern the fragments, for the narratives foreground other matters.

Among the fragments within these narratives about other matters are stories of violence against women. Taken together, the stories of Bathsheba, Tamar, and the *Pilagshim* form a coherent story of gender injustice. We can imagine this story being told, but it is a story that has been redacted by those with other interests, so we are left with fragments, albeit prophetic fragments. These fragments of economic injustice and gender injustice have yet to find each other in the narratives of 2 Samuel, even when we might have imagined them coalescing around the figure of Ahithophel, an elder from among the *'am ha'arets*. But, alas, Ahithophel failed to intersect injustices. We should not miss, as Ahithophel does, how the verb לק״ח, "to take" is used in these texts both for economic exploitation and for the exploitation of women.

---

[79] Roland Boer, "The Sacred Economy of Ancient 'Israel,'" *SJOT* 21 (2007): 29–48; Gerald O. West, "Tracking an Ancient Near Eastern Economic System: The Tributary Mode of Production and the Temple-State," *Old Testament Essays* 24 (2011): 511–32.

BIBLIOGRAPHY

Appiah-Kobi, Kofi, and Sergio Torres, eds. *African Theology En Route: Papers from the Pan-African Conference of Third World Theologians, December 17–23, 1977, Accra, Ghana.* Maryknoll, NY: Orbis Books, 1983.

Baird, Jennifer, and Claire Taylor. *Ancient Graffiti in Context.* London: Routledge, 2010.

Boer, Roland. "The Sacred Economy of Ancient 'Israel'." *SJOT* 21 (2007): 29–48.

Brett, Mark G. "Narrative Deliberation in Biblical Politics." Pages 540–49 in *The Oxford Handbook to Biblical Narrative.* Edited by Danna Nolan Fewell. New York: Oxford University Press, 2016.

Davies, Philip R., ed. *Yours Faithfully: Virtual Letters from the Bible.* London: Equinox, 2004.

Dube, Musa W. "African Biblical Interpretation." Pages 8–17 in *The Oxford Encyclopedia of Biblical Interpretation.* Edited by Steven L. McKenzie. Oxford: Oxford University Press, 2013.

———. "Divining Ruth for International Relations." Pages 179–95 in *Other Ways of Reading: African Women and the Bible.* Edited by Musa W. Dube. Atlanta: Society of Biblical Literature and Geneva: WCC Publications, 2001.

———. "Looking Back and Forward: Postcolonialism, Globalization, God and Gender." *Scriptura* 92 (2006): 178–93.

———. *Postcolonial Feminist Interpretation of the Bible.* Saint Louis, MO: Chalice, 2000.

———. "Reading for Decolonization (John 4:1–42)." *Semeia* 75 (1996): 37–59.

———. "Toward a Postcolonial Feminist Interpretation of the Bible." *Semeia* 78 (1997): 11–26.

———. "The Unpublished Letters of Orpah to Ruth." Pages 145–50 in *Ruth and Esther: A Feminist Companion to the Bible.* Edited by Athalya Brenner. Sheffield: Sheffield Academic, 1999.

Fabella, Virginia, and Mercy Amba Oduyoye, eds. *With Passion and Compassion: Third World Women Doing Theology.* Maryknoll, NY: Orbis Books, 1988.

Fabella, Virginia, and Sergio Torres, eds. *Doing Theology in a Divided World.* Maryknoll, NY: Orbis Books, 1985.

———, eds. *Irruption of the Third World: Challenge to Theology. Papers from the Fifth International Conference of the Ecumenical Association of Third World Theologians, August 17–29, 1981, New Delhi, India.* Maryknoll, NY: Orbis Books, 1983.

Fiedler, Rachel NyaGondwe. *A History of the Circle of Concerned African Women Theologians 1989–2007.* Zomba, Malawi: Mzuni Press, 2017.

Frostin, Per. *Liberation Theology in Tanzania and South Africa: A First World Interpretation.* Lund: Lund University Press, 1988.

Harding, James E. "Homophobia and Rape Culture in the Narratives of Early Israel." Pages 159–78 in *Rape Culture, Gender Violence, and Religion: Biblical Perspectives.* Edited by Caroline Blyth, Emily Colgan, and Katie B. Edwards. Cham: Palgrave Macmillan, 2018.

Marcuse, Herbert. *One-Dimensional Man: Studies in the Ideology of Advanced Industrial Society.* Boston: Beacon, 1964.

Mbembe, Achille. *On the Postcolony.* Berkeley: University of California Press, 2001.

Melanchthon, Monica. "Bathsheba Reconfigured: Sexual Violation and After." Pages 77–100 in *Gender, Religion und Kultur*. Edited by Renata Jost. Stuttgart: Kohlhammer, 2010.
Metz, Johann Baptist. *Faith in History and Society: Toward a Practical Fundamental Theology*. New York: Seabury, 1980.
Mosala, Itumeleng J. *Biblical Hermeneutics and Black Theology in South Africa*. Grand Rapids: Eerdmans, 1989.
Mukonyora, Isabel, James L. Cox, and Frans J. Verstraelen, eds. *Re-Writing the Bible: The Real Issues*. Gweru: Mambo, 1993.
Nzimande, Makhosazana K. "Postcolonial Biblical Interpretation in Post-Apartheid South Africa: The *Gebirah* in the Hebrew Bible in the Light of Queen Jezebel and the Queen Mother of Lemuel." PhD diss., Texas Christian University, 2005.
———. "Reconfiguring Jezebel: A Postcolonial *Imbokodo* Reading of the Story of Naboth's Vineyard (1 Kings 21:1–16)." Pages 223–58 in *African and European Readers of the Bible in Dialogue: In Quest of a Shared Meaning*. Edited by Hans de Wit and Gerald O. West, Leiden: Brill, 2008.
Oduyoye, Mercy Amba. "Reflections from a Third World Woman's Perspective: Women's Experience and Liberation Theologies." Pages 246–55 in *Irruption of the Third World: Challenge to Theology*. Edited by Virginia Fabella and Sergio Torres. Maryknoll, NY: Orbis Books, 1983.
Oduyoye, Mercy Amba, and Musimbi Kanyoro, eds. *Talitha, Qumi! Proceedings of the Convocation of African Women Theologians 1989*. Ibadan: Daystar, 1990.
Oppenheim, A. Leo, ed. *Letters from Mesopotamia: Official, Business, and Private Letters on Clay Tablets from Two Millenia*. Chicago: University of Chicago Press, 1967.
Retzlaff, Georg. *The Other Side: Hitherto Unpublished Letters by Biblical Heroes*. Bloomington, IN: AuthorHouse, 2009.
Ruether, Rosemary Radford. "Feminist Theologies in Latin America." *Feminist Theology* 9 (2000): 18–32.
Tombs, David. "Abdonment, Rape, and Second Abandonment: Hannah Baker in *13 Reasons Why* and the Royal Concubines in 2 Samuel 15–20." Pages 117–41 in *Rape Culture, Gender Violence, and Religion*. Edited by Caroline Blyth, Emily Colgan, and Katie B. Edwards. Cham: Palgrave Macmillan, 2018.
Torres, Sergio, and Virginia Fabella, eds. *The Emergent Gospel: Theology from the Underside of History*. Maryknoll, NY: Orbis Books, 1978.
Trible, Phyllis. "Depatriarchalization in Biblical Interpretation." *JAAR* 41 (1973): 30–49.
———. *Texts of Terror: Literary-Feminist Readings of Biblical Narratives*. OBT. Philadelphia: Fortress, 1984.
Welch, Sharon D. *A Feminist Ethic of Risk*. Minneapolis: Fortress, 1990.
West, Gerald O. "Between Text and Trauma: Reading Job with People Living with HIV." Pages 209–30 in *Bible through the Lens of Trauma*. Edited by Elizabeth C. Boase and Christopher G. Frechette. Atlanta: SBL Press, 2016.
———. *Biblical Hermeneutics of Liberation: Modes of Reading the Bible in the South African Context*. 2nd ed. Maryknoll, NY: Orbis Books and Pietermaritzburg: Cluster, 1995 (1991).
———. "Deploying the Literary Detail of a Biblical Text (2 Samuel 13:1–22) in Search of Redemptive Masculinities." Pages 297–312 in *Interested Readers: Essays on the Hebrew*

Bible in Honor of David J. A. Clines. Edited by James K. Aitken, Jeremy M. S. Clines, and Christl M. Maier, Atlanta: Society of Biblical Literature, 2013.

———. *The Stolen Bible: From Tool of Imperialism to African Icon*. Leiden: Brill and Pietermaritzburg: Cluster, 2016.

———. "Tracking an Ancient Near Eastern Economic System: The Tributary Mode of Production and the Temple-State." *OTE* 24 (2011): 511–32.

West, Gerald O., and Phumzile Zondi-Mabizela. "The Bible Story That Became a Campaign: The Tamar Campaign in South Africa (and Beyond)." *Ministerial Formation* 103 (2004): 4–12.

Wittenberg, Gunther H. *Resistance Theology in the Old Testament: Collected Essays*. Pietermaritzburg: Cluster, 2007.

"Women Resist Triple Oppression." South African History Archive. Accessed February 5, 2021. https://tinyurl.com/rnkhxxme.

12

Terror of Texts: Orality and the Reclaiming of Daughters' Land Rights (Numbers 27:1–11 and 36:1–12)

Jione Havea

Letters travel. Move. Shift. Drift, across time and space, over lands and waters. Letters cross over. Cross into. Enter. Invade? Letters communicate and make correspondences between individuals, collectives, interests, and worlds. From in-between fingers in-to eyes and minds, letters negotiate limits. Private limits. Public limits. Political limits. Cultural limits. Ideological limits. Some letters announce and advocate life. Some letters deny life and even call for death. Some letters go out in order to remember and some in order to forget. Some letters spam and scam, and many letters spam for many other reasons. Some letters reach their destinations and are received, while some reach but get ignored. Some letters go out but do not arrive. Lost letters. Some letters do not come out at all but are lost letters nonetheless. A few letters reach scripturality, canonized as epistles, and they live longer than others. Whatever the occasion and the consequence, letters go and come within the timing and spacing of lands and waters.

Some time back, somewhere close to the gathering places of the five Indigenous Australian Kulin Nations—Wurundjeri, Boonwurrung, Taungurong, Dja Dja Wurrung, Wathaurung—i wrote four letters to intersect flashbacks in the Hebrew Scriptures (Num 27:1–11 and Num 36:1–12) with concerns, struggles, and memories in the oral worlds of the dead and the living in Pasifika (for Oceania, Pacific Islands).[1] These letters, later touched up and shared in this chapter, were written on the "wings of *talanoa*," an expression that refers to complex and significant events in the oral preferring cultures of Pasifika.

---

[1] When i am the first person subject, i use the lowercase because i use the lowercase for all other subjects—you, she, he, it, we, they, other—and i look forward to the day when i will not need to explain why.

In several (but not all) of the native Pasifika languages, *talanoa* refers to three interflowing events: story, telling (of story), and conversation (around story and telling). One needs a story (*talanoa*) in order to relate and reciprocate with others, and one tells (*talanoa*) one's story (*talanoa*) in order for the conversation (*talanoa*) and the resulting relationship to come alive and prevail. Without story (*talanoa*) and telling (*talanoa*), the conversation (*talanoa*) is empty, and the relationship is meaningless; without telling (*talanoa*) and conversation (*talanoa*), the story (*talano*a) is dead; and without story (*talanoa*) and conversation (*talanoa*), the telling (*talanoa*) is abusive (or a "telling off"). On the wings of *talanoa*, my letters crossed between the textual worlds of scripture and the oral worlds of Pasifika; because my letters are addressed to two dead relatives ('Ana Loiloi and Sela Kakala) and two living females (Diya Lākai and Auntie Caroline), the letters come out at the intersection of the world of the living and the world of the dead (read: ancestors). The latter is not difficult to see and feel in the Pasifika world of *talanoa*, where the ancestors are not removed from the world of the living. In fact, we who are still alive live in the world of the (dead) ancestors. On the wings of *talanoa*, firstly, my letters oralize the textualized worlds of ancient scripture in a context where the living and the dead cor*respond*.

On the wings of *talanoa*, secondly, this chapter is not a reading of texts of terror, as has been done in the world of the living by Phyllis Trible, whose readings have been revisited and extended by several of the contributions to this collection. It is rather an offering that contains clusters of *talanoa* (story, telling, conversation) on the terror of texts. I explain in the letters below what the expression "terror of texts" means for me, but at this juncture i quickly note that texts have the power to create and change realities, uphold and hide memories, weave and unravel interests, and nurture and violate dreamings, as well as soothe and terrorize the living and the dead.[2] When the paired qualities of texts named in the sentence above tip in favor of one over the other, the terror of texts nags.

On the wings of *talanoa*, thirdly, i hope that this chapter assists in making more fluid the divide between formality (and formalism) and *casua*lity. In the form of letters, the tone of this chapter may be casual, but the drive is no less serious than more rigid and formalist attempts (associated with the old line of western scholarship). In addition, since this chapter comes out on a platform reserved for academic works, it is a simple reminder that academic works are dead if they do not engage in *talanoa* (and the gifts of orality).

The following letters, which are not free of the terror of texts, started off as my attempt to introduce the stories of five female biblical characters—Mahlah,

---

[2] For Indigenous Australians, "dreamtime" refers to the occasion when ancestral spirits created life and designed the air, water, and landscapes (some of which are set aside as ceremonial sites). The accounts and teachings of the dreamtime are preserved in "dreamings," which are sources of wisdom and meaning (similar to the scriptures of book cultures).

12. Terror of Texts 203

Noah, Hoglah, Milcah, Tirzah (Num 27)—to two dead relatives ('Ana Loiloi and Sela Kakala), an Indigenous Australian elder (Auntie Caroline), and a living relative (Diya Lākai).[3] The letters were written for oral presentation and were delivered to a live audience (at the Australian Collaborators in Feminist Theologies conference held at Melbourne on May 11, 2018), and then *talanoa* spread its wings.

LETTER 1

Somewhere close to the gathering places of the Kulin Nations (for non-Indigenous Australian readers, this means that i write somewhere in Melbourne, Victoria, Australia), a place that was never ceded by its traditional owners.

May 04, 2018

Dear 'Ana Loiloi,

You'd be surprised that i am writing to you after many years. The last time i wrote to you was a text message when you were still alive. My excuse for taking so long to write again is simple: i don't know which address you use these days. I trust that you are chilling with and *talauhu'i* to the ancestors, and that you will have time at some point to receive and read this letter.[4] Of course, you have all the time in the world! You have been dead for over ten years now, and time must mean something different to you these days.

I want to tell you the story of five sisters whom you would appreciate. I am not sure if their story is true or made up, but that does not matter to me. What matters is that they have a story, and a story has the capacity to create reality. In our language, *'oku 'i ai honau talanoa, ko honau koloa ia*—they have *talanoa*, and that is their wealth. In other words, their *talanoa* gives them worth. In our Pasifika oral cultures, *talanoa* does not have to reflect history or the truth (both of which could be faked, anyway). *Talanoa* has the capacity to create history and truth. So, these sisters have *talanoa*, and that's enough for me.

Their story is in the Bible, a book that does not tell many stories of women. Occasionally, some women are mentioned but mainly in the interests of their fathers, brothers, uncles, husbands, or sons. Moreover, many of those women are nameless, which is a way of making them subjects (they are in a story) and at the same time non-subjects (they are not named); in this way, to borrow a term that

---

[3] Together, these letters echo the spirit of the poem that Kathy Jetñil-Kijiner wrote for her seven-month old child, Matafele Peinam; see Jetñil-Kijiner, "United Nations Climate Summit Opening Ceremony—A Letter to My Daughter," *Kathy Jetñil-Kijiner*, September 24, 2014, https://tinyurl.com/vjtpckyc. The letters are addressed to the dead and the living, but they go out seeking the next and future generations.

[4] The word *talauhu'i* is Tongan for when young people disturb old people.

Julia Kristeva used a fair bit, they are *abjects*.[5] In that light, these sisters are special—they have a story, and they are named: Mahlah, Noah, Hoglah, Milcah, and Tirzah. Remember their names in case you run into them, or run into wo/men named after them, at some point.

I am sure that each of them has her own sets of *talanoa*, but the biblical narrator is not interested in those or in each of them as individuals. They are named in relation to their dead father, Zelophehad. Their *talanoa* is about a dead person, and that gives me the permission to write to you, my dead niece. I suspect that the sisters were named—Mahlah, Noah, Hoglah, Milcah, and Tirzah—only because their father Zelophehad did not have any sons.

They have a story in the Bible because they did not have a brother. If they had a brother, these sisters would have been forgotten like many unnamed and untold women. Please don't blame me for that. That's how the Bible operates, and this is part of what i call the "terror of texts." I am playing with the concept "texts of terror" that a white US biblical scholar, Phyllis Trible, introduced (1984). I identify her as white because color matters, and there are scholars of other colors in the United States. You died too early and did not experience the developments (but i can't say that they are advances) in social media. Recently, there has been the #BLM (Black Lives Matter) movement in response to racial discrimination in the United States. For people of color in North America, the color on their skin makes a difference with respect to privileges and discrimination. I'm sure you can understand this, given your experiences in a university where the faculty and student bodies were predominantly white.

Back to Trible: she was working on biblical texts of terror—that is, texts that are terrible and terrorizing of women. Yes, there are many of those in the Holy Bible, and i remember our conversations while you were still in hospital about how the Bible does not answer many of your questions about life. I appreciated that you found meaning in Buddhist scriptures and very grateful to your parents for putting a Buddhist saying on your tombstone.[6] It's radical that a Buddhist scriptural text has entered a Christian cemetery, thanks to you!

Building on but also diverting from Trible, my focus is on the terror of texts. Texts (writings, letters) are tools for remembering, but also for forgetting. It's when texts are written in order to forget that the terror of texts becomes evident. I'll explain this more in my next letter (to your aunt Sela) ... but wish you could see the faces to whom i'm reading this letter for the first time: i'm in a theological hall with feminists, mostly women, but there are a few men, the majority of whom are white, and they are probably more interested in hearing the story of the five sisters

---

[5] Julia Kristeva, *Powers of Horror: An Essay on Abjection*, trans. Leon S. Roudiez (New York: Columbia University Press, 1982), 1–4.

[6] "A journey of a thousand miles begins with a single step."

than in my ruminations about the terror of texts. Before i do that, do you remember the time you showed me the text messages from your gay friend, and from that other guy you thought was interested in you? Those boys didn't know i was reading their text messages! This is a curious thing about texts and letters: they are written for specific person(s), but the writers have no control over who reads them. In this case, i'm reading the letter written for you to others. I think that's a good way to control private letters: make them public. I am pointing this out because there is a tendency to think that the public and private spheres are gendered and divided. That's not how *talanoa* works. *Talanoa*, communication, and media make the private-public divide ridiculous.

Now, back to the story. Zelophehad has no sons to inherit his wealth, and his land would have been lost from his household had the five daughters—Mahlah, Noah, Hoglah, Milcah, and Tirzah—not raised their voices. Thank God they spoke up…right? They approach Moses and the authorities, the elders and "all the congregation," with a multi-plied claim concerning their dead father:

> Our father died in the wilderness; he was not among the company of those who gathered themselves together against the LORD in the company of Korah, but died for his own sin; and he had no sons. Why should the name of our father be taken away from his clan because he had no son? Give to us a possession among our father's brothers. (Num 27:3–4 NRSV)

Moses presents their claim to the LORD, who not only approves but also encodes a decree for all of the Israelites. There are two points to stress in relation to the claim of these sisters. First, the LORD recognizes them as right: "And the LORD spoke to Moses, saying: The daughters of Zelophehad *are right in what they are saying*; you shall indeed let them possess an inheritance among their father's brothers and pass the inheritance of their father to them" (Num 27:6–7). This is great affirmation! But it is also problematic. The sisters actually call attention to six matters, but the LORD passes judgment on only one of those. The sisters point to the facts that (1) their father died in the wilderness, (2) their father did not participate in Korah's rebellion, (3) their father died for his own sin, (4) their father did not have a son, (5) the name of their father should not be lost because he did not have a son, and (6) a possession from their father's family should be given to them. They said six things, but the response from the LORD makes it sound as if they were interested only in receiving an inheritance (#6). This is one example of the terror of texts: the LORD reduces the charge of the sisters to the material world (and, unfortunately, jumping to one of the songs you used to like, Madonna's "Material Girl" also falls into the trap of materiality!).

I don't like what the LORD does here, and i encourage you not to enter the LORD's theological closet. I want to believe that the five daughters—Mahlah, Noah, Hoglah, Milcah, and Tirzah—are smarter and more ideologically loaded than the LORD wants readers to believe. Most readers go along with the LORD because they do not think that women—like Mahlah, Noah, Hoglah, Milcah, and Tirzah—have something complex in mind. So, i don't think the LORD does justice to the claim of these five women, and i'll come back to it another time.

For now, i need to move to the second important point to make: because of the daughters' claim, a law was decreed for all of the Israelites:

> If a man dies but has no son, then you shall pass his inheritance on to his daughter. If he has no daughter, then you shall give his inheritance to his brothers. If he has no brothers, then you shall give his inheritance to his father's brothers. And if his father has no brothers, then you shall give his inheritance to the nearest kinsman of his clan, and he shall possess it. It shall be for the Israelites a statute and ordinance, as the LORD commanded Moses. (Num 27:8b–11)

This is radical. How many laws have been established because of the story or claim of women? No, i'm not asking about how you used to boss and lay the law over your brothers. Rather, i'm asking about public laws. There are so many laws established to silence, to control, and to violate women, but in the case of these five daughters—Mahlah, Noah, Hoglah, Milcah, and Tirzah—a law was decreed because of them. I think that this is worth celebrating, wherever you are now, and with whomever is in your company. Tell them the story of these sisters—Mahlah, Noah, Hoglah, Milcah, and Tirzah—and ask them to stand up for their rights. And for your rights. Your rights do not end simply because you are dead.

In the course of your celebration, also ask your mob if they are satisfied with what the LORD decrees. Why should women inherit only if they do not have a brother? Why don't women inherit alongside their brother(s)? And what about those women and men whose fathers and mothers have nothing to pass on to them? What good is a law about inheritance for people who have nothing to inherit? Why didn't Moses and the LORD think of them as well?

See what they think. And let me know.

Until the next time, uncle J (i stopped being Uncle Scar after you died)

ps (read "psst"): If you have not noticed, i am writing from somewhere close to the gathering places of the Kulin Nations—which means that we have shifted to Melbourne—the land that received your blood when you were embalmed, and i trust that the ancestors of this land received you in your rest.

ps2 (added after March 20, 2019): Your sister-in-law Amy gave birth to a beautiful girl, and they gave her a beautiful name: Loiloi Georgina.

LETTER 2

Still somewhere close to the unceded gathering places of the Kulin Nations

Still May 04, 2018

Just passed the breaking of my fast

Dear Sela Kakala,

You've been gone for over two years, and we occasionally think of and talk about you. I will not lie to you: we forget you sometimes, but we will not forget you forever. When we hear the mention of your name, we remember you. So it is important to have a name, right? And it is also important to have *talanoa*.

I just wrote to Loiloi explaining the *talanoa* of five sisters—Mahlah, Noah, Hoglah, Milcah, and Tirzah. You know where Loiloi is buried, so you can crawl over and ask her about my letter if she has not already told you. These sisters were the subjects of a chapter in my *Elusions* (2003) but reading their story this time made me realize how badly they were trapped in the theological closets of the Bible. This time also, i am more troubled with the absence of their mother. So, my mind has been wandering/wondering. And in wandering/wondering about their absent mother, i automatically think of you and how your two children (who are now fourteen) will grow up without you in their lives. They will bring fresh flowers to your grave on most Saturdays, but that will not be the same as having you in their daily lives. We can't change that now, but i hope that, when their *talanoa* is told, you will be named as well as remembered and not be like the story of the biblical sisters—Mahlah, Noah, Hoglah, Milcah, and Tirzah—whose mother is nowhere in their story.

As my mind wonders/wanders, i am troubled by several questions: Do the five sisters—Mahlah, Noah, Hoglah, Milcah, and Tirzah—share the same mother? How might their story be different if their mother(s) were named and had a say? Or do they make their claim at the urging of their hidden mother(s)? I'll tell you what i think about those questions…and you can decide to agree or not. Give me a signal if you wish, but don't freak out my audience!

I want to keep both possibilities: that the mother (and i'll be conventional and stick to one mother) is silent and absent, and that she is the prime mover behind the daughters. These possibilities are not contradictory—the mother could be silently (as far as the text is concerned) driving things through her daughters. I do not want to mix up the two possibilities, because they identify some of the differences between you and me. You are the one who will not be silenced, except (even?) by death, and i'm the one who lurks in the background, waiting to greet death. But this is not about you and me; this is about the ignored mother of the sisters.

The mother is silent and absent. And she is nameless. So, i say that we first give her a name. I propose that we call her Kulin! Why Kulin? Because, as you know, we live close to the gathering places of the Kulin Nations—consisting of the Wurundjeri, Boonwurrung, Taungurong, Dja Dja Wurrung, and Wathaurung people—these nations have systemically been silenced in this context. I should ask one of the traditional owners of this land for permission to use the name Kulin, and i'll do that when i find the appropriate opportunity. For the time being, in this *talanoa*, Kulin the mother of the five sisters represents the five peoples of the Kulin Nations. Beyond them, Kulin represents indigenous nations that are silenced and absent in this land, and in the texts and the readings of the Bible.

Kulin's silence and absence is another example of the terror of texts. I began *talanoa* on this to Loiloi, so please explain to her this also: When texts are written in order to silence, to remove and to hurt, and to forget, we have more evidence of the terror of texts. Numbers 27 exhibits the terror of texts by silencing and removing Kulin from the view of readers, but we can resist by reclaiming her presence, by giving her a name, and by giving her a place in the story. The fact that Kulin is absent from the biblical text does not mean that she should be absent from our reading.

Now, about the second possibility: that Kulin is the prime mover behind the daughters, pushing them to take their claim to Moses and to the congregation. Kulin is pushing the cause of her husband into public recognition and communal reception. This is a likely possibility on the basis of reading the story closely. As i explained in my letter to Loiloi, the sisters say six things, but the LORD's response only deals with one (#6).

> The sisters pointed to the fact that (1) their father died in the wilderness, (2) their father did not participate in Korah's rebellion, (3) their father died for his own sin, (4) their father did not have a son, (5) the name of their father should not be lost because he did not have a son, and (6) a possession from their father's family should be given to them.

There is something in the details that suggests to me that Kulin is motivating and pushing her daughters along. The daughters appear to want to clear their father from two possible charges: that he was part of a rebellion, and that he should be punished for not having a son. When we take the daughters out of the LORD's closet, we can hear them being more concerned about their father and his name (#1–5) than about them receiving his inheritance (#6). These matters are interrelated but emphasizing the inheritance (#6) silences Kulin. To emphasize the "vindication" and "name" of Zelophehad is to be trapped in the patriarchal frames of the Bible, but those acts can give Kulin a place in the *talanoa* of her daughters. What do you think about this suggestion, Sela? Could a trap (in the bible) be a release (in Indigenous Australia)?

I have two excuses for suggesting this reading. Firstly, i know that you would do everything possible to vindicate the name of your husband. My brother is lucky in this way. And secondly, there is a biblical story (Mark 6:14–29) in which a mother drives her daughter along. It's actually a sad story that explains the beheading of John the Baptist. Herodias was not Tongan, and i am not suggesting that you are like her. My point is simply this: there is biblical precedent for the view that a mother influences her daughter. And there are biblical stories in which mothers play active roles in their sons' lives: Hagar, Sarah, Rebekah, Rachel, Leah, Jochebed, Zipporah, Hannah, Naomi, and many others, both named and unnamed. God forbids that we recognize strong mothers only in the stories of sons but not in the stories of daughters as well.

So let's not stop at giving the mother of Mahlah, Noah, Hoglah, Milcah, and Tirzah a name—Kulin—let's also give her a place and a will in their *talanoa*. Would those be enough, Sela?

I am not a woman, so i should not pretend to know what daughters and mothers go through in the manly/blokey world. By the way, next Sunday is Mother's Day and i see a lot of mothers in my audience. Some of them have healthy children, and some don't; some are more privileged than others; some are expecting, and others are in pain and grieving; some look forward to Mother's Day, and some do not. I don't assume that all women share the same thinking, or that all mothers have the same expectation or emotion…but i wish you and these ladies a happy Mother's Day all the same.

I also do not assume that some women could speak on behalf of all women, or that some mothers should speak on behalf of all mothers. That would not be a very feminist thing to do. And who am i to explain what it means to be a woman, to be a mother, or to be a feminist? I hope that, in the next life, you would do some of that on our behalf.

Your brother in law, jione

ps: *sai tau 'ilo* (in Tongan, "good to know").

ps2 (added after July 30, 2019): Your husband has remarried, to Mele, and i fully understand if that made you turn in your grave.

LETTER 3

Still somewhere, close to the unceded gathering places of the Kulin Nations[7]

May 14, 2018

(a foggy morning, the day after Mother's Day)

Dear Auntie Caroline,

I am a migrant to your country, and i must first apologize that i did not seek your permission and the blessing of your peoples before our family settled down. Our family comes from two lands, India and Tonga, and we are privileged to be in your land.

Last Friday, i made a presentation at a conference organized by the Australian Collaborators in Feminist Theologies on "The State of Feminist Biblical Scholarship." In my presentation, i suggested (as you can see in Letter 2 above) that the name "Kulin" be given to the unnamed, unrecognized mother of the five daughters in a story split between Num 27:1–11 and Num 36:1–12. So i am writing to you for two reasons:

Firstly, to inform you of what i publicly suggested at this conference. I suggested Kulin in recognition of how your people are also unrecognized in the stories of this country, so, in this way, i aim to bring the attention of scholars and researchers both to the unnamed mother of the sisters in Num 27 and Num 36 and to the struggles of your people.

Secondly, to ask for your blessings on this naming exercise. It is intriguing to me that your Kulin Nations consist of five nations (Wurundjeri, Boonwurrung, Taungurong, Dja Dja Wurrung, Wathaurung), and that there are five sisters (Mahlah, Noah, Hoglah, Milcah, Tirzah) in Num 27 and Num 36. It would be *deadly* (in the indigenous sense) if there were an opportunity to undertake a series of bible studies on the stories of these five sisters with members of your five nations. Would that be possible? Or are you like some of my dead relatives, who would rather give the Bible a rest?

With respect, and in solidarity,

Jione (a recent settler in your land)

ps: Please let me know when, where, and how i could join in celebrating the gifts of your people. I understand that your people have struggles and pain, but i know that you also have wisdom and charm to share with the rest of us.

---

[7] This letter was written after the next one (letter 4), but it is culturally more appropriate to place it at this point (after letter 2).

ps2: when some of us forget the worth and joys of your people, we participate in what i call the terror of texts. Please don't let us get away with this.

LETTER 4

Still somewhere, close to the unceded gathering places of the Kulin Nations

May 07, 2018

(day after FakaMē, a Sunday that Tongan churches set aside for children)

After lunch

Dear Diya Lākai,

You don't know how to read long letters yet, and, at four years old, you might be too young for this kind of letter (despite Kathy Jetñil-Kijiner's poem to her much younger child, which you can view on YouTube). So save this letter for later. I know that if your mother has her way, you will be a radical feminist. Time will tell, and i might not be there to find out. So you have to write to me wherever the hell i'll be then.

I just wrote to two of your dead relatives, but i did not tell them all that needs to be told about the daughters of Kulin and Zelophehad—Mahlah, Noah, Hoglah, Milcah, and Tirzah. I saved the most troubling part for you, because this part is not for the dead but for the living. Besides, *talanoa* is not an exercise in telling everything. No one knows everything, and no one can tell everything. *Talanoa* can only be particular and partial (pun intended), and the best *talanoa* always holds something back.

The story of the sisters continues in Num 36:1–12. The elders on their father's side are not happy with the law that the LORD decreed, so they come with a counter claim:

> The LORD commanded my lord to give the land for inheritance by lot to the Israelites; and my lord was commanded by the LORD to give the inheritance of our brother Zelophehad to his daughters. But if they are married into another Israelite tribe, then their inheritance will be taken from the inheritance of our ancestors and added to the inheritance of the tribe into which they marry; so it will be taken away from the allotted portion of our inheritance. And when the jubilee of the Israelites comes, then their inheritance will be added to the inheritance of the tribe into which they have married; and their inheritance will be taken from the inheritance of our ancestral tribe. (Num 36:2b–4)

The elders are concerned that the tribe's ancestral portion will be lost if the daughters marry into a different tribe. Their concern is legit and reasonable. However, it reveals that the elders are also trapped in the LORD's material closet. Without anyone consulting the sisters or their mother, Moses declares the LORD's decision:

> Let them marry whom they think best; only it must be into a clan of their father's tribe that they are married, so that no inheritance of the Israelites shall be transferred from one tribe to another; for all Israelites shall retain the inheritance of their ancestral tribes. Every daughter who possesses an inheritance in any tribe of the Israelites shall marry one from the clan of her father's tribe, so that all Israelites may continue to possess their ancestral inheritance. No inheritance shall be transferred from one tribe to another; for each of the tribes of the Israelites shall retain its own inheritance. (Num 36: 6b–9)

Case closed. Mahlah, Tirzah, Hoglah, Milcah, and Noah marry sons of their father's brothers. "They were married into the clans of the descendants of Manasseh son of Joseph, and their inheritance remained in the tribe of their father's clan" (Num 36:12).

As for this story, there are several matters that i hope will irritate you in due time and inspire you to do something at the relevant occasion. Irritation is opportunity, always. Firstly, i hope you will respect your elders, but this does not mean that you have to always buy into their values or please their wishes. *See, judge*, and *act* (on this complex call by liberation thinkers, read Uncle Gerald's letter) as you find appropriate for your time and your company. When you need inspiration, listen and dance to the Caribbean Pulse's version of "Stand Up" and Bob Marley's "Redemption Song."

Secondly, the first point applies to what your parents instill in you. We condition and try to control your thinking and desires, but feel free to be different. Rebellion was not welcomed during the days of Kulin's daughters, but resistance is necessary when and where there is injustice. Resistance is difficult and tiring if you go at it alone, so find sisters and brothers to join you in your struggle. And collaborate with others in similar struggles. Resistance is good. Solidarity is empowering. And, when you need inspiration, listen to Miriam Makeba's "La luta continua."

Thirdly, don't be afraid to challenge the written [laws]. Legal revisions and rewritings are common in life and in biblical literature. Elders can change their minds; the LORD also changes her mind. It is best to seek revision and rewriting in the interests of minority and minoritized people, creatures, and creations. Don't limit yourself to the cause of humans. Join the struggle of all minoritized subjects. Watch *Moana* again, for it is not only about Maui and Moana but also about restoring the heart of Te whiti so that the island of Motunui will again be inhabitable. You will see many islands become uninhabitable in your lifetime. Grieve for them, and fight for the survival of other islands.

Fourthly, don't worry about your father's name. I don't have much of an inheritance anyways. And do not get trapped in the material world or in YHWH's closet. Struggle for creation, but do not be trapped in materiality. Fight for the health of creation, but do not be ruled by the checks of the donors and supporters.

Fifthly, find more mothers for Mahlah, Tirzah, Hoglah, Milcah, and Noah. There is something empowering about having two or more mothers. But don't let the second mother take over the place of Kulin. Kulin has been written off before, and it's time to put an end to the terror of texts. Find a second mother for the sisters, and even a third and a fourth, but don't replace their first mother. Of course, i'd be pleased if you find them Indian and Tongan mothers. Your Indian mother could help you out.

As for you, you may marry whoever you wish when you grow up. Read carefully—*when you grow up*—but don't wait for too long. And when you grow up, don't forget to be young. Learn to write letters. And don't wait until people are dead before you write to them. If you want help with writing short and meaningful letters, read Musa Dube's "The Unpublished Letters of Orpah to Ruth." You can find it online. Finally, see, judge, and act for yourself whether what i'm saying in this long letter might work for you or not—live beyond the shadows of your father.

As always, your "silly papa"

ps: read your Bible carefully

ps2: add your own postscripts

PS

Letters do not finish or (are) complete(d) on their own. Readers have a role to play, and they may add their own postscripts to those of the writers. When letters leave the fingers of writers, they shift from private and personal spaces to public intersections where they may be read by readers who were not intended (or implied) by the writers. These additional readers may add their own postscripts and consequently, to return to my musings on the wings of *talanoa*, letters *continue* unfinished and uncompleted.

The letters presented above are addressed to four individuals, but the four letters flow from and into each other.[8] Because my letters *write into* each other, it would be appropriate to read them together. In my case, letters also need other letters but not for the sake of being finished or complete(d). Rather, letters need other letters in order to gain lives of their own. And even when writers are finished, the letters continue.

---

[8] In Pasifika, an individual is already communal, even after death, so the letters are addressed to individuals, but they welcome readers who are communal.

At this juncture, i shift with one more postscript (ps). Like letters, scriptural texts need readers and other texts.[9] Like letters, scriptural texts are not finished, complete(d) or closed. To obstruct the interflow between scriptural texts, readers and other texts contribute to the terror of texts. And so does the assumption that scriptural texts are closed. That, too, contributes to the terror of texts. Like letters, scriptural texts travel. Move. Shift. Drift…

BIBLIOGRAPHY

Dube, Musa W. "The Unpublished Letters of Orpah to Ruth." Pages 145–50 in *Ruth and Esther: The Feminist Companion to the Bible*. Edited by Athalya Brenner. Sheffield: Sheffield Academic, 1999.

Havea, Jione. *Elusions of Control: Biblical Law on the Words of Women*. Atlanta: Society of Biblical Literature and Leiden: Brill, 2003.

Jetñil-Kijiner, Kathy. "United Nations Climate Summit Opening Ceremony—A Letter to My Daughter." *Kathy Jetñil-Kijiner*. September 24, 2014. https://tinyurl.com/vjtpckyc.

Kristeva, Julia. *Powers of Horror: An Essay on Abjection*. Translated by Leon S. Roudiez. New York: Columbia University Press, 1982.

Trible, Phyllis. *Texts of Terror: Literary-Feminist Readings of Biblical Narratives*. Philadelphia: Fortress, 1984.

---

[9] I understand the term "texts" to include oral, crafted, and embodied media.

13

Gender, Violence, and the Dalit Psyche: The Jephthah Story (Judges 11–12) Reconsidered

Monica Jyotsna Melanchthon

> In the social jungle of human existence, there is no feeling of being alive without a sense of ego identity.
>
> — Erik Erikson

Caste as a status marker is a unique feature of Indian society.[1] While its origin is obscure and debated, its manifestation in social and political life is visible and complex. It is difficult to describe caste or reasonably explain it as a system with rules. It is a lived experience, justified by a series of scriptural sanctions that stratify society into a hierarchical order (*varna* system). For a variety of intricate reasons, Indian society has kept the caste practice alive. Despite the many and massive changes brought by industrialization, urbanization, and migration, the caste system shows few signs of decline. Additionally, the policy of positive discrimination enshrined in Article 15 of the Indian Constitution has led to a further crystallization of caste identities even if the aim of that constitutional provision was to eliminate inequality and discrimination arising out of the marginalization of certain castes.[2]

Caste therefore continues to make its poisonous impact on every aspect of Indian life, affecting the lives of at least sixteen percent of India's population (approximately 250 million people), who are the Dalits. Relegated to the lowest jobs and professions, which are considered polluting, they live in constant fear of being publicly humiliated, paraded naked, beaten, and raped with impunity by

---

[1] For the epigraph, see Erik Erikson, *Childhood and Society*, 2nd ed. (New York: Norton, 1963), 130.

[2] Article 15, sections (1) and (2) of the Indian Constitution prohibit the state from discriminating against any citizen on the basis of religion, race, caste, sex, place of birth, or any combination of these factors.

dominant-caste groups seeking to keep them in their place. Consigned to a segregated position that is characterized by poverty and misery for nearly three millennia, they continue to be the most disadvantaged among the Indian population, with Dalit women experiencing the most heinous forms of sexual crimes and violence.

In this chapter, I attempt to read the familiar text of terror about Jephthah in Judg 11 from the perspective of caste, using insights gained from Sharankumar Limbale's disturbing and evocative autobiographical account of complex and intersecting forms of exclusion entitled *Akkarmashi* (*The Outcaste*) and Dalit experience in general.[3] I do not seek to revisit or review all scholarly discussions on this narrative. I do note that many interpreters seem to focus on the violence (virtuous or otherwise) of Jephthah but do not sufficiently analyze the violence that he experiences and the possible psychological impact of such violence on an individual. In this exercise, I seek to highlight issues that help me understand both Jephthah and his daughter, the main characters in this narrative. It is my hope that this approach will offer a new vantage point from which to look at the text, raise new questions, and help us understand the text from the lived experiences of marginalized and colonized communities, in this case the Dalit community.

THE OUTCASTE: AKKARMASHI

> My mother is an untouchable, while my father is a high caste.... Mother lives in a hut, father in a mansion. Father is a landlord, mother, landless. I am an "akkarmashi" (half-caste). I am condemned, branded illegitimate. I regard the immortality of my father and mother as a metaphor for rape. My father had privileges by virtue of his birth.... My mother was not an adulteress but the victim of a social system.... A violation anywhere in the country, I feel, is a violation of my mother.
>
> I have put in words the life I have lived as an untouchable, as a half-caste, and an impoverished man. There is a Patil in every village who is also a landowner. He invariably has a whore. I have written this so that readers will learn the woes of the son of a whore. High caste people look upon my community as untouchable, while my own community humiliated me, calling me "akkarmashi."... I have always lived with the burden of inferiority. And this book is a tale of this burden.

---

[3] Sharankumar Limbale, *The Outcaste: Akkarmashi*, trans. Santosh Bhoomkar (New Delhi: Oxford University Press, 2008).

Limbale's 1984 life narrative *Akkarmashi*, written in the Mahar dialect of Maharashtra and now translated into English, begins with this note.[4] Limbale portrays the miserable life he lived as an untouchable, an impoverished half-caste male. He describes his miseries as the son of a whore. Considered an untouchable by the high caste, he was an *akkarmashi*, or "an outcaste" in his own community. He therefore lived with the burden of humiliation, inferiority, and untouchability. While it is considered a curse to be a Dalit in a caste-ridden society, to be born of an illicit union within the Dalit community is to be doubly cursed. While Dalits are the outcasts in the Indian society, to be a half-caste among them is to be less than human. In reading through the book, one cannot miss that Limbale's condition was compounded by abject poverty, humiliation, subjugation, and constant hunger as the all-pervasive context. A crucial reminder here is that a Dalit autobiography is a narrative not only of the self but also of the protagonist's community.[5] Hence, in the preface to the first edition of this autobiography, he writes, "This is the story of my life, an expression of my mother's agony and an autobiography of a community."[6] Even as the story highlights the plight of many Dalits, it also showcases his agonizing search for identity. "Half of me belongs to the village, whereas the other half is excommunicated. Whom am I? To whom is my umbilical cord connected?"[7]

Limbale is insistent that sexual exploitation of lower caste women is part and parcel of the caste system, a structure that inherently involves human beings exploiting other human beings. He regards the relationship and act of his father and mother behind his birth explicitly as a "metaphor of rape":

> The sexual exploits of the men among the wicked exploiters draw legitimacy from their authority, wealth, society, culture and religion. But what of the exploited woman? She has to carry the rape in her womb. That rape has to be born, fed, and reared. And this rape acquires and lives a life. My autobiography holds in it the agony of such a life.[8]

---

[4] Limbale, *Outcaste*, ix. The Mahar are a caste-cluster, or group of many endogamous castes, chiefly from Maharashtra state in India. They belong to the lowest group of the Hindu caste system, and their duties include street sweeping and removing of carcasses. See "Mahar," Brittanica.com, accessed February 4, 2021, https://tinyurl.com/zafa59bd.

[5] Mangalam, "A Disturbing Tale," *The Book Review Literary Trust*, accessed January 12, 2020, https://tinyurl.com/sdfh5uwk.

[6] In the preface to the first print of *Akkarmashi* (1984) as cited by G. N. Devy, introduction to *The Outcaste: Akkarmashi* by Sharankumar Limbale, trans. Santosh Bhoomkar (New Delhi: Oxford University Press, 2008), xxiii.

[7] Limbale, *Outcaste*, 39.

[8] In the preface to the first print of *Akkarmashi* (1984) as cited by Devy, introduction, xxiii.

Limbale's *Akkarmashi* is a disturbing tale that offers significant insights into the identity of Dalits and their vulnerability. It also highlights the Dalit propensity to internalize the oppressor's ideology and the consequent alienation from one's own community.

JEPHTHAH: THE CHILD OF A PROSTITUTE

The Jephthah narrative has received a lot of scholarly attention because of its many ambiguities, gaps, and silences, as well as the disturbing questions and issues it raises. Phyllis Trible identifies Judg 11 as a "text of terror" because of the inhuman sacrifice of a young girl.[9] The text has polarized interpreters. Some condemn Jephthah the man and question the ethics of his action, while others laud his faithfulness to YHWH to the extent that he was willing to offer his only daughter. Many others have praised the daughter's faithfulness, her sacred responsibility and loyalty to her father and his oath.

Limbale identifies himself thus:

> I was born of her affair (Masamai) with Hanmantha Patil. …My father and his forefathers were Lingayats. Therefore, I am one too. My mother was Mahar. My mother's father and forefathers were Mahar, hence I am a Mahar…. How can I be high caste when my mother is untouchable? If I am untouchable what about my father who is high caste?… Half of me belongs to the village, whereas the other half is excommunicated. Who am I? To whom is my umbilical cord connected?[10]

While Limbale struggles to determine where he belongs, Jephthah is identified as a Gileadite (Judg 11:1), an identity ascribed to him by virtue of the one who fathered him, and as a mighty warrior and experienced fighter.[11] Limbale longed to be invited into his father's house, but Jephthah, we are told, was raised by his father who is a "subject who slides from an individual named Gilead to the entire town called by that name. In other words, Jephthah's father might be any man in

---

[9] Phyllis Trible, *Texts of Terror: Literary-Feminist Readings of Biblical Narratives* (Philadelphia: Fortress, 1984), 93–118.

[10] Limbale, *Outcaste*, 38–39.

[11] This expression was used even before he proved his prowess as a military man, leading some to speculate that he was already a well-established warrior within the household of Gilead before he was ousted by his brothers; see Renate Jost, *Gender, Sexualität und Macht in der Anthropologie des Richterbuches* (Stuttgart: Kohlhammer, 2006), 170 as cited by Mercedes L. Garcia Bachmann, *Judges*, Wisdom Commentary 7 (Collegeville, MN: Liturgical Press, 2018), 120.

the town of Gilead. The town maintains the prostitute, sires a son by her."[12] Gilead's wife and the sons born to her did not like having Jephthah around. He was cast out by his half-brothers who did not want to share the inheritance with him because he was "the son of another woman" (Judg 11:2).

Limbale asks, "Why didn't he speak to me? It was difficult for me to think of Kaka as my father. I was angry with him.... I was livid with rage."[13] I ask, Why did Gilead not speak up for his son Jephthah?[14] Economic concerns alongside the stigma associated with birth result in rejection of the offspring by both the father and the extended family (Judg 11:2).[15] His mother was referred to as the "other woman." The only thing we know is that she is identified as a זונה (*zonah*), a "harlot" (Judg 11:1) and referred to as "another woman" by the brothers (Judg 11: 2). We do not know her name, her age, or her ethnicity.[16] What were the circumstances which led to her to sell sex? Was Gilead unmarried or married at the time of their meeting? What role did she play in Jephthah's life? Had she died? Is that why Gilead took him in? There are no answers. For the biblical narrator, Jephthah's nameless mother is only incidental to the plot. The mystery surrounding her and her sex work, however, are determinative in cementing Jephthah's identity. A part of who he is will always be ambiguous; the ambiguity buttresses his vulnerability and enables the community that sired him and the narrator to control how he is perceived and received—namely, as being somehow inferior.

Sex workers and mistresses bear children out of desire for tangible human relationships that are genuine, meaningful, and lasting. These children are often both economic and emotional necessities. Studies on mixed marriages—whether they involve caste, race, religion or nationality—provide evidence of the anxieties that offspring face, especially surrounding identity. These anxieties are quite complicated and go beyond just the identity question. As victims of their circumstances

---

[12] Danna Nolan Fewell and David M. Gunn, *Gender, Power, and Promise: The Subject of the Bible's First Story* (Nashville: Abingdon, 1999), 126. If we proceed with this line of thinking, it is possible to assume that the identity of Jephthah's father is now known.

[13] Limbale, *Outcaste*, 46.

[14] Perhaps he was already dead, too; see Garcia Bachmann, *Judges*, 121.

[15] Was she a sex worker or just a promiscuous woman? The ambiguity heightens the mystery surrounding his birth. In determining why Jephthah was disinherited, I. Mendelsohn, "The Disinheritance of Jephthah in the Light of Paragraph 27 of the Lipit-Ishtar Code," *IEJ* 4 (1954): 118 suggests that Jephthah's mother was neither a concubine nor a concubine slave (a "servant first and concubine last") but a "professional harlot who bore a son to one of her visitors."

[16] Athalya Brenner, "Women Frame the Book of Judges—How and Why?" in *Joshua and Judges: Texts and Contexts*, ed. Athalya Brenner and Gale Yee (Minneapolis: Fortress, 2013), 133, 127 suggests that most women in the book are nameless because they are not in fact important enough to have names, even fictive ones, a "pointed hint as to female intrinsic worth," but "important for the plot and message."

from birth, they are rarely allowed the opportunity to forget or be free of their background. Prevailing discourses of religious fundamentalism, as well as racial and caste discrimination, influence and shape the lives of the children of these so-called transgressive matrimonies.[17] They are not seen as "pure" because of their low caste or undesired ethnicity, and/or the different religion of their mothers. "Stained" and stigmatized as "internal others," they do not always obtain indisputable acceptance into paternal kin groups and communities. The intergenerational stigma affects their everyday interactions and psychological well-being and creates hurdles in life, including in their ability to find marriage partners.[18] "They are deprived of an environment conducive to healthy physical and psychological development, suffer from nutritional deficiencies, minimal health care, non-availability of basic needs, and social handicaps."[19]

Jephthah—his name, יפתח, means "he opens"—and Limbale are both born to a sex worker or mistress and experience discrimination, humiliation, and rejection by their families (father's side) and their communities. Raising children while being engaged in sex work or being the "other woman" is complicated and challenging.[20] But there is no tone of cursing or blaming the mother in either narrative. Her life and status in life is accepted. As Limbale says, "Children born to a whore have no legal father because there is an unbridgeable gap between such a father and son. The prestige of the father is at stake!"[21]

As children, neither Jephthah nor Limbale exhibit any anger or hatred toward their mothers for the choices they have made. In fact, studies have shown that children born to sex workers understand and, despite the challenges, do not seek to be separated from their mothers.[22] Again, Limbale: "What sort of life had she been living, mortgaging herself to one owner after another and being used as a commodity? Her lot has been nothing but the tyranny of sex."[23] I imagine that Jephthah, like Limbale, lived life as an outcast, burdened by the circumstances of his birth and wrestling with his identity and rejected status. While his father was not condemned for sleeping with another woman, both he, as the child of their

---

[17] Cf. Reena Kukreja, "An Unwanted Weed: Children of Cross-Region Unions Confront Intergenerational Stigma of Caste, Ethnicity and Religion," *Journal of Intercultural Studies* 39 (2018): 382–98, DOI: 10.1080/07256868.2018.1484345.
[18] Kukreja, "Unwanted Weed."
[19] Cf. Madan Mohan Das, "Giving the Children of Prostitutes their Due," *Indian Council of Child Welfare News Bulletin* 39.3–4 (1991): 31–37.
[20] Christine M. Sloss and Gary W. Harper, "When Street Sex Workers Are Mothers," *Archives of Sexual Behavior* 33 (2004): 329–41.
[21] Limbale, *Outcaste*, 59.
[22] Geeta S. Pardeshi and Sanjoy Bhattacharya, "Child Rearing Practices amongst Brothel Based Commercial Sex Workers." *Indian Journal of Medical Sciences* 60 (2006): 288–95.
[23] Limbale, *Outcaste*, 59.

union, and his mother were discriminated against. Limbale describes his experience as follows: "While walking through the village I looked for Kaka's mansion. Expecting to be noticed and invited in, ... but the moment he noticed me he shut the door, I returned home with a sad face."[24]

TOB: A GOOD PLACE—A SANCTUARY?

Upon being kicked out, Jephthah attempts to reconstruct his life in a location away from home, "in the land of Tob" (Judg 11:3).[25] He becomes "a magnet for other 'empty men'."[26] I am intrigued by this place named Tob and the ambiguities surrounding it. How or why does a "good" land become a sanctuary for "outlaws" and "empty people"? Were they disenfranchised men, unhappy with their place of origin? In 2 Sam 10:6, 8, we are told that that it was a place from which the Ammonites were able to recruit twelve thousand men to fight against David. Was it a gathering place for mercenaries who could be hired? Perhaps. But this still does not explain how this place acquired this name. Was it so named by the residents themselves? Did they do so in order to counter how others saw it—namely, as a hangout of outlaws and scoundrels? Could it be "good" because it is a space of tolerance and plurality? Can we imagine this to be an in-between space where individuals, irrespective of where they were from, could interrogate their cultural, ethnic, and political identity? A place open to one another, a land of imagination that provided one with a thrilling sense of imagination, a point of intersection? Is it a place where one can enjoy their self-esteem and give expression to the strength that comes from it? Individuals formed by a minority culture while participating in the culture of the dominant have to negotiate their own identity in such in-between spaces. Is that why it was called the land of Tob? As Limbale notes, "Those days when we went around the village and walked with pride, the high caste people hated our confidence. They didn't want us to enjoy any self-esteem. But we realised that self-esteem had unusual strengths."[27]

---

[24] Limbale, *Outcaste*, 46.
[25] Literally, "a good land." The land of Tob was apparently back country and served as an asylum for outlaws, based perhaps on the Judges text; see "Tob," Jewish Virtual Library, accessed February 4, 2021, https://tinyurl.com/uv97h69s. Its location is unclear, but it was perhaps an area that bordered Gilead and Ammon, southeast of the Sea of Galilee. Cf. Edward Lipiński, *On the Skirts of Canaan in the Iron Age: Historical and Topographical Researches* (Leuven: Peeters, 2006), 298–99.
[26] Fewell and Gunn, *Gender, Power, and Promise*, 126. The expression אנשים ריקים (*'anashim reqim*) is translated "outlaws" (NRSV), "gang of scoundrels" (NIV), "worthless fellows" (RSV), "men of low character" (JPS), or "gang of rowdies" (CJB).
[27] Limbale, *Outcaste*, 76.

I wonder if those who congregated around Jephthah are considered outlaws because they resist and rebel against the discrimination they experience based on birth or some other social factor.[28] Jephthah can therefore be classified as a subject on the margins, most probably a disenfranchised individual or a subaltern subject, deprived of community and belonging with a half-baked identity—the son of a sex worker, cast out by family and community, a non-hegemonic subject excluded from the dominant ideology's representation of society and its history.[29] As Limbale notes: "We felt no affection for our village. ...we were scared and tense. Our caste had been thrust upon us even before we were born."[30]

I see Jephthah as a subject colonized by tribal and cultural superiority, victimized by accident of birth. Seen and treated as a person of low birth, he lived in exile with this burden of inferiority and sought to address it while living in Tob with like-minded individuals.[31] One way Jephthah can cope is by engaging in behavior that the author characterizes as deviant, which is also a detour, an alienated way to find a way around alienation. As Limbale notes: "But some day we ought to rebel. How long can we mutely suffer all this?... Some time we ought to reject all this."[32]

These so-called empty people banded together to challenge the status quo, to address the unending trauma of having to juggle hyphenated identities and belongings, and to resist daily discrimination, which is depicted as "raiding" and living off the spoils of these raids.[33] There are many who consider groups that are struggling for justice and personhood as terrorists, outlaws, or antisocials. But should all criticism of and resistance to structures of authority or government be seen as treason? Is resistance to an oppressive establishment an evil act? I have doubts as to whether Jephthah is antisocial, as the narrator would like us to believe. It is unclear what type of resistance Jephthah adopts. He is resistant perhaps, but intentionally disruptive? I am not sure.

---

[28] Cf. Garcia Bachmann, *Judges*, 122 n.18.
[29] On the subaltern, see Cristina Garcia-Alfonso, "Judges: Subaltern Women," in *Postcolonial Commentary and the Old Testament*, ed. Hemchand Gossai (London: T&T Clark, 2019): 106–21.
[30] Limbale, *Outcaste*, 76.
[31] Pamela J. Milne, "From the Margins to the Margins: Jephthah's Daughter and her Father," in *Joshua and Judges: Texts and Contexts*, ed. Athalya Brenner and Gale Yee (Minneapolis: Fortress, 2013), 219.
[32] Limbale, *Outcaste*, 76.
[33] Is he, perhaps, a Robin Hood kind of figure?

THE ELDERS OF GILEAD

In verses 4–11, the elders of Gilead request that Jephthah, a social outcast with proven military skill, return to his homeland and head up the opposition. Does he acquire these skills before being ousted or while negotiating life in Tob? His martial prowess erases all that made him unacceptable.[34] In my mind, Jephthah is approached for his ability to fight but also because he is expendable.[35]

The elders offer him military leadership and to fight alongside him (Judg 11:6). But Jephthah does not accede immediately. He reproves them first for ousting him (verse 7), which perhaps unnerves them. Without giving him an answer, they say that they have now "turned back" to him so that Jephthah may fight the Ammonites. They up their offer: he will "become head over us"—namely, over all Gilead. They will not join him. Jephthah will fight this war on their behalf. The "we may fight" of verse 6 becomes "you may fight" in verse 8. He seals the deal with a constructed and conditional contract, which perhaps outlines the terms, and which is then formalized through a ritual at Mizpah in which Jephthah says all "his words before YHWH…" (Judg 11:11). Jephthah takes an oath to abide by it in the presence of YHWH and the community at Mizpah. He is made commander and leader (verse 11). The bargaining with the elders is both "bitter and protracted" and "self-interested," and the "animosities" between the two parties emphasizes "the power and importance of the contract" made between them.[36] But Jephthah does not allow his vulnerable position or the inferiority imposed on him to deter him from standing his ground. He knows they need him, and they do!

JEPHTHAH NEGOTIATES WITH THE AMMONITES

Jephthah does not attack the Ammonites immediately. He begins a dialogue with the Ammonite king (Judg 11:12–28). He sends two messages (verses 12 and 14–27) through messengers to the king of Ammon and receives a response in between (verse 13).[37] Jephthah makes "spectacular use of language as a means of trapping"

---

[34] J. Cheryl Exum, *Tragedy and Biblical Narrative: Arrows of the Almighty* (Cambridge: University Press, 1992), 48.
[35] This is reminiscent of many Hollywood movies, in which criminals consigned to a lifetime in prison are recruited in order to fight a war or for a cause. Their skill is welcomed and needed but their death is not mourned. From the perspective of those who have hired them—the state, security forces, etc.—they are expendable!
[36] It is clear here that there is no love lost between the parties. Cf. John C. Yoder, *Power and Politics in the Book of Judges: Men and Women of Valor* (Minneapolis: Fortress, 2015), 103.
[37] Pamela Tamarkin Reis, "Spoiled Child: A Fresh Look at Jephthah's Daughter," *Proof* 17 (1997): 280–81 identifies this section of the narrative as a "recruiting speech," which he

his adversary in this exchange with the king of Ammon.[38] The dialogue reveals the historical sequence of events that led to the war between the two communities as recorded in Numbers 20–21. The circumstances under which Israel came to occupy Ammon provide continuing grounds for tension and give historical legitimacy—namely, just and right cause for the current battle.[39] By naming both Chemosh and YHWH as parties to the original land partition, Jephthah projects the "moral correctness of a human agreement" onto the realm of the divine.[40] Jephthah asserts that he has done no wrong and asks that YHWH as judge decide (Judg 11:14–27). Pamela Tamarkin Reis asks if Jephthah is seeking a negotiated peace with the Ammonites and concludes that this might not be the case because there is no evidence of a military leader who has "sought a mediated settlement with its attackers; the Bible does not approbate compromise with idolaters and endorse ceding God granted land to pagans. Therefore, I believe Jephthah's lengthy, detailed, and accurate exposition of the historical events recorded in Numbers 20–21, justifying Israel's right to the land, is intended as a morale booster and a recruiting speech."[41] Reis continues by noting that the dialogue shows not only how clever Jephthah is, but also that Jephthah does not waste words on "intransigent Ammonites." It is a ploy to keep them at bay while he educates the Gileadites on "the legality of Israel's claim, and the righteousness of their cause." He uses "the pretext of briefing messengers" to persuade the Gileadites, who he knows may not listen to him, given that he is an "outcast and an exile" and that they already indicated their hesitancy to join him in war.[42]

Reis's argument is persuasive. I accept that the dialogue in Judg 11:12–28 is a morale booster, a recruitment speech that is motivational and educational, and that it provides justification for military intervention. I am hesitant, however, to accept that Jephthah was not also seeking "negotiated peace" with the Ammonites.[43] I lean toward John C. Yoder's reading, which notes that "during this

---

delivers in order to boost the morale of his own people. She suggests that the use of messengers is a tactful and clever strategy adopted by Jephthah. Instead of speaking directly to his people, who might not hear him because of who he is, he orients his messengers and succeeds in motivating his people to join his army.

[38] Robin Baker, "Double Trouble: Counting the Cost of Jephthah," *JBL* 137 (2018): 35.
[39] This is no ordinary war—it is a holy war!; see Reis, "Spoiled Child," 281.
[40] Yoder, *Power and Politics*, 105.
[41] Reis "Spoiled Child," 280.
[42] Reis "Spoiled Child," 281. Cf. also Garcia Bachmann, *Judges*, 126.
[43] There may indeed be no other evidence of Israelite leaders seeking to arbitrate peace through diplomatic negotiation, as Reis, "Spoiled Child," 280 suggests, and it may be true that patriarchy is much more at ease with war than dialogue, as suggested by Garcia Bachmann, *Judges*, 125. Why do these factors have to deny Jephthah from adopting this strategy?

closely argued discourse, Jephthah made no reference to power or pragmatism."[44] Jephthah seems to appeal to what might today be considered international law, and he does not use "raw power to arbitrate" but he calls on a higher and just authority—namely, YHWH.[45] He comes across as one who is particular about "legal rectitude" than with the exercise of "military threat."[46] He attacks the Ammonites only after these diplomatic negotiations fail. And *only* after this attempt at negotiation does "the spirit of YHWH come upon him" (Judg 11:29). Jephthah's action here presents a very different understanding of the warrior God, a God who does not rush into war without considering options for arriving at a peaceful settlement.[47]

Jephthah traverses across Gilead into Manasseh and on to Mizpah of Gilead and from Mizpah to the Ammonites (Judg 11:29). Again, Reis suggests that this is an indication of the difficulty Jephthah has in forming an army, that he has to travel to all these places in order to recruit.[48] While it might have been necessary in order to gather an army, it is also a way of introducing himself and impressing upon the community that he is their head, akin to an election campaign. The enormity of the task finally hits home, and he realizes how important it is for him to achieve success. Perhaps the effort he has to put into forming an army gives rise to the doubt that results in the vow to YHWH (Judg 11:30–31).

Before we proceed to look at the rest of the story, a question: How are we to evaluate Jephthah on these two exchanges, with the elders and the king of Ammon? Several scholars see Jephthah as an able, skilled, and shrewd negotiator, a devout follower of YHWH, knowledgeable about the history of his people, a gifted statesman and diplomat, an articulate and passionate defender of his community, a liberator and judge, and one who weighs his options before acting.[49]

Such readings seem to be giving in to the narrator's agenda of projecting Jephthah as a deviant character.

[44] Yoder, *Power and Politics*, 105.
[45] Yoder, *Power and Politics*, 105.
[46] Yoder, *Power and Politics*, 105.
[47] Cf. discussion of the God who sanctions warfare and effects victory and defeat in war by Eric A. Siebert, *Disturbing Divine Behavior: Troubling Old Testament Images of God* (Minneapolis: Fortress, 2009), 156–60.
[48] Reis "Spoiled Child," 281.
[49] Richard E. DeMaris and Carolyn S. Leeb, "Judges—(Dis)honor and Ritual Enactment: The Jephthah Story—Judges 10:16–12:1," in *Ancient Israel: The Old Testament in Its Social Context*, ed. Philip F. Esler (Minneapolis: Fortress, 2006), 184 and Fuchs, *Sexual Politics*, 193. On Jephthah as a devout follower of YHWH, see Esther Fuchs, *Sexual Politics in the Biblical Narrative: Reading the Hebrew Bible as a Woman*, JSOTSup 310 (Sheffield: Sheffield Academic, 2003), 193.

WHAT DOES JEPHTHAH WANT?

What factors motivate Jephthah to yield to the request of the elders of Gilead? Is it love for Gilead and its inhabitants? A sense of duty? Why give in to a community that has disowned him? The elders assume that he is doing this for money, being the outlaw that he is.[50] Jephthah perhaps agrees in order to correct his inconsistent honor status.[51] Renita Weems suggests that Jephthah is "consumed with what he thought he lacked"—namely, power and prestige, as well as his ambition to acquire them, made him hungry, impulsive, and blind.[52]

I wonder if we might find an answer to what it is that Jephthah is seeking if we take inspiration from the theory of Frantz Fanon, for whom psychoanalysis and socioeconomic analysis are central. Fanon maintains that psychopathological conditions are created by the colonizing process and compounded by pressures—economic, social, religious, or political.[53] The colonial world of caste or tribe is a Manichaean world: the upper caste (read "colonizer") turns the Dalit, the colonized, into a sort of quintessence of evil, of impurity, of being less than human. In such oppressive systems, the subaltern adopts varied ways to respond, ranging from armed insurrection to nonviolent collective struggle. In discourse around caste, analysts speak of the "dalit psyche as the psyche of the oppressed," which is a wounded psyche.[54] The teachings about caste and inferiority are internalized and lived out. The impacts of oppression, such as cultural depreciation, and the removal of core cultural identity, continued violence, and fear in the Dalits leads to self-hatred, internalizing negative group identities, and low self-esteem. To counter this, some resort to embracing practices and lifestyles that would make

---

[50] Reis, "Spoiled Child," 281.
[51] DeMaris and Leeb, "Judges."
[52] Renita Weems, *Just a Sister Away: A Womanist Vision of Woman's Relationships in the Bible* (San Diego, CA: LuraMedia, 1988), 54–55.
[53] Frantz Fanon, *Black Skin, White Masks*, trans. Charles Lam Markmann (London: Pluto, 1967), 3–4 writes in his introduction, "I believe that only a psychoanalytic interpretation of the black problem can lay bare the anomalies that are responsible for the structure of the complex.... The analysis I am undertaking is psychological.... It is apparent to me the effective disalienation of the black man entails an immediate recognition of social and economic realities. If there is an inferiority complex, it is the outcome of a double process:—primarily economic—subsequently, the internalization—or, better the epidermalization—of this inferiority."
[54] Felix Wilfred, *Dalit Empowerment* (New Delhi: ISPCK, 2007), 173–74. For the quotation, see Jose Pulickal, "Dynamics of Dalit Psyche Meanings and Paradigms" (unpublished manuscript), 107, https://tinyurl.com/s89shbdd.

them more acceptable to the oppressor; this is termed the "mimetic drive/desire."[55]

In the Indian experience, the mimetic drive is akin to the concept of "Sanskritization," which is an integral part of social mobility.[56] It describes the attempt at cultural mobility by lower castes seeking to raise their status in the caste hierarchy by adopting some cultural ideals of the Brahmins.[57] Fanon sees this as the desire of every colonized people—namely, to be liked by the oppressor.[58] While Sanskritization is, in the first instance, a tactic for escaping from the dominant community's stereotype of the oppressed person, it also requires the oppressed individual, in their attempt to become white, upper caste, to reject their own "black/dalit" view of society, including their own family. Limbale, for instance, writes of finishing high school and college, getting married, and securing a job as a telephone operator away from where he grew up. His name led some to believe that he was of a higher caste. He played along and instructed his Dalit friends to refrain from using the greeting *jai Bhim* around him; if they did, he would respond by saying *namaskar*. *Jai Bhim* is a greeting used by followers of B. R. Ambedkar, an Indian jurist, economist, politician, and social reformer and the principal architect of the Indian Constitution. *Jai Bhim* literally means "victory to *Bhim*," which refers to Ambedkar. Limbale hid all books by Ambedkar and began to read novels written by dominant caste authors, avoided meeting with Dalit friends, ate meat secretly and at night, and kept his caste a secret. He was ashamed of his past and used fake and high caste names when he spoke of his in-laws.[59]

Mangalam writes:

---

[55] From *mimesis*, a term with several possible meanings, including "representation" and "imitation." René Girard is most well-known for the concept of *mimetic desire*, which he developed in several books over the years; see, e.g., Girard, *Violence and the Sacred*, trans. Patrick Gregory (Baltimore, MD: John Hopkins University Press, 1977).

[56] Sanskritization of the Dalits embodies a strong "element of protest against the high castes"... both "Sanskritization and emulation challenge the position and authority of higher castes," according to M. N. Srinivas, introduction to *Caste: Its Twentieth Century Avatar*, ed. M. N. Srinivas (Gurgaon, India: Penguin, 1997), xiv–xv.

[57] As a result, they cease to observe some of their ideals, traditions, and food habits considered to be impure by the dominant castes. Dalit scholars have pointed out that this emulation of upper castes is always the result of collective will, one that is given expression in an individual act—it is a social tendency rather than a political act. In addition, the emulation of dominant castes by a nondominant caste depends not so much on the rank of the dominant caste in the Brahminical hierarchy but on their economic and political power and their numerical strength.

[58] Fanon, *Black Skin*, 148, 178.

[59] Limbale, *Outcaste*, 103–5.

At the end, Limbale stands alone, burdened by a growing family (a wife and three kids), his middle-class aspirations and his fears regarding a place in society. But he also stands condemned—not on account of his illegitimate birth but rather for allowing himself to be sucked into the legitimacy of bourgeois respectability.[60]

Might Jephthah have internalized a similarly imposed negative identity? Does Jephthah accede to the request because it presents him the opportunity to become like one of them, to be accepted and included? I imagine that Jephthah is responding to the Gileadites out of his own struggle for survival amidst insecurity and rejection and perhaps poverty and need. He wants to taste a little of that economic and political power, but, more importantly, he seeks acceptance and belonging. This also explains his traversing the land to be seen, to be recognized and accepted. The desire to be liked by the oppressor produces various forms of alienation simply because in some ways it is a fantasy—that all perception of oneself and others is made unreal by being filtered through the ideal of power, whether caste, whiteness, or ethnicity, or birth.

DOES JEPHTHAH SUCCEED IN HIS DESIRE TO BECOME ACCEPTED?

We would like to think so. But there is some doubt regarding this once we arrive at the last ten verses of Judg 11. Jephthah makes a vow that he will offer as an עולה (ʿōlah), or burnt offering, the first thing that comes out of his doors to greet him upon his victorious return from war with the Ammonites and the aftermath.[61] The vow has been understood to be a "pre-battle vow" or "a traditional Israelite war custom."[62] I therefore understand why the vow is made and why it includes the offering of a sacrifice. It is the "whoever comes out of the doors of my house" that is problematic. How can something so ridiculous come out of his mouth? Is it desperation? Or fear of failing which led to this foolish vow? I think it is a combination of both—the ultimate sacrifice and worth the risk.

---

[60] Mangalam, "Disturbing Tale."
[61] As Lauren A. S. Monroe, "Disembodied Women: Sacrificial Language and the Deaths of Bat-Jephthah, Cozbi and the Bethlehmite Concubine," *CBQ* 75 (2013): 36 notes, עולה (ʿōlah) is not the term used in biblical prohibitions against child sacrifice (Lev 18:21; 20:2–5; Deut 12:31; 18:17; 2 Kgs 23:10). The verbs used are "give," "offer," "burn," and "pass through fire"; hence, Judg 11 needs to be seen apart from these legal prohibitions. The type of offering that Jephthah seeks to make is not the same as that which is prohibited by these laws.
[62] A "pre-battle vow" would be akin to that found in Num 21:2. Cf. Reis, "Spoiled Child," 281. For war customs, see Alice Logan, "Rehabilitating Jephthah," *JBL* 128 (2009): 677.

This section of the chapter has received much attention and has divided scholarship into sacrificialists and nonsacrificialists. I do not intend to repeat these varied scholarly positions. But I would call attention to the work of Lauren Monroe who locates Jephthah's offering of his daughter in the context of other narratives where child sacrifice is at issue.[63] Monroe argues that Judg 11:30–40 are a secondary addition to the narrative in verses 1–29.[64] From a narratological standpoint, the vow interrupts the account of Jephthah's military success, which is signaled by the descent of the "spirit of YHWH" in verse 29 and continues through the description of victory in verse 33. She writes:

> Elsewhere in Judges, reference to the Spirit of YHWH descending on a warrior indicates that his enemies will be given into his hand (3:10; 14:6;) In 11:29–32, these two elements are separated from each other by reference to the vow in 11:30–31. Furthermore, since the descent of the spirit of YHWH is a guarantee of victory, the vow itself is unnecessary and casts doubt on Jephthah's faithfulness and integrity in a narrative that otherwise reflects well on him.[65]

She concludes that Judg 11:30–31 and 34–39a constitute an interpolation made to malign Jehpthah, to cast doubts on his credentials as a model warrior and tribal chief.

Monroe's analysis resonates with the Dalit experience. Caste is a source of embarrassment and shame among middle class Indians, and they are rarely allowed to ignore or forget their roots. Dalit and racialized minorities are often subject to a more rigorous form of "predatory scrutiny," monitoring, and assessment by the dominant group.[66] Although Jephthah's success saves the Gileadites, his position as leader, the son of a prostitute, an illegitimate child, and a socially deviant person, jars on their sensibilities.[67] They need to tarnish his image. Such a portrayal faithfully contributes to the picture of Israelite wickedness in the period of the judges. By including the ambiguous section on the sacrifice of the daughter, which surprisingly goes unchallenged, Jephthah is cast as an individual who practices customs and rituals that are non-Israelite, alluding to Mesha's sacrifice of his firstborn to Chemosh to stave off the Israelite army (2 Kgs 3).

---

[63] Monroe, "Disembodied Women," 37.
[64] Thomas Römer, "Why Would the Deuteronomists Tell about the Sacrifice of Jephthah's Daughter?," *JSOT* 77 (1988): 30–31 concludes that the addition is a "Post-Deuteronomic addition under Hellensitic influence," as cited by Monroe, "Disembodied Women," 36.
[65] Monroe, "Disembodied Women," 37.
[66] Danna Nolan Fewell, *The Children of Israel: Reading the Bible for the Sake of Our Children* (Nashville: Abingdon, 2003), 82.
[67] Fewell, *Children*, 77.

Let us assume that these verses are not an interpolation, that Jephthah does in fact make the vow.⁶⁸ What then? My own sense is that he does it because of his intense desire to succeed, to become acceptable, and to provide his daughter a chance at life free from discrimination. He does not anticipate that he will have to sacrifice (burn) his daughter.⁶⁹ Discrimination and oppression are insidious, cumulative, and have impact across generations. The daughter and her unnamed mother are not oblivious to Jephthah's ancestry, or the treatment meted out to him. They, too, experience the humiliation of his birth. The daughter's submission falls into the hierarchical intent of the text.⁷⁰ She does not question her father but emerges as "the perfect daughter whose loyalty and submissiveness to her father knows [sic] no limits."⁷¹ She agrees for the sake of her father and for the sake of the family. It is a desperate vow, reckless for sure, but it is made under pressure for personal survival, for victory, for acceptance and without enough thought. It has to be carried out and is the only way to save the family.⁷² She repeats the words of her father and, by doing so, communicates that her father is doing a "just and venerable deed."⁷³

Elisheva Baumgarten calls attention to a medieval Spanish reading of this text, which claims that the sacrifice of the daughter was bloodless.⁷⁴ Rather than being sacrificed, the daughter dedicates her life to God. From the perspective of caste, this is reminiscent of the devadasi system in India, an ancient custom of "marrying" low-caste girls to a goddess.⁷⁵ The practice is particularly interesting

---

⁶⁸ See David Marcus, *Jephthah and His Vow* (Lubbock, TX: Texas Tech Press, 1986), 47, who suggests that Jephthah was unaware of the Israelite law against human sacrifice; he was influenced by Ammonite religion and assumed that it would be acceptable to YHWH as well.

⁶⁹ Fewell *Children*, 81 suggests that she was the only one who came out onto the street to receive her father.... The community was silent, and there was no celebration over his victory because of who he was. The daughter knew or had heard of his oath and wanted to ensure he could keep it.

⁷⁰ L. Juliana M. Claassens, *Claiming Her Dignity: Female Resistance in the Old Testament* (Collegeville, MN: Liturgical Press, 2016), 71.

⁷¹ Esther Fuchs, "Marginalization, Ambiguity, Silencing: The Story of Jephthah's Daughter," in *A Feminist Companion to Judges*, ed. Athalya Brenner (Sheffield: Sheffield Academic, 1993), 126.

⁷² Fewell, *Children*, 80–81.

⁷³ Fuchs, "Marginalization," 125.

⁷⁴ Elisheva Baumgarten, "Remember that Glorious Girl": Jephthah's Daughter in Medieval Jewish Culture," *JQR* 97 (2007): 202–4.

⁷⁵ The term *devadasi* is a Sanskrit word that literally means "female slave of God." Women who were dedicated to God/goddess as Devadasis enjoyed higher status by extending their services to the temples. That is no more the case. It has often led to sexual exploitation of these women—often very young girls, almost children—dedicated to the goddess by temple

and resistant to reform, as it arises out of a crossroads of religion, poverty, caste and societal norms, all of which perpetuate its survival, but more importantly, it is a practice to which these low-caste girls subscribe because they view it as their only way to rise in India's rigid caste system.

The fact that neither the daughter nor the mother is named—not by the narrator and not by the community in the narrative—speaks volumes about what the community of Jephthah's time thought of these women. By allowing him to sacrifice his daughter, they know they are effectively closing all possibility of continuation of his family line. Margaret C. Hunt explains this as the community's fear of Jephthah or acceptance of male prerogative or preeminence when it comes to women.[76] I lean toward understanding it as a period of near-anarchy, as suggested by Anne Michele Tapp.[77] I think Jephthah's cry in Judg 11:35 is not irritation or blame upon his daughter but a lament and a recognition of the systems of power and oppression in which he, his wife, and his daughter are trapped.

Women's rituals around her memory give meaning to her sacrifice. The detail of her virginal status is used to construct and reconfigure the female body.[78] One can draw many parallels between Jephthah's daughter and girls dedicated to the *devadasi* practice.

Jephthah rules for only six years but is buried among the Judges (Judg 12:7). He is a son of Gilead and has to be recognized for his contributions. Were he not one, he would have been written off. The shortness of his rule is also indicative of the battering that the body and the mind take when they have to function under and against the constant struggle to survive and exercise self-respect.

---

patrons and higher caste individuals. The practice was imbued with great respect, as the girls chosen to become *devadasis* are subject to two great honors: by being literally married to the deity, they were treated as if they were the Goddess herself, and they were considered "auspicious." See Ankur Shingal, "The Devadasi System: Temple Prostitution in India," *UCLA Women's Law Journal* 22 (2015): 109, https://tinyurl.com/264rnbhy.

[76] Margaret C. Hunt, "Dutiful Daughters and the Fathers Who Fail Them: The Application of Feminist Insights and the Retrieval of Resistance Strands of Women's Traditions via a Narrative Analysis of Four Unmarried Daughter Texts in the Hebrew Bible" (PhD diss., Flinders University Faculty of Education, Humanities, Law and Theology, Adelaide, South Australia, April 2010, https://tinyurl.com/mk6s45m).

[77] Anne Michele Tapp, "An Ideology of Expendability: Virgin Daughter Sacrifice in Genesis 19:1–11, Judges 11:30–39 and 19:22–26," in *Anti-Covenant: Counter Reading Women's Lives in the Hebrew Bible*, ed. Mieke Bal (Decatur, GA: Almond Press, 1989), 157–74.

[78] Gerald West, "The Bible and the Female Body in Ibandla lamaNazaretha: Isaiah Shembe and Jephthah's daughter," *OTE* 20 (2007): 489–509.

CONCLUSION

Jephthah suffers discrimination, deprivation, exploitation, and marginalization like Limbale. What is the psychological impact of these practices on him and his family? How does a text such as this impact readers who suffer constant humiliation under oppressive and discriminating structures—social, religious, and political? While the ambiguities, silences, and gaps within the text contribute to the troubling, traumatizing, and terrorizing legacy of Hebrew texts, the very same ambiguities provide opportunity to read the text from various vantage points. I have chosen to read it from the perspective of Dalit experience, privileging the psychological impact that the Gilead treatment has on Jephthah and his family. Dalit readers will easily empathize with this character. What the text offers to such a reader is the risks that individuals will take to preserve themselves, protect self-respect and self-esteem, and preserve the family. The text, I believe, is a call to recognize these strategies and mechanisms, disturbing as they are, as well as the systems that necessitate them, and it seeks to launch a journey of resistance in the reader. When reading this terrorizing text, a Dalit is invited to resist and not to succumb to the ideology of the oppressor.

What this paper has not done is discuss God as character in this narrative for want of space. But I leave you with a question of Limbale's which I think is similar to what Jephthah may have asked himself while he was in Tob, and I invite you to answer it for him: "God discriminates between man and man. He makes one man rich and the other poor. One is high caste, the other untouchable.... We are all supposed to be the children of God, then why are we considered untouchable?"[79]

BIBLIOGRAPHY

Baker, Robin. "Double Trouble: Counting the Cost of Jephthah." *JBL* 137 (2018): 29–50.
Baumgarten, Elisheva. "Remember that Glorious Girl": Jephthah's Daughter in Medieval Jewish Culture." *JQR* 97 (2007): 180–209.
Brenner, Athalya. "Women Frame the Book of Judges—How and Why?" Pages 125–38 in *Joshua and Judges: Texts and Contexts*. Edited by Athalya Brenner and Gale Yee. Minneapolis: Fortress, 2013.
Claassens, L. Juliana M. *Claiming Her Dignity: Female Resistance in the Old Testament*. Collegeville, MN: Liturgical Press, 2016.
Das, Madan Mohan. "Giving the Children of Prostitutes their Due." *Indian Council of Child Welfare News Bulletin* 39, nos. 3–4 (1991): 31–37.

---

[79] Limbale, *Outcaste*, 62.

DeMaris, Richard E., and Carolyn S. Leeb. "Judges—(Dis)honor and Ritual Enactment: The Jephthah Story—Judges 10:16–12:1," Pages 177–90 in *Ancient Israel: The Old Testament in Its Social Context*. Edited by Philip F. Esler. Minneapolis: Fortress, 2006.
Devy, G. N. Introduction to *The Outcaste: Akkarmashi*, by Sharankumar Limbale. Translated by Santosh Bhoomkar. New Delhi: Oxford University Press, 2008.
Erikson, Erik. *Childhood and Society*. 2nd ed. New York: Norton, 1963.
Exum, J. Cheryl. *Tragedy and Biblical Narrative: Arrows of the Almighty*. Cambridge: University Press, 1992.
Fanon, Frantz. *Black Skin, White Masks*. Translated by Charles Lam Markmann. Forewords by Ziauddin Sardar and Homi K. Bhabha. London: Pluto, 1967.
Fewell, Danna Nolan. *The Children of Israel: Reading the Bible for the Sake of Our Children*. Nashville: Abingdon, 2003.
Fewell, Danna Nolan, and David M. Gunn. *Gender, Power, and Promise: The Subject of the Bible's First Story*. Nashville: Abingdon, 1993.
Fuchs, Esther. "Marginalization, Ambiguity, Silencing: The Story of Jephthah's Daughter." Pages 116–30 in *A Feminist Companion to Judges*. Edited by Athalya Brenner. Sheffield: Sheffield Academic, 1993.
———. *Sexual Politics in the Biblical Narrative: Reading the Hebrew Bible as a Woman*. JSOTSup 310. London: Sheffield: Sheffield Academic, 2003.
Garcia-Alfonso, Cristina. "Judges: Subaltern Women." Pages 106–21 in *Postcolonial Commentary and the Old Testament*. Edited by Hemchand Gossai. London: T&T Clark, 2019.
Garcia Bachmann, Mercedes L. *Judges*. Wisdom Commentary 7. Collegeville, MN: Liturgical Press, 2018.
Girard, René. *Violence and the Sacred*. Translated by Patrick Gregory. Baltimore, MD: Johns Hopkins University Press, 1977.
Hunt, Margaret C. "Dutiful Daughters and the Fathers Who Fail Them: The Application of Feminist Insights and the Retrieval of Resistance Strands of Women's Traditions via a Narrative Analysis of Four Unmarried Daughter Texts in the Hebrew Bible." PhD diss., Flinders University Faculty of Education, Humanities, Law and Theology, Adelaide, South Australia, 2010. https://tinyurl.com/mk6s45m.
Jost, Renate. *Gender, Sexualität und Macht in der Anthropologie des Richterbuches*. Stuttgart: Kohlhammer, 2006.
Kukreja, Reena "An Unwanted Weed: Children of Cross-Region Unions Confront Intergenerational Stigma of Caste, Ethnicity and Religion." *Journal of Intercultural Studies* 39 (2018): 382–98.
Limbale, Sharankumar. *The Outcaste: Akkarmashi*. Translated by Santosh Bhoomkar. New Delhi: Oxford University Press, 2008.
Lipiński, Edward. *On the Skirts of Canaan in the Iron Age: Historical and Topographical Researches*. Leuven: Peeters, 2006.
Logan, Alice. "Rehabilitating Jephthah." *JBL* 128 (2009): 665–85.
"Mahar." Brittanica.com. Accessed February 4, 2021. https://tinyurl.com/zafa59bd.
Mangalam. "A Disturbing Tale." *The Book Review Literary Trust*. Accessed January 12, 2020. https://tinyurl.com/sdfh5uwk.
Marcus, David. *Jephthah and his Vow*. Lubbock, TX: Texas Tech Press, 1986.

Mendelsohn, I. "The Disinheritance of Jephthah in the Light of Paragraph 27 of the Lipit-Ishtar Code." *IEJ* 4 (1954): 116–19.
Milne, Pamela J. "From the Margins to the Margins: Jephthah's Daughter and her Father." Pages 209–34 in *Joshua and Judges: Texts and Contexts*. Edited by Athalya Brenner and Gale Yee. Minneapolis: Fortress, 2013.
Monroe, Lauren A. S. "Disembodied Women: Sacrificial Language and the Deaths of Bat-Jephthah, Cozbi and the Bethlehmite Concubine." *CBQ* 75 (2013): 32–52.
Pardeshi, Geeta S., and Sanjoy Bhattacharya. "Child Rearing Practices amongst Brothel Based Commercial Sex Workers." *Indian Journal of Medical Sciences* 60 (2006): 288–95.
Pulickal, Jose. "Dynamics of Dalit Psyche: Meanings and Paradigms." Unpublished manuscript. https://tinyurl.com/s89shbdd.
Reis, Pamela Tamarkin. "Spoiled Child: A Fresh Look at Jephthah's Daughter." *Proof* 17 (1997): 279–98.
Römer, Thomas. "Why Would the Deuteronomists Tell about the Sacrifice of Jephthah's Daughter?" *JSOT* 77 (1988): 30–31.
Shingal, Ankur. "The Devadasi System: Temple Prostitution in India." *UCLA Women's Law Journal* 22 (2015): 109–27. https://tinyurl.com/264rnbhy.
Siebert, Eric A. *Disturbing Divine Behavior: Troubling Old Testament Images of God*. Minneapolis: Fortress, 2009.
Sloss, Christine M., and Gary W. Harper. "When Street Sex Workers Are Mothers." *Archives of Sexual Behavior* 33 (2004): 329–341.
Srinivas, M. N. Introduction to *Caste: Its Twentieth Century Avatar*. Edited by M. N Srinivas. Gurgaon, India: Penguin, 1997.
Tapp, Anne Michele. "An Ideology of Expendability: Virgin Daughter Sacrifice in Genesis 19:1–11, Judges 11:30–39 and 19:22–26." Pages 157–74 in *Anti-Covenant: Counter Reading Women's Lives in the Hebrew Bible*. Edited by Mieke Bal. Decatur, GA: Almond Press, 1989.
"Tob." Jewish Virtual Library. Accessed February 4, 2021. https://tinyurl.com/uv97h69s.
Trible, Phyllis. *Texts of Terror: Literary-Feminist Readings of Biblical Narratives*. OBT. Philadelphia: Fortress, 1984.
Weems, Renita J. *Just a Sister Away: A Womanist Vision of Woman's Relationships in the Bible*. San Diego, CA: LuraMedia, 1988.
West, Gerald O. "The Bible and the Female Body in Ibandla lamaNazaretha: Isaiah Shembe and Jephthah's Daughter." *OTE* 20 (2007): 489–509.
Wilfred, Felix. *Dalit Empowerment*. New Delhi: ISPCK, 2007.
Yoder, John C. *Power and Politics in the Book of Judges: Men and Women of Valor*. Minneapolis: Fortress, 2015.

Afterword
Scriptures of Terror

The so-called wars on terror have been and continue to be waged, rhetoricized, and resisted, with scriptural(ized) verses and references. Those verses and references are, as Phyllis Trible has coined, *Texts of Terror*. The application and defense of those verses and references are, also, texts of terror. Under the covers of scriptures, interpretations require and justify wars of weapons and words. Interpretations too are texts, and terror flow through the covers between texts (scriptures, interpretations).

Since Trible's study was published (1984), scriptural(ized) texts continue to inspire terror all over the world, from the White House(s) to the shithole(s), thus making this work crucial and relevant. As long as there are texts of terror, we need works like this one. We need more works like this one, and more frequent.

Texts of terror are not limited to scriptures, and this work opens windows for seeing and reading texts of terror around, and in front of, communities of scriptural(ized) readers. At a different platform, but all around and all over, COVID-19 script(ualize)s terror. The SARS-CoV-2 virus is not a visible body nor a living organism (with its own metabolism), but a parasite that invades and diseases its hosts (the current data of COVID waves and curves, however, focus on human hosts). In the face of resistance, the virus mutates and continues its colonial expansion. Faster, and wider. Yonder, and beyond. COVID, in itself (as parasite), crosses between living and nonliving—it is not alive, but it is not dead; and in its paths, COVID inscribes terror upon its living hosts (read: colonized bodies). At the middle of 2021, COVID-19 is a text of terror that scriptural(ized) readers have not quite figured out how to read.

Climate change is another text of terror. Its wrath has not reached many (in)lands, but many shores and islands are already terrorized because they are diseased, day by day, by the effects of this invasion. In a world that is terrorized by COVID-19 and Climate change, this work embodies an invitation for scriptural(ized) readers to look beyond the noses of our sacred texts. And beyond the limits of the living.

One of the highlights of this work is its feminist commitments, including contributors who are not women. This is controversial, as the editors noted in their introduction, and hopefully this will invite healthy conversations. Historically and collectively speaking – Womanists, Mujeristas, African women, Queer, and other fellowships of women readers, were nurtured in feminist criticism and at some point, they needed to step out further and take on additional concerns. This work is similar—by staying in the shadows of feminist criticism and taking on additional concerns—but also different, for it provides space for some non-women to offer interpretations of texts related to women. It thus feels like an exercise in sleeping with the enemy. At the same time, on the other hand, this work is not trapped by the male/female dichotomy, and thus it is an opportunity to embrace the fluidity of gender. The question is thus simple: How is this work, as a collection, not feminist? I thus hope that this work will become a platform for discussing the future of feminist criticism.

The international composition of voices, with seasoned and youngish contributors, set this volume as a standard for future IVBS projects. Biblical studies, as a discipline, is an international venture, and IVBS is a platform where less-heard voices are hosted, public-ized and, more importantly, engaged.

Jione Havea
General Editor, IVBS

List of Contributors

Adela Yarbro Collins is the Buckingham Professor Emerita of New Testament Criticism and Interpretation at Yale Divinity School.

Karen Eller is a candidate for Minister of the Word with the Uniting Church in Australia and former Uniting Church chaplain at the Royal Children's Hospital (Melbourne) and the Royal Melbourne Hospital.

Rachelle Gilmour is Bromby Senior Lecturer in Old Testament, Trinity College, University of Divinity and research fellow at the Centre for Public and Contextual Theology, Charles Sturt University.

Laura Griffin is the managing editor of the *Australian Feminist Law Journal* and a lecturer at LaTrobe University Law School.

Jione Havea is a research fellow with Trinity Theological College (Aotearoa New Zealand) and the Public and Contextual Theology Research Centre (Charles Sturt University, Australia)

Dorothy A. Lee is the Stewart Research Professor of New Testament at Trinity College Theological School, University of Divinity.

Monica Jyotsna Melanchthon is Associate Professor of Hebrew Bible/Old Testament and Academic Dean at Pilgrim Theological College, University of Divinity.

Brent Pelton holds graduate degrees in linguistics and theology. He is a high school educator and currently a candidate for ordained ministry in the Uniting Church in Australia.

Angela Sawyer is Lecturer in Old Testament and Dean of Students at Stirling Theological College. Her PhD is in the area of Isaiah, exile, and postchurch Australia.

David Tombs is the Howard Paterson Chair of Theology and Public Issues and Director of the Centre for Theology and Public Issues at the University of Otago.

Phyllis Trible is Baldwin Professor Emerita of Sacred Literature at Union Theological Seminary, New York.

Gerald O. West is Professor of Old Testament/Hebrew Bible and African Biblical Hermeneutics in the School of Religion, Philosophy, and Classics at the University of KwaZulu-Natal, South Africa and Director of the Ujamaa Centre for Community Development and Research.

Robyn J. Whitaker is Senior Lecturer in New Testament at Pilgrim Theological College, University of Divinity.

Ancient Sources Index

Hebrew Bible / Old Testament

Genesis
1:27	44
2:22	44
3:6	44
16	x
18–19	48
19	48, 146, 155, 156
19:1–29	146
19:37	38
21	x
22:1–19	42, 75, 146
22:10	146
27	43
32:26	x
34	47, 58
34:1	46
34:18	59
38	44
39	44
41:45	26
41:50	26
46:20	26

Exodus
2:21	23
3:7	185
7–12	40
14	40
15:25	40
16	40
17:1–7	40
20:13	42
23:9	42
32	40
32:1–6	40
32:11–14	40
34:15–16	23

Leviticus
18:21	228
20:2–5	228

Numbers
11:10–35	40
11:11–15	42
12:2	40
12:13	40
20–21	224
21:2	228
22–25	116
23:19	43
25	9, 10, 17, 19, 19, 21, 22–23, 23, 26, 27, 33, 37, 38, 39, 40, 41, 42, 44–45, 47–48, 52
25:1	17, 21, 45, 52
25:1–5	19, 21, 38
25:2	20
25:3	20
25:4	41
25:6	17
25:6–9	39
25:7–8	40

25:8	20, 21	11:2	219
25:10–13	39, 41	11:3	221
25:13	42	11:4–11	223
25:14–18	19, 39	11:6	223
25:16–18	44	11:7	223
25:17–18	39	11:11	223
27	xi, 13, 203, 208	11:12–28	223–24
27:1–11	13, 201, 210	11:14–27	224
27:3–4	205	11:29	225
27:6–7	205	11:29–32	229
27:8b–11	206	11:30–31	225, 229
30–31	48	11:30–40	229
31	17, 18, 19, 23, 25, 26, 27, 33, 52	11:34–39a	229
31:9	23	11:35	231
31:15	17	11–12	215
31:15–18	23	12:7	231
31:17	17	14:6	229
31:18	26, 43	19	x, xi, 11, 12, 48, 139, 140, 142, 144, 146, 148, 150, 155, 156, 157, 161–64, 173, 174, 175
36	xi, 13, 210		
36:1–12	13, 201, 210, 211		
36:2b–4	211	19:1	140, 166
36:6b–9	212	19:1–8	164–65
36:12	212	19:3	145, 163, 167, 169, 172
		19:6	145
Deuteronomy		19:8	145
5:17	42	19:9	166
7:3	108	19:12	170
12:31	228	19:19	143
18:17	228	19:19–21	155
22	57	19:20	141
22:24–27	57	19:22	155
22:28–29	57	19:22–26	155
24:13	172	19:23–24	155
25:5–10	60	19:24	141
29:1–30:20	xii	19:25	144, 144, 155, 156, 157
30:19	xii	19:25c	141, 143
		19:25d	143
Judges		19:26–27	172
1	155	19:27	172
3:10	229	19:28	172–73
11	x, 49, 147, 216, 218, 228	19:29	141, 146, 163
11:1–29	229	19–21	144, 194
11:1	218, 219	20:4	166

20–21	142	13:6–8	57
20:5b	146	13:7–8	62
		13:10	62
Ruth		13:12	62
1:1–2:13	75	13:12–13	63, 192
		13:13	58, 185
1 Samuel		13:13–14	62, 184
8:5	187	13:16	62
8:10–18	196	13:14	55, 58
8:11	183	13:15	62
8:11–17	187, 196	13:17	62
8:13	184, 185	13:19	59, 64, 184
8:13–17	183	13:20	60, 62, 184
8:20	187	13:21	191
19	111	13:22	62
24:14	69	13:23–37	56
31:4	157	13:32	59
		14:23–27	59
2 Samuel		14:27	184
2:11	188–89	14:33	188
3:2	58	15	59
3:6–11	58	15:1	188
5:3–4	191	15:1–6	188
5:9	187, 191	15:3	188
5:9–13	191	15:6	188
6:12	187	15:6a	188
7:2	187, 191	15:6b	188
10:6	221	15:7–11	188
10:8	221	15:10	188, 189
11	x, 111	15:11	189
11:1	182, 187, 191	15:12	189
11:2	182	15:13–30	189
11:3	182	15:16	63
11:4	182, 191	15:28	190
11:5	182	15:30	64
11:14	182	15:31	64
11:15	191	15:31–37	190
12	61	16–17	63
12:10–11	61	16:1–4	190
13	x, 10, 55, 59, 60–63, 65	16:5–15	190
13:1	62	16:15	64
13:1–22	102	16:15–17:14	64
13:3	63	16:16–20	191

16:21	63, 191, 192	21:4	109
16:21–22	185	21:5–16	44, 109
16:22	58, 63, 192	21:19–20	109
16:23	64, 192	21:23–24	109
17	64	21:25	109
17:1–3	192, 193		
17:4	193	2 Kings	
17:7–13	193	3	229
17:14	64, 65, 193	9	109
17:23	188, 194	9:7	109
20:1–22	196	9:26	109
20:3	63, 194	9:30	109
20:24	195, 196	9:30–37	26, 44, 110
20:25–26	196	9:33–34	110
21:10–14	185	9:36	110
23:34	182	23:10	228
24:1–9	196		
		1 Chronicles	
1 Kings		2:3–55	23
1:1–4	58	23:16–17	25
1:11–40	195		
4:6	195	Ezra	
5:13–14	195	2:59–62	23
9:15	195	7:1–6	41
9:21	195	9–10	43
11	43	9:2	43
11:26–28	195	10	43
11:28	195		
12:1–19	196	Nehemiah	
12:2	195	7:61–65	23
12:4	195	8:1–12	50
12:18	195	10:30	108
16	108		
16:31–33	108	Esther	
16:31–36	44	3:7–4:17	75
17–19	26		
18	108	Job	
18:4	108	1:1–19	75
18:13	108	2:9	184
19:2	108		
19:16	108	Psalms	
21	26	106:28–31	39, 40, 41
21:1–16	109, 180	108:34–36	23

Proverbs		23	21, 115
1–9	162	40:46	41
7:10–13	162	43:19	41
7:18–20	162	44:15	41
9:1–6	162, 169	48:10	41
31	166		
22:2	186	Hosea	
29:13	186	1:2	21, 114
		2:2	115
Song of Songs		2:13	115
1:5	50		
6:13	50	Malachi	
8:6–7	50	2:10–16	23

Isaiah		Deuterocanonical Books	
40:1–2	93		
40:2	95	Tobit	
47	95, 96, 98	6:2	69
49	94	11:4	69
49:14–26	93, 94, 94, 95, 96, 97, 99, 103		
		2 Maccabees	
49:20–21	93	7	156
50:1	93, 95		
50:1–3	94	New Testament	
51:17–20	93		
51:17–52:3	93	Matthew	
51:17–52:6	94	2:16	156
51:22–23	95	6:24	ix
52:1–2	96	7:6	69
52:2	93, 96	10:5–6	71
53	98	15	10
54	93, 94, 96	15:21–28	70
54:1–3	93, 94	15:28	71
54:5–8	93, 95	20:19	156
56:10	69 fn.12	25	150
		26:26–29	155
Jeremiah		27	157
2–3	21	27:1–26	155, 156
		27:17	155
Ezekiel		27:21	155
3:25–26	116	27:26	152, 155
4:7–8	116	27:27	154
16	21, 115		

27:27–31	12, 139, 142, 150, 151, 152, 155, 157	6:14–29	209
		6:21	79
27:28–29	153, 156, 157	6:21–29	83
27:31	156	6:30–44	79
27:35	152	6:34–44	83
27:35	152	6:45–8:26	70
27:41	156	7:1–23	70, 79, 83
27:42–43	156	7:13	75
27:44	156	7:18	76
		7:24	69
Mark		7:24–31	67, 68
1:1–8:21	81	7:25	68, 69
1:12–13	75	7:26	69
1:15	72	7:27	72
1:21	74	7:28	76, 82
1:21–27	68	7:27	69
1:25	69–70	7:28	69
1:27	74	7:29	69, 75
1:31	69–70, 128	7:31–37	79
1:34	68	7:34	69–70
1:41	69–70	8:1–10	79, 83
1:45	75	8:11–21	79
2:11	69–70	8:22–10:52	81
2:15–17	72, 83	8:23–25	69–70
2:23–3:5	72	8:27	81
3:5	69–70	8:38	75
3:7–12	72	9:7	81
3:8	70	9:10	75
3:11	68	9:14–29	68
3:14	78	9:25	69–70
3:35	84	9:30–31	81
4:11	76	9:37	83
4:14–20	75	10:22	75
4:33	75	10:32–34	81
4:39	69–70	10:34	156
5:1–20	68, 72, 80	10:38–39	82
5:8	69–70	10:42–45	81, 82
5:34	69–70, 78	10:46–52	78
5:36	75, 78	12:36	82
5:41	69–70	13:31	75
6:6b–8:21	72	14:12–25	83
6:7	68	14:26–42	150
6:13	68	14:36	82

14:39	75	14:34–35	133
14:41	150	15	124
15:16–24	151, 152	15:7	124
16:1	78	16:19	123
16:8	78		

2 Corinthians
		1:1	123
Luke		3:6	129
14:29	156	11:5	124
18:32	156	11:13	124
		11:23	129
John		12:11	124
4:1–42	70	12:28	125
4:42	70		

Galatians
Acts		1:1	123
6	128	1:17	124
6–8	129		
10	70	Ephesians	
18:1–3	123	5:6–18	114
18:18–19	123	5:22–23	98

Philippians
Romans		1:1	125, 129, 131, 132
1:1	123	3:2	69
9:3	124	4:18–19	114
11:13	123		
15	131	Colossians	
15:25	129	4:15	123
16	131		
16:1–2	129	1 Timothy	
16:3–5	123	2:9–15	11
16:7	124	2:11–12	133
16:21–23	131	3	129, 132
		3:1	126
1 Corinthians		3:2	126, 127
1:1	123	3:1–7	131
1:11	123	3:8–13	131
3:5	129		
8:7–8	112	2 Timothy	
9	124	3:1–9	114
9:1	123		
9:1	124		
9:5	124		
10:27	112		

Titus		17–18	115
1:7	126	18:23	112
		19:20	112
Hebrews		22:15	69
6:4–8	114		

Early Christian Writings

2 Peter			
1:4–9	114	Didache	
2:1–22	114	15:1	129
3:3–4	114	15:1–2	126

1 John		1 Clement	
2:18–19	114	42:4	129
4:1–4	114		

Ephrem, *Nisibene Hymns*

Jude		67	118
3–18	114		

Epiphanius, *Panarion*

Revelation		49.2.5	128
1:9–20	112, 113, 116		
1:16	117	Ignatius, *To the Smyrnaeans*	
2	115, 118	13.2	127
2:2	113		
2:12–17	116	Ignatius, *To Polycarp*	
2:14	112, 113, 114, 116, 117	8.2	127
2:16	117		
2:18	116	Tertullian, *Exhortation to Chastity*	
2:18–29	111, 112, 117	10.5	133
2:20	111, 112, 113, 114		
2:20–23	11	Tertullian, *The Soul*	
2:22–23	115, 117	9.4	133
2:24–26	117		
3:14	113	Tertullian, *The Veiling of Virgins*	
12:9	112	9.1	133
12:17	113		
13:14	112		
17	115		

www.ingramcontent.com/pod-product-compliance
Lightning Source LLC
Chambersburg PA
CBHW022028240426
43667CB00042B/1364